7/03

Distinguished Native American Spiritual Practitioners and Healers

Distinguished Native American Spiritual Practitioners and Healers

TROY R. JOHNSON

Distinguished Native Americans Series

ORYX PRESS
Westport, Connecticut • London

The rare Arabian Oryx is believed to have inspired the myth of the unicorn. This desert antelope became virtually extinct in the early 1960s. At that time, several groups of international conservationists arranged to have 9 animals sent to the Phoenix Zoo to be the nucleus of a captive breeding herd. Today, the Oryx population is over 1,000, and over 500 have been returned to reserves in the Middle East.

Library of Congress Cataloging-in-Publication Data

Johnson, Troy R.
    Distinguished Native American spiritual practitioners and healers / Troy R. Johnson.
        p.   cm.—(Distinguished Native Americans series)
    Includes bibliographical references and index.
    ISBN 1–57356–358–7 (alk. paper)
    1. Indians of North America—Biography.   2. Indians of North America—Religion.   3. Healers—North America—Biography.   4. Shamans—North America—Biography.   I. Title. II. Series.
E89.J7   2002
299′.7′0922—dc21   2001036637
[B]

British Library Cataloguing in Publication Data is available.

Library of Congress Catalog Card Number: 2001036637
ISBN: 1–57356–358–7

First published in 2002

Oryx Press, 88 Post Road West, Westport, CT 06881
An imprint of Greenwood Publishing Group, Inc.
www.oryxpress.com

Printed in the United States of America

The paper used in this book complies with the Permanent Paper Standard issued by the National Information Standards Organization (Z39.48–1984).

10 9 8 7 6 5 4 3 2 1

Contents

Preface

Distinguished Native American Spiritual Practitioners and Healers is a compendium of the lives and practices of 100 Native healers and spiritual leaders, both well-known and obscure individuals, of the historical and contemporary periods. Each entry is divided into sections that answer the questions most commonly asked by researchers and students. Entries open by providing the individual's full name at birth, date and place of birth and death, education, and leadership title. Entries are then divided into a summary of the individual's life, a history of the person's early life, a description of the leadership highlights of the person's career as a healer or spiritual practitioner, and recommendations for further reading. Where possible, the entries are also illustrated with photos of the individual. Because of the historical nature of the material and the fact that many early Native Nations relied on oral history, some information is not available. For instance, dates and places of birth and death are often unknown or have been arrived at by consulting numerous sources that are themselves in disagreement. Similarly, the early life histories of some of the practitioners and healers presented here were not recorded. In all cases, I have attempted to provide the most accurate and complete information available.

Besides a detailed bibliography and subject index, the volume also includes two appendixes. Appendix A lists the Native American spiritual practitioners and healers in this volume by birth date, and Appendix B lists them by Nation or group.

Introduction

Few universals are common to all Native Nations. What is true and sacred to one Nation may not be recognized or practiced by another. Just as Native Nations are not related by blood, one to another, neither are the prescribed roles of their spiritual practitioners or healers similar. In some cases, they differ in small ways; in others, they differ greatly. These differences should not be criticized but celebrated, just as Native Nations celebrated their unique relationship to the Creator or Great Spirit. Nor should Native traditional healing practices be viewed through the lens of Eurocentric biases. Readers must understand the realities of the Native world and the role the healer or practitioner fulfilled as an intercessory between the physical and spiritual worlds.

The role of the Native American spiritual practitioner or healer in Native societies has often been relegated to that of a mystic shaman or some type of magical medicine man. I am reminded of a visit I made to a former California mission where a docent told her audience at one point, "This is where the medicine man practiced his voodoo."

Nonnative writers and filmmakers have created the public perception that there is a "oneness" among these practitioners from which a universal paradigm can be drawn or visualized. Nothing could be further from the truth. As you read and use *Distinguished Native American Spiritual Practitioners and Healers*, you will discover that the Native men and women it profiles do not fit into a precise description. The role of the Native healer was largely prescribed by the religious and, in some cases, cultural traditions of each individual Nation. Some individuals fulfilled a hereditary obligation, while others obtained healing powers through dreams, visions, or as the result of supernatural events such as earthquakes or solar eclipses. In some Native societies, the practice of a spiritual practitioner or healer was rewarded with food, animal skins, horses, or utilitarian items given either as gifts or payment. In some societies, healing was a responsibility that required no remuneration. However, in almost all societies, the act or art of healing carried tremendous social obligations and consequences. Becoming a spiritual healer or practitioner was not an action taken lightly or without great deliberation. Those who filled a hereditary position had little choice, but others carefully weighed the obligations and consequences. Although a practitioner or healer who could meet the needs of his or her people and cure their sicknesses was respected and, in some cases, feared, he or she was also generally recognized as an extremely powerful person who enjoyed a special relationship with the Creator. A healer who could not heal sometimes was met with criticism, disdain, and censure. In extreme cases, a healer suspected of practicing "black medicine" might be put to death.

The Native Americans presented in this volume include figures from the distant and recent past, as well as contemporary healers and spiritual practitioners. The role of the healer has changed over time as Native societies have moved into the twenty-first century. Today, I doubt that any fear being put to death; however, their actions still carry tremendous religious and cultural significance and consequences. The sacred among Native people and Native Nations remains alive today even though the form and practice may differ.

Throughout this text I have used the terms *Indian*, *American Indian*, and *Native American* interchangeably. It should be understood that none of these terms or labels accurately describes the name that Native people or Native Nations would have applied to themselves. Tribal names such as Navajo, Mohawk, Papago, and Delaware are inaccurate as well. These are names assigned to Native Nations by "others." Native Nations have names for themselves that predate European contact on this continent. I have used these names whenever possible.

Profiles

Aiowantha (Hiawatha)

Full Name at Birth: Aiowantha (Hiawatha, Hienwentha, Aryonwartha; "He Who Combs")
Birth: ca. 1525 in the Mohawk River valley in present-day New York State
Death: ca. 1575
Education: no formal education
Leadership Position: Onondaga shaman, visionary, tribal leader, diplomat, and orator

Summary

Aiowantha was a member of the Onondaga Nation by birth but a Mohawk by adoption. Much of what is known about him has been passed down as the history of the formation of the Iroquois League. The League originally consisted of five independent Indian Nations: the Mohawk, Oneida, Onondaga, Cayuga, and Seneca. The Tuscarora Nation was later adopted by the League, and the Indian people belonging to the League are often referred to as Six Nations people.

Prior to the formation of the League, the Mohawk, Oneida, Onondaga, Cayuga, and Seneca Nations participated in devastating blood feuds. The death of a tribal member demanded the death of a member of the offending Nation. Over time, this requirement increased to the level that the existence of the individual Nations was threatened. In the mid- to late 1500s, the Mohawk shaman Aiowantha met a Huron shaman by the name of Deganawida* (the Peacemaker). Deganawida had received a vision in which the Creator instructed him to introduce a new concept of peace titled the Great Law of Peace and a religion called the Longhouse religion. Deganawida had a speech impediment, however, and he turned to Aiowantha as his speaker because of Aiowantha's oratory skills. Together they carried out the Creator's plan and established an alliance among the five Nations of what is now upstate New York. Aiowantha became the principal spokesman and traveled from tribe to tribe, preaching the Creator's message of unity, and negotiating agreements.

Early Life

There is no recorded history of Aiowantha's early life. It is believed that he was born in approximately 1525 among the Onondaga Nation in present-day New York State and flourished as a visionary and shaman in the 1570s. It is believed by many Six Nations people that Aiowantha was the earthly manifestation of Ta-ren-ya-wa-gon, "The Upholder of Heaven," who became mortal and came to earth to unite the Mohawk, Oneida, Onondaga, Cayuga, and Seneca Nations into a confederation and to bring an end to the blood feuding that was destroying the five nations.

Leadership

Aiowantha was a shaman or mystic of exceptional oratory skills who devoted his life to assisting Deganawida in ending the bloodshed among the Mohawk, Oneida, Cayuga, Seneca, and Onondaga Nations. The formation created what is known as the Iroquois League, the Iroquois Confederation, the Confederation of Five Nations, or simply the Six Nations.

Aiowantha was adopted by the Mohawk Nation, where he became a medicine man and magician. Prior to his meeting with Deganawida, Aiowantha was distressed at the constant warfare and never-ending feuds among the five tribes. After having met Deganawida and hearing about the Great Law of Peace, Aiowantha emerged as a reform leader, advocating the unification of the tribes and the end of blood revenge.

Aiowantha, together with the Huron prophet Deganawida, developed plans to end tribal feuding by establishing laws and ceremonies for peacefully settling disputes among the Five Nations. Aiowantha's early efforts to end the violence plaguing the Iroquois Nations were thwarted by a powerful Onondaga opponent named Tadodaho, who opposed the reform movement and confederation plan. When Aiowantha's message fell on unreceptive ears among his own people, he left his home to preach his message among the Mohawk, Oneida, and Cayuga, who embraced his ideas. His association with Deganawida increased his legitimacy, and eventually the Onondaga, and Tadodaho himself, were convinced of the benefits offered by Aiowantha's plan.

Deganawida and Aiowantha's visionary confederacy shaped a framework for lasting peace based on democratic and representative principles. The U.S. founding fathers were aware of and discussed the example of the Iroquois League. Benjamin Franklin and John Adams were certainly familiar with the concept of unification as practiced by the Six Nations. Franklin and Adams visited with the member tribes of the Iroquois League and invited representatives of the League to New York for questioning. They borrowed a number of concepts from the League, including political equality, separation of governmental powers, checks and balances on political powers, and the emphasis on political freedom. The new states of the United States were viewed as being similar to the Five Nations, and the senators were like the fifth Iroquois sachems that were nominated by clan matrons.

It was ultimately Aiowantha who translated the concepts and principles of the Gret Law of Peace into political action, and thus he is credited with organizing the League of the Iroquois. The three principles of the Great Peace were *Skenno* (health of body and sanity of mind), *Gaiiwiyo* (righteousness in conduct, thought, and deed), and *Gashedenza* (knowledge of, and faith in, the spiritual power connected to governing and maintaining self-defense).

In the nineteenth century, Henry Wadsworth Longfellow collected a number of the Iroquois legends and published them in such a way that Aiowantha was identified as Ta-ren-ya-wa-gon, "The Upholder of Heaven." Longfellow based his famous poem, *Hiawatha*, written in 1855, on these legends, and the name Hiawatha became identified with a fictionalized Chippewa god and hero. Despite Longfellow's erroneous intrusion, both Aiowantha and Deganawida are highly esteemed figures among Six Nations people today.

See also Deganawida.

Further Reading

A Hiawatha and Deganawida Bookshelf: http:// www.aaronshep.com/book-shelves/Hiawatha.html

A Native American Legend: Hiawatha and Mondamin: http://detnews.com/ menu/ stories/17152.htm

Champagne, Duane, ed. *The Native North American Almanac: A Reference Work on Native North Americans in the United States and Canada*. 1994. Detroit: Gale Research.

Dictionary of Indians of North America. 1978. St. Clair Shores, Mich.: Scholarly Press.

Hirschfelder, Arlene, and Paulette Molin. *The Encyclopedia of Native American Religions*. 1992. New York: Facts on File.

Lyon, William S. *Encyclopedia of Native American Shamanism: Sacred Ceremonies of North America*. 1998. Denver: ABC-CLIO.

Markowitz, Harvey, Ed. *American Indians. Vol. 1*. 1995. Pasadena, Calif.: Salem Press.

Waldman, Carl. *Who Was Who in Native American History*. 1990. New York: Facts on File.

Akikita

Full Name at Birth: Akikita
Birth: early nineteenth century
Death: nineteenth century
Education: no formal education
Leadership Position: Oto shaman

Summary

Akikita was a noted Oto shaman who flourished in the mid-nineteenth century. Among the Oto, there were classes of people: the chiefs, the people invested with secular or supernatural power (the shaman), and the common people. The chiefs represented secular control, while the shaman was believed to possess supernatural power and was responsible for religious ceremonies, healing rituals, and the spiritual well-being of the entire tribe.

As opposed to many other Indian tribes, the role of the shaman in Oto society was not necessarily a hereditary role. Although it was common for a child of a shaman to follow in his footsteps, the responsibilities of the shaman were very demanding and dangerous, and some family members elected not to participate. If a shaman's son was not interested, the position was offered to the grandson on the father's side. If necessary, the position was also offered to children in the mother's clan to retain the power within the family. If no family member was interested, then a tribal person outside of lineage was selected by the outgoing shaman and tribal leaders.

The story of Akikita's rise to the role of Oto shaman was passed on to an anthropologist, William Whitman, who was conducting fieldwork in the spring of 1935. Akikita's *hitáwa* (grandson) was the informant. His father was Akikita's *hjtós'ke* (nephew).

Early Life

There are no written records of Akikita's early life. Because he became a prominent Oto shaman, we may safely assume that he was raised in a traditional Oto family of the nineteenth century. Akikita would have received his name when he was about four days old in a "Bear naming ceremony." Tobacco was sprinkled in the four sacred directions, and a member of the Bear Clan, or Akikita's uncle, then gave him a name. Following this, Akikita would have been raised in one of the small Oto villages located along the Nemah and Missouri rivers in present-day Nebraska. As a youth, he would have traveled to the neighboring Indian territories that now form the states of Iowa, Kansas, and Missouri.

The Oto had strong family blood ties and lived within a clan village structure where all residents were related. The social and economic activity of the village was carried on within these kinship groups. Because of the strong family ties, his grandparents, aunts, and uncles, all of whom shared the responsibility along with Akikita's parents, would have cared for Akikita. Akikita would have had an extremely strong bond with his father's brother (a patrilineal society), and the uncle probably assigned Akikita a nickname and offered him advice on important matters. Akikita's uncle was responsible for him on hunting trips and when on a war party, even at the peril of his own life.

Oto children were highly prized among tribal members; however, they were rarely disciplined in the Western sense. It was believed that children learned best by example, so Akikita would have been encouraged to model himself after one of his uncles.

As a youth, Akikita would have traveled alone to a secluded area to fast and seek a vision that would provide him with guidance for his future. Akikita would have appealed to *Wakointa* (the Creator) for guidance and a spiritual helper.

Leadership

Akikita acquired his call to shamanism and his supernatural power while in a dream state. The Oto were on a buffalo hunt and had made numerous camps—perhaps as many as a dozen over a period of twenty or thirty days. They moved in search of the buffalo but were unsuccessful. One morning, Akikita arose at about four o'clock and left the camp. Intent on fasting, he ate no breakfast. After a period of time, Akikita began to feel weak. His *hitákwa* (grandson) relates the story from that point: "There was a big tree there, and he [Akikita] lay against it, thinking that he was hungry. Akikita was facing east. He heard a gun go off, way off. He could just barely hear it. Then he heard the bullet coming whistling, hum, hum. It said to Akikita, 'Akikita, I'm coming.' While he was sitting there the bullet rolled in front of him. It said: 'Akikita, I pity you. If you have any difficulty, any hard trouble, you must think about me. If you are in battle and think about me, they won't kill you. Get a little bell and tie it to your wrist. When you are in battle, even if you have no gun, or tomahawk, just use a club. You are going to be a big man among your tribe." This bullet said, "God is going to pity you, and you are going to live to an old age."

While on a later trip to hunt beaver, Akikita received doctoring powers from a white wolf. He got lost while on the hunt and spent four days trying to find his way home. After four days without food, he had a vision in which a white wolf gave him a sacred wolf skin. Akikita said, "The white wolf said, 'I pity you. You are a big man. I have heard about you. I pity you. I am going to give you something. This is holy, what I am going to give you. The sun sees us. The gods see us. What I am going to tell you, I am not going to lie to you about. I am going to give you something.' " The white wolf said, "Among the wolves I am head chief. You are going to be like me, a big chief. If you have any difficulty in fights or in battle, you are not going to be killed. Now you are going home. Your are going to meet a wolf just like me. You kill him. You skin him. You take the hide, tan the hide, cut a hole in the middle and put it over your head. . . . There is another thing I am going to give you. Whenever any disease or sickness is among the tribe, hang the wolf skin up. A wind is going to blow hard for four days without stopping, but the wind is going to blow that sickness away." Akikita told his people the white wolf had also said: "Whenever you are in war, put on the hide and go and fight." After the war he came home. They found four bullets in each of the four corners of the hide, bur not one had pierced it.

Both the bullet and the white wolf hide served as amulets to protect Akikita in warfare and the tribe in time of sickness. In the early 1830s, when the whole tribe suffered from smallpox, it is said that Akikita hung his wolf hide up. The wind blew hard for four days and blew away the sickness.

Akikita received additional power from a vision where he met four buffalo spirits. "They [the buffaloes] said, 'We sent for you. You came here. We showed you this. If people are sick from being shot, you doctor them. You know the weeds. You use them.' Then the four said, 'God made you. God made us for you to live on. You kill us, you eat, and you live. But what we have shown you, what we have told you, when you get home and people are sick and want you, they must bring a pipe and you must smoke first. Think about us. Don't always receive gifts. Sometimes give them back. Then God will pity you.' "

Further Reading

Edmunds, R. David. *The Otoe-Missouria People*. 1976. Phoenix: Indian Tribal Series.

Lyon, William. *Encyclopedia of Native American Shamanism: Sacred Ceremonies of North America*. 1998. Denver: ABC-CLIO.

Waldman, Carl, and Molly Braun. *Encyclopedia of Native American Tribes*. 1988. New York: Facts on File.

Whitman, William. *The Oto*. 1937. New York: Columbia University Press.

William Apes

Full Name at Birth: William Apes

Birth: January 31, 1798, near present-day Colrain, Massachusetts

Death: ca. 1839

Education: attended formal schooling for six winters, 1803–1809

Leadership Position: Pequot Methodist missionary

Summary

William Apes was a Pequot Methodist missionary and author who worked among the Mashpee people near present-day Cape Cod, Massachusetts. As a young man, he served in the American army in the War of 1812. In April 1829 he was formally ordained a minister in the Protestant Methodist church.

Shortly after 1829, Apes visited the Mashpee and found them in need of community services and leadership. Apes not only became a member of the Mashpee tribe but also championed the rights of the Mashpee Nation throughout the 1830s. He encouraged the Mashpee people to adopt a number of measures, including the dismissal of the white missionary who was ministering to the non-Indian congregation rather than to the Mashpee people.

Throughout his life, Apes championed the rights of the Mashpee people. In May 1833, he traveled to the Massachusetts community of Mashpee, where he took part in a revolt against the Massachusetts Commonwealth. In the context of this revolt, he published an account of Indians' grievances in *Indian Nullification of the Unconstitutional Laws of Massachusetts, Relative to the Mashpee Tribe* (1835).

Apes was the author of several other publications as well. In 1829, he produced the first published autobiography by an American Indian, *A Son of the Forest*. He also authored *The Experiences of Five Christian Indians* (1833), *Eulogy on King Philip* (1836), and the *Indian Nullification of the Unconstitutional Laws of Massachusetts Relative to the Mashpee Tribe: or, the Pretended Riot Explained* (1835). At some point in his life Apes added an "s" to his surname, and some references to him can be found under the name Apess.

Early Life

Apes' father was of mixed-blood Pequot and European ancestry. His mother was descendant of the famous Wampanoag leader King Philip (also known as Metacomet). He was the first of five children. Shortly after his birth, the family moved to Colchester, Connecticut. His father had become an apprentice shoemaker, and the family lived in what Apes described as "comparative comfort" for about three years. As a child, his parents were often separated. As a result, he was virtually orphaned along with his brothers and sisters. It appears that Apes and his siblings were poorly fed and poorly clothed. They suffered in the cold weather and depended on the charity of nearby neighbors, who took pity on them.

Apes spent his first four years with his grandparents, who treated him brutally. He stated in his autobiography, "Now my grandparents were not the best people in the world—like all others who are wedded

Image of William Apes. Courtesy, American Antiquarian Society.

to the beastly vice of intemperance, they would drink to excess whenever they could procure rum, and as usual in such cases, when under the influence of liquor, they would not only quarrel and fight with each other but would at times turn upon their unoffending grandchildren and beat them in a most cruel manner." On one occasion, Apes was severely beaten by his grandmother and was saved by the intervention of an uncle who was living in the house. His arm was broken in three places, and it took him nearly a year to recover.

After his grandmother broke his arm, his uncle and a neighbor rescued him. He was removed from his family and never again lived with his parents or any other relatives. Apes became a ward of the town, which then indentured him out to Mr. Furman, the friendly neighbor. While growing up, Apes recalled that his indenture was sold several times to different families in Connecticut. Mr. Furman, a cooper by trade, was a poor man but, by Apes' own account, a good man. He allowed Apes to attend school for six winters, the extent of his formal education.

Apes lived with the Furmans until his indenture was sold to Judge William Hillhouse. This arrangement lasted less than one year, at which time Apes ran away and was sold to William Williamses of New London, Connecticut.

Leadership

Apes was a Pequot Methodist minister and author who worked among the Mashpee people. Most of what is known of him comes from his autobiography, which recounts his youth and early life.

As a young man, Apes served in the American army in the War of 1812. He was a soldier, a Methodist preacher, and a writer and on one occasion was identified as a leading figure in an Indian "rebellion" in Massachusetts. He was a great orator as well. In 1836, he delivered a speech in present-day Boston eulogizing his grandfather, Chief Metacomet, giving a very different view of the Pequot War of 1637. Most New Englanders believed that the Pequot had been exterminated in 1637 and that Indians had disappeared from the region after King Philip's War of 1675–1676. Apes informed his Boston audience that both notions were false.

The spiritual strivings that resulted in Apes' conversion to Christianity began while he was indentured to Mr. Furman and were stirred into a deep Christian conviction while he was indentured to William Williamses. Methodist missionaries held meetings in the neighborhood, and Apes attended. The Williamses were Congregationalists, however, and they disavowed the Methodist religion and forbade Apes to continue to attend meetings. His solution was to run away in late March or April 1813. A fifteen-dollar reward was offered for his capture.

While on the run, Apes met up with a recruiter of militiamen for the War of 1812 and enlisted in the army as a drummer boy. He later served as an infantryman and was involved in several abortive efforts to capture Montreal and in the successful Battle of Lake Champlain on September 11, 1814. Apes was addicted to drinking rum in his early life and throughout his army service. He was released from the army around mid-March 1815.

On December 16, 1821, Apes married a devout Methodist woman, Mary Wood, whom he had met in Connecticut. In April 1829 he was formally ordained a minister in the Protestant Methodist church and in 1831 was sent by the New York Annual Conference of Protestant Methodists to preach to the Pequot. It was in this role as a preacher that Apes came to Mashpee, the only surviving Indian town in present-day Massachusetts.

In addition to his religious duties, Apes became involved in a longstanding struggle between the Mashpee and the white overseers imposed on the community. Three non-Indians had the power to lease out grazing and haying lands to neighboring whites; grant woodlot rights; bind out Mashpee men, women, and children for employment in the community; and control who entered and who could stay in the township. Equally disconcerting to the Mashpee was the appointment of a non-Indian minister whom they did not choose. The missionary had been appointed to minister the Mashpee by Harvard College and had obtained several hundred acres of land. He was working instead among neighboring non-Indians.

In May 1833, William Apes took up the battle. The local newspapers called the confrontation a revolt against the Massachusetts Commonwealth. In the context of leading this revolt, Apes authored perhaps his most important book, *Indian Nullification of the Unconstitutional Laws of Massachusetts, Relative to the Mashpee Tribe* (1835), an account of the Mashpee grievances. Apes encouraged the Mashpee people to adopt a number of measures, including the dismissal of the white missionary and overseers. Under his encouragement, the Mashpee issued the Indian Declaration of Independence, proclaiming that after July 1, 1833, "we as a tribe, will rule ourselves, and have the right to do so; for all men are born free and equal, says the Constitution of the country."

Massachusetts governor Levi Lincoln threatened to call out state troops and declared a state of insurrection. On July 1, 1833, Apes and several Mashpee confronted a group of whites who had come to cut wood on tribal land; they were forbidden by law to do so. When the whites ignored the order, Apes and the others began to unload the wood from the cart. Apes was arrested and charged with riot, assault, and trespass even though they were on Mashpee land. On July 4, Apes received a thirty-day jail sentence, paid a hundred dollar fine, and had to post bond for another hundred dollars in a promise to keep the peace for six months. The case received widespread attention, and the legislature later reversed the conviction based on evidence presented by the Indian people. Apes filed libel suits against his opponents, compelling them to apologize.

Mashpee remained home for Apes and his family for some time after the revolt. He seemed to have left Mashpee in 1838, and nothing is known of his later life.

Further Reading

Calloway, Colin G. *First Peoples: A Documentary Survey of American Indian History.* 1999. New York: St. Martin's.

Hirschfelder, Arlene and Paulette Molin. *The Encyclopedia of Native American Religions.* 1992. New York: Facts on File.

Markowitz, Harvey. *American Indians, Vol 1: Abenaki—Hayes, Ira Hamilton.* 1995. Pasadena, CA: Salem Press.

O'Connell, Barry O., ed. *On Our Own Ground: The Complete Writings of William Apess, a Pequot.* 1992. Amherst: University of Massachusetts Press.

Reuben, Paul P. *PAL: Perspectives in American Literature: A Research and Reference Guide.* Early Nineteenth Century: William Apes or William Apess (Pequot) (1798–1839): http://lead.csustan.edu/english/reuben/pal/chap3/apess.html.

Aripeka

Full Name at Birth: Arpeika (Apayaka Hadjo, Sam Jones)

Birth: ca. 1765

Death: 1860

Education: no formal education

Leadership Position: Seminole-Miccosukee medicine man and war chief in the Second Seminole War, 1835–1842

Summary

Aripeka was a Seminole medicine man during the Second Seminole War of 1835–1842. He was also a war chief of the Miccosukee, the most feared warrior element of the Florida Seminole. Although his exploits have not been well publicized, Aripeka is believed by some to have been more important to the internal Seminole war machine than the famous Seminole leader Osceola. At various councils, Aripeka was noted for his oratory skills and hesitance to forced removal of the Seminole from Florida. He joined with Seminole leaders Osceola, Alligator, and Wild Cat in resisting removal to the Indian Territory. In his role as medicine man, Aripeka was a revered and powerful spiritual leader who used his "medicine power" to whip Seminole warriors into a fighting frenzy.

Aripeka directed Seminole forces in several successful battles, including the famous 1837 Battle at Okeechobee. On December 19, 1837, approximately 250 warriors under the leadership of Osceola and Aripeka withstood the largest battle of the Second Seminole War. Colonel Zachary Taylor directed the U.S. attack. Outnumbered two to one, the Seminole inflicted serious casualties; the U.S. forces 26 killed and 112 wounded compared to the Seminole 11 killed and 14 wounded. General Taylor and his forces withdrew to Fort Bassinger, a short distance from the battleground. Cherokee friends who had voluntarily relocated to the Indian Territory attempted to convince Aripeka and others to relocate peaceably. Aripeka refused and was the only major Seminole leader to remain in Florida after the Second Seminole War. Following the Third Seminole War of 1855–1858, he moved farther south, to Lake Okeechobee in Big Cypress Swamp.

Early Life

Aripeka was born in the present-day state of Georgia around 1765. At an early age, he and his family migrated to the present-day state of Florida and became members of the Seminole Nation. The Seminole Nation is not an original American Indian Nation but was formed in Spanish Florida by remnants of tribes such as the Muskogee, Euchee, Yamasee, Timugua, Tequesta, Abalachi, Coca, and Lower Creek and escaped black slaves from the slave plantations in the southern United States. All of these various groups had suffered severely under the oppression of the non-Indian population and sought refuge outside U.S. jurisdiction.

The date often given for the founding of the Seminole Nation is 1763. The language spoken was Mas´kogi and the word *isli siminoli* meant "free people." English speakers ignored the separate tribal affiliations and called them all "the Seminole."

Although Aripeka traveled widely in Florida, his principal Florida residence was somewhere near the present-day town of Aripeka, on the Pasco-Hernando County line. A present-day historical site on the Weekiwachee River in Hernando County is thought to have been his home village. Prior to the Second Seminole War, 1835–1841, Aripeka fished in present-day Silver Springs, Marion County, Florida and sold part of his catch to U.S. troops at nearby Fort King. Soldiers at the fort gave Aripeka the nickname "Sam Jones" after a popular northern song of the period about Sam Jones the Fisherman. Aripeka is often referred to as Sam Jones in historical writings.

Leadership

Aripeka was one of the important leaders of the Miccosukee band of Seminole Indians. His name (also recorded as Arpeika, Arpiucki, and Appaicca) is taken from his Corn Dance title of Apayaka Hadjo, meaning "Crazy Ratsnake." Called Sam Jones by the whites, Aripeka was both a war leader and a medicine man. Because of his age (nearly seventy at the outbreak of the Second Seminole War), his medicine was powerful, and he exerted great influence among his people. His role was to use his medicine to stir the warrior determination to fight, assist in planning the actions, make medicine to ensure victory, and then retire to tend the wounded. He was inflexible in spirit and in his rage against whites.

Aripeka is thought to have been born in Georgia and to have migrated south to Spanish Florida with other Miccosukee at a very early age. The Seminole Nation came into existence just two years before his birth, and the move south was probably to join with the Seminole people.

Along with Osceola, Alligator, and Wild Cat, Aripeka was the most militant of the Seminole chiefs in resisting removal from Florida to the Indian Territory. At various councils, Aripeka was noted for his refusal to leave Florida.

He counseled the great Seminole leader Osceola to take revenge on the Indian agent Wiley Thompson who in 1835 was attempting to relocate the Seminole. Throughout the Second Seminole War, Aripeka warned his fellow chiefs to beware of white treachery and not to trust truce flags (several leaders had been captured or killed while under a flag of truce). On one occasion, he and Osceola kidnapped three Seminole chiefs—Micanopy, Jumper, and Cloud—who were planning to immigrate to the Indian Territory.

Aripeka took part in many battles of the Second Seminole War. On one occasion in December 1837, he and Osceola led 250 warriors on an attack against Colonel Zachary Taylor at the Battle of Lake Okeechobee. After a day-long battle, both the U.S. and Seminole had been driven from their prepared position, but at a terrific price.

Aripeka came to represent the Seminole resistance against the U.S. Army, and Lieutenant Colonel William Selby Harney was given the task of capturing or killing him. In response, Aripeka is said to have declared that any messenger sent to him by the whites would be put to death. Harney set out with great enthusiasm but was successful only in causing the death of more soldiers. The small number of Indians avoided the troops and escaped on numerous occasions. Congress became restless over the cost of the war—$9 mil-

lion—and the failure to remove the Seminole. Lieutenant John Sprague wrote, "They [the Seminole] have been so often deceived and entrapped, that they place no confidence in the most faithful assurances of any white man."

In December 1840, tired of pursuing Aripeka, General A. Walker Keith Armistead, commander of the Florida command, passed the word to all field commanders to inform Aripeka that he could have a tract of land and remain in Florida if he would cooperate in ending hostilities, but Aripeka continued to counsel resistance.

Aripeka remained a thorn in the side of the U.S. Army and the removal program. On October 12, 1841, Colonel William Jenkins Worth of the Eighth Infantry and commander in Florida, along with 211 men, set out to locate and bring in Aripeka, the last of the Seminole leaders. Their efforts were directed especially at trying to bring in Aripeka, "by fair means or foul." Ultimately, the army had to admit that they could not capture Aripeka, and they were forced to permit a handful of unconquered Seminole to remain in the Florida Everglades, where their descendents reside to this day.

Aripeka and his band were never relocated. At the beginning of the Third Seminole War in 1855, he was living near the Kissimmee River in southern Florida. Now too old to lead in battle, he relinquished his authority to a subchief, Billy Bowlegs. Billy Bowlegs and his followers immigrated to Oklahoma after being paid a large sum of money. Aripeka, however, still refused to go west, and instead moved his few followers to Henrdry County, at the northern edge of what later became the Big Cypress Reservation. Aripeka died in approximately 1860 at about the age of 100.

Following is an excerpt from a poem written by Aripeka that captures his strong spirit:

"Ever since the creation
By the best calculation
The Florida War has been raging
And 'tis our expectation
That the last conflagration
Will find us the same contest
    waging. . . .

For augt we see while ocean rolls
(As though these crafty Seminoles
Were doubly nerved and sinewed)."
Nor art nor force can e'er avail
But, like some modern premium tale,
The war's "to be continued."

Further Reading

A Brief Summary of Seminole History: Osceola and Aripeka: http://www.seminole tribe.com/history/osceola_abiaka. shtml.

Dictionary of Indians of North America. 1978. St. Clair Shores, Mich.: Scholarly Press.

Mahon, John K. *History of the Second Seminole War*. 1967. Gainesville: University of Florida Press.

Waldman, Carl. *Who Was Who in Native American History*. 1990. New York: Facts on File.

Walton, George. *Fearless and Free: The Seminole Indian War, 1835–1842*. 1977. Indianapolis: Bobbs-Merrill.

Washburn, Wilcomb E. *Handbook of North American Indians, Vol. 4*. Washington, D.C.: Smithsonian Institution.

Thomas Banyacya

Full Name at Birth: Thomas Banyacya

Birth: June 2, 1909, in the Hopi village of Moencopi in northeastern Arizona

Death: February 6, 1999, in Keane Canyon, Arizona, about forty miles from his home in Kykotsmovi on the Hopi reservation

Education: attended Sherman Indian School in Riverside, California, and Bacone College, Oklahoma

Leadership Position: Hopi tribal and spiritual leader

Summary

Thomas Banyacya was born into a traditional Hopi family in the village of Moencopi in northeastern Arizona. The Hopi are a Pueblo tribe whose Native territory is located in northeastern Arizona. As a youth, Banyacya attended Sherman Indian School in Riverside, California, and Bacone College in Oklahoma. When he reached the age of eighteen, he refused to register for the U.S. military draft on the grounds of Hopi principles, which forbid the bearing of arms. In 1948, Banyacya was appointed by the Hopi Tribal Council as interpreter and spokesman for traditional Hopi leaders. In his role as representative of the Hopi Nation, he produced the first Hopi passport, which was recognized by the many countries that he visited.

Much of Banyacaya's life was spent in an effort to protect the earth from pollution and destruction, especially that portion given by the Creator to the Hopi people. Throughout his life, Banyacya spoke out against the relocation of Navajo Indian people and other possible effects of U.S. Public Law 93–531, which mandated that the Navajo should be relocated, ostensibly so that the land could be returned to the Hopi.

Thomas Banyacya speaking at the Indigenous Uranium Forum during the Global Radiation Victim's Conference in New York City in 1987. Photo by Kerry Richardson.

Banyacya was one of four young men chosen by Hopi elders in 1948 to tell the outside world of certain dire warnings contained in the ancient Hopi prophecies. Among other things these prophecies mentioned a "gourd full of ashes" (the atomic bomb) and predicted that the world would end in a global "explosion or '"purification" unless human beings changed their destructive ways and prayed to the Great Spirit.

Banyacya, who died in 1999, was the last surviving member of the group, and in his last years he was recognized as a major spokesman for the traditionalist viewpoint on controversial issues, such as the so-called Hopi-Navajo land dispute. That dispute involves an area of 1.8 million acres of high desert plateau where Navajo herders have lived on little-used Hopi land for generations. In 1972, the Congress passed Public Law 93–531, which involved the forced removal of more than ten thousand Navajo and the erection of a barbed wire fence 285 miles long.

Banyacya, his son Thomas Banyacya, Jr., and many others believed that the government was primarily interested in clearing the land so mining companies could gain access to the area's immense deposits of coal, uranium, and oil shale. Banyacya preached that the depredations of the Americans and their ultimate self-destruction were all revealed ages ago in traditional Hopi prophecies.

Banyacya fulfilled his commitments to his elders, and for over forty years he carried the Hopi message of peace and prophecies to the world.

Early Life

Thomas Banyacya was born in the Hopi village of Moencopi in northeastern Arizona. He was born into the Fox, Coyote, and Wolf Clan on his mother's side. His father was of the Corn and the Water clans, and it was from his father's lineage that he received his name, Banyacya, which can be translated as "corn in the fields standing in water after the rains."

As a youth Banyacya attended Sherman Indian School in Riverside, California, and in keeping with Bureau of Indian Affairs policy, his Indian name was dropped and he was assigned the name Thomas Jenkins. Later in life, he reclaimed the name of Banyacya as a symbol of commitment to the Hopi life and culture. After attending the Sherman Indian School, he received a two-year scholarship to study at Bacone College, Oklahoma, one of the first all-Indian colleges. He studied to become a clergyman before changing his mind and decided to become an athlete. He excelled in athletics and was a noted long-distance runner.

Leadership

Banyacya was a Hopi elder and traditionalist who warned world leaders that they had to begin correcting their destructive behavior on earth, the raping of the land, and the destruction of indigenous peoples. At a meeting of the United Nations in 1993, Banyacya told the leaders that they had four days, four weeks, four months, and four years in which to act if they failed to act responsibly, natural disasters would increase. Floods, fires, earthquakes, volcanoes, and deadly sicknesses would occur at an unprecedented level. Banyacya predicted nature was going to begin its retaliation in 1997. With each catastrophe that the world witnessed, such as plane crashes, earthquakes, tornadoes, oil spills, and governmental mistreatment of Indian

tribes, Banyacya saw a warning that people needed to clean up pollution and return to living within the natural laws known to the Native people of the past and the elders of his time.

While he attended Bacone College, Banyacya felt there was a need for Native people to have their own spiritual development and to study their own culture, religion, and traditional ways of life. Because there was no Native American studies program at Bacone, Banyacya, together with Medicine Crow, a Crow colleague from Montana, set up an Indian lodge at the college and began performing songs and ceremonies.

The year 1941 was a turning point in Banyacya's life. At the onset of U.S. involvement in World War II, he refused to register for the military draft on the grounds of Hopi principles, which forbid the bearing of arms. For refusal to register for the draft, he was imprisoned for seven years. Upon release from prison, Banyacya wrote a letter to President Eisenhower requesting a meeting between the U.S. military and Hopi leaders on the subject of Hopi exemption from the armed services. In 1953, Banyacya, together with a group of traditional Hopi spiritual leaders, met in Holbrook, Arizona, with officials from the Selective Service Department and succeeded in obtaining conscientious objector status and the release of Hopis from compulsory military service.

In 1948, Banyacya was appointed an interpreter and spokesman for traditional Hopi leaders. This followed a decision by the *Kikmongwis*, or spiritual leaders, who felt the need and responsibility to put into action certain aspects of Hopi teachings that had been handed down in oral tradition since ancient times. In keeping with these teachings, Banyacya was instructed to travel to the UN's "Great House of

Mica" in New York City carrying a message of peace to the world. The Hopi believed that tht UN headquarters was the "House of Mica" predicted in Hopi prophecy.

Banyacya's efforts to speak before the United Nations were ignored and rebuffed until 1992, when on his fourth attempt, he was allowed to make a brief speech at the General Assembly Hall but on a day when the General Assembly was in recess. To achieve this end, Banyacya wrote a letter to Javier Perez de Cuellar, secretary general of the United Nation, on October 22, 1991 in which he stated, "This is my fourth and final attempt to open the door of the Great House of Mica. If it is not opened as we humbly request so that the red, white, yellow and black peoples might work together for a peaceful world, then we will return to await the inevitable time of purification." On December 10, 1992, Banyacya was allowed to address the General Assembly. He was preceded by three shouts by Oren Lyons, Faithkeeper of the Iroquois League. Banyacya then sprinkled cornmeal next to the podium of the General Assembly and delivered his address in the Hopi language which was translated into English. On April 26, 1993, Banyacya wrote to Boutros Boutros-Ghali, sixth Secretary-General of the United Nations, and thanked him for the opportunity to speak before the United Nations on behalf of the traditional Hopi leaders. Banyacya emphasized that the Hopi are "the original caretakers of this Earth, working through prayer, fasting, meditation, and ceremonies." He stated that there was still an opportunity for many nations and peoples to be saved but that the well-being of the earth depended on the Hopi, the spiritual center at the Four Corners area, and the balance for Mother Earth. (The full text of his address can be read at http://www.welcomehome.org/rainbow/prophecy/hopi.html.)

Banyacya is also recognized as having been the driving force behind a series of six caravans that traveled across the United States beginning in the summer of 1952. The purpose of the caravans was to encourage interest among Indian people in their culture and religion. The caravans attracted the greatest thinkers, spiritual leaders, and medicine people of the era and had a lasting effect on the regeneration of Indian languages, cultural pride, and spiritual development.

In addition to his work in the United States, Banyacya spent much of his life taking the Hopi message to the international community. He received numerous awards and accolades and was widely recognized for his involvement in programs and projects that enriched the lives of indigenous peoples. Banyacya drafted the Hopi Declaration of Peace that ends with the statement, "The True Hopi People declare that Hopi power be a force which will bring about world change." Banyacya died on February 6, 1999.

Further Reading

Champagne, Duane, ed. *The Native North American Almanac: A Reference Work on Native North Americans in the United States and Canada*. 1994. Detroit: Gale Research.

Remembering Thomas Banyacya: http://www.sonic.net/~kerry/banyacya/thomas.htm.

The Hopi Message to the United Nations General Assembly: http://www.welcomehome.org/rainbow/prophecy/hopi.html.

Thomas Banyacya: Hopi Interpreter: http://www.angelfire.com/on/GEAR2000/tbhopi.html.

Thomas Banyacya: Hopi Traditional Elder: http://www.alphacdc.com/banyacya/banyacya.html.

Big Ike

Full Name at Birth: Big Ike "the Rainmaker"
Birth: date and place of birth unknown; flourished around 1889–1890
Death: date and place of death unknown
Education: no formal education reported
Leadership Position: Yurok weather shaman

Summary

Big Ike, also known as the Rainmaker, was a weather shaman who flourished among the Yurok Nation in the late 1880s. The Yurok people traditionally lived along the wooded banks of the lower Klamath River in present-day northern California, as well as along coastal areas to the north and south of the river's mouth.

The Yurok were late to experience the influx of gold miners who inundated present-day California beginning in 1849. During the winter of 1889–1890, gold miners trespassing in Yurok territory on the lower Klamath River became concerned by the lack of rain, which they needed for their gold mining operations. Claims could not be worked because they required water to hydraulic and fill the sluices. Merchants who depended on the gold miners became worried as well because no gold had yet been taken out of the ground. As the situation worsened and there was no sign of rain, the miners decided to hire Big Ike to make it rain. Various Indian Nations have shamans who have the power to bring rain, and Big Ike belonged to one such priesthood.

A trusted white man volunteered to be the go-between who would approach Big Ike with the request and ensure that he was paid for his services. Upon receiving assurances that he would be recognized for his services, "Big Ike told them he would make rain enough for them to work all winter, that much and no more. . . . He agreed to make rain for twenty dollars paid to him by each miner, they were to pay him when the rain began to fall, and the bargain was made."

After the deal was consummated, Big Ike retreated alone to Medicine Rock, where he made his rain medicine. On the afternoon of the third day, the clouds began to gather, and it began to rain. Big Ike then went to collect his fee. However, one miner refused to pay and insulted him and his wife. The miner told Big Ike "that he had nothing to do with making rain; called him a savage and his wife a squaw." Big Ike responded by making his rain medicine stronger. He told the white men and Indians as well that the rain would continue until the fee was paid in full. When the money was not forthcoming Big Ike informed them, "Now you go home, take my advice, and sharpen some good strong stakes and stake down your houses; for as each day goes by it will rain harder until the white men come to Medicine Rock, and are willing and ready to proclaim to the world that Big Ike, the Rainmaker, can make rain when he promises to do so, and must be paid for making this rain. Then, and not until then will the rain cease."

Early Life

There is no recorded history of Big Ike's early life. His entry into written history begins when he is an adult and is described as "a giant of a man."

Leadership

Big Ike was a recognized and respected weather shaman among his people, the Yurok. His position required that he perform religious ceremonies at various times throughout the year to ensure that the seasons remained in balance and that the world continued to renew itself.

The Yurok people were overrun by gold miners in the 1890s but tried to remain alive by making accommodations to white men. Insofar as possible, they remained in the mountains and shunned personal contact with whites.

In 1889, gold miners and merchants began to be concerned for their own survival—not from Indian attack, but because of lack of water with which to operate their hydraulic equipment and fill the sluices to separate the gold from other river materials. A recommendation was made that an Indian rainmaker should be engaged to bring rain. The miners agreed on a price of twenty dollars each to be paid to the rainmaker when the rain began to fall. The deal was struck, and a respected white man approached Big Ike. Big Ike had made rain for his own people many times but had never done so for the whites. He agreed to bring rain even though he expressed doubts that he would be paid because "the whites never did what they promised, and thought that if they could cheat an Indian it was the proper thing to do." He told the miners that it would take three days of ceremony, after which time the rains would begin. Big Ike then retreated alone to a sacred cave in Medicine Rock and made his "rain medicine." On the evening of the third day, the rain began to fall.

Big Ike was typical of Native American shamans in that he was sensitive to criticism of his power and expected that he would be paid for his services. Shamans generally did not participate in the sustenance activities of the tribe and depended on such payment for their daily needs. Big Ike allowed the rain to continue until the next day, at which time he went down to receive his pay. All of the miners paid except for one, who refused and insulted both Big Ike and his wife.

Insulted by the miner's degrading treatment, Big Ike returned to the cave on Medicine Rock and proceeded to call for more rain. In his prayer to his power helper, he stated, "This is the first and only time an Indian has asked his Rain God to help the paleface; and what is his reward? He is called a savage, and his wife a squaw; my children don't like to hear their mother called a squaw."

Soon it began to rain harder, and several Yurok tribesmen went to him and asked him to stop, fearing that their own village would soon be flooded. He told them "that this rain was going to fall until such time as the paleface miners were willing to pay him in full; that even though he was, in the eyes of the white man, a savage and his wife a squaw, they would have to come to him there at Medicine Rock before the rain would stop." The Yurok then went to the miners and informed them "that the Rainmaker was in an ugly mood; that their homes were about to be carried away and that if the rain was not stopped soon the mountain-side would surely go and that there would not be a mine left." Upon hearing this, the miners went up to Medicine Rock to ask Big Ike to cease his rainmaking. Big Ike's reply was as follows:

Go back to your claims and make that white man, who said that I did not make this rain, pay for the trouble that you have all been to, and when you are through, tell him to leave this camp and never return. I am Big Ike, the Rainmaker, and no savage, neither is my wife a squaw. Tell that white man to sharpen one hundred stout stakes and drive them into the ground. I see that the mountain has started to slide already. You will have to hurry before the slide gains momentum; otherwise, the stakes will not hold back the slide.

The miners went back to confront the one who had refused to pay. He started to ridicule Big Ike, telling the miners that was nothing but Indian talk—that "if the Indian rainmaker wanted the mountainside staked down he would have to do it himself." By this time, however, a landslide appeared close at hand. A few strong words were passed, and the miners soon convinced the troublemaker that he had better get to driving the stakes as Big Ike had instructed and as soon as the last stake was driven, to leave the camp. The stakes were driven, the mountainside remained intact, and the dishonest miner departed, never to return.

Further Reading

Graves, Charles S. *Lore and Legends of the Klamath River Indians.* 1929. Yreka, Calif.: Press of the Times.

Hirschfelder, Arlene, and Paulette Molin. *The Encyclopedia of Native American Religions.* 1992. New York: Facts on File.

Lyon, William S. *Encyclopedia of Native American Shamanism: Sacred Ceremonies of North America.* 1998. Denver: ABC- CLIO.

Josie Billie

Full Name at Birth: Josie Billie ("go around," "crazy spherical puma")

Birth: ca. 1887, place unknown

Death: date and place unknown

Education: enrolled at the Florida Baptist Institute in 1946 but period of attendance unknown

Leadership Position: Seminole medicine maker and assistant Baptist pastor

Summary

Josie Billie was a member of the Mikasuki (Miccosukee) band of Seminole and lived on the Big Cypress Reservation at the tip of the present-day Florida peninsula. Billie's interest in medicine began about 1902, and he acquired knowledge from various tribal doctors for approximately two years. One of them, Tommy Doctor, instructed him to undertake a fast as preparation for receiving training to become an *ayikcomi*, or medicine man. During four days of fasting, Billie was taught sacred songs, beliefs, and the ceremonies necessary to induce healing. He became an apprentice to another powerful Seminole shaman, Old Motlow, and repeated the training for the next two years. During Billie's apprenticeship, he learned how to diagnose illness, how to collect and prepare various herbs and healing remedies, and the sacred Seminole healing songs. Billie apprenticed with Old Motlow for four years. Following Old Motlow's death in 1920, Billie took over his practice.

A 1958 photo of Seminole Healer Josie Billie sitting in front of a depiction of the Wheel of Life. Courtesy of the Florida State Archives.

During his career, Billie also held a number of ceremonial positions. He served for four years as an assistant to a medicine man who was in charge of a Busk or Green Corn ceremony, the annual religious observance that ushered in the Seminole new year, recognized as one of the oldest unbroken ceremonial traditions practiced by Native American people. The ceremony is generally held when the green corn ripens and is associated with agricultural growth and fertility. The ceremony celebrated a period of renewal, thanksgiving, and amnesty. The ritual elements included preparing a sacred fire, fasting, praying, offerings, stomp dancing, traditional ball games, and a feast of traditional corn dishes.

Billie later became affiliated with another medicine man, eventually acquiring his medicine bundle (a container for objects and substances which had special significance to the owner; for the healer,

these were objects from which to draw healing powers) and conducting the Busk ceremony associated with it. About 1943, Billie moved to the Big Cypress Reservation after a period of trouble, including the accidental killing of a relative.

Early Life

In accordance with Seminole tradition, Billy was given a boyhood name shortly after birth. The name is translated as "go around" and is an allusion to the avoidance of a military camp during an earlier Seminole encounter. He acquired the name Josie, at the age of about four months when his father visited white friends at Fort Myers in present-day Florida. He received his Seminole name, translated as "crazy spherical puma," at the age of fifteen. As is customary among the Seminole, this was to remain his name for life.

Billie was a member of the Seminole Tiger Clan on his mother's side of the family and a member of the Miccosukee Wind Clan from his father. In his early youth, he was strongly influenced by his maternal grandmother, Nancy Osceola, a descendant of the famous Seminole leader Osceola.

Billy became interested in the Seminole medicine ways at an early age and asked many questions about the healing songs and medicine rituals. Because of his inquisitiveness, he attracted the attention of Old Motlow, a Seminole shaman, and at the age of seventeen, he began his formal training. Billie began his apprenticeship by going on a four-day fast. Old Motlow visited each day and instructed Billie in the secret medicine ways. On the first day, Old Motlow taught the songs necessary to cure various sicknesses. On the second day, he taught the theory that sickness is caused by the wandering of the soul during dreams. On the third day, he reviewed the songs of the first day and added more powerful songs to Billie's training. On the fourth day, Old Motlow taught Josie some of the more powerful spells and magical formulas needed for personal protection and power.

The following year, Billie returned for more teachings under the guidance and direction of Old Motlow. In addition to observing his practice, Billie learned herbal medicines and spiritual powers.

Leadership

Josie Billie was a noted medicine man and healer (doctor) among the Miccosukee band of Seminole Indians. The two roles are not necessarily the same in Seminole culture and require different training and sources of power. The doctor's role involves healing, while the medicine man serves as keeper of the sacred Seminole medicine bundle, among other duties.

Tommy Doctor and Old Motlow, both powerful Seminole shamans, recognized that Billie possessed special medicine that gave him extra curing power. At the age of seventeen, Billie began his four-year apprenticeship with Old Motlow. During this time, he was instructed in the sacred ways and knowledge necessary to fulfill his calling as both a healer and a medicine man. He was taught special medicines, ceremonies, and special songs that transfered the power of living medicine into his body, where they became alive. To keep his medicine alive and strong, Billie was required to renew his spiritual strength every month or two by fasting and taking an emetic made with special ingredients that constituted his "living medicine." If he attempted to cure a patient but failed, he concluded that his living medicine had become weak, and he was required to fast and take the emetic to restore his power.

In 1945, the Reverend Stanley Smith converted Billie to the Baptist faith, and on January 2, 1945, Billie was baptized. In 1946 Billie enrolled in the Florida Baptist Institute for formal religious training outside his own culture. He was later licensed to preach by the Southern Baptist Association and in July 1948 became an assistant pastor of a church on the Big Cypress Reservation. After his conversion to Christianity, he continued to serve as a doctor but not as a medicine man.

In addition to his role as a medicine man, healer, and Baptist pastor, Josie Billie was identified as an innovator who adopted a number of new ways. It is said that he introduced changes in the dress of Seminole men, including the practice of sewing appliqué strips of cloth on shirts now identified and popular among Native American people nationwide as "ribbon shirts." Billie also possessed extensive sacred knowledge, including botanical data, ceremonial songs and dances, oral traditions, and diagnostic abilities. In September 1958, an article in *Time* magazine highlighted Billie's abilities as a maker of medicines. This was followed by his work with the Upjohn Pharmaceutical Company in Kalamazoo, Michigan, where he was working on a tranquilizer made from several plants. When visited by botanist John K. Small in 1921, Josie had approximately thirty plants he was using in his treatments. By 1958 he was reputed to be the most skilled and powerful of the Seminole healers, having about 225 different plants in his repertoire.

Further Reading

Hirschfelder, Arlene, and Paulette Molin. *The Encyclopedia of Native American Religions.* 1992. New York: Facts on File.

Lyon, William S. *Encyclopedia of North American Healing.* 1996. Santa Barbara, Calif.: ABC-CLIO.

Black Elk

Full Name at Birth: Hehaka Sapa (Black Elk)
Birth: December 1863
Death: August 19, 1950, Manderson, South Dakota
Education: no formal education
Leadership Position: Lakota holy man

Summary

Black Elk was born at a time of great change and upheaval for the Lakota Nation and is considered by many to have been one of the greatest holy men ever born. At age five, he experienced a vision in which he was visited by the Thunder-beings, who would be his power helpers throughout his life. In 1881, Black Elk moved to the Pine Ridge Reservation in present-day South Dakota to live with his people, and in 1886 he joined Buffalo Bill's Wild West show as a performer and traveled to New York and to England. Black Elk returned to the Pine Ridge Indian Reservation in 1889 in time to witness the Ghost Dance of 1890 and the end of Indian power on the Great Plains.

Early Life

Black Elk was born in the Moon of the Popping Trees (December), 1863, on the

The Lakota holy man Black Elk (Hehaka Sapa) in a 1947 photo. Joseph Epes Brown, National Anthropological Archives, Smithsonian Institution.

Little Powder River, probably in present-day Wyoming. His father's name was Black Elk, as was his grandfather and his great-grandfather's, so he was the fourth to bear that name. His mother's name was White Cow, and they were members of Oglala tribe of the Lakota Nation. The band to which his family belonged hunted in the most westerly portion of Lakota country, beyond the Black Hills.

Black Elk was born into the traditional Lakota culture in which the Lakota people lived in a sacred relationship with the land, the animals, and the sky, as well as the seen and the unseen spirit forces of the universe. At age five, Black Elk experienced a vision in which he was visited by the Thunder-beings, who were the embodiments of the powers of the West. He had a more powerful vision at age nine. Although he did not understand the meaning or significance of these visions at his early age, they foretold the special powers he would have to use later in life to cure his people from illness and aid them in time of war. The power of the Thunder-beings imbued Black Elk with prophetic powers that would become manifest as he grew to adulthood. As a result of his visions, Black Elk felt different and apart from other children, and his life was overshadowed by the sacred knowledge made known to him.

Leadership

Black Elk was born at a time of great change and upheaval for the Lakota and other Indian Nations of the Great Plains. He and his people were accustomed to an unregimented lifestyle that included the pursuit of the buffalo, raiding for horses, magnificent age-graded societies (social organizations to which all boys of the same age group belong; they own songs, dances, regalia, and are taught tribal customs and duties appropriate to their age; there are a number of these groups beginning in childhood and progressing into manhood) that honored the warrior, and the freedom to move about freely, limited only by a person's own power. In the mid- to late 1800s, the invasion of white men challenged and then changed all of this. Military confrontation and a U.S. government policy of concentration of Indian people on reservations to subsist on government handouts in the form of treaty annuities threatened the survival of a way of life that Indians revered and whites misunderstood. Warfare was inevitable.

Back Elk was too young to take part in the fighting with the U.S. Army during the 1860s and 1870s. He could, however, remember December 1866, the "winter of the Hundred Slain," when Captain William Fetterman and eighty-one U.S. soldiers were killed on Peno Creek near Fort Phil Kearney. The fort was one of three that had been illegally built to support and protect white gold mining traffic on the equally illegal Bozeman Trail running through the heart of unceded Lakota territory. He could also remember how he felt as a thirteen-year-old boy witnessing the defeat of the Seventh Cavalry at the Battle of the Little Bighorn. Black Elk has been quoted as saying that he was not sorry at all. The white man had come to kill Indian men, women, and children and to take their land.

The wars over the Bozeman Trail brought the Oglalas into active conflict with the white men that would continue until 1877. In 1877, after the Oglala war leader Crazy Horse was killed at Fort Robinson, Nebraska, Black Elk's people fled to Canada to seek refuge from the U.S. government. They remained in Canada for about three years but because of food shortages and relentless pressure from the United States, they returned to the United States, only to be confined on the Pine Ridge Indian Reservation.

During the summer of either his sixteenth or seventeenth year, just after returning with his family to the United States, Black Elk was troubled by the visions that he had experienced in his early life and was overcome by obsessive fear of the Thunder-beings. In Lakota belief, a person who had had a vision of the Thunder-beings was required to enact the thunder rituals on earth, to humble one's self before the people, and to use the power he had been given for healing or for war. Black Elk had heard the voice of the Thunder-beings but was unsure what they wanted. With the encouragement of his family, he consulted Black Robe, a prominent Lakota medicine man, who then consulted a number of other prominent medicine men. They were astonished by the greatness of Black Elk's vision and instructed him to enact the Horse Dance, a public demonstration of a portion of the vision. Black Elk followed the instructions of the holy men and in 1881 performed the Horse Dance ceremony at Fort Keogh, Montana. This public manifestation of his vision put Black Elk in harmony with the spirit world and announced his spiritual calling to the Lakota people.

Following his public performance of the Horse Dance, Black Elk moved to the Pine Ridge Reservation in present-day South Dakota to live with his people. In 1883, he participated in a traditional vision quest and was blessed with a vision of his power helpers, the Thunder-beings. Black Elk performed part of this vision in a traditional ceremony known as the *heyoke* ceremony in which a person who has dreamed of Thunder-beings dressed as a sacred clown performed the dance and other rituals in an opposite or contrary way. The *heyoke* possessed great spiritual powers, and his actions were considered holy. Black Elk also repeated his earlier performance of the Horse Dance.

In 1886, Black Elk joined Buffalo Bill's Wild West show as a performer and traveled to New York and England. In England, he left the show and joined another troupe and visited Germany, France, and Italy. While in Europe, Black Elk studied Christianity and expressed a desire to visit the Holy Land but was unable to do so.

Black Elk returned to Pine Ridge in 1889 in time to witness the Ghost Dance of 1890 and the end of Indian power on the Great Plains. Some of the Lakota people had embraced the Ghost Dance religion given to the Paiute Indian prophet Wovoka* by the Great Spirit. The religion foretold the return of the good times when the white man would be removed from the earth and all of the Indian dead would return and rejoin their relatives. The buffalo would once again be plentiful, and the Lakota would no longer be confined to reservations, where they suffered from hunger and despair. Army agents misinterpreted the Ghost Dance as a call for new Indian warfare and massacred 250 Lakota men, women, and children at Wounded Knee Creek in 1890. In his old age, when he looked back at Wounded Knee he said that when he looked upon the dead at Wounded Knee, that he wished that he had died too. He said that something else died at Wounded Knee also. He said that the dream of the Lakota people died there.

Black Elk was married twice, in 1893 and 1906, and fathered seven children. He died on August 19, 1950 at Manderson, South Dakota.

Further Reading

Beck, Peggy V., Anna Lee Walters, and Nia Francisco. *The Sacred Ways of Knowledge, Sources of Life*. 1990. Flagstaff: Northland Publishing Co.

Black Elk, A Great Religious Leader: http://www.cwrl.utexas.edu/~mmaynard/Voices/ blackelk.html.

DeMallie, Raymond J., ed. *The Sixth Grandfather: Black Elk's Teachings Given to John G. Neihardt*. 1984. Lincoln: University of Nebraska Press.

Gill, Sam D. *Native American Religions: An Introduction*. 1982. Belmont, Calif.: Wadsworth Publishing Company.

Hirschfelder, Arlene, and Paulette Molin. *The Encyclopedia of Native American Religions*. 1992. New York: Facts on File.

Neihardt, John G. *Black Elk Speaks*. 1979. Lincoln: University of Nebraska Press.

Vecsey, Christopher, ed. *Handbook of American Indian Religious Freedom*. 1993. New York: Crossroad Publishing Company.

Walker, Paul R. *Spiritual Leaders: American Indian Lives*. 1994. New York: Facts on File.

Wallace Black Elk: http://www.blackelk.com/.

Washburn, Wilcomb E. *Handbook of North American Indians*. Vol. 4. 1988. Washington, D.C.: Smithsonian Institution.

Black Hairy Dog

Full Name at Birth: Black Hairy Dog or Black Hair Shepherd Dog

Birth: ca. 1823, place unknown

Death: ca. 1883, place unknown

Education: no formal education

Leadership Position: Cheyenne medicine man and keeper of the Sacred Arrows

Summary

Black Hairy Dog was a keeper of the Cheyenne Sacred Arrows who succeeded his father, Stone Forehead, to that position in 1876. The Sacred Arrows, the most sacred possession of the Cheyenne people, symbolize the collective existence of the tribe. Traditionally, the passing of the Sacred Arrows from one medicine person to another requires a religious apprenticeship and prescribed ceremony. At the time of Stone Forehead's sudden death, Black Hairy Dog was away from home. Stone Forehead's widow cared for the Sacred Arrows until Black Hairy Dog returned. Due to his absence, Stone Forehead was prevented from conducting the traditional ceremonies that included the cutting of holy symbols on the successor's skin, marking him as the new keeper of the Sacred Arrows.

The Southern branch of the Cheyenne had four Sacred Arrows, given to them by the Creator, who first gave them to Sweet Medicine,* a revered Cheyenne medicine person. As the arrows prosper, the Nation prospers. Along with the Sacred Arrows came sacred teachings, laws, and prophecies. The Sacred Arrows are considered to be the living manifestation of spiritual power for the Cheyenne people and are known as Maahotse (also Mahuts), or simply "The Creator." Two of the arrows have power over human beings, and two of the arrows have power over buffalo. Black Hairy Dog was also a Cheyenne medicine man and healer.

Early Life

There is no recorded history of Black Hairy Dog's early life. He was probably raised in one of the small, permanent Cheyenne villages on the shores of the Cheyenne River in present-day South Dakota. The Cheyenne lived in substantial earth-lodge villages that were built over shallow, excavated floors, above which were raised wooden frames. It is impossible to know how large the early Cheyenne villages may have been or how many of them there were. It was not a large tribe, however, and the likelihood is that not more than three hundred people would have made up a good-sized village. They were a sophisticated people with a rich and dramatic ceremonial life that included shamanism and healing ceremonies.

A mainstay of the Cheyenne diet was wild rice, harvested from canoes, hulled, and roasted. The country was filled with bison, elk, moose, deer, bear, wolves, raccoons, fox, and otter. Ducks and geese were plentiful, as were fish, which were taken in great quantities. As a youth, Black Hairy Dog would have learned to hunt deer, rabbits, and other small game snared or hunted with bow and arrow. As he grew older, he would have hunted the forest bison and larger game animals.

From oral history, it appears that Black Hairy Dog was either a blood or clan brother of the revered Southern Cheyenne Peace Chief, Black Kettle. Lieutenant Colonel George Armstrong Custer killed Black Kettle and one hundred other Cheyenne during an unprovoked attack at the Washita River, in present-day Oklahoma, in 1868.

Leadership

Black Hairy Dog rose to the position of medicine man and keeper of the Cheyenne Sacred Arrows following the sudden death of his father, Stone Forehead, in 1876. Black Hairy Dog was not with his father at the time of his death but rather was in the village of Dull Knife, a famous Northern Cheyenne war chief. In 1876, army troops attacked Dull Knife's village. Two Moons, another Northern Cheyenne war leader, was there, as was Coal Bear, the keeper of the Northern Cheyenne Sacred Buffalo Hat. When the Cheyenne leaders learned that the solders were planning an attack, Black Hairy Dog recommended that they move the camp to the foot of the mountains, to join up with the larger Sioux camp. But Last Bull, chief of the Fox Soldier Society, said, "No, we will stay here and fight." Colonel Ranald MacKenzie took the village, destroyed provisions, and killed forty Cheyenne warriors. Black Hairy Dog was not among those killed and lived to assume guardianship of the Sacred Arrows.

The Southern branch of the Cheyenne had four Sacred Arrows, and the Northern Cheyenne had a Sacred Buffalo Hat. The Sacred Arrows are the most sacred possession of the Cheyenne people and are considered to be the living guardian and guiding force of Cheyenne spiritual power. When the arrows are ritually pointed toward animals, the animals become confused and helpless and are easily killed. When the arrows are carried into battle or are ritually pointed at the enemy before an attack, the enemy becomes disoriented. When used in battle, the Sacred Arrows were said to possess the power to blind the enemy.

Associated with his duties as keeper of the Sacred Arrows, Black Hairy Dog was also a medicine man among the Cheyenne people, which meant that he possessed supernatural power that could be used for the welfare of his people. A person who wanted personal power for healing or immunity in battle had to acquire spiritual power. The main road to supernatural power was through acquisition of ritual knowledge learned from one who was already a medicine person. This is most commonly done by participating in a vision quest.

A Cheyenne vision quest is best described as a fast in a lonely place where one begs the spirits for indulgence and spiritual aid. If favored by a spirit, the person receives a blessing, along with instructions on to how to prepare power objects (such as amulets), how to paint himself, and what songs to sing to release the power. Visions and supernatural powers also come unsought in time of trouble. The individual Cheyenne who wishes to become in tune with the animistic powers (the belief that all things in nature have souls independent of their physical being of the universe) does it through fasting, vision seeking, and sacrificial offering. The pledging to participate in a ceremony such as a Sun Dance is one such offering.

Black Hairy Dog and his wife were among those who escaped when U.S. soldiers and buffalo hunters attacked Little Bull's band of Southern Cheyenne on April 23, 1875, on Sappa Creek in present-day Kansas while the group was en route to the territory of the Northern branch of their people. Pursued by soldiers, Black Hairy Dog and his wife each took two Sacred Arrows and followed different routes. Black Hairy Dog joined Dull Knife's band which was attacked by General Mackenzie's forces on November 26, 1876. Black Hairy Dog saw the enemies approaching first, however, and alerted the people. During the attack, he positioned himself at a point where he could turn the power of the Sacred Arrows against the military soldiers and scouts. Black Harry Dog, his wife, and other families who survived eventually joined up with the Southern Cheyenne in Indian Territory, the present-day state of Oklahoma.

Further Reading

Grinnell, George Bird. *The Fighting Cheyennes.* 1956. Norman: University of Oklahoma Press.

Hirschfelder, Arlene, and Paulette Molin. *The Encyclopedia of Native American Religions.* 1992. New York: Facts on File.

Hoebel, E. Adamson. *The Cheyennes: Indians of the Great Plains.* 1978. New York: Holt, Rinehart and Winston.

Moore, John H. *The Cheyenne Nation: A Social and Demographic History.* 1987. Lincoln: University of Nebraska Press.

James Blue Bird

Full Name at Birth: James Blue Bird

Birth: 1887, place unknown

Death: date and place of death unknown

Education: attended Carlisle Indian Industrial School in Pennsylvania, 1907–1911

Leadership Position: Lakota peyote religious leader

Summary

James Blue Bird was an influential peyote religious leader among the Lakota people. There are two primary ceremonies in the peyote religion: the Half-Moon and the Cross-Fire, or Big Moon, ceremony.

The Half-Moon and Cross-Fire (practiced by James Blue Bird) ceremonies shared many commonalities, and both incorporated aspects of Indian culture and Christianity. Both ceremonies emphasized the divine role of peyote and its power to teach and heal; both opposed the use of liquor and believed that peyote destroyed the taste for it. In both ceremonies, peyote was eaten to concentrate and to learn, not to induce visions. Women could ingest the peyote button; however, most women and children participated in the ceremony by drinking peyote tea. Both ceremonies included preaching, prophecy, baptism, and other similarities to the Christian religion. The Half-Moon ceremony limited tobacco use, whereas the Cross-Fire ceremony prohibited the use of tobacco entirely. Other shared features were the use of elaborate altars on which the peyote was placed, ashes formed into ceremonial designs, and ultimately the construction of permanent churches and altars.

Opposition to the peyote religion was manifested at the federal and state levels, and in 1918 followers of the religion who sought to protect their religious practices from attack organized the Native American church.

James Blue Bird became one of the earliest and most influential peyote leaders among the Sioux and other northern tribes and was one of the prime movers of South Dakota peyotism for many years.

Early Life

James Blue Bird was born in 1887 and attended Carlisle Indian Industrial School in Pennsylvania from 1907 to 1911. While attending Carlisle, he was introduced to the Christian religion. Blue Bird attributed his faith in the Bible to his father, however, who had become an Episcopal minister when Blue Bird was five years of age.

After attending Carlisle Industrial School, Blue Bird spent several years touring the eastern United States with Wild West shows. These shows, popular in the eastern United States, were staged reenactments of western Indian life, including buffalo chases, Indian craft work, and mock battles between Indians and U.S. cavalry. The cavalry always won.

When Blue Bird was fifteen years old, he was introduced to the peyote religion at a meeting conducted by the famous Comanche peyote roadman Quanah Parker,* held in Calumet in present-day Oklahoma. The peyote roadman is the leader of the all-night Peyote ceremony or peyote meeting. The term *roadman* comes from the peyote road, represented on the ceremonial peyote altar by a line. From 1904 to 1907, he attended services on the Pine Ridge Reservation in South Dakota conducted by John Rave and Albert Hensley,* two Peyote roadmen from the Winnebago Nation. In 1916, Blue Bird again attended peyote meetings led by Rave and Hensley, who inspired him to become a roadman of the Cross-Fire peyote ritual. That year he became an acknowledged leader of the peyote religion among the Lakota people.

Leadership

James Blue Bird was one of the earliest and most influential peyote roadmen among the Sioux Nation and other northern Great Plains tribes.

Blue Bird first learned of peyote in 1902 when he was fifteen years of age at a meeting led by the Comanche Peyote Roadman Quanah Parker. From 1907 to 1911 Blue Bird attended Carlisle Indian School, where he was subjected to the Christian religion, but he attributed his faith in the Bible to his father, who had become an Episcopal minister in 1892 when Jim was five. His father did not try to change James's decision because he recognized Christian elements in the Cross-Fire peyote beliefs.

After Carlisle, James spent a number of years with Wild West shows, but in 1916 he attended peyote meetings in Nebraska with John Rave and Albert Hensley, and it was from them that he learned to be a peyote roadman. When Blue Bird returned home in 1916, he was the acknowledged leader of the peyote religion among the Sioux. He subsequently became the organizer and director of the Native American church of South Dakota, headquartered in Allen, South Dakota and maintained the position for fifty years.

As a peyote roadman, Blue Bird was the leader of the all-night peyote ceremony or peyote meeting. During the ceremony, participants centered their concentration on "Father Peyote," a button from the peyote cactus, placed on an earthen altar. A line, called the peyote road, was also drawn on the altar. It is believed that concentration on Father Peyote and the peyote road will lead the prayers of the worshippers to the Creator.

Roadmen may also be healers, or medicine men, and may hold other leadership roles within the tribe. They learn to conduct peyote ceremonies from other roadmen, and from the experience of taking on the duties of the role. It is then their responsibility to instruct others who are interested in learning the necessary skills. Generally, roadmen are paid for their services with gifts since no set fees are charged for conducting a peyote ceremony. Other participants in the ceremony include a chief drummer, a fireman, who builds and tends the ceremonial fire, and a cedarman, who places cedar in the fire to consecrate ritual objects.

Blue Bird's form of peyotism was the Cross-Fire ceremony, and he was very much against the use of tobacco. He attributed the Sioux Half-Moon ceremony to the Lakota roadman Willie Running Hawk and his brother, who lived on the Pine Ridge Indian Reservation. They had learned the ceremony while in present-day Oklahoma. When Blue Bird traveled south to Pine Ridge to attend peyote meetings, he was usually in the company of established peyotists, and his role was that of a student. When he returned home in 1916, he was the acknowledged leader of the peyote religion among the Sioux. In 1918 the Native American church was founded and incorporated to protect the adherents of the peyote religion, who sought to protect their religious practices from attack by federal and state authorities.

From 1928 to 1931, Blue Bird drove a truck for the South Dakota Highway Department in the vicinity of Sisseton, South Dakota. While he was there, ten Sisseton Sioux families joined together to found a Cross-Fire peyote church. Blue Bird was their roadman.

James Blue Bird was one of the prime movers of South Dakota peyotism for many years. He became the organizer and director of the Native American church of South Dakota, and his church had sixteen local chapters. On January 13, 1948, Blue Bird wrote: "I became a member of the peyote religion in July, 1902, in Calumet, Oklahoma. Pine Ridge Sioux in South Dakota and commenced to use Peyote in 1904." In 1971, at age eighty-four and still in good health, and possessing a remarkable memory, he provided details of names, places, and dates concerning the spread of peyote among the Sioux.

Some of James's ideas were emphasized in his prayers and sermons, one of which follows:

The old time Sioux went out to get visions so that they could go and scalp their enemies, but I am against all killing because I believe in the Bible. . . .

My boys in the Korean War carried Peyote all the time. . . .

The Bible guides us in life just like doctors' instruction—it is our prescription for life. . . .

We put the staff in a hold in front of the altar so that it stands upright and points to heaven. . . .

Peyote is an awful wonderful thing. When you eat peyote you feel guilty in your conscience for being a sinner. You think about yourself and try to lead a better life and be a brother to all. . . .

Something around us tells us how far we stand from God. Then it is revealed to us what we should do and what we should not do. . . .

We don't try to convert. . . . Let them come themselves.

Further Reading

Hirschfelder, Arlene and Paulette Molin. *The Encyclopedia of Native American Religions*. 1992. New York: Facts on File.

Steinmetz, Paul B. *Pipe, Bible, and Peyote Among the Oglala Lakota: A Study in Religious Identity*. 1990. Knoxville: University of Tennessee Press.

Stewart, Omer C. *Peyote Religion: A History*. 1987. Norman: University of Oklahoma Press.

James Chrysostom Bouchard

Full Name at Birth: Watomika ("Swift Footed One")

Birth: 1823 in the village of Muskagtola, in the Leni-Lanape (Delaware) Reserve, a portion of the Indian Territory southeast of present-day Leavenworth, Kansas

Death: December 27, 1889, San Francisco, California

Education: attended Marietta Collegiate Institute and Western Teachers Seminary in Marietta, Ohio, fall 1834–May 1847

Leadership Position: Leni-Lanape (Delaware) Indian priest

Awards: first American Indian ordained to the Roman Catholic priesthood in the United States

Summary

James Bouchard (Watomika) was the son of the Leni-Lanape (Delaware) chief Kistalwa and his French wife, Marie-Elizabeth Bucheur. Following his father's death in 1834, Bouchard relocated to Ohio. Bouchard attended the Marietta Collegiate Institute in Ohio, where he first studied for the ministry of Christianity in the Presbyterian church. In 1846, he joined the Catholic church in St. Louis, Missouri, and began his studies for the Jesuit order. In 1848, he became a Jesuit, and in 1855, he became the first Indian to be ordained a Catholic priest. In 1861, he began serving as a missionary to miners in San Francisco even though his preference was to minister to his own people. Bouchard served in the American West for nearly three decades. He became a distinguished orator of the Golden City and preacher in numerous cathedrals and country churches. Father

A c. 1880 photo of the Leni-Lanape (Delaware) priest father James Chrysostom Bouchard, S. J. Courtesy of Midwest Jewish Archives, St. Louis, Mo.

Bouchard also lectured on both his Native American heritage and Christianity.

Early Life

Little is known of his early life among the Leni-Lanape people; however, he reported that his childhood was happy. He lived the life of a traditional Indian youth and became proficient in the use of bow and arrow and tomahawk. He participated as a warrior in an 1834 revenge attack on the Lakota (Sioux) and took pride in his part in the battle. It was during this battle that his father, Kistalwa, was mortally wounded. A short time after, Bouchard's mother returned to live among the Comanche people, and Bouchard traveled with a Mr. Williamson, a Protestant minister, to Ohio, where he was enrolled in Marietta College to be instructed in the human sciences and Christianity.

Leadership

Raised as a traditional Leni-Lanape (Delaware) Indian, Bouchard, whose Indian name was Watomika, emerged from a Native American background to become an outstanding figure in the history of Roman Catholicism in the American West.

Bouchard was born in 1823 into the family of a prominent Leni-Lanape family. He was the son of Kistalwa, the tribal chief, and his wife, Marie-Elizabeth Bucheur, whose Indian name was Monotawan, meaning "White Fawn." Marie-Elizabeth was the daughter of a Frenchman by the name of Bucheur who immigrated to the United States, where he settled on the Rio Frio branch of the Nueces River in present-day Texas. In 1815, a party of Comanche Indians kidnapped Marie-Elizabeth, who was about seven years of age at the time. She remained with the Comanche tribe for about six years and was then traded to the Leni-Lanape (Delaware) tribe, where she was courted by and later married Kistalwa. She was about fifteen years old at that time. The tribe soon relocated to present-day Kansas, and it was in the village of Muskagola that Marie-Elizabeth gave birth to Bouchard.

What is known of his early life among the Leni-Lanape comes from his own recollections as written in letters and in conversations with Father James Defouri, a secular priest who recorded some of his conversations. We know that his childhood was a happy one and that he was raised in the traditional ways of an Indian youth of the Leni-Lanape Nation. He learned the skills associated with fishing and hunting, and became proficient in the use of bow and arrow and the use of the tomahawk. At eleven years of age, he participated as a warrior in an 1834 revenge attack on the Lakota (Sioux) who had recently captured and tortured to death a Leni-Lanape warrior. He took pride in his part in the attack and recounts the horror, bloodletting, and confusion of battle, as well as his father's leadership role. It was during this battle that his father, Kistalwa, received a mortal wound. A short time after, Bouchard's mother elected to return to live among the Comanche people, her first captives.

Following his father's death, Bouchard elected to pursue an education and traveled with a Mr. Williamson, a Protestant minister, to Ohio, where he attended Marietta Collegiate Institute and Western Teachers Seminary. It was there that he first studied for the ministry of Christianity in the Presbyterian church. In 1846, he joined the Catholic Church in St. Louis, Missouri, and began his studies for the Jesuit order. In 1848, he became a Jesuit and in 1855 became the first Indian to be ordained a Catholic priest. "The Jesuit Order in the United States had now received into the ranks of its priestly sons the first American Indian ever to reach sacerdotal dignity within the limits of the country. To James Chrysostom Bouchard belonged this distinction and this honor" (McGloin 69). In 1861, he began serving as a missionary to miners in San Francisco even though his preference was to minister to his own people.

Bouchard served in the American West for nearly three decades and retained his Native language into his Jesuit years. He became a distinguished orator and preached in numerous mining camps, cathedrals, and country churches. His stirring sermons and eloquent delivery earned him high praise and filled churches, often reported as standing room only. The *Santa Clara Redwood* reported that "the West had never heard such soul-stirring, feeling eloquence. . . . The church was altogether too small to contain the crowds anxious to drink in the burning words of the new Orator of the Golden City." As his reputation grew, Father Bouchard was in great demand. The year 1886 is given as representing an average year's schedule in which he preached in sixteen different cities in the Far West. Among the sites of his lectures and sermons, were San Francisco, California; Virginia City, Nevada; Victoria, British Columbia; Butte City, Montana; Portland, Oregon; and Walla Walla, Washington.

Father Bouchard celebrated his last mass on December 8, 1889, in the Father's Chapel of the Jesuit residence in San Francisco. He died on December 27, 1889, in San Francisco. The *San Francisco Chronicle* stated that "Father Bouchard's addressees made him known as one of the best pulpit orators in the country. He had an imposing appearance and a pleasing address. His long white beard . . . gave him a venerable appearance." The Indian Jesuit, the Orator of the Golden City, was now gone.

Further Reading

Ballantine, Betty and Ian Ballantine, eds. *The Native Americans: An Illustrated History.* 1993. Atlanta: Turner Publishing.

Hirschfelder, Arlene and Paulette Molin. *The Encyclopedia of Native American Religions.* 1992. New York. Facts on File.

McGloin, John Bernard. *Eloquent Indian: The Life of James Bouchard, California Jesuit.* 1949. Stanford: Stanford University Press.

San Francisco Chronicle, December 18, 1889.

Santa Clara Redwood. January 1906.

Waldman, Carl. *Who Was Who in Native American History.* 1990. New York: Facts on File.

Box Elder

Full Name at Birth: Box Elder (Mitskim')
Birth: ca, 1795, place of birth unknown
Death: ca. 1892, near present-day Birney, Montana
Education: no formal education
Leadership Position: Cheyenne holy man, keeper of the Sacred Arrows, and medicine lodge priest

Summary

Box Elder was a Cheyenne holy man and Keeper of the Cheyenne Sacred Arrows. He was a leader of the Cheyenne Medicine Lodge ceremony and was highly respected for his ability to prophesy and predict future events. As was customary among Native American holy men, Box Elder was the caretaker of a very powerful medicine bundle that he used throughout his life. His power was so revered that his medicine bundle continued to be used in the Medicine Lodge ceremony even after his death. Box Elder's bundle was also used in the Cheyenne Massaum lodge ceremony, to renew the covenant between the Creator and the Cheyenne people.

Early Life

No records exist of Box Elder's early years. Having been born in approximately 1795, when the Cheyenne were a powerful Nation, he was probably raised in the traditional Cheyenne way. He was probably raised in one of the small, permanent, and substantial earth lodge Cheyenne villages on the shores of the Cheyenne River in present-day South Dakota. It is impossible to know how large the early Cheyenne villages may have been or how many of them there were. It was not a large tribe, however, and the likelihood is that not more than three hundred people would have made up a good-sized village. They were a sophisticated people with a rich and dramatic ceremonial life that included shamanism and healing ceremonies.

A mainstay of the Cheyenne diet was wild rice, harvested from canoes, hulled, and roasted. The country was filled with bison, elk, moose, deer, bear, wolves, raccoons, fox, and otter. Ducks and geese were plentiful, as were fish, which were taken in great quantities. As a youth, Box Elder would have learned to hunt deer, rabbits, and other small game that he snared or hunted with bow and arrow. As he grew older, he would have hunted the forest bison and larger game animals.

Leadership

Box Elder was a highly respected and feared Cheyenne holy man, warrior, and chief. He was the son of Old Horn (later called Blind Bull), a great holy man of the Suhtai band of the Cheyenne Nation. Besides learning sacred knowledge from his father, he was instructed regarding the relationship of power between the animal and human world. Box Elder possessed gifts of prophecy as well as the ability to summon spirit helpers and communicate with them. One spirit helper told Box Elder that he would be bulletproof in war against the white man. As a warrior, he was fearless in battle because of this power.

Box Elder was so respected as a holy man that he was one of two individuals chosen to make the shafts for the Sacred Arrows, to replace those captured by the Pawnee in 1803.

The Southern branch of the Cheyenne had four Sacred Arrows, the most sacred possession of the Cheyenne people, which symbolize the collective existence of the tribe. As the arrows prosper, the Nation prospers. As the arrows are neglected, so too is the Cheyenne Nation neglected.

The four arrows were given to the Cheyenne by the Creator, who first gave them to Sweet Medicine,* a revered Cheyenne medicine person. Along with the Sacred Arrows came sacred teachings, laws, and prophecies. The Sacred Arrows are considered to be the living manifestation of spiritual power for the Cheyenne people and are known as Maahotse (also Mahuts), or simply "The Creator." Two of the arrows are considered to be "male" and have power over human beings, and two of the arrows have power over buffalo.

Box Elder's spiritual powers were displayed in prophetic visions and the ability to foretell the future. On one occasion in 1876, he demonstrated his power by alerting the people of approaching soldiers. He again demonstrated his sacred powers during Colonel Ranald MacKenzie's attack against the Cheyenne in 1876.

Box Elder was also a Medicine Lodge or Sun Dance priest. The Medicine Lodge ceremony is the midsummer ceremony practiced by many of the Plains Indian Nations and is called the Sun Dance by many of the tribes because it includes a "sun-looking" or "sun gazing" dance. It is one of the best-known religious ceremonies conducted by Native Americans and was practiced in some form by almost all tribal groups of the Great Plains regions, including the Cheyenne, Arapaho, Arikara, Blackfeet, Comanche, Crow, Cheyenne, Lakota, and Dakota. The ceremony has many variations; however, for most tribes, the sacred ceremony is held to pray for the renewal of the people and the earth, to give thanks, to fulfill a vow, and to protect the people from danger or illness. It was also an important social event that traditionally brought scattered tribal bands together during the summer for social as well as religious activities. The annual ceremonial period was a time for courting, renewing friendships, exchanging information, visiting relatives, and holding traditional games.

The Medicine Lodge ceremony is one of the most sacred of the Cheyenne healing ceremonies and lasts for three days. During the ceremony, Box Elder's bundle was placed on the south side of the buffalo skull. This bundle was recognized as having great medicine power. It contained, among other things, the straight pipe used in the Medicine Lodge, some red-painted braids of sweet grass, a beaded deerskin sack that held yellow paint, a sphere of buffalo dung, and a small bundle of old buffalo sinew wrapped up in red flannel.

In the healing ceremony in the Medicine Lodge, Box Elder's bundle was taken from the south side of the buffalo skull and opened. The straight pipe was removed, as were a piece of sinew and some plaits of sweet grass. A medicine man used these sacred elements to heal various illnesses.

Box Elder's bundle was also used in the Cheyenne Massaum lodge ceremony. (The name *Massaum* comes from the Cheyenne word *massáne* and is part of the Cheyenne earth-giving ritual.) Like the Sacred Arrows, the Massaum was given to the Cheyenne by the great prophet Sweet Medicine, and each summer the Cheyenne bands gathered for the annual Massaum ceremony to renew the sacred covenant between the creator and the Cheyenne people. The ceremony lasted for five days in which the creation of the universe was reenacted. Religious activities included the smoking of the straight pipe from Box Elder's medicine bundle.

Box Elder lived to an old age. He died near present-day Birney, Montana in about 1892. Box Elder's other names include Maple, Maple Tree, Dog on the Range, Dog on the Ridge Dog Standing, and Old Brave Wolf.

Further Reading

Grinnell, George Bird. *The Cheyenne Indians: Their History and Ways of Life.* 1962. New York: Cooper Square Publishers.

Hirschfelder, Arlene, and Paulette Molin. *The Encyclopedia of Native American Religions.* 1992. New York. Facts on File.

Llewellyn, K. N., and E. Adamson Hoebel. *The Cheyenne Way: Conflict and Case Law in Primitive Jurisprudence.* 1941. Norman: University of Oklahoma Press.

Moore, John H. *The Cheyenne Nation: A Social and Demographic History.* 1987. Lincoln: University of Nebraska Press.

Waldman, Carl. *Who Was Who in Native American History.* 1990. New York: Facts on File.

Brave Buffalo (Tatan' ka ohi' tika)

Full Name at Birth: Brave Buffalo (Tatan' ka ohi' tika)
Birth: ca. 1840 near present-day Pollock, North Dakota
Death: date and place of death unknown
Education: no formal education
Leadership Position: Lakota (Sioux) shaman and medicine man

Summary

Brave Buffalo was one of the most powerful healers on the Lakota Standing Rock Reservation in present-day South Dakota at the turn of the twentieth century. His power to heal came in a dream in which sacred round stones appeared to him and told him that the maker of all was Wakan Tanka (the Great Spirit of the Sioux) and that to honor him he must honor the Creator's works in nature.

Brave Buffalo reported that a shaman's medicine "is a very sacred thing—not to be discussed lightly or with just any person. Some people, he said, never reveal to anyone the details of their personal spiritual power."

In diagnosing the sickness of his patients, Brave Buffalo used a four- by six-inch mirror encased in a wooden frame. On the surface of the mirror were the sacred symbols of the new moon and a star symbol. Brave Buffalo reported, "I hold this mirror in front of the sick person and see his disease reflected in it; then I can cure the disease." He reported that his healing powers were "the strongest during the full moon," and "when the moon dies my strength is all gone until the moon comes back again."

Early Life

There is no written history of Brave Buffalo's early years. We do know that he was the son of Crow Bear, also an important medicine man. The remainder of our information comes from a story that Brave Buffalo told shortly before his death:

> When I was 10 years of age I looked at the land and the rivers, the sky above, and the animals around me and could not fail to realize that they were made by some great power. I was so anxious to understand this power that I questioned the trees and the bushes. It seemed as though the flowers were staring at me and I wanted to ask them "Who made you?" I looked at them but they could not answer me. Then I had a dream and in my dream one of these small round stones appeared to me and told me that the maker of all was Wakan Tanka (the Great Spirit of the Sioux) and that in order to honor Him I must honor his works in nature. The stone then said that by my search I had shown myself worthy of supernatural help and that it would provide for me this help.

Following his dream, Brave Buffalo searched for a stone similar to the stone of his dream. He covered the stone with an eagle down feather and wrapped it in a piece of buckskin. The stone served as a reminder of the supernatural help promised in his dream.

Leadership

In his treatment of the sick, Brave Buffalo was a sucking shaman. He would perform sacred ceremonies over the sick person while singing healing songs that had been given to him in a dream. Once the disease-causing agent or the diseased area was made known to him, he would suck the object from the patient using a hollow bone tube. The object would then be disposed of in a manner that had been made known to him.

Brave Buffalo reported, "Some diseases are affected by the day and others by the night. I use this song [obtained in his wolf dream] in cases which are worse at night. I composed it myself and always sing it at night, whether I am treating a sick person or not. I offer smoke to the four winds and sing this song." In his wolf dream, Brave Buffalo was surrounded by a pack of wolves, each of which had its nostrils and paws painted red. The wolves took him to their den on top of a high hill, where they taught him a song to be used in his healing ritual.

Brave Buffalo went on to state:

> Some people have an idea that we medicine-men, who get our power from different sources, are the worst of human beings; they even say that we get our power from the evil one, but no one could disregard such dreams as I have had, and no one could fail to admire the sacred stones (*tunkan*). Wakan Tanka (Creator) is all-powerful, and if we reverence his work he will surely let us prove to all men that these things are indeed his doing. It is a very strict requirement that a medicine-man shall act out his dream [or vision], and that he maintain absolute integrity of character. If he fails to do this he will be punished and will not live long. I am not required to fast, only to smoke, showing that I am at peace with all men. Dreams come to me now in a natural way. Often during the day when I am alone on a journey and my mind is on many things, I stop to rest awhile. I observe what is around me and then I become drowsy and dream. Often I see the sacred stone in my dreams. When I was ten years of age, I looked at the land and the rivers, the sky

above, and the animals around me. I felt that all this must have been made by some great power. I wanted to understand this power. I looked at the trees, the bushes and the flowers. They all seemed to be staring at me and I wanted to ask them, "Who made you?" I looked at the moss-covered stones; some of them looked like a man, but they could not answer me. Then I had a dream, and one small stone told me that the maker of all things was the Great Spirit, Wakan Tanka.

"The stones," Brave Buffalo said, "are like the sun and the moon, not buried in the ground, but on top of the hill."

Further Reading

Brave Buffalo and the Sacred Stones: http://members.aol.com/MNicholas2/native/buffalo.htm.

Brave Buffalo's Dream: http://www.cybersuds.co.jp/ge/INDIAN/brave.html.

Lyon, William S. *Encyclopedia of Native American Healing.* 1996. Denver: ABC-CLIO.

Fanny Brown

Full Name at Birth: unknown

Birth: ca. 1870, place unknown

Death: date and place of death unknown

Education: no formal education

Leadership Position: Wintu shaman

Summary

Brown was an influential Wintu shaman who flourished in the late 1800s and early 1900s in the upper Sacramento area of present-day California.

Shamanism was extremely important among the Wintu and combined the most important social and religious aspect of Wintu culture. Shamanistic power was usually acquired during a *lahateonos* (initiation ceremony), which was open to both men and women. As many as twenty persons might try to become a shaman during the *lahateonos*; however, only a small number (two to five) obtained the shamanistic power. Every shaman was required to be a good singer and possess a number of doctoring songs associated with her various spirits. There were other avenues to become a shaman as well. In about 1934, Brown told Cora Du Bois, an ethnologist, how she received her first power:

My nephew died of consumption while I was holding him in my arms. When he died my heart jumped up. For about two minutes my body got stiff. I was crying. I felt as if I were drunk. I saw a tattooed woman standing about twenty yards away from me. She was a spirit and wanted to take the boy away. . . . That night I went home to sleep. Every little while something made me sing. I don't know what made me sing. I would half sleep for a little while, then I would sing some more. That went on all night. That was the first time I felt the spirit. I was pretty old already. I was married and had lost a child. I think maybe it was my baby's spirit which came back to me. After I sang I came to. My heart was making me do this all the time. I was like this for about three weeks. I sang every night. During those three weeks I didn't know anything. I felt a hot and cold pain come in one ear, go through me head, and come out the other. The pain lasted all the time during those three weeks. Whenever I doctor now that pain comes back, but it goes away as soon as I come to.

Brown also acknowledged that she inherited shamanistic healing powers from her brother and sister. She stated, "My brothers and my sister were doctors. . . . I got all their powers and their spirits. They came to me little by little. My brother had two spirits. My sister had two—a sucker spirit and a human one."

Early Life

There is no recorded history of Brown's early life. Because she flourished as a shaman, it is reasonable to assume that she was raised in the traditional Wintu tradition. Brown would have been nursed from birth to the age of two to four years. During her infancy, her mother would have rubbed and stretched her body to make it shapely. Brown would have spent a great deal of time with her grandparents or a near relative, who, following traditional Wintu practices, may have adopted her and raised her equal to their own children. Like all other Wintu girls, Brown would have been taught to sit when in the presence of men, with her legs stretched straight out in front or drawn up to one side. She would have displayed shyness and avoided contact with men. In keeping with band and clan affiliation, her ears were pierced and her chin tattooed so that her lineage could be established by viewing her face.

Leadership

In her early career as a shaman, Brown was primarily a sucking doctor who cured illness by sucking the intrusion from the patient's body. To effect the cures, she used the spirits that she had obtained from her brother and sister. In addition to their spiritual helpers, Brown also claimed their doctoring materials. Among the Wintu, it was permissible for a relative to claim the materials from a deceased relative providing she knew how to "talk to them right." Brown had that ability. After she claimed the doctoring materials, Brown stated,

> I have a bunch of feathers to use in doctoring. It was hidden in the mountains by a great old-time doctor. My brother found it and brought it [the bundle] in the house to me and left there. The feathers should all come from the wings of eagles. Tail feathers are too short. If a man who isn't a good doctor holds a bunch of these feathers, he will get a headache. It is dangerous for him to handle them. I made my own headdress (yellow-hammer) and necklace (of rattlesnake rattles). I killed my own rattlesnakes. A person who is a good doctor isn't afraid of rattlesnakes. I don't know what a "pain" looks like. Some people say it looks like a sliver of bone. . . . When I suck out a pain I chew it up and kill it with my teeth, then I spit it out into a bundle of grass. I never swallow it. I hide the bundle of grass in the bushes. Once I doctored a man three days and nights and I got out a pain every time I sucked.

Brown was known to have clairvoyant abilities as well. At one point in her life, one of her sons was killed, and she was told that he had drowned. Brown went into a trance and told all that had happened. She said that her son had been murdered and that his body had been kept under the house for two days, after which it was thrown into the river. She told the informants that the body would be found in the river between Kennett and Keswick, on the Sacramento River. People looked for the body and found it.

Shamanistic power can be used for both good and evil. Following the murder of her son, Brown gained the reputation of being a "poisoner" and was rarely called to attend a patient. Most of the material concerning Brown's poisoning was anecdotal, however, and focused on an ongoing feud between Brown and another shaman, Charles Klutchie. Klutchie had a large family. Brown had had ten children, all but one of whom were dead. It was said that Brown was jealous of Klutchie, and Brown and Klutchie accused each other of "shooting poisons" at their respective houses. Klutchie proved to be an equal match to Brown, and in an attempt to hurt him, Brown poisoned his close friend Tilly Griffen. When Griffen became ill, she implicated Brown as the person who had sent poison against her. Following this event, Brown fades from history.

Further Reading

Du Bois, Cora. *Wintu Ethnography.* 1935. Berkeley: University of California Publications.

Hirschfelder, Arlene, and Paulette Molin. *The Encyclopedia of Native American Religions.* 1992. New York: Facts on File.

Lyon, William S. *Encyclopedia of Native American Shamanism: Sacred Ceremonies of North America.* 1998. Denver: ABC-CLIO.

Bull Lodge

Full Name at Birth: Bull Lodge (Buffalo Lodge)

Birth: ca. 1802, place of birth unknown

Death: ca. 1886, place of death unknown

Education: no formal education

Leadership Position: Gros Ventre holy man, Keeper of the Flat Pipe, Chief Medicine Pipe (also known as the Feathered Pipe), and a Gros Ventre warrior

Summary

Bull Lodge was a Gros Ventre holy man and warrior who possessed gifts of healing and prophecy. His mother was Cook Kill, or Good Kill, a Gros Ventre woman who was married to a French trader, High Crane (or Crooked Rump).

Bull Lodge was the keeper of two of the most sacred symbols in Gros Ventre religious cosmology: the sacred Flat Pipe and the sacred Feathered Pipe, or Chief Medicine Pipe. The pipes were symbols of creation and the Gros Ventres' place in the universe.

The Gros Ventre considered their religion integral to their identity as a people; however, there was also a great emphasis on bravery and fortitude as displayed in warfare. Bull Lodge was described in 1879 by the Indian agent Wyman Lincoln as "a kind of a renegade Gros Ventre who used bad medicine and spent much of his time with the Crow Indians."

Holy men who were called keepers were trained to care for and perform the rituals associated with the two sacred pipes. A man such as Bull Lodge could be a keeper, but he was obligated not to use his power to harm others.

Early Life

Little is known of Bull Lodge's life. His mother, Cook Kill, left his father, High Crane, to rejoin her people who had moved to another area. Bull Lodge never knew his father and was brought up among the Gros Ventre. As a youth in the early 1800s, he would have belonged to an age-graded society, where all of the youth of one age progressed together through instruction and preparation for their roles in Gros Ventre life. They would be taught games, songs, dances, and hunting skills appropriate to their age group, and as the cohort advanced in age, they were instructed in the religious cosmology and their role and responsibility as warriors. At about age twelve, Bull Lodge would have participated in a vision quest, which was a way to acquire a spiritual or war helper. (A helper was a spirit power that could be called upon for guidance by the individual.) In preparation for the vision quest, a medicine person would have instructed Bull Lodge to go alone to a distant place where in the past successful vision quests had taken place. Snake Butte, on the Fort Belknap Indian Reservation in present-day Montana, is one such place. The young Bull Lodge would have taken nothing with him to eat or for comfort. The vision quest generally lasted from one to four days during which the participant fasted and "cried for a vision." Alone, hungry, and in tune with the spiritual world, the seeker usually had a vision or dream in which a spirit person, animal, or supernatural force was made known to

him. This would be his spirit helper throughout his life and could be called on in time of need.

Religious leaders such as Bull Lodge often participated in numerous vision quests and had a number of spirit helpers.

Leadership

Bull Lodge was a Gros Ventre holy man and warrior who possessed gifts of healing and prophecy. In his early life, he was known as a highly skilled warrior and for ten years led war parties against neighboring plains Indian tribes. His success, bravery, and leadership in battle resulted in his recognition as a Gros Ventre war chief at the age of forty.

As a youth, Bull Lodge participated in the vision quest, fasting to experience a vision. He eventually received spiritual instructions to undertake fasts in seven different sacred areas within the Gros Ventre traditional homelands. Each fast resulted in increasingly complex visions that were to sustain him and the Gros Ventre people throughout his life. Based on this experience, Bull Lodge began preparing to become a medicine man, dedicating his life to the teachings of the sacred Flat Pipe and the Feathered pipe.

As keeper of the Flat Pipe, Bull Lodge had various powers in the area of weather control, as well as in protecting the people from illness or danger. There were seasonal rites associated with the Flat Pipe that were discontinued in the 1800s, but the face-painting rite was continued. During this rite, children and many adults had their faces painted with sacred red paint in a design that symbolized creation and the Gros Ventres relationship with the Great Mystery (the Creator).

The Gros Ventre considered their religion integral to their identity as a people, and their religious beliefs and rituals both shaped and validated the group's political and military actions. The two tribal medicine pipes served to hold the tribe together.

Actually, the two pipes are better described as pipe bundles. The pipes themselves were wrapped in bundles containing other sacred objects and then wrapped in outer coverings. They were symbols of creation and of the Gros Ventres' place in the universe. The more powerful and the older bundle was the Flat Pipe, which was given to the Gros Ventre when the world was created. This bundle represented their link with, obligation to, and blessing from the Great Mystery Above. The Flat Pipe's sacred objects, songs, and origin history represented the events of creation and the instructions and knowledge given to the first Gros Ventre people about how to make their living, get along with one another, and obtain supernatural aid. The contents of the Feathered Pipe bundle also were important symbols of the Gros Ventres' relationship with the Great Mystery, and the rites associated with this bundle were important to their success.

Bull Lodge began his healing career when he was forty years old by healing his uncle, Yellow Man, who was suffering from a serious illness. After he had completed nineteen cases of doctoring, he was given the Chief Medicine Pipe, which also conferred on him the sacred office of Pipe Chief medicine man. Bull Lodge's power was such that he was able to heal a broad range of illnesses and injuries. One unique power that Bull Lodge possessed that was not shared by many other medicine people was the ability to heal gunshot wounds.

Bull Lodge once had a vision in which he saw a war shield descend from the sky. The shield was painted with the image of a thunderbird. Bull Lodge heard a voice that instructed him to make a shield just like the one that he had seen, and the power of the shield would protect him. War shields of the Plains Indian tribes were considered to be sacred and were often painted with powerful spirit images, such as supernatural bears, buffalo, or, as in Bull Lodge's case, thunderbirds.

There was a great emphasis on bravery and fortitude among the Gros Ventre warriors. Sanctions against lazy or unassertive behavior were particularly harsh. This aggressiveness often resulted in special emphasis being placed on fierceness and competition to gain prestige and admiration by tribal members. These were most often displayed in exploits of war, but in the absence of war could become ritualized in enemy-friend relationships between bands of the same tribe. An ethnographer, Regina Flattery, recorded one such competition between Bull Lodge and another famous Gros Ventre, Sits Like a Woman, exemplifying the way the relationship encouraged tenaciousness and unyielding aggressive behavior in battle. In this instance, Bull Lodge insulted Sits Like a Woman's record as a leader of war parties. Shortly afterward, Sits Like a Woman returned from a successful war party and insulted Bull Lodge and then challenged him saying: "If you choose to pay me back in the way I have treated you, go ahead. But first lead a successful war party. If you then do to me what I have done to you, I won't be mad. But I'll lead still another war party and do far worse to you that second time than I have done this time."

Bull Lodge foretold his own death and was about eighty-five when he died. An account of his life was obtained from one of his daughters, Garter Snake (In-nietse), through a Works Progress Administration writing program conducted by Frederick Gone, another tribal member. It was edited by George Horse Capture and published in 1980 as *The Seven Visions of Bull Lodge*.

Further Reading

Champagne, Duane, ed. *The Native North American Almanac: A Reference Book on Native North Americans in the United States and Canada*. 1994. Detroit: Gale Research.

Fowler, Loretta. *Shared Symbols, Contested Meanings*. 1987. Ithaca, N.Y.: Cornell University Press.

Hirschfelder, Arlene, and Paulette Molin. *The Encyclopedia of Native American Religions*. 1992. New York: Facts on File.

Horse Capture, George. *The Seven Visions of Bull Lodge*. 1980. Lincoln: University of Nebraska Press.

Jesse Bushyhead

Full Name at Birth: Jesse Bushyhead (Unaduti, Tas-the-ghe-te-hee, or Dta-ske-gi-di-hi)

Birth: 1804, place of birth unknown

Death: July 17, 1844, place not recorded

Education: attended the American Board Mission School at Candy Creek, Tennessee

Leadership Position: Cherokee Baptist minister

Summary

Jesse Bushyhead was the first Cherokee Indian to be ordained a Baptist minister and the first to be pastor of his own church in the Indian Nations, the present-day state of Oklahoma.

After overcoming an early addiction to strong drink, Bushyhead was converted to Christianity at an early age. At the age of twenty-five, he began to have doubts about the practice of infant baptism as preached by visiting Catholic missionaries and after reading the Bible carefully concluded that the Baptists were correct in their interpretation of the Bible. In January 1832, Bushyhead felt called to preach and traveled to Valley Towns, in present-day North Carolina, to meet the Baptist evangelist Evans Jones. Jones was very much impressed by Bushyhead's intelligence and strength of character and persuaded the Baptist Mission Board to employ him. Bushyhead was licensed by the Baptist church in 1831 or 1832 and was hired as a missionary assistant to the Cherokee in 1833. When Bushyhead became a missionary assistant, Jones's church added another thirty-five members to its congregation.

It appears that Bushyhead collaborated with John Buttrick Jones, Evan Jones, and possibly Sequoyah (the inventor of the Cherokee Syllabary) in the translation of the Bible into Cherokee. As a result, Bushyhead became one of the most popular and influential leaders of the Cherokee Nation.

Early Life

Very little is known of Bushyhead's early life. He was born in 1804 and was of mixed ancestry. His father was John Stuart, a British army officer and an agent to the Cherokee Indians, and his mother was a Cherokee woman. His father was called by the Cherokee Oo-no-dota, meaning "bushy head."

As the result of his mixed ancestry, Bushyhead grew up speaking both Cherokee and English fluently and attended the American Board Mission School at Candy Creek in present-day Tennessee. Bushyhead was raised in the Tennessee region of the Cherokee Nation at Achaia, seventy-five miles west of Valley Towns in the Hiwasssee Valley in present-day southwestern North Carolina.

Leadership

Jesse Bushyhead was a highly respected religious leader and translator among the Cherokee people. Born shortly after 1800 in the Great Smoky Mountains, Bushyhead was of mixed Cherokee and white ancestry. His father was John Stuart, a British army officer who had married a Cherokee woman while he was serving as Indian agent to the Cherokee. Bushyhead could speak and read the English language, and he studied the Bible. As the result of his study, he decided to follow the teachings of the Baptist faith and be baptized by immersion. In 1830, a Baptist preacher from Tennessee conducted the baptism. After attending the American Board Mission School at Candy Creek, Bushyhead returned to Amohee, his hometown, located on the western edge of the Great Smoky Mountains, as a devout Christian, where he began preaching to his people.

Bushyhead became a close associate of the Reverend Evan Jones, an itinerant evangelist who recommended him for an assistant missionary position with the Baptist Board of Foreign Missions in 1832. The recommendation was accepted, and Bushyhead was ordained a Baptist minister in April, 1833. Following his ordination, Bushyhead served as pastor of the Amohee Baptist Church while working with Jones to further missionary efforts and translate religious works into the Cherokee language. In 1836, Bushyhead and Jones were traveling two full church circuits every four or five weeks where they preached, baptized, and instructed new Christians regarding Christianity and the discipline of the church. Between circuit trips, Bushyhead and Reverend Jones traveled to Cherokee communities near Bushyhead's home for religious meetings. Bushyhead spent his evenings and nights translating the Christian Bible into the Cherokee language using the Cherokee Syllabary. He was considered to be one of the best interpreters in the Cherokee Nation and possessed the full confidence of his people.

After having been addicted to alcohol early in his life, Bushyhead served as a founder and president of the National Temperance Society among his people. He traveled widely, and on one trip to New York City he addressed fellow Baptists at an annual meeting of the Baptist Board of Foreign Missions

Bushyhead also held a number of high offices in the Cherokee Nation and on several occasions served as his nation's delegate to Washington, D.C. He was a member of the Cherokee delegation to Washington that testified against Cherokee removal to Indian Territory, in present-day Oklahoma. In 1834 he was appointed a justice of the Cherokee Supreme Court, and in 1837 the primary chief of the Cherokee Nation, John Ross, appointed Bushyhead to go to Florida to study the Seminole Nation's resistance against removal west of the Mississippi River. After his arrival in Florida, Bushyhead volunteered to serve as an intermediary between the Seminole and the U.S. government. The Cherokee were interested in Bushyhead's efforts to mediate in the Seminole War because of the similarity between the removal efforts the United States was exerting on the Seminole and the Cherokee nations. The Senate had ratified fraudulent removal treaties with both nations signed by small, nonrepresentative factions to give the cover of legitimacy to President Andrew Jackson's removal of the tribes. The treatment of the Seminole served as a precursor to the experience of the Cherokee. U.S. Army General Thomas Jesup imprisoned the Seminole chiefs, whom Bushyhead had persuaded to negotiate under a flag of truce. The Cherokee experienced the same type of imprisonment.

Bushyhead and his family were among those arrested and confined at Camp Hetzel in Tennessee on June 16, 1838. Cherokee people by the thousands were dragged from their homes and confined in forts and stockades and placed under military guard all over the Cherokee Nation as a result of President Jackson's Indian removal policy. Bushyhead and Stephen Forman, also a convert, held regular services in the stockade. "On one Sabbath, by permission of officers in command, they went down to the river and baptized five males and five females. They were guarded to the river and back. Some whites present affirm it to have been the most solemn and impressive religious ceremony they ever witnessed."

The Cherokee Nation, now numbering about fourteen thousand, were divided into contingents of one thousand each, and leaders were placed in charge of each detachment. Bushyhead and Reverend Evans were chosen to lead removal groups to Indian Territory (present-day Oklahoma) during the forced migration known as the "Trail Where They Cried," or, more commonly, Trail of Tears. An eye-witness who saw Bushyhead's detachment as they passed through Kentucky later commented on President Van Buren's message that "they have emigrated without any apparent reluctance. When I read the President's message that he was happy to inform the Senate that the Cherokees were peaceable and without reluctance removed, I wished that the President could have been there in Kentucky with me that very day, and have seen the comfort and willingness with which the Cherokees were making the journey." The Cherokee removal dragged on into midwinter, across frozen lakes and rivers. A few of the Cherokee were on horseback, and the sick and feeble were carried in wagons. Most were on foot. "Even aged females, apparently nearly ready to drop into the grave, were traveling with heavy burdens attached to the back, sometimes on the frozen ground and sometimes on muddy streets, with no covering for the feet except what nature had given them." One-fourth of the Cherokee people perished during the forced relocation.

Bushyhead died on July 17, 1844. His family included his eldest son, Dennis, who served as a principal chief of the Cherokee Nation for two terms between 1879 and 1887.

Further Reading

Brown, John. *Old Frontiers: The Story of the Cherokee Indians from Earliest Times to the Date of Their Removal to the West, 1838.* 1938. Kingsport, Tenn.: Southern Publishers.

Carter, Samuel, III. *Cherokee Sunset: A Nation Betrayed, A Narrative of Travail and Triumph, Persecution and Exile.* 1976. Garden City, N.Y.: Doubleday.

Hirschfelder, Arlene and Paulette Molin. *The Encyclopedia of Native American Religions*. 1992. New York: Facts on File.

McLoughlin, William G. *Champion of the Cherokees: Evan and John B. Jones*. 1990. Princeton: Princeton University Press.

Calf Shirt

Full Name at Birth: Calf Shirt
Birth: ca. 1844, place unrecorded
Death: December 1873 at Fort Kipp, Montana
Education: no formal education
Leadership Position: Blood shaman

Summary

Calf Shirt was a shaman in the Blood Tribe of the Blackfoot Confederacy. The Blood lived on the northeastern Great Plains and received their name because they painted their bodies with red clay. Calf Shirt was also a noted war leader and rose to the position of chief of the Lone Fighters Band during the 1800s. As a youth, he acquired a second name, Impervious to Bullets. Calf Shirt had a weakness that was common to Indians who had had no exposure to distilled liquor: he became drunk very easily. Calf Shirt was subject to prolonged bouts of drinking during which he displayed a terrible temper. Because of his violent behavior, he was given the nickname Wild Person. The name fit him well. He was convinced of his dual powers of bear strength and the ability to shed bullets and knives. Only his mother could calm him when he was under the influence of the whisky trader's brew. Fellow Blood tribesmen were in awe of his power. In 1871 he helped repulse a Cree war party that had come on a horse-raiding foray. Calf Shirt discovered the raiders, and despite heavy gunfire directed at him, he routed the horse stealing party, receiving no wounds. In December 1873 it appears that his powers had deserted him. Calf Shirt was gunned down at Fort Kipp, Montana, after he entered the fort to seek revenge for an insult by the white traders there.

Early Life

Little is known of Calf Shirt's early life. He was born at a time when the Blood tribe was very powerful and a force to be reckoned with. It appears that he was raised in a traditional Blood society with close tribal and kinship ties. His mother's name was Tight Eyes, and his father's name was the Shoulder. Calf Shirt's mother was an influential woman and provided a steadying influence on Calf Shirt throughout his life.

Calf Shirt's powers were given to him during a vision quest when he traveled to a remote area near the Sweetgrass Hills in Northern Montana. The hills (actually mountains reaching 6,914 feet) were a sacred place for the Blackfoot, the first to refer to the area as "Hills of Sweet Smelling Grass." Calf Shirt fasted alone for four days, hoping to be given a spiritual helper. During his fast, a grizzly bear spirit visited him and told him to perform certain tasks, after which no bullet, arrow, or knife could penetrate his body. After informing the tribal shaman of his vision, Calf Shirt was given a new name, "Impervious to Bullets." Because of his bravery he gained a reputation of invincibility and became known as a great warrior.

Leadership

Many stories had been told that told of Calf Shirt's power, but he is best remembered for his ability to rise from the dead. In December 1873, Calf Shirt visited the Baker trading post on the Marias River near present-day Shelby, Montana. He had returned to the post to claim a shield that he had left as security some time earlier. Joe Kipp, the post sutler, demanded that Calf Shirt purchase the shield; Calf Shirt replied that he had no money and went on to say that he was going to be involved in a fight and needed his shield. Kipp went for his weapon, but Calf Shirt drew his own pistol first. Calf Shirt realized the danger in shooting Kipp, so he left the trading post. He did, however, feel that he had been insulted. Kipp's slight boiled within Calf Shirt for three or four days and finally came to the surface. Calf Shirt wanted his shield and was convinced that he was impervious to Kipp's weapons. He painted his body for war, stripped to his breechcloth and moccasins, and began his medicine dance. He then returned to the trading post, ready for war. As Calf Shirt approached the trading room, a group of four whisky traders promptly opened fire. The traders looked on in amazement as they hit Calf Shirt with lead balls time after time. Rather than falling, he turned and walked out the main gates of the fort for 100 yards before collapsing into a deep hole from which earth sodding had been taken for building the roof of the fort. "There were sixteen bullet holes in his body, every one of them a fatal shot; he had evidently possessed the vitality of grizzly bear." To rid themselves of Calf Shirt

once and for all, the whisky traders picked the deceased Calf Shirt up and pushed his body through a hole in the ice in the Marias River while Calf Shirt's wives stood by.

Calf Shirt had prophesized that in the event of his death, he had the power to come back to life four days later. After Calf Shirt had been dead two days, his wives began to sing songs that he had taught them to hasten his rebirth. When the songs failed to revive Calf Shirt, another Blackfoot medicine man from Crowfoot's village stepped forward and claimed that he could bring Calf Shirt back to life through the use of four drinks of whisky. The medicine man began his sacred dance and poured some whisky into the mouth of the dead shaman, after which it was observed that one of Calf Shirt's legs began to straighten out as if about to stand. The medicine man continued his sacred incantations and claimed that with more whisky, he could complete the task of calling Calf Shirt back from the other world.

The pending rebirth of Calf Shirt caused great concern among the Bloods and the traders. They recalled the problems that he had caused while alive and under the influence of whisky, plus he had foretold his return, this time as a grizzly bear. Out of fear of Calf Shirt and the unknown, they pleaded with the medicine man to stop his magic and leave Calf Shirt in the spirit world. The medicine man complied with their wishes. His wives were left to mourn and prepare the body for burial.

Calf Shirt had a nephew by the same name who was also a shaman. The younger Calf Shirt received the powers from the rattlesnake during a vision quest. The snakes became his brothers and the younger Calf Shirt had the ability to go out onto the prairie and secure large numbers of rattlesnakes, some of which he would carry inside his shirt or blanket. It is reported that the younger Calf Shirt would show his powers to the whites for money. An unidentified journalist reported, "Calf Shirt claims to have some subtle power over snakes and to see him take his present specimen up, she measuring about three feet long, catch it by the neck and cram about eight inches of it, the deadliest reptile in America, head first down his throat, is calculated to make the marrow in any man's bones shiver." The younger Calf Shirt died in 1901.

Further Reading

A Blackfoot Winter Count: http://www. lethfhc.org/winter.htm.

Dempsey, Hugh A. *The Amazing Death of Calf Shirt and Other Blackfoot Stories.* 1994. Saskatoon: Fifth House.

Lyon, William S. *Encyclopedia of Native American Shamanism: Sacred Ceremonies of North America.* 1998. Denver: ABC-CLIO.

Peter Catches

Full Name at Birth: Peter Catches
Birth: date and place of birth unknown
Death: date and place of death unknown
Education: raised in a Catholic mission school
Leadership Position: Lakota medicine man and healer

Summary

Peter Catches was an influential peyote religious leader among the Lakota people. The two primary ceremonies in the peyote religion or the Half-Moon and the Cross-Fire (or Big Moon) ceremony, shared many commonalities, and both incorporated aspects of Indian culture and Christianity. Both ceremonies emphasized the divine role of peyote and its power to teach and heal; both opposed the use of liquor and believed that peyote destroyed the taste for it. In both peyote was eaten to concentrate and learn, not to induce visions. Women could ingest the peyote button; however, most women and children participated in the ceremony by drinking peyote tea. The adherents of both ceremonies included preaching, prophecy, baptism, and other similarities to the Christian religion. The Half-Moon ceremony limited tobacco use, whereas the Cross-Fire ceremony prohibited the use of tobacco entirely. Other shared features were the use of elaborate altars on which the peyote was placed, ashes formed into ceremonial designs, and ultimately the construction of permanent churches and altars. Opposition to the peyote religion was manifested at the federal and state levels and in 1918 followers of the peyote religion who sought to protect their religious practices from attack organized the Native American church.

Peter Catches became one of the earliest and most influential peyote leaders among the Lakota and other northern tribes and was one of the prime movers of South Dakota peyotism for many years.

Peyote, a spineless cactus, originally was one of the offerings made to the gods in Aztec temples, where the buttons of this small, hallucinogenic cactus plant were ritually consumed. Down through the ages, peyote flourished in other regions of Mexico and in South Texas.

Leadership

Peter Catches was a Lakota medicine man and healer who also served as a Catholic catechist and a peyote roadman (person who is in charge of a peyote religious ceremony) on the Pine Ridge Reservation in South Dakota. Catches, an orphan, was brought up in a Catholic mission school and became a teacher of catechism. He eventually turned to traditional Lakota beliefs, becoming a healer and adviser, while continuing to practice Catholicism. Instructed by a holy man in the generation before his, Catches began conducting Eagle Ceremony (a ceremony conducted by a religious leader whereby he called upon the power of the eagle—which was considered to be the most powerful and spiritual animal—for assistance in the healing ceremony) power rituals and training apprentices. He also became a Sun Dance leader (the person who calls for a sun dance to take place; his responsibility was to ensure that all appropriate ceremony and traditions are followed to the letter; he must select and secure the place where the ceremony is to take place, construct the arena and the arbor, oversee the selection of the Sun Dance pole) and undertook a number of responsibilities in connection with the sacred ceremony, including service as chief dancer and the instruction of candidates.

Among the Lakota, the Sun Dance is one of the seven sacred rites handed down by White Buffalo Calf Woman. Before beginning the ceremony, the Lakota people must undergo four days of preparation. These preliminary activities include gathering the required objects, teaching holy songs to designated singers, selecting persons to search for a sacred cottonwood tree, choosing a man for the honor of counting coup on the tree and ritually cutting down the tree. Counting coup was a procedure whereby warriors struck the enemy, either with their hand or with a "coup stick." The bravery required to do this brought great honor and the event was retold in ceremony. Often an eagle feather would be awarded. No honor was bestowed for the killing of the enemy because touching a live enemy took much more courage and daring. The ritual elements of the Sun Dance included fasting, purification, and dancing before the sacred tree. One aspect of the ceremony included piercing the chest of the male dancers who had pledged to undergo sacrifice. Conducted by a holy man on the final day of the Sun Dance, the process was done in various ways. The piercing represents the giving of the body for the people. Participants participate in the Sun Dance in response to a promise they had made to the Creator in return for something that the Creator has done for them. The Sun Dance is a world renewal ceremony. After the ceremony, the participants concluded the sacred ceremony with sweat lodge purification.

According to Thomas H. Lewis, a psychiatrist and anthropologist who wrote about Catches, the medicine man started altering some of his religious practices in the 1970s. He advised against using white-introduced objects, including metal and glass, and began rejecting rides in automobiles. Living close to the natural world with few material possessions, he reached destinations distant from his home by walking. At this time, his involvement with Catholicism diminished and then ended.

Lewis further noted that Catches, who had earlier rejected peyotism, began to add Half-Moon peyote ceremonies to his religious practices. The devout holy man is also known to have conducted regular fasts at Bear Butte and other sacred sites, sweat lodge purification rituals, eagle curing ceremonies on a regular basis, and other traditional observances.

He was interviewed by David Zimmerly in 1969, and the important interview was published as "On Being an Ascetic."

Further Reading

DeMallie, Raymond J., and Elaine A. Jahner, eds. *Walker, James R.: Lakota Belief and Ritual.* 1991. Lincoln: University of Nebraska Press.

Hirschfelder, Arlene, and Paulette Molin. *The Encyclopedia of Native American Religions.* 1992. New York. Facts on File.

Lewis, Thomas H. *The Medicine Men: Oglala Sioux Ceremony and Healing.* 1990. Lincoln: University of Nebraska Press.

Nels Charles

Full Name at Birth: Nels Charles
Birth: ca. 1887, place unknown
Death: date and place of death unknown
Education: attended Chemawa Indian School in Oregon, 1900–1911
Leadership Position: Wintu shaman

Summary

Shamanism was the most important religious aspect of Wintu culture. The shaman was the primary means by which people communicated with the supernatural. Wintu shamanism was open to both men and women, and shamanistic powers were acquired in an initiation ceremony. In the spring or late autumn of each year, all persons who wished to acquire shamanistic powers presented themselves to recognized shamans for initiation into the society. Some candidates might already have had preshamanic dreams or experiences, but they were not required to become a candidate.

The initiation ceremony began in the evening. The shamans and the candidates danced naked around a manzanita wood fire all night and sang to invoke the sacred spirits. Those who failed to gain a supernatural experience dropped out after a few hours and went to bathe. There was no shame attached to not having received a spirit.

For those few who were chosen, the arrival of a spirit was announced by a whistling sound above the smoke hole of the earth lodge. The tribal chief or a skilled interpreter stood in the lodge and told from where the spirits were coming. If a spirit found a candidate suitable, it entered his body, at which time the behavior of the initiate became frenzied. The older shaman then instructed the newly selected shaman in the nature and requirements of the spirit that had possessed him, the songs appropriate to that particular spirit, and the taboos that had to be observed. Nels Charles was one such shaman.

Early Life

There is no record of Charles's early life but because of his acceptance into the shaman society, some general assumptions can be made. We do know that Charles was born into the Wintu tribe in a family of shamans. Both his father and grandfather were shamans. The Wintu are a northern California tribe, and Charles probably grew up along the McCloud and Sacramento rivers. He would have been raised in a bark house, one of several such houses that would have composed a Wintu village, and shared the house with his biological family of three to seven people. Everyone within the village was in some way related. A sense of sharing was present among the Wintu, and as Charles grew into his teens, he was expected to share the game that he killed or fish that he caught in common with all other village members. He received his Wintu education from his grandparents and near relatives and was frequently instructed "to be a *wita* [a man]." The term *wita* included "having the skills in hunting, fishing, gambling, oratory, respect for the aged, and a democratic attitude."

Charles and his family moved several times throughout the year, along with the other village members, to take advantage of the seasonal ripening of fruits, berries, acorns, and tubers. In winter, the village reassembled in the more permanent winter village, where food was stored and firewood was collected in large quantities.

Charles attended Chemawa Indian School in Oregon from 1900 to 1911, where he was taught by teachers provided by the YMCA. At Chemawa, he learned to bake and taught other boys there to bake as well. In 1907 or 1908, he was hurt while lifting weights. He had a hemorrhage and was taken to the school hospital for care.

Leadership

When Charles was interviewed in 1933, he was reported to be forty-six years of age. His grandfather, father, and one uncle had been shamans, and Charles was about 25 when he began dreaming in 1912. He stated that a person appeared in a dream and sang sacred songs and asked him questions. Although he felt stronger after the experience, he did not know who the spirit was. Over the next two years, different spirits came to him, but he never knew how many spirits came. When Charles began his shamanic doctoring, he drew on the spirits that had visited him. The spirits continued to come to Charles in his sleep and present various medical problems to him and quiz him as to what remedies he would use. On occasion, the spirits would show him a dead person, and in his dreams he could return the person to life.

Charles had no clear picture of who was appearing to him other than that he looked like church pictures that he had seen of God, only with a crown. After he dreamed that dream, he made a decision to follow the shaman road. Charles continued his communication with the spirits through dreams and followed their instructions. Sometimes a spirit was too strong for Charles, so another shaman had to be called in. On one occasion, an evil spirit, possibly sent by a jealous shaman, abused Charles, and he ran away from his family. Charles was sick, he could not eat, and his spirit was not right. He was spiritually lost, and nothing was right for him. It was reported that a hostile shaman had "ruined" Charles and taken away his power. Charles requested that two other Wintu shamans, Charlie Klutchie and Tilly Griffen, strengthen him by singing their shaman songs. Charles paid them to sing for him, as was the customary practice when requesting help from another shaman.

After this experience, Charles' shamanic powers were diminished. He stated:

> My power is not so great because my spirits worry. They don't know what to do with themselves. When they were strong, I was strong and could cure patients. But after I lost my sister and some aunts, I was worried and that bothered my spirits. I was weakened. My spirits aren't sure whether they can cure a sick person and they are weakened by not being sure. If a person abuses me I mustn't wish him to be sick, or die, or have bad luck. That would ruin me. My spirits might think differently and that would weaken my power. Spirits talk to my heart and know what I think.

Following this experience Charles was considered to be a shaman of weakened ability. He "went out of his head" on several occasions and would escape from his family and disappear in the hills for several days. The white people of the Napa, California area became concerned because of Charles's erratic behavior. On one occa-sion, the townspeople had him admitted to an insane asylum at Napa, where he re-mained for an undetermined period of time. Informants agreed that there was nothing wrong with him, and when he re-turned home, he returned to being a sha-man with no onus whatsoever. The Napa, California State Hospital records state that Nels Charles was diagnosed as an "ep-ileptic psychotic (equivalent)."

There is no history of Charles after this experience, although it was reported that he returned to the Wintu people and was treated with guarded respect.

Further Reading

Du Bois, Cora. "Wintu Ethnography." In A. L. Kroeber and R. H. Lowe, eds. *American Archaeology and Ethnology, Vol. 36 1935–1939*. 1940. Berkeley: University of California Press.

Lyon, William S. *Encyclopedia of Native American Shamanism: Sacred Ceremonies of North America*. 1998. Denver: ABC-CLIO.

Native American Medicine: http://www.alternativetherapies.com/select/past/45c.html.

Coocoochee

Full Name at Birth: Coocoochee

Birth: ca. early 1740s, southeast of Montreal, Canada

Death: 1800s, place of death not recorded

Education: no formal education

Leadership Position: Mohawk medicine woman and visionary

Summary

Coocoochee was born into the Bear clan of the Mohawk Nation, southeast of present-day Montreal, Canada, in the early 1740s. She married a Mohawk war-rior and gave birth to one daughter and three sons. In 1769, she and her family relocated to Ohio to avoid the white colo-nists who were encroaching ever closer to her Mohawk traditional homelands. Coocoochee and her family settled among the Shawnee Indian Nation on the west bank of the Scioto River, where she joined the camp of Shawnee chief Blue Jacket, and settled in his village. As the result of this move, she lived most of her life among the Shawnee.

The white colonists continued encroaching on Indian lands, however, and in 1774, Lord Dunmore, governor of the Virginia Colony, destroyed the Shawnee villages in the Muskingum Valley, just one hundred miles from Coocoochee's new home.

During her years with Chief Blue Jacket's people, Coocoochee was taught medicine ways, herbal healing, and the role and function expected of a medicine woman. Because of her "far-seeing power," Coocoochee was sought on many occasions by the tribal council for various matters concerning the welfare of the people.

Early Life

Little is known of Coocoochee's early life. She was born into the Bear Clan of a Mohawk Indian village southeast of present-day Montreal, Canada. She married a Mohawk warrior, Cockundiawsaw, and they had one daughter and three sons. In 1792, one of her sons, White Loon, captured a ten-year-old white boy by the name of Oliver Spencer, and he was taken into Coocoochee's family. Although Spencer lived in the Shawnee camp for only seven months (July 1792–February 1793), he maintained contact with Coocoochee and her family throughout his lifetime. It is from Spencer's writing that we gain our knowledge of Coocoochee.

Leadership

Coocoochee and her husband attempted to avoid open confrontation with the encroaching white colonists by relocating from their traditional Mohawk lands to that of the friendly Shawnee chief Blue Jacket. In 1774, only five years later,

word came of the total destruction of the Shawnee villages in the Muskingum Valley by the colony governor, Lord Dunmore. It became clear that Coocoochee and her family were no longer safe in that location. With the outbreak of the American Revolution in 1777, Chief Blue moved his people, including Coocoochee and her family, to the Mad River along the Ohio-Kentucky frontier. Upon settling at this location, Chief Blue Jacket's village became a refuge for many Native tribes fleeing the fighting between colonists and British.

Coocoochee was not immune to the war, however. Her husband and oldest son, Wapanoo, were pro-British and participated in anti-American expeditions during the Revolutionary War. They were joined by more and more Indians from various tribal groups and battled against the colonial encroachers.

Coocoochee and her family were forced to flee again before the press of the military expeditions of Benjamin Logan in 1786. The family settled near the Miami Towns along the Maumee River near present-day Fort Wayne, Indiana, where they lived in relative peace until 1790, at which time the Miami towns were torched by the forces of General Josia Harmar. It was during this raid that her husband, Cokundiawsaw, was killed. Coocoochee was forced to relocate once again, and with her children she traveled along the Maumee River where they were taken in by a large intertribal group known as the Glaize at present-day Defiance, Ohio. Four years later, a raid (known as the Battle of Fallen Timbers) by General "Mad" Anthony Wayne forced this large community to scatter to survive.

While Coocoochee is identified as a Mohawk medicine woman and visionary, it was during her years with Chief Blue Jacket's people, the Shawnee, that Coocoochee was taught her medicine ways, herbal healing, and the role and functions expected of a medicine woman. Her position as a medicine woman gave her special status, and it was probably because of her ability to heal and foretell the future that she was so highly regarded and prized by Chief Blue Jacket. Because of her "far-seeing powers," Coocoochee's advice was sought on many occasions by the chief and his council for various matters concerning the welfare of the people. This included frequent relocations to avoid the relentless pursuit and destruction by the American colonists.

Further Reading

Bataille, Gretchen M. *Native American Women: A Biographical Dictionary*. 1993. New York: Garland Publishing.

White, Julia. *Woman Spirit*: http://www.meyna.com/mohawk2.html.

George Copway

Full Name at Birth: George Copway (Kah-Ge-Ga-Gah-Bowh ["stands fast"]), also Kahgegagebow

Birth: 1818 near the mouth of the Trent River near Ontario, Canada

Death: 1869, at Lake of Two Mountains, a mission in Quebec, Canada

Education: attended a Methodist mission school at Rice Lake, Canada, dates unknown, and graduated in 1839 from Ebenezer Manual Labor School in Illinois

Leadership Position: Chippewa missionary and writer

Summary

George Copway was born near Ontario, Canada. During his early years, Methodist missionaries were actively trying to convert the Ojibwa people to Christianity, and Copway was converted when he was twelve years old. When he was twenty years old, he attended Ebenezer Academy in Illinois and worked on religious translations from English into the Algonquian language. Copway explained that he believed that Christianity offered hope to American Indians. He later helped his cousin Enmegahbowh* and another Ojibwa convert, Peter Marksman, to establish a Methodist mission at Lac Courte Oreilles near present-day Hayward, Wisconsin. Copway eventually worked at a number of other missions, including the Lake Superior Mission, Keweenaw Mission, Saugeen Mission on Lake Huron, and his home mission of La Pointe on the Rice Lake Reserve, where he assisted the Reverend Sherman Hall with biblical translations.

In the fall of 1837, Copway, Enmegahbowh, and Marksman entered the Ebenezer Manual Labor School in Illinois, under the auspices of a Methodist missionary society. Following his 1839 graduation from Ebenezer, Copway returned to Upper Canada, where he met and married a young English woman, Elizabeth Howell.

In 1846 Copway traveled in the United States and in 1847 published his autobiography, *The Life, History, and Travels of Kah-Ge-Ga-Gah-Bowh*, which was reprinted six times in its first year and reissued in 1850 as *Recollections of a Forest Life: The Traditional History and Charac-*

teristic Sketches of the Ojibwa Nation. Copway eventually lived in poverty for several years in New York City, attempting to support his family on the income he made as a lecturer. In 1864, he and his brother David helped recruit Canadian Indians into the Union Army during the Civil War. Copway also became a healer or herbal doctor, advertising his cures in the *Detroit Free Press* in 1867. That same year, Copway returned to Canada, going to Lake of Two Mountains, a mission in Quebec, among the Iroquois and other tribal people.

Early Life

George Copway was born in Ontario, Canada, into the Mississauga band of the Ojibwa Nation, and was raised in a traditional Native American family. During his early years, Methodist missionaries were trying to convert the Ojibwa people to Christianity. The Ojibwa missionary Peter Jones persuaded his parents to convert to Christianity, and in 1830 Jones and Copway's mother converted Copway to Christianity. After his conversion, Copway, still a teenager became involved in missionary work among his people.

Leadership

George Copway was converted to Christianity at the age of twelve by Methodist missionaries who were trying to convert the Ojibwa people to Christianity. Once converted, Copway became a missionary himself. Copway believed that Christianity offered the only hope for survival for American Indians. Following his conversion, Copway attended a Methodist mission school at Rice Lake, where one of his teachers was the missionary John Clark. When Clark requested four native workers to assist in the work at the Lake Superior Mission of the American Methodist church, Copway, and his cousin Enmegahbowh were among those selected. Copway worked at the Keweenaw Mission the first winter and then at La Pointe, where he assisted the Reverend Sherman Hall with biblical translations. Copway later helped Enmegahbowh and another Ojibwa convert, Peter Marksman, establish a Methodist mission at Lac Courte Oreilles near present-day Hayward, Wisconsin. In the fall of 1837, Copway, Enmegahbowh, and Marksman entered the Ebenezer Manual Labor School in Illinois under the auspices of a Methodist missionary society. Following his graduation from Ebenezer in 1839, Copway returned to Upper Canada, where he met and married a young English woman, Elizabeth Howell. He and his wife moved to New York City, where he found employment with religious publishers. While pursing a career as a writer, he also lectured extensively in the United States and Europe.

Copway eventually worked at a number of other missions, including the Saugeen Mission on Lake Huron and his home mission on the Rice Lake Reserve. In 1846, he traveled to the United States and subsequently published a number of books, including: *The Life, History, and Travels of Kah-Ge-Ga-Gah-Bowh* (1847, reprinted six times in its first year and reissued in 1850 as *Recollections of a Forest Life*; *The Traditional History and Characteristic Sketches of the Ojibwa Nation*, then in 1858 as *Indian Life and Indian History*; *The Ojibwa Conquest* (1850); *The Organization of a New Indian Territory East of the Missouri River* (1850); and *Running Sketches of Men and Places in England, Germany, Belgium, and Scotland* (1851), and a weekly newspaper entitled *Copway's American Indian* (1851).

Copway's autobiography and his history of the Ojibwas were undoubtedly responses to efforts of the Lake Superior Ojibwa to resist removal from 1847 through 1849. In his writings, Copway emphasized the basic humanity and generosity of the Ojibwa toward one another, values that non-Indian Christians would recognize as similar to their own. He also humanized his people by citing examples of how Ojibwa parents cared for and loved their children. These examples counteracted the stereotype of bloodthirsty Indians, depictions that were common in the captivity narratives popular well into the 1830s. While pursing a career as a writer, he also lectured extensively in both the United States and Europe.

Copway eventually lived in poverty for several years in New York City, supporting his family on the income he made as a lecturer. In 1864, he and his brother David helped recruit Canadian Indians into the Union Army during the Civil War. Copway also became a healer or herbal doctor, advertising his cures in the *Detroit Free Press* in 1867. Later that year he returned to Canada, going to the Lake of Two Mountains, a mission in Quebec. Copway was baptized a Catholic there shortly before his death in 1869.

Further Reading

Champagne, Duane, ed. *The Native North American Almanac: A Reference Book on Native North Americans in the United States and Canada*. 1994. Detroit: Gale Research.

Copway, George: http://www.georgetown.edu/bassr/heath/syllabuild/guide/copway.html.

Hirschfelder, Arlene, and Paulette Molin. *The Encyclopedia of Native American Religions*. 1992. New York. Facts on File.

Waldman, Carl. *Who Was Who in Native American History*. 1990. New York: Facts on File.

Crazy Mule

Full Name at Birth: Crazy Mule
Birth: date and place of birth unknown
Death: ca. 1889
Education: no formal education
Leadership Position: Cheyenne holy man and warrior

Summary

Crazy Mule was a Northern Cheyenne of great spiritual power. He was a respected holy man and head man of the Crazy Dog Society; its members were the organized military force of the camp and acted as its police force. Members of the Crazy Dogs also enforced the orders of the chiefs. Crazy Mule was so respected as a holy man that he was chosen together with another holy man, Box Elder,* to assist in the work of replacing the Sacred Arrows captured by the Pawnee in 1830. The Sacred Arrows are the most sacred possession of the Cheyenne people and symbolize the collective existence of the tribe. As the arrows prosper, the Nation prospers. As the arrows are neglected, so too is the Cheyenne Nation neglected. The four arrows were given to the Cheyenne by the Creator, who first gave them to Sweet Medicine,* a revered Cheyenne medicine person. Along with the Sacred Arrows came sacred teachings, laws, and prophecies. The Sacred Arrows are considered to be the living manifestation of spiritual power for the Cheyenne people and are known as Maahotse (also Mahuts), or simply "The Creator." Two of the arrows are considered to be "male" and have power over human beings, and two of the arrows have power over buffalo.

Crazy Mule was also a warrior who fought against the enemies of the Cheyenne. He claimed the power to make himself invulnerable to bullets and on two occasions his bulletproof powers were demonstrated during battles against U. S. military soldiers. Crazy Mule was also known to have the power to kill enemies by merely looking at them and on one occasion killed two soldiers at a great distance by concentrating on the soldier and staring at them until they fell dead. Because of the strength of his power Crazy Mule was obliged to use great caution to keep from injuring his own friends by looking at them.

In 1867, Crazy Mule was slightly wounded after being shot by a soldier near the Big Horn River fort. Having lost his invincibility to bullets, Crazy Mule retired from active warfare and lived among the Southern Cheyenne in Indian Territory (present-day Oklahoma). Crazy Mule is said to have been in the tribal delegation that traveled to Washington in 1873 to negotiate an agreement with the U.S. government.

Early Life

No records exist of Crazy Mule's early years. Having fought as a warrior in the United States and Cheyenne wars of 1866, Crazy Mule would have been a youth when the Cheyenne were yet a powerful Nation. He was probably raised in a traditional Cheyenne lifeway in one of the small, permanent, and substantial earth-lodge Cheyenne villages on the shores of the Cheyenne River in present-day South Dakota. The Cheyenne were not a large nation, however, and the likelihood is that not more than three hundred people would have made up a good-sized village. They were a sophisticated people with a rich and dramatic ceremonial life that included shamanism and healing ceremonies.

A mainstay of Crazy Mule's diet was wild rice, harvested from canoes, hulled, and roasted. The country was filled with bison, elk, moose, deer, bear, wolves, raccoons, fox, and otter. Ducks and geese were plentiful, as were fish that were taken in great quantities. As a youth, Crazy Mule would have learned to hunt deer, rabbits, and other small game that was snared or hunted with bow and arrow. As he grew older, he would have hunted the forest bison and larger game animals and learned the skills of a holy man.

Leadership

Crazy Mule was a Northern Cheyenne of great spiritual power. He was also a warrior who fought against the enemies of the Cheyenne. Crazy Mule claimed to be impervious to bullets and in 1865 and again in 1866 his bulletproof powers were demonstrated during battles against U.S. military soldiers. In 1866, the Cheyenne were camped on Muddy Creek, in the Dakota Territory and Crazy Mule was exhibiting his power to those around him. Different people were shooting at him but the bullets and the arrows did not enter his flesh. Not one of them had succeeded in harming him. A witness to this event told the story as follows,

> I saw a test made upon him, at a time when our tribal camp was far up Tongue River. I was then 29 years old. He [Crazy Mule] dressed his body with only a muslin shirt, painted with his special medicine colors, and on his feet he wore a pair of moccasins beaded in a certain way, according to his medicine plan. Thus prepared, he placed himself in front of a big tree. Twenty-seven Cheyenne who had rifles were chosen to take a position a short distance in front of him. They rested their rifles in an upright forked stick and fired at the painted muslin shirt. As soon as the shots had been fired, Crazy Mule reached down and pulled off his moccasins. From them he emptied out the 27 bullets.

Crazy Mule was also known to have the power to kill enemies merely by looking at them. On one occasion it was reported that Crazy Mule killed three cavalry captains, "each one a long distance away, too far for bullets to carry. He just stood on a hill and looked steadily at them. They became dizzy, staggered in their walk, then were paralyzed and fell dead." Crazy Mule once related that he was obliged to use great caution to keep from injuring his own friends by looking at them.

Among the Northern Cheyenne, Crazy Mule was noted for his strong, mysterious power. He could use his power at any time he might choose, but it was reported that he was a good-hearted man and never harmed any Cheyenne. On one occasion, a certain white man came to a Cheyenne camp pretending to have strong powers. The man could swallow a bunch of needles, and then when he jumped and shook himself, the needles would fall, scattering from his clothing. He repeated the trick several times, and the people looked at him in awe. Sensing a challenge to his power, Crazy Mule studied the white man's performance. The next time, the stranger swallowed the needles, Crazy Mule circled behind him, twirled his fingers toward the white man's back, and drew all of the needles into his own hands. When the white man jumped up and down, to make them fall from him, the needles did not come. He jumped and jumped, but nothing was shaken from his body. Crazy Mule then stepped into view, extended his hand, and showed the needles lying there in his own open palms. The visitor trembled and turned pale as a ghost. He mounted his horse, rode away, and never returned. He was afraid of Crazy Mule's medicine.

During the Medicine Lodge celebration in the summer of 1862, a ceremony, was held at which a man was tied with bowstrings and then covered up and the light extinguished. Under the covering was placed a whistle and a pipe. The whistle sounded during the period of darkness. In a few moments the light was renewed, and the man was found to be untied. During the ceremony, the spirits that came in response to Crazy Mule's invitation visited the bound person. The ceremony was undertaken for the purpose of learning the location of some property lost from a wagon a few days before. The spirits came in response to Crazy Mule's invocation and talked with the man who was tied up.

In 1867, Crazy Mule was slightly wounded after being shot near the Big Horn River fort. For the most part, he then lived among the Southern Cheyenne in Indian Territory (present-day Oklahoma). In 1874 Crazy Mule held a medicine lodge ceremony at the head of the Washita River in present-day

Oklahoma. The Comanche under the influence of a healer by the name of I sa tái visited Crazy Mule's medicine lodge and convinced the Cheyenne to join with them on an attack against the buffalo killers camped at Adobe Walls, on the staked plains, in present-day Texas. The results were devastating for the Indian people; sixty died, and I sa tái was discredited.

It is not certain that Crazy Mule was involved in the Custer battle on the Little Big Horn in 1876. In 1877 he was a member of Two Moon's Band of Cheyenne who fought against General Nelson Miles at Tongue River, and he went in with Two Moon and White Bull to surrender. Two Moon and White Bull fought in the Custer battle, so it is probable that Crazy Mule was present as well. Crazy Mule is said to have been in the tribal delegation that traveled to Washington in 1873 to negotiate an agreement between the Cheyenne Nation and the U.S. government. The respected holy man, healer and warrior died among the Southern Cheyenne about 1889.

Further Reading

Grinnell, George Bird. *The Cheyenne Indians: Their History and Ways of Life*. 1962. New York: Cooper Square Publishers.

Grinnell, George Bird. *The Fighting Cheyennes*. 1956. Norman: University of Oklahoma Press.

Marquis, Thomas B. *The Cheyennes of Montana*. 1978. Algonac, Mich.: Reference Publications.

Waldman, Carl. *Who Was Who in Native American History*. 1990. New York: Facts on File.

Henry Crow Dog II

Full Name at Birth: Henry Crow Dog II

Birth: September 2, 1899, place of birth unrecorded

Death: winter of 1985 at Crow Dog's Paradise in South Dakota

Education: attended an unidentified Indian board school for a short time in his childhood

Leadership Position: traditional medicine man of the Lakota Sioux.

Summary

Henry Crow Dog II was the third member of his family to carry that name. He was born after the demise of Indian military power on the Great Plains. The last great battle—a massacre—had taken place in 1890 at Wounded Knee Creek, and by the time of his birth, Crow Dog's people had been confined to the Rosebud Indian Reservation in South Dakota. In Leonard Crow Dog (Henry's son) and Richard Erdoes' book *Crow Dog: Four Generations of Sioux Medicine Men*, Crow Dog admonishes the authors to let him tell his story "his way." Crow Dog related,

> The world I was born in, it was the *wasichus'* [white man's] world. There were no buffalo anymore, no game, nothing to be happy about. We were starving people. . . . The tipis were all gone. Some people lived in dirt huts, and some fixed up shelters like sweat lodges, bent sticks covered with hides. . . . We used to go to the creek and hunt

two kinds of rabbits. The little one, the cottontail, and out on the prairie the big one, the jackrabbit. . . . My father and grandfather had learned the old way. They could still use the bow. They could make a fire with flint and tinder. They still had all the survival skills. . . . When I was a kid most everybody had horses. We learned to ride almost before we could walk. . . . My father taught me everything I need to know. . . . He taught me how to use white man's tools, saws, drills, crowbars. . . . I had trouble in school. I didn't speak a word of English, and the teacher didn't speak a word of Sioux, so how could we learn. . . . I worked for a while for the railroad, laying track. From 1934 to 1950 I worked in Nebraska harvesting grain, digging spuds, and picking beets. I made two or three dollars a day.

When Crow Dog was a youth, all Indian religious and cultural ceremonies were forbidden by the U.S. government. The Sun Dance and Ghost Dance were outlawed. Crow Dog stated,

When I was young, Indian ceremonies, even a sweat lodge, were forbidden. . . . So you talked and listened to the yuwipi spirits (spirits that arrived during the course of a yuwipi ceremony) at night, in the darkness. By day you put up a good front, toting your Bible around, crossing yourself—that was a shield behind which a medicine man could hide. And we also kept our medicine bundles hidden where the missionaries couldn't see them.

The Sun Dance one of the most important religious ceremonies conducted by the Lakota people, was held to pray for the renewal of the people and the earth, give thanks, fulfill a vow, and protect the people from danger or illness. The Sun Dance also brought scattered tribal bands

together during the summer for social as well as religious activities. The Yuwipi ceremony was a nighttime curing ceremony conducted in a darkened room by a medicine man such as Crow Dog. A person seeking help with a problem, such as an illness, would approach the medicine man and request a Yuwipi ceremony. During the ceremony, the Yuwipi spirits would come and minister to the sick person.

Crow Dog's son Leonard recounts that people would listen to his father for hours: "He led a hard life, but he did not let it conquer his spirit. Under all the poverty and suffering, he was proud of who he was. . . . The Crow Dogs are royal blood that is, full bloods. We are the people of the center."

Early Life

Crow Dog's father's name was Henry Crow Dog, and his mother was Jumping Elk. In telling of his early life, he said, "I wasn't born in a hospital. I was born the old way [in a tipi]."

There is little recorded history of Crow Dog's early life. He was raised on the Rosebud Reservation in South Dakota at a time when the dominant society operated under the general principle that Indian people were a defeated people and would ultimately die out or be assimilated into white society. Crow Dog's parents taught him survival skills, and combined with his spiritual calling as a Lakota Medicine Man, was able not only to survive himself, but to ensure the survival of the Great Sioux Nation.

Leadership

Crow Dog was a Lakota holy man and mediator between the quiescent Indian people barely surviving on Indian reservations in the early 1900s and the rise of Indian activism, pride, and self-determination that began in the late 1960s.

In 1887 President Grover Cleveland signed the Dawes Act, the chief provisions of which were to destroy the tribal structure, break up Indian reservations, and give fee-simple title to land to Indian people. Excess land would revert to ownership by the federal government. Crow Dog and others who received title to allotted lands were under constant pressure to sell or lease their lands to non-Indian entrepreneurs—the land-grabbers.

Crow Dog was able to withstand the constant efforts exerted by numerous individuals to sell his land allotment, and his parcel became known as Crow Dog's Paradise. The land allotment was located on what remained of the Rosebud Reservation and was described as being a paradise "with little houses along a creek, surrounded by pines, cottonwoods, and lush green plants of every kind." Henry Crow Dog, the renowned medicine man lived there with his son, Leonard Crow Dog, and his family until his death.

In the 1970s, Crow Dog's Paradise became the spiritual center for members of the American Indian Movement (AIM). On February 27, 1973, AIM occupied the trading post at Wounded Knee in protest over the treatment of Indian people, specifically the failure of law enforcement officials to prosecute white people who were murdering Indians on the Pine Ridge Reservation. AIM supporters for the occupation initially traveled to Crow Dog's Paradise, where they found about five hundred people waiting for them. They went first into the purification lodge, where Henry Crow Dog led them in a ceremony. AIM members Russell Means and Leonard Peltier joined Crow Dog on his land, where he once again led a traditional Sun Dance. Crow Dog and other reserva-tion traditionalists had taken AIM activists under their tutelage.

In an attempt to arrest AIM members suspected of firing guns at FBI agents at Wounded Knee, FBI agents rushed commando style through the buildings and the tents at Crow Dog's, tearing everything apart. Crow Dog came over to a bunch of FBI agents, and he drew a circle in the dust in front of them. He then drew a line through the middle of the circle. Crow Dog stated, "This is you with your guns over on this side," he told them, "and this is us over here with our sacred pipe." And then he was quiet while they just stared at him. "The circle is turned," he said after a while, and walked away "and their mouths were just hanging open."

Crow Dog died in the winter of 1985. Crow Dog always said, "I am the last real Sioux left."

Further Reading

Champagne, Duane, ed. *The Native North American Almanac: A Reference Work on Native North Americans in the United States and Canada.* 1994. Detroit: Gale Research.

Crow Dog, Leonard, and Richard Erdoes. *Crow Dog: Four Generations of Sioux Medicine Men.* 1995. New York: HarperCollins.

Henry Crow Dog II: http://www.humanrights.de/u/usa/lpart/hcd.html.

Matthiessen, Peter. *In The Spirit of Crazy Horse.* 1992. New York: Penguin Books.

Means, Russell, with Marvin J. Wolf. *Where White Men Fear to Tread: The Autobiography of Russell Means.* 1995. Los Angeles: General Publishing Group.

Myths and Legends: http://www.santeedakota.org/mythsand.htm.

Waldman, Carl. *Who Was Who in Native American History.* 1990. New York: Facts on File.

Curley Headed Doctor (or Curly-Headed Doctor)

Full Name at Birth: unknown; the name Curley Headed Doctor was probably given to him by early California settlers with whom the Modoc traded and worked.

Birth: date and place of birth unknown; first recorded appearance in 1869

Death: 1890 on the Modoc leased section of the Shawnee Reserve in Indian Territory (present-day Oklahoma)

Education: no formal education

Leadership Position: Modoc medicine man, shaman

Summary

Curley Headed Doctor was a capable Modoc religious leader and prominent shaman who used his magic and ritual to support the followers of Captain Jack, a modoc warrior, in the 1873 Modoc war against the army and California settlers. He was Captain Jack's spiritual adviser and had a powerful influence on the Modoc leader. Prior to the lava bed (a volcanic area in Northern California where the modoc went to live after they left the Klamath reservation) fights, Curley Headed Doctor demonstrated his power by drawing a line beyond which the enemy supposedly could not pass. He performed numerous other rituals to render the Indians bulletproof. He was ultimately discredited when a Modoc warrior was killed while attempting to disarm a cannon ball. Curley Headed Doctor promoted a military confrontation with the U.S. Army and used his oratorical skills to prod Captain Jack into killing General Edward R. S. Canby in April 1873. Following his surrender, Curley Headed Doctor guided the U.S. Army to Captain Jack's hiding place in the Modoc stronghold. Following the Modoc war, he and the remaining Modoc were forced to relocate to the Indian Territory, where he died.

Early Life

No records exist that speak of Curley Headed Doctor's early life. He emerges onto the pages of history in December 1869.

Leadership

In the 1860s, the U.S. government was aggressively pursuing its Indian policy of separation and consolidation. Indian tribes were to be separated away from the general U.S. population and consolidated onto Indian reservations, where they were to be detribalized and prepared for assimilation into white society. In the rugged Lost River valley of present-day northern California lived the Modoc, a small tribe of some four hundred to five hundred people. The Modoc had experienced the migrant influx brought about by the California gold rush and were attempting to live in harmony with the miners who had invaded their traditional lands. The Modoc traded and worked with the miners and shared an uneasy peace that existed from 1851 to 1872. As with most other Native nations, the Modoc were fiercely attached to their homelands. The relationship was both a physical and spiritual relationship and one they refused to abandon. In the 1870s, the refusal of the Modoc to be relocated became a major obstacle to peace between the tribe and the United States.

The Modoc, under the leadership of Captain Jack (Kintpuash), wanted peace and removed to the Lost River, near Tule Lake, in northern California. The federal government, represented by Superintendents of Indian Affairs Alfred B. Meacham and T. B. Odeneal, insisted that the Modoc remove and settle on the Klamath Indian reservation on the California-Oregon border. The Modoc and the Klamath tribes had existed as antagonistic but acceptable neighbors in the past, however, the Klamath had not given permission nor did they want the Modoc relocated onto their already strained reservation. Their relocation onto the limited land base with insufficient food, water, and employment caused increased resentment toward the uninvited Modoc. The Klamath were superior in number and made life unpleasant for the Modoc. As a result, Captain Jack and his followers left the Klamath reservation and returned to Lost River, near Tule Lake, where they again lived in an uneasy peace with the white miners, now turned settlers and farmers. In December 1869, Superintendent Meacham traveled to Lost River to convince Captain Jack to return to the Klamath reservation. It was on this occasion that Curley Headed Doctor emerges onto the pages of history.

On December 23, 1869, during discussions between Meacham and Captain Jack, it is reported that Curley Headed Doctor jumped to his feet and said in the Modoc language "We will not go there." Up to this point, some progress had been made to convince Captain Jack to lead his followers back to the Klamath reservation. The shaman's abrupt statement, however, threw the conference into confusion, and the atmosphere changed. Captain Jack immediately deferred to the shaman and informed Meacham that the Modoc were through talking. Other Modoc in attendance leaped to their feet, and many of them drew pistols. The situation had become precarious. Meacham and his people now feared for their lives and realized that if Curley Headed Doctor had his way, they would probably be killed. Meacham and his party removed themselves from the negotiations, and Captain Jack called his party into caucus, where Curley Headed Doctor used all of his oratory skills to urge the assassination of Superintendent Meacham and his party. The discussions continued well into the night while additional soldiers arrived to support Meacham and his party. Because of the additional troops, the Modoc now feared for their lives and fled to the lava beds on the south shore of Tule Lake, where they were joined by some forty-five additional Modoc who became eager supporters of Curley Headed Doctor and the war policy that he now promoted. Curley Headed Doctor seemed to have won a complete victory and was backed by prominent Modoc leaders such as Shacknasty Jim, Bogus Charley, and Ellen's Man. It appears that Captain Jack was in favor of passive resistance, however, he was under the influence of Curley Headed Doctor.

The Modoc were now ensconced in the lava beds, also known as the land of burnt-out fires because of their volcanic origin. Modoc warriors, seeking revenge for the killing of a Modoc, left their stronghold to attack both the northern and eastern shores of the lake. In December 1872, Curley Headed led a number of Modoc in a raid against a ranch to retaliate for an earlier attack by white ranchers. After killing fourteen people, they returned to the lava beds and rejoined Captain Jack. Jack and his group provided them refuge and refused to meet the military's demand that they be turned in to the authorities. On January 16, 1872, the army deployed a force of 335 army troops and militiamen around Captain Jack's stronghold in an attempt to bring the hostilities to an end. Still the army was unable to dislodge the Modoc from their stronghold.

In March 1873, President Grant appointed a peace commission headed by General R. S. Canby to treat with the Modoc. In April 1873, Modoc leaders met in council with General Canby and two other peace commissioners. Prior to the meeting, Curley Headed Doctor and Hooker Jim encouraged Captain Jack to kill General Canby. Captain Jack pointed out that the act would result only in more troops being sent and most likely the annihilation of the Modoc. Curley Headed Doctor berated Jack as a coward and shamed Jack by putting a shawl and woman's hat on him. He thus goaded Jack into killing Canby. On April 11, 1873, when General Canby next met with Captain Jack, he refused to meet the demands of the Modoc to give them back their land, and Jack drew a pistol and killed the general. Captain Jack's prediction proved true. Following the murder, a force of 1,500 troops were dispatched to the lava beds with instructions to bring the war to an end. General William Tecumseh Sherman stated that "any measure of severity to the savages will be sustained" (Axelrod 216).

Following the Canby murder, the pursuit was relentless. Still, the Modoc stronghold proved formable and impenetrable. As the attacks intensified and morale became strained, Curley Headed Doctor faced his greatest test. He had been boasting for some time that if the warriors would believe his prophecies, no

harm would befall them. He now ordered a rope of tule, several hundred feet in length, to be laid entirely around the stronghold. The rope was painted red to indicate that this was a magic circle into which no white soldier should come the next day. Curley Headed Doctor then had a central fire built and a medicine pole erected. He placed a medicine flag on the pole as well as the tail feathers of a great hawk, an otter skin, and the skin of a white weasel. A magic fire was built on the dance ground, and the Modoc began their drumbeat. Curley Headed Doctor began to dance and was followed by others in the one-step, drag-step that characterized the Ghost dance, which had spread to the Modoc from the Paiute in the Great Basin area. Following a night of dancing and magical performance, the Indians were properly prepared.

On the morning of April 15, Major John Green led an assault on the stronghold. Soldiers from Green's command crossed the magic red tule rope that Curley Headed Doctor had placed as a guarantee that no one would enter the stronghold. During the second night of fighting, a Modoc warrior tried to defuse a cannon ball by pulling the detonator out with his teeth. Curley Headed Doctor had assured his followers that no one protected by his magic would be killed. His medicine failed, and he was now discredited among his people. His medicine flag was abandoned as worthless and left for the soldiers. While the Modoc fought on, Curley Headed Doctor surrendered on May 23, 1873, and was among those who ultimately led the army to Captain Jack's hideout. Following the war, the shaman and other Modoc were exiled to Indian Territory (present-day Oklahoma), where he died in 1890. Prior to his death, he stated, "As soon as I die, the spirits leading me will cause the greatest storm you have ever seen." He was more accurate in this prophecy than he had been in the lava beds, with his bulletproofing promises. Quapaw, Modoc, and Shawnee Indians were lashed by a great storm when Curley Headed Doctor died.

Further Reading

Axelrod, Alan. *Chronicle of the Indians Wars from Colonial Times to Wounded Knee.* 1993. Englewood Cliffs, N.J.: Prentice Hall.

Dillon, Richard H. *Burnt-out Fires: California's Modoc Indian War.* 1973. Englewood Cliffs, N.J.: Prentice-Hall.

Gibson, Arrell Morgan. *The American Indian Prehistory to the Present.* 1980. Lexington, Mass.: D. C. Heath.

Hirschfelder, Arlene and Paulette Molin. *The Encyclopedia of Native American Religions.* 1992. New York. Facts on File.

Modoc Shadows: http://www.multimedia.calpoly.edu/libarts/denglund/1994.html.

The Modoc Wars: http://education.opb.org/learning/ofg/modoc/soldiers.html.

Murray, Keith. *The Modocs and Their War.* 1959. Norman: University of Oklahoma Press.

Waldman, Carl. *Who Was Who in Native American History.* 1990. New York: Facts on File. Inc.

Davéko

Full Name at Birth: Davéko

Birth: ca. 1818, place of birth not recorded

Death: 1897/1898; place of death not recorded

Education: no formal education

Leadership Position: Kiowa-Apache shaman

Summary

Davéko was a renowned shaman who was born around 1818 and died in 1897 or 1898. According to the informant and writer J. G. McAllister, Davéko received his powers during a four-day vision quest during which "some medicine, something, like rattlesnake, like owl, like little whirlwinds, came toward him, causing the ground to tremble like an earthquake. . . . Davéko could not recognize it. It was like the approach of a great storm; rains were coming, and there was a great black cloud with a tail touching the ground. This was the small, soft turtle, with the long tail that took pity on him." Thus, he acquired powers from the snake, owl, and turtle. Thereafter, Davéko wore the rattles of a rattlesnake tied to his scalp lock.

Early Life

Little is known of Davéko's early years other than that his father was also a shaman. Davéko was most likely born when the Kiowa lived south of the Arkansas River in territory that is now southern Kansas and northern Oklahoma. To the south of the Kiowa lived the Comanche, a tribe with which they became closely allied. An Apache band relocated near the Kiowa as well and came to be so closely associated with the Kiowa that their leaders became part of the Kiowa camp circle. From that union came the tribe that

Davéko was born into, the Kiowa-Apache.

While still a young boy, Davéko would have participated in a vision quest, where he would have been taken by his uncle or a medicine person to an isolated spot where he would have fasted and prayed for a vision. In the vision he would have been shown a spirit person, animal, or force that guided him and would support him for the remainder of his life.

Leadership

A typical account of Davéko's healing follows. According to McAllister:

Davéko first sang his medicine song. Then his stepson, Sam, who was assisting him, sang. . . . When they sang it became foggy over the man who was sick. There was something in him. Davéko put his mouth in the regions of the man's navel and sucked out a piece of rough skin as tough as that from a man's heel. The young man had not moved, but after Davéko took that out the young man stirred. They sang again and the sick man wanted to be raised up. It was after sundown and getting dark. . . . They had been singing all day and he [Sam] was tired. He [Sam] went to bed. After he left, the sick man sat up and asked for water. They gave him a drink. Davéko sang a *Klintidie* song. The sick man was sitting up and his friends were feeling good, so they all sang. . . . The next morning he was up and walking around in the tipi.

When looking for a disease object within a patient's body, it was reported that Davéko would use a black handkerchief that enabled him to locate the ob-ject, which he then sucked out. In curing snakebites, he sucked out snake teeth from the wound. He was also known to use herbs and roots in his healing rituals.

The above account is congruent with Davéko's call as a sucking doctor. A sucking doctor, or shaman would perform sacred ceremonies over a sick person while singing healing songs that had been given to him in a dream. Once the disease-causing agent or the diseased area was made known to him, he would suck the object from the patient using a hollow bone tube. The object would then be disposed of in a manner that had been made known to him in a dream. In addition to being a sucking shaman, Davéko doctored by blowing water onto his patients, a power that he most likely received from his turtle spirit helper. He also used deer hoof rattles with the wing feathers of a hawk attached to it.

Davéko was well known for the many power feats that he could perform, including the ability to find lost persons or objects. As was common among Kiowa-Apache shaman, Davéko was well paid for his services and was, for the most part, greatly feared.

Further Reading

Kiowa Drawings: http://nmnhwww.si.edu/naa/kiowa/kiowa.html.

Lyon, William S. *Encyclopedia of Native American Healing*. 1996. Denver: ABC-CLIO.

McAllister, J. G. *Davéko Kiowa Apache Medicine Man*. 1970. Austin: Texas Memorial Museum.

Waldman, Carl, and Molly Braun. *Encyclopedia of Native American Tribes*. 1988. New York: Facts on File.

Deer Bird

See Juan de Jesus Romero

Deganawida

Full Name at Birth: Deganawida ("Heavenly Messenger")
Birth: date and place of birth unknown
Death: date and place of death unknown
Education: no formal education
Leadership Position: Huron spiritual leader

Summary

Deganawida was a prophet, statesman, and lawgiver who cofounded the Five Nations Confederacy, also known as the Iroquois League. Based on his instructions from the Giver of Life, Deganawida composed the laws of the Great Peace that would unite the Five Nations into a peaceful confederacy and planted the Great Tree of Peace at what is now Syracuse, New York. Deganawida placed a bundle of arrows—one for each member tribe of the Iroquois Confederacy—tied together with deer sinew, alongside the Great Tree of Peace to signify that all the men and women of the confederacy had become united as one person.

Early Life

Little is known of Deganawida's early life. Called "Heavenly Messenger," according to ancient belief, he was born to a virgin mother who had been informed in a dream by a messenger from the Creator that she was to bear a son destined to plant the Tree of Peace. Some say Deganawida came from north of Lake Ontario. In some oral traditions, he was a Huron, in others he was an adopted Mohawk, and still in others he was a healing spirit who had assumed human form. In any event, he became a cultural hero to the Iroquois peoples and was known as the Peacemaker. According to oral history, Aiowantha (Hiawatha),* an Onondaga chief, first encountered Deganawida when Hiawatha was wandering the forests in grief over the death of his three daughters. According to Onondaga traditions of avenging the deaths of relatives, their deaths now required the taking of the life of an enemy.

Establishing a new covenant, Deganawida assuaged Hiawatha's grief with words of sympathy and the giving of beads of wampum, symbolically wiping his tears and easing the pain of his loss. This ritual became part of the protocol of the Iroquois League and the foundation of the Iroquois Great League of Peace.

Leadership

Deganawida is generally credited as the founder of the Iroquois Confederacy, which is more correctly identified as the Five Nations of the Haudenosaunee, which means "People of the Longhouse." The exact date of origin is unknown, but it is generally dated prior to European contact in the Americas even though recent scholars suggest that the Confederacy formation was not completed until the early 1500s.

In Iroquois history, Deganawida lived when there was little peace among the Iroquois-speaking nations: the Mohawk, Onondaga, Oneida, Cayuga, and the Seneca. These nations were often at war with one another because there was no agreed-on means of resolving conflict among the nations. A murder of one person by a member of another nation led to revenge raids, known as blood feuds, which often resulted in raids and war between nations. Bringing an end to these blood feuds was a matter of self-preservation.

At the dawn of creation, the Great Spirit had commanded all people to live in peace with one another, however, the message had been lost. Deganawida received a vision from the Master of Life that instructed him to give the Great Law, a set of rules and procedures for working out differences and settling hostilities between nations. Oral history states that Deganawida, the Peacemaker, set out across Lake Ontario in a stone canoe. When he landed on the southern shore, he came upon Hiawatha, a clan leader of the Iroquoian-speaking Mohawk nation who had lost his three daughters to intertribal strife and discord. Deganawida offered words of condolence and dried his tears. These same words of condolence would hereafter be repeated at Iroquois council meetings to promote amenity and goodwill among the nations.

Having met and assuaged Hiawatha's grief, Deganawida and Hiawatha composed the laws of a great peace that would restore order and preserve harmony in Iroquois country. Deganawida's words of

sympathy offered to Hiawatha were accompanied by the giving of beads of wampum. The ritual of giving of wampum became part of the protocol of the Iroquois League and their diplomatic dealings with outsiders. The giving of wampum in the form of wampum belts assuaged grief and redressed wrongs. Wampum belts could also be used to carry messages of peace and war. The great laws of peace were recorded, each on a string of wampum, so that future generations would remember and observe them.

Deganawida emerged as a spiritual leader of powerful vision in spite of a speech impediment. Hiawatha possessed the gifts of oratory and thus became the spokesperson for the message of Deganawida and the Great Spirit. Together, they set out on a journey to spread the message of the Great Law and the Tree of Peace among the Iroquois Nations in present-day New York and Ohio.

Deganawida and Hiawatha traveled among the Iroquois Nations, and after some resistance among the Onondaga, convinced the Seneca, Cayuga, Onondaga, Oneida, and Mohawk to form a confederacy of forty-nine chiefs. The five nations that entered the league retained full autonomy over their own affairs; however, matters of mutual importance were debated by a confederated council. Through ceremonies and agreements, they settled their disputes peacefully at the annual gatherings of the council, which met at Onondaga, near present-day Syracuse, New York. The first meeting took place under a giant evergreen tree that symbolized the Great Tree of Peace of which Deganawida and Hiawatha had spoken.

The Confederated Council consisted of a governing body of fifty male council members—ten from each of the five tribes in the league. Fifty tribal leaders attended the first confederation meeting; however, in later years, only forty-nine representatives were seated, saving the empty seat symbolically for Hiawatha. In the council process, each tribe had one vote, and decisions were always unanimous, reached by consensus, usually after lengthy discussion. Each tribe retained its autonomy and was not obligated to accept a conclusion they did not agree with.

Elderly tribal matrons of the individual tribe selected each of the council members. Following the teachings of Deganawida, each tribal leader wore a deer headdress with antlers as his mantel of authority. The elderly clan matrons nominated the council members and could depose, or "dehorn," the council representative of their own lineage from office if he did not conform to the will of the lineage. In the event of death or removal of a leader from office, the clan matrons selected the successor. When decisions came before the Confederated Council, the clan matrons solicited input from tribal members, caucused together, and advised the tribal chiefs of the will of the people. Failure to follow the advice of the clan matrons could result in removal from office.

Deganawida delivered the Great Law of the League to the members of the Confederated Council. The law was preserved for generations through oral tradition before it was written down and published in the nineteenth century. Having delivered the laws of the confederacy, which charged each of the leaders, among other things, to cultivate good feelings of friendship, love, and honor among themselves, Deganawida stated that he would go home, conceal and cover himself with bark, and charged that there should be no other person called by his name.

Further Reading

Ballantine, Betty, and Ian Ballantine, eds. *The Native Americans: An Illustrated History*. 1993. Atlanta: Turner Publishing.

Calloway, Colin G. *First Peoples: A Documentary Survey of American Indian History*. 1999. New York: St. Martin's Press.

Champagne, Duane, ed. *The Native North American Almanac*. 1994. Detroit: Gale Research.

Deganawida: http://www.louisville.edu/k-12/camden/conroy/ deganawi.html.

Deganawida: http://web. onramp.ca/ rivernen/nation_1.html.

Gibson, Arrell M. *The American Indian*. 1969. Lexington, Mass.: D. C. Heath.

Hirschfelder, Arlene and Paulette Molin. *The Encyclopedia of Native American Religions*. 1992. New York: Facts on File.

Snow, Dean R. *The Iroquois*. 1996. Cambridge, Mass.: Blackwell Publishers.

Trigger, Bruce G. and Wilcomb E., Washburn, eds. *The Cambridge History of the Native Peoples of the Americas, Vol. 1: North America Part 1*. 1996. Cambridge: University of Cambridge Press.

Washburn, Wilcomb E. *Handbook of North American Indians*, Vol. 4. 1988. Washington, D.C.: Smithsonian Institution.

Philip Joseph Deloria

Full Name at Birth: Tipi Sapa ("Black Lodge"); Philip Joseph Deloria

Birth: December 25, 1853, on the Grand River in northern South Dakota

Death: 1931

Education: attended Shattuck Military School in Faribault, Minnesota, and Nebraska College for two years

Leadership Position: Dakota Episcopal priest and missionary

Summary

Philip Deloria was one of the most prominent Native American clergy in the Episcopal denomination. The family name, *Deloria*, is an anglicized form of the name Phillippe des Lauriers, who was a French fur trader. Des Lauriers settled in a Yankton Sioux village and married the daughter of a Yankton headman.

As a young man, Tipi Sapa (Philip) was an apprentice to his father in his work as a medicine man and assisted in his healings. At the age of sixteen, he decided, with his father's encouragement, to pursue an academic education and fulfill his religious vocation by becoming an Episcopal priest. It was the hope of Tipi Sapa and his father that by entering the priesthood, he could better help his people adjust to the changing circumstances of reservation life. Upon his confirmation, Tipi Sapa was baptized Philip Joseph Deloria and left home to attend an Episcopal mission school in Nebraska. He later attended a military academy in Minnesota. After receiving his degree, Deloria served as a catechist and was an Episcopal priest and missionary among his people. He became a deacon of the church in 1874 and was ordained a priest in 1892. His ministry included forty years of service on the Standing Rock Reservation, where he was instrumental in establishing St. Elizabeth's School at Wakpala, South Dakota. Honored as one of the "Saints of the Ages" by his denomination, Reverend Deloria's statue was placed in the National Cathedral in Washington, D.C. He died in 1931. He was married to Mary Sully Bordeau, their family included five daughters and one son, Vine Deloria, Sr.

Early Life

Philip was raised in the traditional Sioux manner and participated in the traditional Sioux ceremonies, including the piercing of his ears, the first ritual performed honoring a son. He was then given the name of Tipi Sapa ("Black Lodge"). His mother, Siha Sapewin, was from the Rosebud band of the Lakota Indians and was one of Saswe's three wives. Philip was one of six children of that marriage.

It is reported that Philip was Saswe's favorite child and was always present when Saswe went to perform his religious and political duties. In 1856, when Philip was about three years old, Saswe had to go on a long trip. When he returned, he found that Philip had died the previous day, suffering from a very high fever. Heavy with grief, Saswe entered the tipi and when he finally emerged, carrying Philip's body, Saswe's arms and legs were bloody from the self-inflicted knife wounds of mourning. Saswe mounted his horse carrying Philip's body, and rode off to a high hill where he dismounted and began to pray. Saswe prayed all that night and the next day, pleading with the spirits to return his son to him. At about sundown, to the surprise of the family members who had accompanied them but mourned from a distance, Saswe descended the hill, hand in hand with Tipi Sapa.

Saswe converted to Christianity a few years before his death in 1876 and encouraged Philip to convert to Christianity.

When Philip was about seventeen years old, he happened to go by an Episcopal mission while they were signing the hymn "Guide Me, O Thou Great Jehovah." According to Tipi Sapa's account, he found the song pleasant to hear and wanted to hear it again, to learn it if possible. He went to the church on three successive Sundays, but the tune was not sung. On the fourth Sunday, he heard the hymn. He stood next to a man who sang the song out of a book. Philip caught the words of the song and learned them. He felt that he was now the possessor of a great treasure. From that day on, he attended the services with regularity. His attendance brought him to the attention of Reverend Joseph Cook, who then worked hard to convert him. Philip said that Cook did not grow weary of talking to him, and finally he compared the two courses that lay ahead: the Indian life and the Christian life. After much deliberation, he converted to Christianity, had his long hair cut off, and assumed the dress of the white man.

Leadership

Tipi Sapa was elected to the position of chief of Band Eight of the Yankton Sioux tribe as a very young man. Even though he chose to become an Episcopal priest, his people elected him chief several times. He was particularly proud of his association with peace efforts because it fulfilled his life's mission of bringing peace and harmony to the Sioux people.

Tipi Sapa was baptized Philip Joseph Deloria and left home to attend an Episcopal mission school in Nebraska. In the spring of 1871, Bishop Clarkson confirmed him, and Deloria returned to his people, equipped with the knowledge of reading, writing, and math. He quickly became a lay reader in the church and was appointed to supervise all Episcopal mis-

sion work on the Standing Rock Reservation. At the same time, he assumed his duties as chief of the Yankton Sioux in the place of his father. Deloria was presented with a medal from the Indian department signifying his authority.

Deloria was one of three young Lakota leaders who in 1873 founded Wojo Okolakiciye (the Planting Society), an organization promoting ecumenical fellowship that later became known as the Brotherhood of Christian Unity.

In 1875 Deloria married Annie Brunot. They had a boy Francis Philip in November 1876, and in 1879 Annie gave birth to a girl, who lived only ten days. Annie died about a month later from complications of childbirth. Deloria remarried in 1881 to Jennie Lamont to provide a home for his son. Tragically, Francis Philip died in 1883 at the age of six. His second wife, Jennie, died shortly after giving birth to their second child.

In 1888 Deloria was placed in charge of the Episcopal missions in South Dakota. He resided at St. Elizabeth's Church and married Mary Sully Bordeaux in 1888. Together they raised a family of six children. Their only son, Vine Victor Deloria,* whose Lakota name was Ohiya (Champion), was born in 1901. Mary died when Ohiya was fifteen years of age. Ohiya was strongly influenced by the stories of the spiritual encounters that were the Deloria family heritage, and he also accepted a Christian vocation.

By the early 1900s Deloria had become a living symbol of the Christian belief that Indians could make progress in civilization. Deloria retired in 1925, by which time he had secured a national reputation as one of the most devoted and respected priests in the history of Episcopal missions. He is one of only three Americans included in the ninety-eight

"Saints of the Ages" carved behind the altar of the National Cathedral in Washington, D.C.

Deloria's cultural reminiscences were collected in a 1918 book written by Sarah Emil Olden titled *The People of Tipi Sapa*.

Further Reading

Deloria, Vine, Jr. *For This Land: Writings on Religion in America*. 1999. New York: Routledge.

Deloria, Vine. Jr. *Singing for a Spirit: A Portrait of the Dakota Sioux*. 1999. Santa Fe: Clear Light Publishers.

Dictionary of Indians of North America. 1978. St. Clair Shores, Mich.: Scholarly Press.

Hirschfelder, Arlene, and Paulette Molin. *The Encyclopedia of Native American Religions*. 1992. New York: Facts on File.

Markowitz, Harvey, ed. *American Indians. Vol 1*. 1995. Pasadena, Calif.: Salem Press.

Vine Victor Deloria, Sr.

Full Name at Birth: Vine Victor Deloria, Sr.; Ohiya ("Champion")

Birth: October 6, 1901, at St. Elizabeth's Mission near Wakpala, South Dakota, on the Standing Rock Reservation

Death: February 26, 1990, in Tucson, Arizona

Education: attended Kearney Military Academy, Kearney, Nebraska; graduated from Bard College, Annandale-Hudson, New York, with a bachelor's degree; attended General Theological Seminary, New York City

Leadership Position: Lakota Episcopal priest, Yankton Sioux minister, first American Indian to hold a national executive post in the Episcopal church

Summary

Deloria was a Yankton Dakota who, like his father, Philip Joseph Deloria,* became an Episcopal priest. He was born in 1901 at Wakpala, South Dakota, on the Standing Rock Reservation to Philip and Mary Sully Bordeau Deloria. His education included attendance at Kearney Military Academy, where he became a cadet colonel and credited his experience as character building. Deloria attended Bard College in New York, where he received a bachelor's degree. Following graduation, Deloria worked in the Colorado mines and then became an Indian school adviser. He later completed General Theological Seminary in New York City and was ordained as a minister in his father's church at Wakpala, South Dakota.

In 1954, Deloria was appointed to the Episcopal National Council in New York City, where he was in charge of all Indian mission work as the Indian secretary for the Episcopal Church of America. He was the first American Indian to hold a national executive post in the Episcopal church. Deloria was later appointed archdeacon of the Niobrara Deaconry and served as archdeacon in Pierre, South Dakota. Deloria was well respected by his people and spent over thirty-seven years ministering to them before his retirement in 1968. A symposium speech that he made in 1982 was published in 1987 as "The Establishment of Christianity Among the Sioux," in *Sioux Indian Religion* (1987). He retired to his home in Pierre, South Dakota. Deloria's children included a son, Vine Deloria, Jr.,* the well-known theologian, attorney, and author who carried on his father's fight for Indian rights, a daughter Barbara, and a son, Sam who has made significant contributions to the field of Indian law.

Early Life

Very little is written about Deloria's early years. His grandfather, François Des Laurias, was a leader of the Ihanktonwan band of Dakota Indians. His father, Philip Joseph Deloria, was a member of the same band and earned a position in the Dakota warrior society. Philip Deloria later converted to Christianity and joined the Episcopal clergy. His mother, Mary died, when he was fifteen. Prior to his father's death in the 1920s, Philip Deloria contacted Bishop Beecher of Nebraska and arranged to have his son admitted to a diocesan school, Kearney Military Academy in Kearney, Nebraska. The young Deloria attended Kearney for five years, mastering English and becoming the cadet major of the student body. Deloria was a gifted athlete and excelled in football, baseball, and basketball. He attended college in New York on an athletic scholarship and envisioned a career as a professional athlete.

Leadership

Vine Deloria, Sr., was the first American Indian to be named to a national executive post in the Episcopal church. His father, Philip Deloria, was a full-blood Sioux and served as a missionary priest at Standing Rock Sioux Reservation, converting thousands of Indians to Christianity during his career. He was honored with a statue in the Episcopal Cathedral in Washington, D.C. As a boy, Vine Deloria attended a military academy, where he rose to the rank of cadet colonel. After he grad-

uated from Kearney Military Academy, his father was able to get him a scholarship to St. Stephens (Bard) College in Annandale, New York. St. Stephens was a small Episcopal college originally established to train men for the Episcopal priesthood. St. Stephens was eager to enroll Deloria, whose athletic reputation had been firmly established at Kearney. Deloria continued to excel in sports and earned honorable mention by Walter Camp in his annual All-American listing. He graduated from St. Stephens in 1926 and returned home.

In 1926, Deloria was one of the translators during the government hearings held in Lake Andes, a small town on the Yankton Reservation and in 1927 at the Pipestone Quarry in Minnesota. The hearings were over the ownership of the Red Pipestone Quarry in Minnesota, where many tribes got the pipestone necessary for making the bowls of their sacred pipes. Congress authorized a hearing, and Deloria was one of the translators. Through the legal expertise of Jennings Wise, a former U.S. attorney general, a bill was finally passed, and the Yanktons received $100,000 and retained the right to gather pipe-making materials at the quarry.

Deloria attended the theological course at General Theological Seminary in New York City and was subsequently ordained in his father's church, where he had been baptized and confirmed. Following his ordination, Deloria was assigned to All Saints Mission. He served there for seventeen years, then spent three years at the Sisseton Mission in eastern South Dakota and three years at an Anglo parish in Iowa.

In January 1940, Deloria went on a speaking tour to raise money to rebuild the All Saints Church that was heavily damaged by a devastating tornado on July 19, 1939. Deloria went east and told the story of the great storm, the church's importance to the Indian people of the Pine Ridge Reservation, and the story of the Sioux people. He raised a large sum of money, and the remainder of the funds were contributed by the cathedral of St. John in Denver; a nice new church and rectory were built in Martin, South Dakota. It was during this tour that Deloria, an obscure priest hidden in the grasslands of South Dakota, became a nationally prominent church leader.

In 1954 he was appointed to the National Council of the Episcopal Church as assistant secretary for Indian missions, the first Indian to serve as a denominational executive. He was also appointed archdeacon of the Indian parishes in South Dakota, a post he occupied until his retirement in 1968. Deloria served in the Indian missions for thirty-seven years and for several years as assistant secretary in the Division of Domestic Missions on the national staff of the Episcopal church in New York City. Before his retirement in 1967, Deloria was made archdeacon of the Niobrara Deaconry and in that position worked among Indian people all over South Dakota.

Further Reading

Bruguier, Leonard R. "A Legacy in Sioux Leadership: The Deloria Family." In *South Dakota Leaders*, Herbert T. Hoover and Larry J. Zimmerman, eds. 1989. Vermillion: University of South Dakota Press.

Champagne, Duane, ed. *The Native North American Almanac: A Reference Work on Native North Americans in the United States and Canada*. 1994. Detroit: Gale Research.

Deloria, Vine, Jr. *For This Land: Writings on Religion in America*. 1999. New York: Routledge.

Deloria, Vine, Jr. *Singing for a Spirit: A Portrait of the Dakota Sioux*. 1999. Santa Fe: Clear Light Publishers.

DeMallie, Raymond J., Douglas R. Parks. *Sioux Indian Religion*. 1989. Norman: University of Oklahoma Press.

Dictionary of Indians of North America. 1978. St. Clair Shores, Mich.: Scholarly Press.

Hirschfelder, Arlene, and Paulette Molin. *The Encyclopedia of Native American Religions*. 1992. New York: Facts on File.

Malinowski, Sharon. *Notable Native Americans*. 1995. Detroit: Gale Research.

Markowitz, Harvey, ed. *American Indians. Vol 1*. 1995. Pasadena, Calif.: Salem Press, Inc.

Vine Deloria, Jr.

Full Name at Birth: Vine Victor Deloria, Jr.

Birth: March 26, 1933, Martin, South Dakota, on the edge of the Pine Ridge Indian Reservation

Education: Martin Elementary School, Martin, South Dakota; the Kent School, a private college preparatory school in Connecticut; Colorado School of Mines, Golden, Colorado; earned bachelor's degree from Iowa State University, 1958; master's degree in theology, Lutheran Seminary, Rock Island, Illinois, 1963; law degree, University of Colorado, 1970

Leadership Position: Standing Rock Sioux writer, lawyer, professor, theologian, and religious protagonist; elected to the Executive Council of the Episcopal Church, 1968

Summary

Vine Deloria, Jr., is recognized as one of the most prolific and influential American Indian authors of the twentieth century and is a strong advocate of education for American Indian people. In a 1974 *Time* magazine poll of the "Theological Superstars of the Future," Deloria was included as one of the eleven religious leaders and scholars identified as "shapers and shakers of the Christian faith."

After receiving his bachelor of science degree from Iowa State University, Deloria studied for a career as a minister, earning a master's degree in theology from the Lutheran School of Theology in Rock Island, Illinois. Upon graduation, he accepted a staff position with the United Scholarship Service, a church-supported educational philanthropy group based in Denver, Colorado. Dissatisfied with the paternalistic approach taken by the leaders of the organization, Deloria resigned and soon became a leader in the reorganization of the National Congress of American Indians (NCAI) where he later served as the organization's executive director. In 1978 Deloria accepted a tenured appointment as professor of law and political science at the University of Arizona. In 1990 he left Arizona for the University of Colorado at Boulder, where he accepted an appointment as professor of American Indian studies and history with adjunct appointment in law, political science, and religious studies.

Deloria burst upon the national scene as a writer of great importance with his politically charged *Custer Died for Your Sins: An Indian Manifesto*, an indictment of the U.S. government's treatment of Indian people. Published in 1969, *Custer Died for Your Sins* became the "Indian bible" for a new generation of American Indian people and served as a manifesto for Indian activists of the 1960s and 1970s. *God Is Red*, written in 1973 and republished in 1992, *Red Earth, White Lies, Native Americans and the Myth of Scientific Fact* published in 1997, and *For This Land: Writings on Religion in America* published in 1999 are Deloria's best books on Indian religion.

Early Life

Very little has been written about Deloria's early life. He was born in 1933, the son of Ohiya, "Vine Deloria, Sr.,*" and Barbara Deloria. He was born in Martin, South Dakota, to an unusually distinguished family. His grandfather was a Yankton Sioux chief. His aunt, Ella Deloria, was a noted scholar of Indian ethnology and linguistics. His father, Vine Deloria, Sr., was an Episcopal minister who served on the National Council of the Episcopal Church as assistant secretary for Indian missions.

Deloria attended an off-reservation school in Martin, South Dakota, and was steeped in Indian culture. One of the most memorable events of his childhood was a visit to the site of the 1890 Wounded Knee massacre of Lakota people by the U.S. 7th Calvary. Deloria left home when he was sixteen years of age to further his education.

Leadership

Vine Deloria, Jr., was the son of an Episcopal minister and studied for the ministry at the Lutheran School of Theology, receiving a master's degree in theology from the Lutheran School of Theology in 1963. He was never ordained because he became disillusioned with the white man's religion. According to Deloria, religion for the white man is something to talk about and something to study; for the Indian, religion is something in his heart, something he feels, and something he lives.

Upon graduation from the Lutheran School of Theology, Deloria accepted a position with the United Scholarship Service, a church-supported educational philanthropy group based in Denver, Colorado. Deloria had a strong sense of the need for education for Indian people, and while with the Scholarship Service he developed a program that placed more than forty Indian students in independent preparatory schools in New England. The program reflected Deloria's concerns that young Indians should become productive members of the general society and still be able to "retain their Indianness."

From 1964 to 1967, Deloria served as executive director of the NCAI, the preeminent intertribal organization in the United States at that time. Deloria oversaw a total reorganization of the organization that had become marked by intertribal conflict, low membership, and near bankruptcy. Deloria understood the need for a national power base for Indian people and moved the NCAI into that position. Deloria began his career as a writer while with the NCAI, where he published a quarterly newsletter, the *Sentinel* that allowed him to give voice to his political and social concerns. It was while writing for the *Sentinel* which he honed his critical and sarcastic barbs aimed at the non-Indian establishment.

Deloria resigned as executive director of the NCAI in 1967 to enroll in the University of Colorado Law School, where he received his law degree in 1970. His first and most well-known book, *Custer Died for Your Sins: An Indian Manifesto*, was published in 1969. The book became an overnight best-seller and awoke a new generation of young Indian people who would lead and participate in the red power movement, then in its nascent stage. Deloria took time from his writing and studies to visit and give advice to the young Indian activists who occupied Alcatraz Island in November 1969.

In the mid-1970s Deloria became chairman of the Institute for the Development of Indian Law in Washington, D.C., where he became deeply involved in the social, economic, political, and legal problems confronting Indian people. Deloria had always maintained that Indian people must remain Indian rather than assimilate into U.S. society and that education and ideology were the keys to achieving dignity and justice for Native American people.

Deloria followed *Custer Died for Your Sins* with *We Talk, You Listen, New Tribes, New Turf*, in 1970. His message of government neglect and abuse resonated throughout Indian country and fed the flames of the Indian renaissance. Deloria became known as a revolutionary thinker who spoke out against the seductiveness and wastefulness of U.S. culture. He insisted that young Indian people receive traditional teachings before being exposed to the dominant Euro-American culture.

Because of his religious and political philosophy and his growing popularity, Deloria was invited to serve on numerous boards and Indian organizations. He filled leadership roles in organizations such as the Citizens Crusade Against Poverty, the Council on Indian Affairs, the National Office for the Rights of the Indigent, the Institute for the Development of Indian Law, and the Indian Rights Association. He taught at UCLA's American Indian Studies Center for four quarters and held visiting appointments at the Pacific

School of Religion, the New School of Religion, and Colorado College. He founded the Institute for the Development of Indian Law in 1971. In 1978 he accepted a tenured appointment as professor of law and political science at the University of Arizona. In 1990, he left Arizona for the University of Colorado at Boulder, where he accepted an appointment as professor of American Indian studies and history with an adjunct appointment in law, political science, and religious studies. He retired from his full-time professorship in 1999 and is now an emeritus faculty member of the University of Colorado.

Through his widely published books Deloria has brought a greater understanding of American Indian religion, history, and philosophy to a vast audience. His books address important political and legal issues concerning Indian-white relations. Deloria also argues that Christian religions have failed and that the United States is in a state of moral and religious crisis. He urges a return to Indian religions, which promote an ecologically sound relationship with the environment. Deloria further argues that white society must adopt a tribal-communal way of life if it is to survive. To achieve this, Deloria calls for a complete change in the social and theological outlook of white society.

Some of Deloria's well-known are: *Custer Died for Your Sins* (1969), *God Is Red: A Native View of Religion, We Talk, You Listen: New Tribes, New Turf* (1970), *Behind the Trail of Broken Treaties* (1974), *The Metaphysics of Modern Existence* (1979), *The Nations Within: The Past and the Future of American Indian Sovereignty* (1984), *The Progression of Civilization: Federal Indian Policy since the 1880s* (1984), *American Indian Policy in the 20th Century* (1985), *For This Land: Writings on Religion in America* (1999), and *Singing for a Spirit: A Portrait of the Dakota Sioux* (1999). He edited *A Sender of Words: Essays in Memory of John G. Neihardt* (1984), a volume that contains essays on *Black Elk Speaks*.

Further Reading

Champagne, Duane, ed. *The Native North American Almanac: A Reference Work on Native North Americans in the United States and Canada*. 1994. Detroit: Gale Research.

Deloria, Vine, Jr. *For This Land: Writings on Religion in America*. 1999. New York: Routledge.

Dictionary of Indians of North America. 1978. St. Clair Shores, Mich.: Scholarly Press.

Markowitz, Harvey, ed. *American Indians. Vol 1*. 1995: Pasadena, Calif.: Salem Press.

Vine Deloria, Jr.: http://www. native authors.com/search/bio/ biodeloria. html.

Charles Alexander Eastman

Full Name at Birth: Hakadah

Birth: February 19, 1858, in the Santee Indian Reservation near Redwood Falls in present-day Minnesota

Death: January 8, 1939, Detroit, Michigan

Education: attended Santee Normal School in Nebraska, 1874–1876; Beloit College in Wisconsin, 1876–1877; Knox College in Illinois, 1877–1880; Dartmouth

College in New Hampshire, 1883–1887; and Boston University Medical School, 1887–1890

Leadership Position: Wahpeton (Santee) Lakota physician and author

Awards: earned M.D. degree at Boston University in 1890; recipient of the first Indian Achievement Award in 1933

Summary

Charles Eastman was the first Native American physician to serve on the Pine Ridge Reservation in South Dakota and a prolific author of works about Indian life and culture. He was raised in a traditional Santee Sioux setting and had little contact with American society. Beginning at age fifteen, Eastman was enrolled in a succession of schools that brought him into contact with U. S. culture for the first time. Eastman attended Dartmouth College and Boston University Medical School, where he received a degree in medicine in 1890. He then became a physician at the Pine Ridge Indian Reservation, the first Native American in a position of authority there. Eastman was active in the Young Men's Christian Association and was one of the founders of the Boy Scouts of America.

Early Life

Eastman was the son of a Lakota warrior, Ite Wakanhdi Ota (Many Lightnings), and his wife, Wakantankanwina (Mary Nancy Eastman). His mother died at about age twenty-eight from lingering complications associated with Eastman's birth. Because of his mother's death, he was given the name Hakadah, "The Pitiful Last." Eastman was raised by his father's extended family. Uncheedah, his paternal grandmother, became most responsible for his early education. Eastman's father was taken prisoner by the U.S. Army during the Minnesota Sioux uprising of 1862 and was one of 303 Sioux who were sentenced to be hanged

Charles Alexander Eastman. Dartmouth College Library.

for the atrocities that had been committed. Unknown to Eastman, Many Lightnings' sentence was reviewed by President Abraham Lincoln and was changed to three years' imprisonment at the federal penitentiary in Davenport, Iowa.

Eastman was four years of age at the time of his father's confinement and was raised by his extended family in the traditional ways of a Lakota youth. He was raised to be a warrior and hunter and to respect the presence of the Great Spirit in all things. In 1862, Eastman's Lakota band chose him to represent them in a lacrosse contest during the Midsummer's Feast. He was victorious in the contest, and his band awarded him a new name, Ohiyesa, "The Winner."

As a result of increased pressure from the federal government to settle on an Indian reservation, Eastman's grandmother and uncles relocated to present-day North Dakota, and then to Ontario, Canada. Eleven years later, his father now named Jacob Eastman, was reunited with his son in Canada. For eleven years, Eastman had believed that his father had been executed. Eastman soon relocated with his father to Flandreu, South Dakota, where he accepted Christianity and was baptized Charles Alexander Eastman.

Leadership

Eastman personifies the image of an American Indian with a foot in both the Indian and white worlds. He was born into the family of a Lakota warrior and was trained in the traditional ways of a Lakota youth. His mother died while he was an infant, and he was raised by his father's patrilineal extended family. At the age of four years, Eastman believed that his father had been hanged along with thirty-seven other Lakota for their alleged part in the killing of seven hundred whites during the Minnesota uprising of 1862. Eastman and his kin relocated to North Dakota and then to Canada, where eleven years later, much to his surprise, he was reunited with his father. Eastman was now fifteen years old and had had little contact with the white world.

Eastman and his father relocated to South Dakota, where his exposure to and education in the white world began. He attended a series of white schools that included Dartmouth College and earned his medical degree at Boston University in 1890. Although Eastman had now been away from his own people for sixteen years, he felt a strong desire to return and use his education to help his people become Christianized and educated. In a letter written to accompany his application as an Indian seeking employment among In-

dians he stated that "the government physician can be the most useful civilizer among the force of government officers placed in any Indian Reservation" (Wilson 40–41).

It was during this time that the Lakota Nation was experiencing extreme pressure from the United States to give up their traditional life of age-graded societies, wealth in horses, and the buffalo pursuit. Indian people were expected to sign treaties and give up their lands in exchange for removal and confinement on small reservations. There, they would be wards of the government, dependent on the federal government for food, shelter, and ultimately assimilation into the dominant white society. One response to the overwhelming oppression was the Ghost Dance that began with Wovoka,* a Paiute shaman in the Great Basin region. This revitalization religion was nonviolent and held forth the promise of a new world where the whites would disappear, the buffalo would return, and the Indian dead would be reborn. The Lakota added to the religion the Ghost Dance shirt, which they believed would stop the white man's bullet. In 1890, the U.S. government, fearing a new Indian war, overreacted and massacred 150 Indian men, women, and children and wounded another 50, all members of Big Foot's peaceful Lakota band. As the agency physician on the Pine Ridge Reservation for the Indian Health Service, Eastman had witnessed the rise of the Ghost Dance movement and was one of the first people to visit Wounded Knee after the massacre and tended to the wounded.

Eastman resigned his position on the Pine Ridge Reservation in 1893 and began a private practice in St. Paul, Minnesota. In 1900, he once again ministered to Indian people and was the agency physician at the Crow Creek Reservation in South Dakota.

Between 1894 and 1897, Eastman was active in the Yong Men's Christian Association and established thirty-two Indian YMCA groups. He was a lobbyist in Washington, D.C., for the Santee Sioux from 1879 to 1899. In 1899, he became outing agent for the Carlisle Indian School in Pennsylvania, headed by Captain Richard Henry Pratt. In 1903, President Theodore Roosevelt assigned Eastman the task of revising the allotment of tribal lands to individuals and assigning the Sioux family names to protect their titles to land. In 1911, Eastman, along with Reverend Sherman Coolidge (Arapaho), Charles E. Daganewtt (Peoria), Laura Cornelius (Oneida), and Thomas L. Sloan (Omaha), was instrumental in the formation of the Society of American Indians. From 1923 to 1925, under President Calvin Coolidge, Eastman was appointed federal Indian inspector, and during the same period, he was a member of the Committee of One Hundred, a reform group that made recommendations to expedite Indian claims against the federal government. In 1910, along with Ernest Thompson Seton, Eastman helped found the Boy Scouts of America.

Between 1902 and 1916, Eastman wrote numerous articles and nine books about Indian history and mythology. He also gave many lectures about his experiences as an Indian. His books include *Wigwam Evenings: Sioux Folktales Retold* (1906), *The Soul of the Indian* (1911), and *From the Deep Woods to Civilization* (1916).

Eastman died of a heart attack at Grace Hospital in Detroit, Michigan, on January 8, 1939, and was buried in an unmarked grave at the Evergreen Cemetery in Detroit.

Further Reading

Calloway, Colin G. *First Peoples: A Documentary Survey of American Indian History.* 1999. New York: St. Martin's Press.

Champagne, Duane, ed. *The Native North American Almanac: A Reference Work on Native North Americans in the United States and Canada.* 1945. Detroit: Gale Research.

Copeland, Marion W. *Charles Alexander Eastman (Ohiyesa).* 1978. Caldwell, Idaho: Caxton Printers.

Waldman, Carl. *Who Was Who in Native American History.* 1990. New York: Facts on File.

Washburn, Wilcomb E. *Handbook of North American Indians, Vol. 4.* 1988. Washington, D.C.: Smithsonian Institution.

Wilson, Raymond. *Ohiyesa: Charles Eastman, Santee Sioux.* 1983. Chicago: University of Illinois Press.

Enmegahbowh

Full Name at Birth: Enmegabowh ("One Who Stands Before His People"); John Johnson

Birth: ca. 1810

Death: June 12, 1902; buried near St. Columba mission, White Earth, Minnesota

Education: attended a Methodist mission school in Jacksonville, Illinois, while a young man; entered Ebenezer Manual Labor School in Illinois in 1837

Leadership Position: Ojibwa-Ottawa Methodist missionary

Summary

Enmegahbowh was a Chippewa-Ottawa Methodist and then an Episcopal missionary and interpreter among the Anishinaabeg Indians. Enmegahbowh, who received the name John Johnson when he became Christianized, was born to Ottawa parents who lived with the Rice Lake band of Ojibwa, located north of Lake Ontario in Canada. He first came to the United States in 1834 as a mission interpreter. Enmegahbowh was baptized into the Methodist religion; when the Methodists closed their mission, he encouraged the Episcopal church to establish one at Gull Lake, which was founded in 1852. He then became the first indigenous ordained ministry in the Episcopal church.

After declining an opportunity to attend college, Enmegahbowh eventually began mission assignments in Minnesota. He subsequently lived and worked among Ojibwa bands at Sandy Lake, Mille Lacs, White Fish Lake, Rabbit Lake, Fond du Lac, Gull Lake, and White Earth. Enmegahbowh later began Episcopal missionary work at Gull Lake, where a temporary church, St. John's in the Wilderness, was eventually replaced by St. Columba. Enmegahbowh was ordained an Episcopal deacon by Bishop Kemper in 1859 and ordained a priest by Bishop Whipple in 1867.

In 1868, when the Ojibwa were removed by treaty from Gull Lake to the newly established White Earth Reservation in Minnesota, Enmegahbowh and about forty of his parishioners began to reestablish St. Columba mission at White Earth. Called to serve the Ojibwa people a year later, he left St. Columba to begin another associate mission on the shores of Gull Lake. In 1869, the Gull Lake mission

Enmegahbowh c. 1900. Courtesy, Becker County Historical Society.

was moved to the White Earth Reservation, and, in 1873, he assisted in the founding of a school to train Indian clergy.

In the early 1840s, Enmegahbowh married an Ojibwa woman, Biwabiko-gizigokwe, or Iron Sky Woman, whose parents agreed to the marriage on the condition that the couple not leave Ojibwa territory. Her parents then consented to the baptism of their daughter, who was renamed Charlotte. In 1849, the Methodist church expelled Enmegahbowh and his wife from the church because Enmegahbowh reportedly fought a white man who had insulted Charlotte.

Enmegahbowh outlived his twelve children, including his son George Johnson, a gifted minister. After Charlotte died on March 30, 1895, Enmegahbowh's constant companion was a young grandson whose death in 1896 was a devastating loss. Enmegahbowh died on June 12, 1902, and was buried near St. Columba mission at White Earth, Minnesota.

Early Life

Very little has been written about Enmegahbowh's early life. He was born to Ottawa parents who lived with the Rice Lake band of Ojibwa, located north of Lake Ontario in Canada. Enmegahbowh was adopted as a boy by the Chippewa (Ojibway). He was educated at a Methodist mission school in Jacksonville, Illinois, and later ordained as Reverend John Johnson. Although Enmegahbowh's year of birth is generally identified as 1810, one Episcopal clergyman stated that he was thirty-six years old when he was ordained a deacon in 1859, making his date of birth as late as 1823.

While a young man, Enmegahbowh's parents sent him to a school run by an Anglican clergyman. He attended classes for a few months until he became homesick and ran away. He later attended a mission school established by the Methodist Episcopal church in the Rice Lake community. The Reverend James Evans convinced Enmegahbowh's parents to allow him to leave for the Methodist mission at Sault Ste. Marie to work as an interpreter. Enmegahbowh left home in 1834, never to see his parents again.

Leadership

Enmegahbowh came to the United States in 1834 as a mission interpreter for the Methodist church. When the Methodists closed their mission, Enmegahbowh encouraged the Episcopal church to establish one at Gull Lake, which was founded in 1852. He served there as an assistant and interpreter, and Enmegahbowh himself became an Episcopal deacon in 1859. After his ordination as a deacon, he played a significant role in a conflict known as the Hole-in-the-Day uprising. Informants claimed that the Ojibwa leader Hole-in-the-Day was planning to unite with Little Crow, a leader from the Mdewakanton band of Dakota, in an effort to drive out encroaching whites. It was reported that Enmegahbowh sent warnings to Fort Ripley, then fled from Ojibwa dissidents. He traveled with his family by canoe down the Gull River, where two of his children later died of exposure from the ordeal. St. Columba's was destroyed during the conflict, leaving Enmegahbowh without a church or position.

In 1863 Enmegahbowh found temporary work accompanying an Ojibwa treaty delegation to Washington, D.C., where he served as an interpreter and conducted tours. His effectiveness as a missionary was later undermined because of his connection with an unpopular treaty agreement, and it took him years to regain the trust he had lost among the Ojibwa.

In 1868, when the Ojibwa were removed from Gull Lake to the newly established White Earth Reservation in Minnesota, Enmegahbowh and about forty of his parishioners began to reestablish St. Columba mission at White Earth. In 1867, he was ordained a priest by Bishop Henry Benjamin Whipple, and he trained several Ojibwa for ordination into the Episcopal ministry.

Enmegahbowh's understanding of Anishinaabe enabled him to interact effectively with band members. He emphasized the traditional values of sharing and reciprocity and gave generously of his own personal belongings and resources. This differentiated him from Euroamerican missionaries who had come before. Important Anishinaabe leaders, none of whom had shown a great deal of enthusiasm for the Episcopal religion, were especially drawn to his message.

Enmegahbowh encouraged the Anishinaabe to take up agriculture, drawing on lessons that he had learned from the Canadian Anishinaabeg. The Anishinaabe band leaders followed his instructions, hoping that intensified farming efforts would help rejuvenate their communities. Those who embarked on the farming experiment succeeded in the early years. Enmegahbowh was encouraged in their efforts and on one occasion stated, "I have never seen them [the Anishinaabe] so willing & ready to work & cultivate the soil."

Enmegahbowh's later life was filled with grief. He outlived all twelve of his children, as well as his wife, Charlotte, who died on March 30, 1895. He found temporary comfort in a grandson, whose death in 1896 was a devastating loss. Enmegahbowh himself died in 1902.

Further Reading

Ballantine, Betty, and Ian Ballantine, eds. *The Native Americans: An Illustrated History*. 1993. Atlanta: Turner Publishing.

Episcopal Diocese of Minnesota: http://www.episcopalmn.org/history.html.

Hirschfelder, Arlene, and Paulette Molin. *The Encyclopedia of Native American Religions*. 1992. New York. Facts on File.

Meyer, Melissa L. *The White Earth Tragedy: Ethnicity and Dispossession at a Minnesota Anishinaabe Reservation, 1889–1920*. 1994. Lincoln: University of Nebraska Press.

Fanny Flounder

Full Name at Birth: Fanny Flounder
Birth: ca. 1840s, place of birth not recorded
Death: 1940s, place of death not recorded
Education: no formal education
Leadership Position: Yurok female shaman

Summary

Fanny Flounder was one of the last of the powerful female *kegoyowor* (shaman) in the twentieth century. Flounder was a sucking doctor and had the ability to move objects at will. She would perform sacred ceremonies over the sick person while singing healing songs that had been given to her in a dream. Once the disease-causing agent or the diseased area was made known to her, she would suck the object from the patient using a hollow bone tube. The object would then be disposed of in a manner that had been made known to her in the dream.

An informant, Harry Roberts, who had spent time with her when he was young, reported:

When Fanny was curing I used to see a blue light coming off the back of her head, and I could see it at the end of her fingers. You see that in a dim room. She'd create a low-keyed hum, "hmmmmmmmm"—and click sticks together, or clap her hands lightly. She'd go on like that for a long time, like a beehive: keep it up for hours. Then suddenly she'd touch a tension spot on her patient's body and lead the tension off. Then she'd [wipe her hands vigorously]. . . .

Some time between 1901 and 1908 an anthropologist took this photo of the Yurok healer Fanny Flounder. Courtesy of the Phoebe Hearst Museum of Anthropology and the Regents of the University of California-photographed by Alfred Kroeber.

During the healing of a young girl, it was reported that

as the evening proceeded, the shaman's activity moved through periods of quiet and periods of song and dance, whistling and clapping, and long almost mournful vocalizations that appealed to remote living powers, spirits. In the darkness with just the glowing light of the fire's embers and in the presence of the villagers, the room seemed to fill with spirits and the sense of power seemed to crush inward with almost overwhelming force. Some times the shaman was kneeling with the girl and almost seemed to carry on a whispered conversation with her, bending down so close to her head. At other times, Flounder's hands moved sensitively across her body. . . . The girl herself seemed to be entering into a trance-like state. The shaman's movements slowly worked toward a kind of frenzied energy and culmination. She rose and sang and danced and whistled and clapped, all with more agitated animation. Then she sank to her knees and swayed over the girl's body with increasing passion. In the end she sucked powerfully at the critical point, discovered by her focused sensitive investigations. She spat a small crystal of evil illness into the small basket in her left hand. The ceremony had ended.

Early Life

There is no recorded history of Flounder's early life. We do know from the historian Lowell Bean that among California Indian tribes, shamans were not only the "principal religious functionaries" but also frequently political administrators simultaneously, as well as being "the principal philosophers, poets, artists, musicians, intellectuals, scientists, doctors, and psychotherapists." Using this insight, we can assume that Flounder served as a mediator between the sacred and profane worlds. According to Bean, Flounder would have participated in "magical fight" to gain mystical power and knowledge about the universe. She would then use this power to "aid the souls of the deceased in their journey to the land of the dead, to relay instructions from the mystical world on proper life-styles in the here and now, and to diagnostic and cure illness."

Leadership

According to Yurok philosophy, the Creator "Wohpekumeu made things as they are in this world; the spirits of old still dance in the faraway land across the ocean or have assumed animal forms . . . the sun and sky were made or repaired." But these were only incidental. What was more important was the person who would serve as an intermediary between humans and the spirit world. These people, like Fanny Flounder, were the Yurok shamans.

Shamanism takes on a peculiar aspect in northwestern California where the Yurok were created. Among the Yurok, shamanistic power resides in control of "pains," small, animate objects that cause illness by entering the bodies of people and also endow the shaman with power when he or she brings them to reside within himself or herself. It should be noted that among the Yurok, almost all shamans are women. The witch or poisoner was usually a man and operated by magic rather than shamanistic power. It was reported that Flounder "ultimately acquired five pairs of telogel (abilities to cure pains or diseases), making her one of the most powerful, famous, and wealthy doctors in memory."

An informant, Florence Shaughnessy, reported witnessing one of Flounder's rituals and the acquiring of a new healing "plan":

We sang and sang and she (Fanny) danced. Finally she spewed up a bloody mess (the telogel) into a basin (keyom) we had there. It looked just like a small swallow all covered with bloody slime. I looked and I could see its little beak, the gold stripes on its shoulder. It was breathing there. I saw it clearly, sitting there breathing.

George put the bowl on the mantle (storage ledge of the semi-subterranean house). Then she drew on her long pipe. There was a thud!—I can still hear it, like flesh hitting flesh. Then the basin came swirling down to the floor, empty. She got up. . . . That bird was a new pain for her, and they said it gave her power over tumors.

Flounder died during the 1940s at close to one hundred years of age.

Further Reading

Bean, Lowell John, ed. *California Indian Shamanism*. 1987. Menlo Park, Calif.: Ballena Press.

Kroeber, A. L. *Handbook of the Indians of California: The Yurok Land and Civilization*. 1925. Washington, D.C.: Bureau of American Ethnology of the Smithsonian Institution.

Lyon, William S. *Encyclopedia of Native American Healing.* 1996. Denver: ABC- CLIO.

Shamanism: http://www.cabrillo.cc.ca.us/~crsmith/shaman.html.

Frank Fools Crow

Full Name at Birth: Frank Fools Crow, called Frank to distinguish him from his father, Fools Crow. His grandfather, Knife Chief, first bestowed the name Fools Crow on Frank's father, passed the name on to Frank. The only son by his father's fist wife, Spoon Hunter, Frank Fools Crow was given his name at a naming ceremony held four days after the death of his mother.

Birth: ca. 1891. All Fools Crow knews for certain was that he was born in the Porcupine community of the Pine Ridge Reservation in South Dakota sometime between 1890 and 1892, either on June 24 or June 27, 1890.

Death: November 27, 1989

Education: At age 13, after Frank began to have strong feelings about becoming a medicine man, his father took him to a well-known Lakota holy man named Stirrup, who became his teacher.

At age 18, an Indian agent attempted to enroll Frank Fools Crow in an Indian boarding school; however, it was discovered during the enrollment process that he was too old to be compelled to attend.

Leadership Position: Lakota holy man and ceremonial chief

Summary

Frank Fools Crow was a revered Sun Dance intercessor, *yuwipi* man, and *wapiye* (healer) for over sixty years. The Sun Dance played a large part in Lakota life; it is their religion and their highest way of paying honor to God. The dance was generally held in July each year and was held so that men who had made a pledge to Wakan Tanka could fulfill the pledge and ensure prosperity for the Lakota Nation. Wakan Tanka is generally interpreted as "The Great Mystery" and is synonymous with the Creator and the Great Spirit. *Yuwipi* is a Lakota term generally used to refer to a nighttime curing ceremony conducted in a darkened room by a medicine man, *yuwipi wicasa*, who has been bound and wrapped tightly from head to toe. *Yuwipi* is a sacred word that has many meanings. *Uwi* means "to bind, to tie up." *Yuwipi* is also the term

for tiny, sacred stones gathered from anthills for use in ceremonies and another name of an ancient spirit. Fools Crow's extraordinary life and healing powers are described in Mails's biography *Fools Crow* and by Fools Crow directly on the recording *Fools Crow* (Tatanka Records, 1977).

In 1917, Fools Crow became a Roman Catholic, finding few problems with differences between Catholicism and his traditional beliefs, and practiced both religions for the remainder of his life. He participated in a European tour in 1921, a Wild West show in 1927, and other traveling shows. In 1931, he was one of the riders in what is described as the last true and sacred Horse Dance. Fools Crow also traveled with a group publicizing western movies, appeared in the film *War Bonnet*, and promoted the film.

Besides his role as a religious leader, Franks Fools Crow assumed civil leader-

Closeup of Frank Fools Crow, photographed at Wounded Knee, South Dakota, in March 1973. © Bettmann/Corbis.

ship of the Porcupine District of the Pine Ridge Reservation in South Dakota in 1925. In later years, he continued to perform his duties as a religious and civil leader. During the Native American occupation of Wounded Knee on the Pine Ridge Reservation in 1973, he sought peace by negotiating with federal officials and the Native American protesters to settle the armed confrontation. Fools Crow served as an intermediary and delivered a document from government officials outlining a proposed settlement of the crisis. Although doubt existed regarding the proposed peace treaty, Fools Crow encouraged the signing of the document. After both sides signed the document, the seventy-six-day confrontation ended.

On September 5, 1975, Frank Fools Crow became the first Indian holy man to lead the opening prayer of a session of the U.S. Senate. In the spring of 1976, Frank Fools Crow, age eighty-five, viewed the sacred buffalo calf pipe, a life-long desire and a rare honor.

Early Life

Frank Fool Crow's mother, Spoon Hunter, died four days after he was born. His father's sister, Runs for Hill, cared for him until he was about five years of age. In 1896, his father married Emily Big Road. Frank's father had a major influence in his early training. He taught him how to ride well and work hard, and often made him run long distances to build up his endurance. He also encouraged Fools Crow to respect and keep the traditional Lakota ways. Two other men besides his father played important roles in the shaping of his early life: his uncle Iron Cloud and the Lakota holy-man Stirrup. Iron Cloud taught him much of what he knew about Wakan-Tanka and how to have a close relationship with him. Iron Cloud also taught him many practical things about how he should live, how to take care of the mind and body, and how to get along with people.

At age thirteen, after Frank began to have strong feelings about becoming a medicine man, his father took him to Stirrup, who became his teacher. The holy man took him on his first vision quest in 1905, where Fools Crow received his spirit helper (a force or being he could turn to in time of trouble). In 1914 Stirrup chose Frank Fools Crow as his choice to carry on his work as a holy man.

Leadership

Frank Fools Crow was a Lakota holy man and ceremonial chief who was born in the Porcupine community of the Pine Ridge Reservation in South Dakota shortly after the Wounded Knee tragedy of 1890. Fools Crow was an Oglala Lakota, a member of the largest and once the most powerful and best known of the seven subtribes of the Teton Sioux. He was the nephew of Black Elk, another noted Lakota holy man, and is considered by many to be the greatest Native American spiritual leader of the past century.

The Fools Crow name came from Frank's grandfather, Knife Chief, whose older son was killed by Crow Indians. Fools Crow was raised in the traditional Lakota way. Most of his boyhood days were spent doing chores for his family such as taking care of his father's horses and other livestock. He rode, fished, and enjoyed swimming with his friends. When Frank Fools Crow was eight or nine years old, Knife Chief made him a bow and some arrows and taught him

how to use them. Following Lakota tradition, he hunted rabbits, prairie dogs, and prairie chickens and became an excellent marksman.

Besides his father and grandparents, two of Fools Crow's teachers were his uncle Iron Cloud, a Lakota leader during the early reservation period, and Stirrup, a well-known Lakota holy man. When Stirrup took Frank Fools Crow on his first vision quest in 1905, he was assisted by Daniel Dull Knife and Grady Dull Knife. The place where he quested was in Yellow Bear Creek, near present-day Kyle, South Dakota. They went early in the morning to prepare for the four-day ordeal. Late in the afternoon of the first day, Frank Fools Crow and his teachers participated in a purification ceremony held in the sweat lodge. They sang songs, chanted prayers, and prayed individually. As the sun was going down, Stirrup placed a black cloth hood over Frank Fools Crow's head so that he could not see where the men were taking him. He was led to a questing pit that was about two feet wide, four feet deep, and six feet long. Sage had been spread on the bottom to purify the pit and make a bed. Frank Fools Crow remained in the vision quest pit for four days and nights without food and water. On the fourth day, he had his first vision. Early on the fifth day, Stirrup came for him and took him back to camp.

Frank Fools Crow told Stirrup about his vision, and Stirrup helped Fools Crow to understand it. Stirrup instructed him to keep the meaning a secret because Wakan-Tanka would not want him to reveal everything that he saw. It was not until after Frank Fools Crow's second vision quest, in 1914, that he received the most profound secrets that he would need to know to begin his career as a holy man. Once again, Stirrup interpreted the meanings for him and taught him some of the sacred ceremonial songs. At this point, Stirrup became Frank Fools Crow's sacred father. Stirrup warned Frank Fools Crow that he would be expected to make sacrifices and that he would be called on to cure people without pay. He was forbidden to participate in drinking, womanizing, and fighting, nor could he openly discuss political issues with Indian people.

In November 1913, Frank Fools Crow conducted his first Kettle Dance, which his grandparents taught him. In the spring of 1913, while riding in the hills near his home, he experienced his first vision in a thunderstorm. This gave him the power to learn to lead the Sacred Kettle Dance Ceremony, a prayer for rain and food. When it was done, it was always the last dance of the day to be performed.

Another important religious dance was the Horse Dance. Frank Fools Crow claims to have been one of the riders of the last sacred Horse Dance, held near Whiteclay, Nebraska, in 1931. The other participants were Poor Thunder, Danny Otheo, and Standing Little Boy. Four singers and four wild horses were used for the dance. One horse was black, one a sorrel, one a buckskin, and one white. The wild horses were led into in a corral set up near the place where they were going to dance. A fire was built next to the corral. Poor Thunder took some red-hot ashes and mixed them with the smoke. When Poor Thunder took the ashes over to the corral and let the wind blow the smoke through the rails and across the horses, they calmed down in moments and were no longer wild.

Each of the four riders wore a costume that consisted of a breechcloth and a black cloth bandanna that covered the entire face. The bandanna was tied in a knot behind the head and was thin enough that they could see through it. A hole was cut in the bandanna so that the riders could insert an eagle bone whistle through it and blow on it. The corral gate was then opened, and the four men walked directly up to the horses. Without the aid of bridle, halter, rope, or anything else, the men mounted the wild horses. The riders prodded the horses with their bare heels, and each of the horses walked calmly through the gate. The participants in the ceremony now began singing, and the horses started dancing. As they danced, clouds formed and thunder began to crash. The lightning struck about ten yards ahead of them, but the horses did not break and run, as might be expected. The horses continued to dance as the lightning moved in a semicircle ahead of them. The riders, Frank Fools Crow included, started to pray, and the storm ended. They halted their horses at each of the four sacred directions. The riders dismounted and released the horses back into the wild.

Frank Fools Crow supported the occupation of Wounded Knee II on February 7, 1973, headed by American Indian Movement (AIM) leaders Russell Means (Oglala Sioux), Clyde Bellecourt (Chippewa), and Dennis Banks (Chippewa). On February 25, 1973, Fools Crow was among a group of chiefs, medicine men, and headmen who supported the group's decision to go to Wounded Knee. Others who participated were Chief Red Cloud, Chief Iron Cloud, Chief Bad Cob, and Chief Kills Enemy. Peter Caches was identified as the medicine man. Frank Fools Crow requested that the Oglala Sioux Civil Rights Organization (OSCRO) and AIM form a provisional government that could speak for the new nation to the outside world. With his encouragement, the

Independent Oglala Sioux Nation (ION) was formed on March 11, 1973, and a Declaration of Independence was issued.

In May 1973, as the occupation of Wounded Knee continued, a White House delegation met with a number of Lakota chiefs at the home of Frank Fools Crow. The intent of the meeting was to solicit recommendations from the Indian leaders as to how the United States might comply with treaty obligations in a way that would end the occupation. Frank Fools Crow was the leading spokesperson during the meeting. The traditional leaders pressed the government to revert to the pre-1871 treaty relationship that existed between the federal government and Indian Nations. They insisted on a referendum ending the Indian Reorganization Act form of government and a reinstatement of the traditional form of tribal organization. The federal representatives replied that no such fundamental change in status was possible.

On May 5, 1873, an agreement signed by Leonard Garment, special counsel to the president, was delivered to Frank Fools Crow for delivery to the Indian occupiers of Wounded Knee. An interpreter read him the document. Fools Crow said he was not happy with the agreement because it failed to reinstate the treaty relationship between the federal government and Indian nations and thus promised little of consequence. Wanting to end the seventy-six-day occupation, however, he agreed to present the proposal to the Indians at Wounded Knee. The occupiers agreed with the terms, and the accord was signed by Leonard Crow Dog, Frank Fools Crow, and AIM members. The occupation of Wounded Knee came to an end.

On May 17, 18, and 19, 1973, representatives from President Nixon met to discuss treaties with Indian leaders from Pine Ridge Reservation, once again at the home of Frank Fools Crow. Before negotiations began, Frank Fools Crow wanted an answer from Patterson to the question of whether the Sioux could be reinstated to the 1868 Treaty. Patterson explained that the 1871 law had eliminated the right of the president to negotiate treaties. Frank Fools Crow and his group were not overawed by the White House pronouncements. "We are not asking for the negotiation of new treaties," Frank Fools Crow stated. "We are merely asking for the treaties that already exist to be enforced." The federal government was without power to grant the treaty negotiations that the Sioux demanded. Further negotiations were cancelled.

During a vision quest at Bear Butte in 1965, Wakan-Tanka told Frank Fools Crow that the time had come for him to tell certain things about himself and his Teton people to a person who would be made known to him. Thomas E. Mails was the person selected. In 1979, assisted by Dallas Chief Eagle, Mails published *Fools Crow* and fulfilled the direction of Wakan-Tanka and left a permanent record of the Lakota holy man and his people.

Further Reading

Beck, Peggy V., Anna Lee Walters, and Nia Francisco. *The Sacred Ways of Knowledge, Sources of Life*. 1990. Flagstaff: Northland Publishing Co.

Chief Frank Fools Crow: http://www.chief.uiuc.edu/foolscrow.html.

Dewing, Rolland. *Wounded Knee II*. 1995. Chadron, Nebr.: Great Plains Network.

Hirschfelder, Arlene and Paulette Molin. *The Encyclopedia of Native American Religions*. 1992. New York: Facts on File.

Johnson, Troy, et al., eds., *American Indian Activism: Alcatraz to the Longest Walk.* 1997. Urbana: University of Illinois Press.

Josephy, Alvin M., et al., eds. *Red Power: The American Indians Fight for Freedom.* 1999. Lincoln: University of Nebraska Press.

Mails, Thomas E. *Fools Crow.* 1979. New York: Doubleday.

Rice, Julian. *Lakota Storytelling: Black Elk, Ella Deloria, and Frank Fools Crow.* 1989. New York: Peter Lang.

Walker, Paul R. *Spiritual Leaders: American Indian Lives.* 1994. New York: Facts on File.

Washburn, Wilcomb E. *Handbook of North American Indians, Vol. 4.* 1988. Washington, D.C.: Smithsonian Institution.

Stephen Foreman

Full Name at Birth: Stephen Foreman

Birth: 1807 in Rome, Georgia

Death: 1881 in the Indian Territory of present-day Oklahoma

Education: attended the College of Richmond; attended a mission school at Candy's Creek, near Cleveland, Tennessee, and the Congregational Mission at New Echota, Georgia; later attended Union Theological Seminary in Virginia and Princeton Theological Seminary

Leadership Position: Cherokee Presbyterian missionary

Summary

Foreman was a well-known mixed-blood Cherokee Indian who worked with the Presbyterian missionaries and was, himself a Presbyterian missionary. He attended the Union Theological Seminary in Virginia and Princeton Theological Seminary in New Jersey and was licensed by the American Board of the Presbyterian Church in 1833 and ordained as a minister in 1835. Foreman translated biblical works and served as an associate editor of the *Cherokee Phoenix*, a weekly newspaper written in English and in Cherokee, and later contributed material to the *Cherokee Advocate*, the official newspaper of the Cherokee Nation.

Foreman worked with Samuel Worcester and Elias Boudinot on translations of the Bible into the Cherokee language. He supported the John Ross party led by Chief John Ross during a critical time in Cherokee history. Ross, Foreman, and others fought against the removal of the Cherokee Indians from their traditional homelands in the southeastern United States. Because he fought against the Cherokee removal west of the Mississippi River, Foreman was imprisoned in 1838. After being released from prison later that year, he helped lead one of the last groups to Indian Territory (present-day Oklahoma). It was Foreman's belief that he could help ameliorate the terrible physical and emotional trauma being experienced by the Cherokee during the removal by being present among them. During the Civil War, Foreman avoided choosing sides and worked as a missionary in Texas. Upon his return to Indian Territory, he purchased the house Elias Boudinot had owned and created the Church in the Woods. He continued his religious activities there until his death in 1881. Foreman had fourteen children by two marriages.

Early Life

Very little has been written regarding Foreman's early life. We do know that he was born in Rome, Georgia, in 1807 and was one of twelve children of a Scottish trader and his Cherokee wife. The family moved to Cleveland, Tennessee, soon after his father died. He attended the mission school at Candy's Creek, and then continued his studies with the Reverend Samuel Worcester, the Congregational missionary at New Echota, Georgia. He went on to attend the College of Richmond in Virginia and the Princeton Theological Seminary in New Jersey.

Leadership

Foreman was licensed by the American Board of the Presbyterian Church in 1833 and ordained as a minister in 1835. He received his license to preach by the Union Presbytery of Tennessee in 1838. Foreman worked with Samuel Worcester, a Presbyterian missionary, and Elias Boudinot, a member of the pro-removal faction of the Cherokee Nation, on translations of the Bible into the Cherokee language. He also worked as associate editor of the *Cherokee Phoenix*, a weekly newspaper written in English and in Sequoyah's Cherokee Syllabary, and the *Cherokee Advocate*, the official newspaper of the Cherokee Nation.

Foreman worked as a missionary among the Cherokee during the turmoil of the removal period, 1833–1838, when the Cherokee were uprooted from their traditional homelands and forced to migrate west of the Mississippi River. He supported the John Ross party led by Principal Chief John Ross, who refused to sign a removal treaty with the U.S. government. Foreman was the clerk of the Red Clay Council of the Cherokee Nation on August 7, 1837. The council endorsed a resolution signed by Ross that nominated certain parties, including Foreman, as delegates to represent the Cherokee Nation before the U.S. government to testify against the Cherokee removal bill. He was vested with full powers to negotiate all existing difficulties by treaty arrangements between the Cherokee Nation and the United States. Because of his antiremoval stance, Foreman was imprisoned in 1838. Soon afterward, he was placed in charge of one of the several detachments of emigrating Cherokees during the Trail of Tears, the forced march to the Indian Territory. It was the belief of John Ross and others, including Foreman, that if Cherokee leaders took charge of the removal process, they could lessen the physical and emotional trauma of the relocation process. This proved to be untrue, however, as inadequate food, supplies, and exposure to freezing winter temperature cost the lives of over four thousand Cherokee people. Once in the Indian Territory, the Cherokee people dedicated themselves to making the best of the bad situation. Foreman continued to act as a tribal and religious leader for the Cherokee people, and in 1841, he helped organize a public school system for his tribe and served as its first superintendent. In 1844, he was elected to the Supreme Court of the Cherokee Nation and between 1847 and 1855 he served as executive councilor.

During the Civil War, Foreman avoided choosing sides and worked as a missionary in Texas. On returning to the Indian Territory, he created a church in the former home of Elias Boudinot, a leader of the proremoval faction of the Cherokee.

In addition to his duties as a Presbyterian missionary, Foreman became secretary of the Cherokee Temperance Society and maintained it as a large and powerful organization for many years. In 1844, in a report to the U.S. agent, he gave the number of members of the temperance society as, 2,473.

In 1851, the American Missionary Association Board discovered that Foreman owned a female slave. The board had found in 1848 that Mrs. Foreman was a slaveholder, but the association was able to overlook the problem because she held her slaves as separate property. The ownership of the slave limited Foreman's future effectiveness with the missionary association.

Foreman continued his religious activities in the Indian Territory until his death in 1881.

Further Reading

Ballantine, Betty and Ian Ballantine, eds. *The Native Americans: An Illustrated History.* 1993. Atlanta: Turner Publishing.

Bass, Althea. *Cherokee Messenger.* 1936. Norman: University of Oklahoma Press.

Hirschfelder, Arlene, and Paulette Molin. *The Encyclopedia of Native American Religions.* 1992. New York: Facts on File.

McLoughlin, William Gerald. *Cherokees and Missionaries 1789–1839.* 1984. New Haven, Conn.: Yale University Press.

Moulton, Gary E. *The Papers of Chief John Ross, Vol. 1: 1807–1839.* 1984. Norman: University of Oklahoma Press.

Stoutenburgh, John L., Jr. *Dictionary of the American Indian.* 1960. New York: Philosophical Library.

Josiah Francis

Full Name at Birth: Francis the Prophet; Hillis Hayo, Hildis Hadjo, Hillishago, Hillishager

Birth: ca. 1770s

Death: April 18, 1818, in St. Marks, Florida

Education: no formal education.

Leadership Position: Creek prophet

Summary

Josiah Francis was a renowned prophet among the Creek people and became an influential war leader during the War of 1812. He traveled with the Shawnee leader Tecumseh in 1811 to seek support for Tecumseh among the Creeks and other southern tribes. Tecumseh was attempting to create an alliance of Indian nations that would block further U.S. expansion onto Indian lands.

Josiah Francis was a leader in the Creek War of 1813–1814 and fought against General Andrew Jackson, who referred to him as the great Seminole prophet. In 1815, he made an unsuccessful trip to England in search of support for his struggle against the United States. He returned to the United States in 1817 and settled near St. Marks, Florida. Andrew Jackson invaded Spanish Florida on April 7, 1818, and burned Josiah Francis's home and the rest of the village. In April

1818, Jackson lured Josiah Francis onto a gunboat flying a British flag. Josiah Francis and Hlimollemico, another native leader, were captured and hanged on April 18, 1818, at St. Marks.

Early Life

Josiah Francis's lineage is uncertain. His father was a white blacksmith, and his mother was perhaps of the Tawasa- or Tuskegee-related tribes, most likely Creek. Little is known of his early life, however, it has been suggested that other Creek children may have teased him because of his mixed ancestry and that he became obsessed with identifying himself with his Native heritage. It is known that Josiah Francis had a historical connection to the Red Stick (warrior) Creeks and the Seminole Indian Nation of Florida that had ancestors among a number of different Southeast tribes. It is highly likely that Josiah Francis received religious inspiration from the Creek medicine man Seekaboo, who flourished during this period. It is known that Josiah Francis traveled with the Shawnee leader Tecumseh, and it is likely that he received religious inspiration from Tecumseh's brother Tenskwatawa,* the Shawnee prophet, as well.

Leadership

Josiah Francis was of mixed blood parentage, born to a mother who was likely of Creek descent and a white father who was a village blacksmith. Choosing to identify with his Native heritage, he became one of the most important Creek prophets of all times. Like many other Indian prophets, Josiah Francis was an ardent advocate of war against the white man and used his spiritual powers to gain support for his cause.

As a major prophet, Josiah Francis had the ability to go into trances in which he visited with and spoke with the Great Spirit. While in a trance state, he received supernatural powers and instructions that the people were to follow to rid themselves of the white intruders and return to the old way of life. Francis was known to disappear under water for extended periods of time, and he claimed the ability to fly through the air. He attributed his powers to a spirit helper who also helped him destroy his enemies. He was a contemporary of Seekaboo, a powerful Creek medicine man who flourished during this period, and probably received religious inspiration and ceremonial instructions from this important holy man.

Francis traveled with the Shawnee leader Tecumseh in 1811 in Tecumseh's quest to garner support among the Creeks and other southern tribes for the Shawnee struggle against the white Americans. Tecumseh was attempting to create an alliance of Indian nations that would create an Indian barrier stretching from the Great Lakes region to the Gulf of Mexico and thus block further U.S. expansion onto Indian lands. Tecumseh's military alliance was coupled with the religious teachings of his brother Tenskwatawa, and it is likely that Josiah Francis was also influenced by this important religious leader.

Josiah Francis opposed white encroachment on Creek lands and advocated a return to traditional ways. In an attempt to stop the loss of further lands, he advocated warfare and became an active participant in the Creek War of 1813 and 1814, fighting against General Andrew Jackson. Following an Indian victory at the Battle of Burnt Corn on July 27, 1813, Josiah Francis began constructing a sacred town where only Indians would live. He asserted that Ecunchattee, or the Holy Ground, would be protected by the Great Spirit, who would surround the village with a barrier and kill any whites who attempted to cross the barrier. The influence of Tenskwatawa is evident in this event. In 1809, Tenskwatawa constructed a sacred town known as Prophetstown at the junction of the Tippecanoe and Mississippi rivers in present-day Indiana. Non-Indian forces eventually destroyed both Ecunchattee and Prophetstown.

In 1815 Francis made an unsuccessful journey to England for the purpose of ratifying a treaty first proposed by Edward Nicholls, a British military officer. The treaty, had it been signed, promised the Indian people an independent state as well as England's protection and trade. Not wanting to upset the precarious peace that existed between England and the United States, Britain failed to ratify the agreement. Francis remained in England for over a year departing for home on December 30, 1816. Upon his return to Florida, he settled near St. Marks, Florida.

On April 7, 1818, General Andrew Jackson led an illegal raid into Spanish Florida in pursuit of Red Stick Creeks and to recapture fugitive southern slaves who had found sanctuary in the Seminole Nation. Jackson's forces captured St. Marks and burned Francis's home and the rest of the village. Although Francis escaped, Jackson lured him onto an American gunboat by flying a British flag. Upon boarding what he believed to be a friendly vessel, Josiah Francis was captured. He was hanged on April 18, 1818, at St. Marks.

Further Reading

Champagne, Duane, ed. *The Native North American Almanac: A Reference Work on Native North Americans in the United States and Canada*. 1994. Detroit: Gale Research.

Hirschfelder, Arlene, and Paulette Molin. *The Encyclopedia of Native American Religions*. 1992. New York: Facts on File.

Owsley, Frank L., Jr. "Prophet of War: Josiah Francis and the Creek War." *American Indian Quarterly: Journal of American Indian Studies* 9 (1985): 273–293.

Waldman, Carl. *Who Was Who in Native American History*. 1990. New York: Facts on File.

Geronimo

See Goyathlay

Goyathlay (Geronimo)

Full Name at Birth: Goyathlay (Jeronimo or Gokhlayeh)

Birth: June 1829, in No-doyohn Canyon in present-day Arizona

Death: 1909 at Fort Sill, Oklahoma

Education: no formal education

Leadership Position: Apache shaman and tribal leader

Summary

Geronimo was a highly respected Chiricahua Apache war leader who gained his political power because of his abilities as a powerful shaman. An unidentified informant stated that "Geronimo got political power from the religious side. He foresaw the results of the fighting, and they used him so much in the campaigns that he came to be depended upon as a war leader. He went through his [religious] ceremony, and he would say, 'You should go here; you should not got there.' That is how he became a leader."

As a shaman, Geronimo had many powers. For healing, he had ghost powers (for ghost sickness) and coyote powers (a coyote was a very powerful spirit—very difficult to kill with the ability to shape shift in times of emergency). An unidentified informant provided the following account of a four-day healing ceremony in which Geronimo used his coyote powers to cure an old man:

> The ceremony began in the evening, as soon as it became dark. It took place in an arbor outside of Geronimo's house. There was a fire. Geronimo and the patient were on the west side of the fire. Geronimo had an old black tray basket before him filled with things he used for the ceremony. He had a downy eagle feather in it and an abalone shell and a bag of pollen. All these things were wrapped up in a bundle before the ceremony began.
>
> He rolled a cigarette and puffed to the directions first of all. . . . After smoking, he rubbed the patient with pollen. He dropped pollen on the patient, just on certain parts of the body. He prayed to the four directions as he did this. These prayers referred to Coyote and were on the same order as the songs, which followed.

This photo of Goyathlay (Geronimo) was taken at Fort Sill in the Oklahoma Territory in the early 1880s. National Archives.

Geronimo started to sing. There were many songs and the songs were about Coyote. They told how Coyote was a tricky fellow, hard to see and find, and how he gave these characteristics to Geronimo so that he could make himself invisible and even turn into a doorway. They told how the coyote helped Geronimo in his curing. Geronimo accompanied his singing with a drum, which he beat with a curved stick. At the end of each song he gave a call like a coyote.

Early Life

Geronimo was born and raised near the headwaters of the Gila River in present-day Arizona. His father was Taklishim, a full-blooded Chiricahua Apache. His mother Juana, also a full-blooded Apache, had been a captive among the Mexicans. Geronimo was the fourth child in a family of eight children—four boys and four girls. In his biography he recalls that "as a baby I rolled on the dirt floor of my fathers' teepee, hung in my tosch [Apache cradle] at my mother's back, or suspended from the bough of a tree. I was warmed by the sun, rocked by the winds, and sheltered by the trees as other Indian babes."

While a young child, Geronimo was taught the legends of his people. He was taught the relationship of the Apache to the sun and sky, the moon and stars, and the clouds and storms. His mother taught him to kneel and pray to Usn (the Creator) for strength, health, wisdom, and protection.

Geronimo's father told him of the brave deeds of Apache warriors, the pleasures of the hunt, and the glories of the warpath.

Geronimo recalled,

> With my brothers and sisters I played about my father's home. Sometimes we played hide-and-seek among the rocks and pines; sometimes we loitered in the shade of the cottonwood trees. . . . Sometimes we played that we were warriors. We would practice stealing upon some object that represented an enemy. . . . Sometimes we would hide away from our mother to see if she could find us, and often when thus concealed we would fall to sleep and perhaps remain hidden for many hours.
>
> When we were old enough to be of real service we went to the field with our parents; not to play, but to toil. When the crops were to be planted we broke the ground with wooden hoes. We planted the corn in straight rows, the beans among the corn, and the melons and pumpkins in irregular order over the field . . . It was common for many families to cultivate land in the same valley and share the burden of protecting the growing crops from destruction by the ponies of the tribes, or by deer and other wild animals.

Although it is not recorded in his biography, the young Geronimo would have taken part in a vision quest at about the age of twelve. The vision quest generally lasted from one to four days during which the participant fasted and "cried for a vision." Alone, hungry, and in tune with the spiritual world, the seeker usually had a vision or dream in which a spirit person, animal, or supernatural force was made known to him. This would be his spirit helper throughout his life and could be called on in time of need. Religious leaders such as Geronimo often participated in numerous vision quests and had a number of spirit helpers.

Leadership

Geronimo came to be considered a medicine man by his people because of his gift of power—the ability to influence people and events. Geronimo also had war medicines such as a "gun ceremony" that he used to make himself invincible to bullets. It was reported that he also had the ability to control daylight. An unidentified informant stated that "when he was on the warpath, Geronimo fixed it so that morning wouldn't come too soon. He did it by singing."

As a young man, Geronimo fought under the Chiricahua Apache leader Cochise and the Mimbreno Apache leader Mangas Colorados, and he gained prestige within the tribe because of his skill and courage in battle. He established his reputation against the Mexicans, who in 1858, killed his mother, wife, and three children in an unprovoked attack. In 1872, Cochise agreed to peace with white officials on being granted the Chiricahua, or Apache

Pass, Reservation along the Butterfield Trail. Geronimo surrendered to General Nelson Miles on September 4, 1886, at Skeleton Canyon, about sixty miles south of Apache, in present-day Arizona.

After their surrender, Geronimo and hundreds of other Apache were sent in chains by train to Fort Pickens and Fort Marion in Florida. After one year, Geronimo and others were relocated to Mount Vernon Barracks in present-day Alabama, where many Apache died from tuberculosis and other diseases. Geronimo accepted the Comanche and Kiowa offer to share their reservation in the Indian Territory, and in 1894 the remaining Apache were shipped to Fort Sill.

In his new home, Geronimo took up farming and joined the Dutch Reformed church. His life story, *Geronimo's Story of His People*, was dictated to S. M. Barrett and published in 1905. Geronimo appeared at the national expositions in St. Louis and Omaha and in Theodore Roo-

sevelt's 1905 presidential inaugural procession. He died of pneumonia in 1909.

Further Reading

Barrett, S. M., ed. *Geronimo's Story of His People*. 1905. Washington, D.C.: National Historical Society.

Champagne, Duane, ed. *The Native North American Almanac: A Reference Work on Native North Americans in the United States and Canada*. 1994. Detroit: Gale Research.

Hirschfelder, Arlene, and Paulette Molin. *The Encyclopedia of Native American Religions*. 1992. New York: Facts on File.

Lyon, William S. *Encyclopedia of Native American Shamanism: Sacred Ceremonies of North America*. 1998. Denver: ABC-CLIO.

Markowitz, Harvey. *American Indians. Vol. 1*. 1995. Pasadena, Calif.: Salem Press.

Meindertsma, P. J. *Geronimo, His Own Story* http://odur.let.rug.nl/~usa/B/geronimo/geronixx.htm.

Waldman, Carl. *Who Was Who in Native American History*. 1990. New York: Facts on File.

Gray Hair

See Wodziwob

Hail

See White Bull

Haná cha-thí ak

See Sitting Bull

Handsome Lake (Skanyadariyoh)

Full Name at Birth: Skanyadariyoh or Skaniadariio ("Handsome Lake")
Birth: ca. 1735

Death: August 10, 1815, Onondaga Indian Reservation, New York

Education: no formal education

Leadership Position: Seneca spiritual leader

Summary

Handsome Lake obtained the title of sachem sometime before 1799 and held it until his death in 1815. While the Iroquois League was experiencing great social and cultural destruction as a result of war with European invaders of their homelands, Handsome Lake reported a series of visions and preached the *Gaíwiio,* or "Good Word," to the Iroquois. His gospel contained several themes: a pending world destruction, a new definition of sin, and a prescription for salvation that included belief in the Good Word. Disciples of Handsome Lake organized his words into a new religion, the Code of Handsome Lake, which were recorded on wampum belts kept at Tonawanda, New York, the present-day headquarters of the Handsome Lake religion.

Early Life

Handsome Lake was born in a Seneca village on the Genesee River in present-day New York State and was the half-brother of the famous Seneca leader Cornplanter. As a young man, Handsome Lake participated in the colonial and Indian wars of the period: the French and Indian War (1755–1759) between the French (in alliance with various Indian Nations) and the English and Pontiac's War (1763) between various Indian Nations and the British, and he fought on the side of the British in the American Revolutionary War (1775–1783). Handsome Lake lived at the end of an era of respect and power of the Seneca Nation and witnessed the devastation of the Iroquois Confederacy.

Leadership

Following the American Revolution, factionalism, death, illness, and land cessions threatened the solidarity of the Iroquois League. This was especially painful for the Seneca, who saw their population decimated and their traditional lands reduced from 4 million acres extending across western New York and Pennsylvania to fewer than 200,000 acres. On June 15, 1799, Handsome Lake, who was living with his half-brother, Cornplanter, was bedridden by prolonged alcoholism and collapsed and appeared to die. Handsome Lake's nephew Blacksnake discovered that Handsome Lake was not dead but was in a coma. It was while he was in this coma that Handsome Lake experienced his first of four visions in which the Creator awakened him to a new religion and a new way of life for Iroquois people.

The Longhouse religion that developed based on his teachings combined traditional beliefs with some Christian additions, adopted from Quaker missionaries who ministered among the Seneca. Before his first vision, Handsome Lake was a heavy consumer of alcohol and suffered from depression and bitterness. In his vision, three messengers told him to preach the message against alcohol, witchcraft, love magic (the manipulating of power to attract a desired partner), and abortion, as well as to tell people guilty of these things that they were to admit publicly their wrongdoing, repent, and never sin again. Upon regaining his health, Handsome Lake preached that the Iroquois people should live in peace with the United States and with one another. He denounced factionalism among the member nations of the Iroquois Confederacy and emphasized the importance of education and farming. Farming was no longer to be just the occupation of women but of men as well. Handsome Lake also encouraged a shift from a matrilineal to a patrilineal society where men would head the nuclear family in place of the clan mothers' longhouses. Longhouses were traditional Iroquois housing structures (sometimes over one hundred feet long) shared by a number of matrilineal-related families. The longhouse belonged to the women, and when a woman married, her husband moved into her longhouse.

On August 7, 1799, after dreaming about a fourth messenger and falling into a trance, Handsome Lake had a second vision of a sky journey. Led by a guide, he visited heaven and hell and was told about the moral plan for the cosmos. He was given a strict moral code and told to take it to his people. His third vision, on February 5, 1800, concerned the Great Spirit's worries about the condition of the Seneca. He was told that they were to return to the practice of important cultural institutions of Seneca life such as adherence to the ancient calendar of ceremonies devoted to the Creator, especially the Midwinter Ceremony. Failure to carry out these ceremonies would result in the destruction of the world by fire. Handsome Lake revived the Midwinter Ceremony and added the Feather Dance, Thanksgiving Dance, Rite of Personal Chant, and the Bowl Game as well.

Following his visions, Handsome Lake traveled widely and preached a new gospel in which he emphasized temperance, peace, keeping land instead of selling it, acculturation, and domestic morality. He favored the adoption of American tools and artifacts and believed that Seneca children should attend school and learn how to farm as Americans did. Handsome Lake's preaching was called "The Good Word," or *Gaíwiio*, to distinguish the movement from the old religion of the Iroquois. Handsome Lake himself did not envision a new religion but believed instead that he was picked to revive the traditional religious observances of the Iroquois.

The Good Word was widely accepted as a new religion, and between 1799 and 1815 a renaissance occurred on many Iroquois reservations. Handsome Lake's gospel contained several themes: forecasts of world destruction, a new definition of sin, and a prescription for salvation that included a complex code of behavior. These included combating the witches (those suspected of manipulating spiritual powers for evil purposes) who were corrupting the Iroquois society, combating those who practiced love magic, and public confession of sin as a major sacrament. The people were told to cease wife beating, fighting, and gambling and to practice strict temperance. Handsome Lake proposed several major ritual changes, such as the disbanding of medicine societies and the elimination of the anniversary mourning ceremony, because he viewed them as being associated with witchcraft.

Before his death, Handsome Lake was able to see spiritual reformation among his people. After a generation of disorder and the proselytizing by Christian missionaries, disciples of Handsome Lake revived his words and organized them into a new religion, the Code of Handsome Lake. His grandson Sosheowa developed a version of the Code in 1840s at Tonawanda, which was to become the standard by which other speakers' versions would be judged. Blacksnake, Handsome Lake's nephew and disciple, also helped formalize the Handsome Lake religion, an amalgamation of ancient tradition, elements borrowed from Christianity, and innovations introduced by Handsome Lake himself. The Code of Handsome Lake was recorded on wampum belts that exist today and are kept at Tonawanda, the headquarters of the Handsome Lake religion. Once a year at the Six Nations (Iroquois Confederacy) meeting, Iroquois leaders who know the Code are called on to preach it. Every Iroquois longhouse has three or four preachers, each charged with the responsibility of knowing the Code. The Longhouse religion is practiced today, and the yearly ritual recalls the time during autumn when messengers were sent from Handsome Lake's headquarters to recite his laws to the Iroquois longhouses.

Further Reading

Ballantine, Betty and Ian Ballantine, eds. *The Native Americans: An Illustrated History.* 1993. Atlanta: Turner Publishing.

Calloway, Colin G. *First Peoples: A Documentary Survey of American Indian History.* 1999. New York: St. Martin's Press.

Champagne, Duane, ed. *The Native North American Almanac.* 1993. Detroit: Gale Research.

Gibson, Arrell M. *The American Indian.* 1969. Lexington, Mass.: D. C. Heath.

Handsome Lake: http://nativenet.uthscsa.edu/archive/nl/9209/0001. html.

Hirschfelder, Arlene and Paulette Molin. *The Encyclopedia of Native American Religions.* 1992. New York: Facts on File.

Snow, Dean R. *The Iroquois.* 1996. Cambridge, Mass.: Blackwell.

Sovereign People: http://www.clpgh.org/cmnh/exhibits/north-south-east-west/iroquois/handsome_lake.html.

Trigger, Bruce G., and Wilcomb E., Washburn, eds. *The Cambridge History of the Native Peoples of the Americas. Vol. 1: North America Part 1.* 1996. Cambridge: Cambridge University Press.

Washburn, Wilcomb E. *Handbook of North American Indians, Vol. 4.* 1998. Washington, D.C.: Smithsonian Institution.

Albert Hensley

Full Name at Birth: Albert Hensley

Birth: ca. 1875; place of birth not recorded

Death: date and place of death not recorded

Education: attended Carlisle Indian School in Pennsylvania, December 22, 1888–June 15, 1895

Leadership Position: Winnebago peyote roadman and missionary

Summary

Albert Hensley was a peyote roadman and missionary among the Winnebago and other tribal groups. According to a brief account of his early life, written for an Indian school superintendent in 1916, anthropologist and Indian agent Alice C. Fletcher arranged for him to attend the Carlisle Indian School in Pennsylvania after he agreed to run away from his father, who was opposed to schooling. He arrived in Carlisle on December 22, 1888, and stayed until June 15, 1895.

After John Rave, the local Winnebago peyote leader, Hensley was one of the most active Winnebago peyote leaders. There is general agreement that the two of them established the northern extension of the Cross-Fire or Big Moon ritual among the Lakota and Ojibwa, and Chippewa. It is also believed by some that Hensley was responsible for introducing the Christian Bible into the Cross-Fire ritual, and the ceremony became stronger and more Christianized under his influence.

There are two primary ceremonies in the peyote religion: the Half-Moon and the Cross-Fire, or Big Moon ceremony. Both the Half-Moon and Cross-Fire (practiced by Albert Hensley) ceremonies incorporated aspects of Indian culture and Christianity; both emphasized the divine role of peyote and its power to teach and heal; both opposed the use of liquor and believed that peyote destroyed the taste for it. In both the Half-Moon and Cross-Fire ceremonies peyote was eaten to concentrate and to learn, not to induce visions. Women could ingest the peyote button, however, most women and children participated in the ceremony by drinking peyote tea. The adherents of both ceremonies included preaching, prophecy, baptism, and other similarities to the Christian religion. Both rituals constructed permanent church buildings and permanent concrete altars on the floors. The Half-Moon ceremony limited tobacco use, whereas the Cross-Fire ceremony prohibited the use of tobacco entirely. Other shared features were the use of elaborate altars on which the peyote was placed, ashes formed into ceremonial designs, and ultimately the construction of permanent churches and altars. The term *roadman* comes from the peyote road that is represented on the ceremonial altar by a line. It is believed that concentrating on the peyote road while participating in the peyote ceremony will lead the prayers of the worshipper to the Creator.

Like the peyotist Quanah Parker,* Hensley was both a political and religious leader. He wrote a number of letters to the Bureau of Indian Affairs on a wide range of issues, including a strong defense of the peyote religion. In 1921, he was a charter member of the peyote church when the Winnebago of Nebraska became the first tribe to incorporate a peyote church outside the state of Oklahoma. The Peyote Church of Christ was renamed the Native American church of Winnebago, Nebraska, in 1922 and included both Cross-Fire and Half-Moon adherents in its membership.

Early Life

Hensley's mother died when he was a baby, and his paternal grandmother raised him until her death when he was five years old. He then lived with various families until he was seven, at which time he went to live in his father's home, where he remained until he was sixteen years of age. Hensley wanted to attend school; however, his father insisted that he remain home and assist with the family labor. In 1887, the Indian allotting agent, Alice Fletcher, assisted him in running away from home so that he could attend Carlisle Indian School. Fletcher provided Hensley with a train ticket and arranged for his entrance into the school. He arrived at Carlisle on December 22, 1888, and attended school until June 15, 1895. He did not graduate, although he was in the senior class for three months.

During the summer months while Hensley was enrolled at Carlisle, he participated in the government "outing" program, whereby Carlisle students were hired out to local farmers. Hensley stated that he worked for two summers for a very mean man for $10 per month and a third summer for a very kind man who paid him $40 per month.

While at Carlisle Indian School, Hensley learned the skills of steam plumber, carpentry, and blacksmithing.

Leadership

Hensley was a peyote roadman and missionary among the Winnebago and other tribal groups. According to a brief account of his early life, written by Hensley in 1916 for Alice C. Fletcher, the superintendent of the Indian School in Sioux City, South Dakota, his mother died while he was "yet a baby," and his paternal grandmother raised him until she died when he was only five years old. He was then "kicked here and there in different families," and when he was seven years old, he went to live with his father, who made him work and was opposed to formal schooling. Fletcher encouraged him to attend school and asked him if he would run away from his father if she got him a ticket to Carlisle, Pennsylvania. Hensley ran away from his father on December 18, 1888, and arrived at Carlisle on December 22, 1888, where he remained until June 15, 1895, broken only by summer employment in the federal government "outing" program. The outing program was one of the government's attempts to assimilate Indian people into the dominant society by having them live and work with local families during the summer months while the students were out of school.

It is generally acknowledged that after John Rave, Hensley was one of the most prominent peyote leaders among the Winnebago Nation. The Winnebago Indians in northeastern Nebraska had learned of peyote about 1889 and soon developed an active ceremonial organization. Rave was the local peyote leader in the beginning, but by 1908 Albert Hensley had become one of the most active leaders.

Although Hensley did not graduate from the Carlisle Indian School, he was well educated, having spent nearly seven years at Carlisle. His concern about the persecution of individuals who practiced the peyote religion led him to write to the commissioner of Indian affairs in 1908 through the agency superintendent, A. H. Kneale, sending some samples of peyote. In his letter, Hensley explained the religious value of peyotism and offered to help the commissioner understand this valuable Indian religion. In March 1910, Hensley wrote to the Bureau of Indian Affairs, this time assisted by two other peyotists, Oliver Lamere and John H. Clay. The commissioner of Indian affairs replied, "You are advised that for the present I have decided to permit any Indians who may wish to secure a supply of the beans [peyote buttons] to purchase a small quantity for his personal use, but any traffic therein will be promptly suppressed." Hensley, Lamere, and Clay again wrote to the commissioner asking him how they were to procure peyote since it grew only in Mexico and Texas and they could not afford to go there. They would have to buy from someone else, and that would violate the prohibition against trafficking. They suggested several alternatives such as placing orders and having peyote shipped by U.S. mail to a dealer in peyote and having that person ship them to the dealer in separate packages. Another suggestion was that the superintendent had an agent dispense peyote to Indian individuals through the doctor on the reservation, not allowing any member to have more than twenty-five peyote buttons at a time or draw peyote buttons more often than once in five weeks. The response displayed the superintendent's displeasure and ignorance of the individualistic nature of the peyote religion. The superintendent stated that the Winnebago Indians could do the same as the Osage Indians, where he allowed only one man of the congregation to use peyote each week, and that person would report the visions that he received with the others. BIA chief special officer William Johnson stated that "if the idea is a purely religious one, that of communing with their God, it seems to me that it is sufficient for one member of the church to become intoxicated [to use peyote] each week."

It is believed by some that Hensley was responsible for introducing the Bible into the Cross-Fire ritual because the Cross-Fire ceremony became stronger and more Christianized under his influence, and he defended and encouraged it all his life.

In 1910 Hensley was called to report to Captain Pratt at Carlisle to answer a question, "Tell me anything else of interest connected with your life." Hensley replied, "I am doing my best to teach my people both young and old, and they are learning too, about God and Jesus."

Hensley was an accomplished leader in economics and politics as well as in religion. He wrote many letters to the BIA on subjects ranging from rule of Indian inheritance and leasing of Indian lands to interference of the Indian agency superintendent in purely private Indian affairs. He married Martha Henry and had five healthy children and stated that they were "always happy and made a good living on farm and independent."

Further Reading

Hirschfelder, Arlene, and Paulette Molin. *The Encyclopedia of Native American Religions*. 1992. New York: Facts on File.
Stewart, Omer C. *Peyote Religion: A History*. 1987. Norman: University of Oklahoma Press.

Hiawatha

See Aiowantha

Emily Hill

Full Name at Birth: Emily Hill
Birth: November 1, 1911, near the Trout Creek on the North Fork of the Little Wind River in Wyoming
Death: January 14, 1988
Education: attended a government boarding school on the Wind River Indian Reservation in Wyoming until approximately age eighteen
Leadership Position: Shoshone medicine woman

Summary

Hill lived most of her life on the North Fork of the Little Wind River in Wyoming. She had no remembrance of her father, who died when she was very young. Her mother remarried, and Emily Hill was the third of nine children. Hill's great-grandmother was a warrior woman whose bravery in combat and defiance of a famous Shoshone leader for mistreating his wife was a great part of the family history passed down through the generations. A woman warrior was a person whose spirit was one with the Creator and whose heart belonged to the People. The foremost responsibility of a woman warrior was to be true to one's self, the People, and the Creator and to ensure the survival and well-being of the People.

Hill and her family lived in tents and small log cabins on the Wind River Reservation. Her family was poor and lived off government rations of meat and other staples issued at the reservation agency.

Shortly after leaving the Wind River Boarding School, Hill married. She had three children, seven grandchildren, and eight great-grandchildren. Following the death of her husband, Hill formed a close relationship with her half-sister, Dorothy, who became her partner for life. She recalled that "we used to go up the mountains, get those great big logs for winter wood." Emily and Dorothy owned their own ponies as well as three horse teams. They cut and stacked hay during the haying season, and Hill herself irrigated their fields. Dorothy Hill suffered a debilitating accident in the 1950s, and Emily cared for her sister for the next thirty years.

Early Life

Hill stated that she was born "maybe in the willows someplace" and lived virtually her entire life on the North Fork of the Little Wind River in Wyoming. She attended a government boarding school on the Wind River Reservation and stated that she "didn't know a thing of white talks." While at the boarding school, Hill played guard on the school's first girls' basketball team. She also worked with other students to make the boarding school self-supporting. Throughout her life, Hill recalled many happy memories from her boarding school years, where she participated in gardening, canning, cooking, baking, and sewing. In 1920, Hill survived a measles epidemic that swept through the boarding school and assisted the school nurse in tending to the sick children. As a result of this experience and seeing the value of Western medicine, she included it with her traditional healing practices when she became a traditional medicine woman.

Leadership

Emily Hill was a Shoshone medicine woman from the Wind River Reservation in Wyoming. Hill's father died when she was a young child. Her mother remarried, and the family eventually included nine children. Hill began attending the Wind River Reservation boarding school at the age of six and continued her education until she was about eighteen. During that period, she was exposed to English and other non-Indian teachings, with students being punished for speaking the Shoshone language. Following her school years, Hill married and had three children. Hill's traditional healing practices included her belief in dreams and prayers, as well as the sacred knowledge she had acquired from an elderly woman who served as her teacher. She used both native and Western medicine to help heal people. Hill maintained her faith in the

Naraya, or Ghost Dance, religion which was practiced at Wind River well into the twentieth century. The Ghost Dance religion was introduced in 1889 by the Paiute Indian prophet Wovoka* and was based on the belief that there would be a time when all Indian people—the living and the dead—would be reunited on an earth that was spiritually regenerated and forever free from death, disease, and all the other miseries that had recently been experienced by Indian people. The Ghost Dance religion included the "avoidance of violent conflicts, avoidance of bad relations with Euro-Americans, the promise of plentiful rain, freedom from illness, return of the dead, and the earthshaking arrival of a new world." The religion was outlawed by the U.S. federal government and was suppressed and brought to a disastrous end by the army massacre of some 250 Lakota people, led by the famous leader Big Foot, at Wounded Knee Creek in South Dakota in December 1890. When the dances were no longer held, she and her sister continued singing the sacred songs.

Hill was also an adherent of the Sun Dance religion and joined with the women singers at the ceremonies until her health declined. The Sun Dance played a large part in Shoshone life; it was their highest way of paying honor to God. The dance was generally held in July each year so that men who had made a pledge to Wakan-Tanka could fulfill the pledge and ensure prosperity for the Shoshone Nation. Wakan-Tanka is generally interpreted as "The Great Mystery" and is synonymous with the Creator and the Great Spirit. As a respected elder, Hill spoke out at tribal council meetings. Hill and four other Shoshone women singers collaborated with an author, Judith Vander, in a book called *Songprints* (1988). It includes information about Hill's life and her extensive collection of Shoshone music, much of which she learned from her mother. Hill entered a nursing home in 1986 and died on January 14, 1988.

Hill was considered to be an extremely knowledgeable and traditional Shoshone medicine woman. She participated in the Ghost Dance songs, Sun Dance songs, Women's Dance, and Wolf Dance songs. Hill considered all of the song associated with these ceremonies as prayer songs that touched on the world of nature, animals, plants, rocks, mountains, stars, the sun, water, and the progress of the soul after death. The songs helped her to acquire the power necessary for healing. She acknowledged but did not participate directly in the Shoshone ceremonial songs of the Pointing Stick, Chokecherry, and Giveaway. While other singers shifted to Euro-American songs in the early twentieth century, Hill kept within the traditional Shoshone musical bounds.

Further Reading

Hirschfelder, Arlene, and Paulette Molin. *The Encyclopedia of Native American Religions*. 1992. New York: Facts on File.

Vander, Judith. *Songprints: The Musical Experience of Five Shoshone Women*. 1988. Urbana: University of Illinois Press.

Voget, Fred W. *The Shoshoni-Crow Sun Dance*. 1984. Norman: University of Oklahoma Press.

Hola Tso

Full Name at Birth: Hola Tso

Birth: May 15, 1890, place of birth not recorded

Death: October 22, 1973; buried in the Damon Family Cemetery in Fort Defiance, Arizona

Education: Albuquerque Indian School, Albuquerque, New Mexico (no record of years attended)

Leadership Position: Navajo peyotist

Summary

Hola Tso was an outspoken member of the Navajo Nation Council and a devout peyotist who spoke in defense of the use of peyote as a sacrament of the Native American church. On June 3, 1940, he was the only peyotist present when the Navajo Tribal Council deliberated an adoption of an antipeyote ordinance. Well aware of the healing properties of peyote, Tso was aware of the sacred powers in the peyote medicine as well. Tso requested that additional evidence and medical testimony about the plant be brought before the council. The council refused his request. He advised the council that he had attended and participated in a peyote meeting conducted by Alfred Wilson, president of the Native American church. Despite his efforts, the Navajo Anti-Peyote Ordinance passed by a vote of 52 to 1. Tso was the only vote against the ordinance.

When the Navajo Tribal Council met to reconsider the peyote ordinance in 1954, Tso was given five minutes to defend the use of peyote. He rejected the council's offer on the grounds that five minutes was insufficient time. The Navajo Tribal Council failed to act, and the ordinance remained in effect. In 1955, Tso and other peyotists petitioned the Navajo Council to amend the ordinance, but that effort failed as well. In 1956, Tso was elected vice-president of the Native American church of North America.

Early Life

Hola Tso was born into the Kiyannii and Dibé lizhinii clans of the Navajo Nation in 1890. This was a period of severe economic hardship for the Navajo people as they attempted to reestablish themselves in their traditional homelands following the United States treaty with the Navajo Tribe, 1868. Tso never knew his birth parents and was raised by extended family members.

Tso grew up around cattle ranches near Houck and Chambers, Arizona, where he became a well-known cowboy under the name Acothle Tso. Tso attended the Albuquerque Indian School, where he excelled in sports; football was his favorite. Because of his athletic ability, he was selected to practice with the Carlisle Indian School football team where the noted Indian athlete Jim Thorpe was playing. Unfortunately Tso lost two fingers from his left hand during an injury in his carpentry class, thus ending his opportunity for an athletic career.

Tso learned his aggressive, competitive, and strong-willed nature while attending the Indian school at Albuquerque.

Leadership

Tso was relentless in his pursuit of and commitment to legalizing the use of peyote in the Native American church. Peyote, is a spineless cactus, and it is believed that it was originally one of the offerings made to the gods in Aztec temples, where the plant buttons of this small, hallucinogenic plant were ritually consumed. Down through the ages, peyote flourished in Mexico and South Texas, too.

Tso's involvement with peyote began in the 1930s when his wife, Susie, introduced him to the medicine. Tso had married Susie Damon in the early 1920s. His family elders selected her to calm Tso's wild and reckless ways. Hola Tso and Susie had nine children—four sons and five daughters. It was from Susie and her family that Tso obtained his strength and spiritual awakening.

Susie's family had established a strong sense of Navajo identity through the use of peyote. They found that the ceremonial use of peyote instilled a sense of sobriety, industry, and independence in the user. For instance, one could not take peyote and subsequently drink alcohol without becoming extremely sick. Because of Susie's influence, Tso sought a closer association with peyote and the Creator, and he was empowered with an uncommon wisdom, given to him by the Holy People. Tso made him a convert to the peyote religion, and he entered a lifelong pursuit to legalize the practice of the religion among the Navajo people. His position as a respected and influential council member contributed to the spread of peyotism by attracting followers to his beliefs.

The spread of peyote use in the late 1930s among the Navajo people alarmed the elected leaders of the Navajo Tribal Council. Peyote was presented as a dangerous substance and foreign to the Navajo traditional way of life. Tso defended the use of peyote against these powerful opponents. During the antipeyote hearing on June 3, 1940, it was stated that peyote "made people crazy; it caused death, and it crippled and deformed infants." Only Tso spoke in support of the religious and medicinal properties of peyote. He went on to fight for the legalization peyote by filing lawsuits in the state and federal courts. He spent years traveling and testifying on behalf of the Native American Church in their legal battles. His wife maintained the family home and raised their children. It is said that "she preached to her grandchildren . . . keeping the fires burning in the home, retaining and teaching the values of the Navajo traditional way of life, praying to the divine Creator, and keeping the family together. Without this understanding and acceptance from Susie, Hola Tso may never have been able to be the legacy of greatness he is today."

Tso spent his last years with his wife, children, and grandchildren. Their lives are grounded on his teaching: "Set a sound and firm foundation early in life by obtaining a good education and following the four principles of the Native American Church: Love, Faith, Hope, and Charity, and then building a lifetime on this foundation."

Further Reading

Hola Tso: http://www.lapahie.com/Hola_Tso.html.

32nd Native American Church Convention: http://members.tripod.com/NATIVELEE/convention.htm.

The Hola Tso Story: http://members.tripod.com/NATIVELEE/hola.htm.

Jake Hunt

Full Name at Birth: Jake Hunt (Titcam Nashat, Earth Thunderer)

Birth: 1860s on the east bank of the White Salmon River near the community of Husum, Washington

Death: sometime between 1910 and 1914 at Spearfish on the Columbia River in Washington State

Education: no record of formal education

Leadership Position: founder of the Klickitat Waptashi or Feather religion

Summary

Hunt was a Klickitat Indian from the Pacific Northwest (present-day Washington State) and the founder of the Waptashi or Feather religion. Hunt was raised in the Washani religion, following the teachings of the Wanapam dreamer-prophet Smohalla. *Washani* is a Shahaptian term meaning "worship." A related word is *washat*, or "dance." Because religious services were held in longhouses, the Washani was also called the Longhouse religion. The longhouse was a long, rectangular structure with a fireplace at or near each end. People sat on rows of benches, possible tiered, that lined both long walls or on benches along the short walls. In the central area, dances and other ritual activities took place, usually accompanied by drumming. Men, women, and children occupied seats in the longhouse according to gender or clan affiliation, depending on the ceremonial occasion. It is believed that Hunt's religious beliefs were strongly influenced by a vision experienced during his son's funeral. Hunt's vision instructed him to stop grieving for his wife and son (who had died within two months of each other), to make a hand drum to use in religious services, and to spread a new religion to seven lands. This resulted in the founding of the Waptashi religion.

The Waptashi religion is referred to in the Shahaptian language as *waskliki* (spin) or *waptashi* (feather) from prominent features of its practices. Hunt incorporated elements of both spinning and the use of feathers in his rituals. He also introduced new practices, including vomiting, to initiate members into the religion. The religion incorporated features of both Washani and Shaker practices. In common with the Indian Shakers, the Feather adherents used curing practices and rejected intoxicants. After establishing the Waptashi religion, Hunt began seeking converts in other areas in keeping with his earlier vision.

Leadership

Hunt was born in the 1860s in the Klickitat community of Husum, in present-day Washington State, on the east bank of the White Salmon River. Almost nothing is known of his early years. He was raised in the Washani religion, following the teachings of the Wanapam dreamer-prophet Smohalla. *Washani* is a Shahaptian term meaning "worship." Accounts vary on the origin of the Washani religion, but many people believe that it began with the prophets, such as Watilki; others believe that it originated after a devastating epidemic. A more contemporary belief is that the Washani religion is a

Christianized variation of the Dreamer religion that was practiced by Smohalla and other dreamer prophets. The Dreamer Religion focused on the belief in an impending destruction and renewal of the world, during which the Indian dead would return. Dreamer-prophets such as Smohalla underwent a temporary death and rebirth experience or vision in which they made a visit to the spirit world and returned to earth with a message from the Creator. The message often included specific songs and dances that became an essential part of the religious ceremony. Some of the early religious leaders foretold the arrival of fair-skinned strangers from across the ocean, told of their trade goods, and the future treatment of Native people. They also pointed to natural signs such as earthquakes to announce the impending destruction of the world.

Following his death and rebirth experience, Smohalla advised his followers to return to Native traditions and reject the religion and trade goods of the intruders. Smohalla taught that Native people would arise from the earth on feathers after the world was renewed and returned to them. His beliefs were manifested in dances, including the Washat Dance with its accompanying ceremonies and observances that included naming ceremonies, weddings, feasts, memorials, and annual observances or rituals.

Hunt was later influenced by the Indian Shaker religion through a leader named Wasco Jim who conducted a healing ceremony for Hunt's ill son. Wasco Jim was unable to cure Hunt's son but succeeded in converting a number of Indian people to the new Shaker religion. Hunt was influenced by a vision told to him by Wasco Jim in which the Shaker healer was instructed to use feathers in his religious services. Hunt converted to the Shaker faith after he was informed that his wife, Minnie Coon, who became ill soon after their son, could not be healed unless he joined that religion. Despite efforts to save her, Hunt's wife died a month after her son's death, and Hunt then turned against the Shakers and withdrew from the group.

Hunt's religious beliefs were also formed by a vision that both he and his niece experienced. In the vision, both saw Lishwailait, the Klickitat prophet, "standing in the center of a circular disk of light, which symbolized an area of land. He [Lishwailait] was dressed in traditional clothing, wore two eagle feathers in his hair and carried a small drum and drumstick." These visions prompted the establishment of the Waptashi faith. Hunt stopped grieving for his wife and son, erected a longhouse in his home community, took the name Titcam Nashat, and began preaching. Hunt had four sisters who helped him to establish the Waptashi religion.

The Feather religion is referred to in the Shahaptian language as waskliki (spin) or waptashi (feather) religion because Hunt incorporated elements of spinning and the use of feathers in his rituals. The proper execution of these rituals was believed to help initiates obtain spiritual assistance and cleanse away impurities and cure illnesses. The eagle was believed to be extremely powerful, and its feathers were held or worn during services. Hand mirrors were also used as part of the worship experience, and it is believed that this element was derived from the prophet Lishwailait, who "was believed to have seen the sins of everyone when he looked into a mirror during religious services."

The Feather religion was an amalgamation of Washani and Shaker religions.

Hunt continued to follow first food ceremonies and other traditional practices of the Washani, but he added the Shaker prohibitions against alcohol use, aspects of the Shaker curing or healing rituals, and the use of the ceremonial longhouse. In common with the Indian Shakers, the Feather adherents used curing practices and rejected intoxicants. First food observances were ceremonies that were held at the first appearance, or first taking, of salmon and other fish, from the natural environment. The ceremony included prayers, offerings, and the giving of thanks. First food ceremonies were viewed as an intricate part of world-renewal and were considered to be essential to the continuation of the food for the people.

In keeping with his earlier vision, Hunt began seeking converts in other areas. He succeeded in gaining followers among the Wishram band on the Columbia River and among the Rock Creek band, also on the Columbia River. After failing to cure a dying young man on the Umatilla Reservation in Oregon, Hunt was retaliated against by an agent of the Bureau of Indian Affairs, who opposed traditional religious practices. The agent ordered Hunt's sacred objects destroyed and ordered the holy man to choose between incarceration or banishment from the Reservation. Hunt chose to leave the Umatilla Reservation and return to Husum, Washington. He died sometime between 1910 and 1914 at Spearfish, on the Columbia River in Washington State.

Further Reading

Hirschfelder, Arlene, and Paulette Molin. *The Encyclopedia of Native American Religions.* 1992. New York: Facts on File.

Notes From "The North American Indian," Vol. 7: http://curtis-collection.com/tribe%20data/klick.

Ice

See White Bull

Peter Jones

See Kah-ke-wa-quo-na-by

Charles Journeycake

See Ne-sha-pa-na-cumin

Kah-ke-wa-quo-na-by ("Sacred Feathers") (Peter Jones)

Full Name at Birth: Kah-ke-wa-quo-na-by, Kahkewagwonnaby ("Sacred Feathers")

Birth: January 1, 1802, in the Credit River Mississauga settlement of Burlington Heights, near Hamilton (Ontario) in the colony of Upper Canada

Death: June 29, 1856, in Branford, Ontario

Education: Although there is no record of Kah-ke-wa-quo-na-by's formal education, early writings indicate that he was formally schooled from the ages of fourteen to twenty-one near Paris, Ontario; however, there is no reference to a specific school.

Leadership Position: Mississauga (Ojibwa) tribal leader and Methodist missionary

Summary

Kah-ke-wa-quo-na-by, or "Sacred Feathers," was a Mississauga (Ojibwa) tribal leader, Methodist missionary, and a writer. He was the son of a Welshman by the name of Augustus Jones and Tuhbenahneeguay, the daughter of the Missisauga Ojibwa chief Wahbonosay. He was raised traditionally until the age of sixteen, at which time he was baptized and began religious studies. While being raised by his father, Augustus Jones, at Grand River near present-day Paris, Ontario, he took the Christian name of Peter Jones. Jones converted to Christianity in 1823 at a revival meeting presided over by the Methodist missionary William Case.

As a young adult, Jones became actively involved in services at the Wesleyan Methodist church, and in 1827 he became the first Native Methodist missionary to the Ojibwa Nation. In 1830, Jones was ordained into the Wesleyan Methodist church. Following his ordination, Jones visited several Ojibwa bands in western Ontario and with his brother, John, provided the first translations of the Bible from English into Ojibwa. He worked again among the Native people at Muncey and New Credit and became a well-known religious leader and spokesman for Native rights.

Jones was the author of *The Life and Journals of Kah-ke-wa-quo-na-by* (1860) and *A History of the Ojebway Indians* (1861). He translated hymns, scripture, and other religious materials into the Ojibwa language. He married an English woman who, with four of their sons, survived him. One son, who bore his name, became editor of an Ontario periodical, the *Indian*.

Early Life

Kah-ke-wa-quo-na-by was born on January 1, 1802, to a Mississauga, Ojibwa woman, Tuhbenahneeguay, and Augustus Jones, a Welshman. He was raised traditionally among his mother's people in her community on the northwestern shore of Lake Ontario until age fourteen. He then went to live with his father and Mohawk stepmother at Grand River near present-day Paris, Ontario, and remained with them for seven years. During that period, Kah-ke-wa-quo-na-by worked on the family farm, attended school, and took the Christian name Peter Jones.

Leadership

Kah-ke-wa-quo-na-by, or Peter Jones, was a well-known Wesleyan Methodist missionary and spokesman for Native rights. He was born on January 1, 1802, in Ontario in the Credit River Mississauga settlement of Burlington Heights, near Hamilton, Upper Canada. His father, Augustus Jones, was born in Wales, and was a surveyor and a friend of the renowned Mohawk Indian leader Joseph Brant. His mother, Tuhbenahneeguay, was born into the Mississauga tribe of the Ojibwa nation and was the daughter of the Mississauga chief Wahbonosay. Jones's Ojibwa name was Kah-ke-wa-quo-na-by, which meant "Sacred Feathers." At the age of fourteen, Kah-ke-wa-quo-na-by was sent by his father to a school in Saltfleet Township, Canada, and at the age of sixteen his father had him baptized into the Episcopal faith, following which he was given the name Peter Jones. As a young adult, Jones became actively involved in services at the Wesleyan Methodist church and became the first Native Methodist missionary to the Ojibwa in 1827.

As a Methodist missionary, Peter Jones visited several Ojibwa bands in western Ontario and with his brother, John, provided the first translations of the Bible from English into Ojibwa. Jones was received on trial for the ministry in 1827; he became a deacon of the Methodist church in 1830 and a minister in 1833. Additionally, Jones was elected chief of two Ojibwa bands and visited New York, London, and several other large cities on behalf of the Ojibwa Nation. He became well known not simply for his religious activities but as an articulate spokesperson for the protection of Native land rights.

In 1823, Peter and his brother, John, were converted at a Methodist mission near Rice Lake in Ontario. In 1825, Jones was invited by William Case to work as a Methodist and was asked to keep a journal of his travels. Jones became the first Canadian Native to keep a journal, the first Native missionary to be appointed to serve the Ojibwa, and, along with his brother, John, the first translator of biblical literature into the Native languages of Ojibwa and Chippewa. Jones was also instrumental in the establishment of a Native mission on the Credit River in 1825. In 1826, he was sent on a missionary tour throughout Ontario and played a part in convert-ing John Sunday and George Copway, two very important Ojibwa tribal leaders.* During these years, he also worked on translations of religious texts into the Algonquian language.

In 1831 Jones continued his travels as both a missionary and chief of the Mississauga, visiting Toronto, New York, London, and other cities. He preached over sixty sermons in Methodist churches throughout Britain and arranged to have translations of the New Testament portion of the Bible published. Jones was received by Queen Victoria in 1837 and delivered a petition from the Ojibwa Indians requesting the title to Indian lands.

Jones translated numerous hymns, scripture, and other religious materials into the Ojibwa language, and his linguistic work benefited other missionaries who followed him. He married an English woman, Eliza Field. They had five sons, one of whom died in infancy; four survived him. Jones was forced by poor health to retire in 1850 and died near his birthplace, in Branford, Ontario, on June 29, 1856. His *Life and Journals of Kah-ke-wa-quo-na-by (Rev. Peter Jones)* and *History of the Ojebway Indians* were published posthumously. In 1857, the Ojibwa in Branford erected a monument dedicated to Jones's memory. One of his sons, who was given Peter Jones's name at birth, became editor of an Ontario periodical, the *Indian*.

Further Reading

Champagne, Duane, ed. *The Native North American Almanac: A Reference Work on Native North Americans in the United States and Canada*. 1964. Detroit: Gale Research.

Hirschfelder, Arlene, and Paulette Molin. *The Encyclopedia of Native American Religions*. 1992. New York: Facts on File.

Jones, Peter: http://128.100.124.81/library/special/jones.htm.

Waldman, Carl. *Who Was Who in Native American History*. 1990. New York: Facts on File.

Kee-Kah-Wah-Un-Ga (Reuben A. Snake, Jr.)

Full Name at Birth: Kee-Kah-Wah-Un-Ga ("He Who Has Arisen")

Birth: January 12, 1937, in Winnebago, Nebraska

Death: June 28, 1993

Education: attended Neillsville Mission School in Wisconsin; Haskell Indian School in Lawrence, Kansas, 1950–1951; Northwestern College at Orange City, Iowa, 1958–1959; University of Nebraska at Omaha, 1964–1965; and Peru State College, Nebraska, 1968–1969

Leadership Position: prayer chief of the Native American church of North America and Winnebago tribal leader

Awards: honorary degree, doctorate of humanities, Nebraska Indian Community College, 1989; Citizenship Award, Nebraska Indian Commission, 1986; Distinguished Nebraskan, 1986; Certificate of Recognition from the U.S. Secretary of Interior, 1986

Summary

Kee-Kah-Wah-Un-Ga was a well-known religious and national leader concerned with issues such as Indian religious freedom and education. He served as national chairman of the American Indian Movement in 1972, national president of the National Congress of American Indians, 1985–1987, and counsel to the Americans for Indian Opportunity, Washington, D.C., 1984. *Your Humble Serpent*, completed by anthropologist and Smithsonian Fellow Jay C. Fikes after Kee-Kah-Wah-Un-Ga's death, is a portrait of this late American Indian political and spiritual leader.

Kee-Kah-Wah-Un-Ga devoted himself totally to the war against cultural and religious destruction, discrimination, and poverty afflicting American Indian people. As a director of the National Indian Education Training Project, Kee-Kah-Wah-Un-Ga was instrumental in training Indian parents, tribal governments, and Indian communities to acquire federal funding to advance the education of Native American people and achieve tribal and individual self-sufficiency. Kee-Kah-Wah-Un-Ga worked diligently to build continuity in economic, educational, and social programs for Indian people and lobbied constantly for legislation to improve and protect the lives of Native people. Passage of legislation such as the American Indian Religious Freedom Act, 1978, the National Museum of the American Indian Act, 1989, the Native American Graves Protection and Repatriation Act, 1990, and the Native American Language Act, 1990, can be attributed to Kee-Kah-Wah-Un-Ga's advocacy. In 1989, Senator Robert Kerrey invited Kee-Kah-Wah-Un-Ga to serve as his legislative assistant with responsibilities of ad-

Reuben A. Snake, Jr. Photo taken by Katy Snake. Kifaru Productions.

vising Kerrey on Native American issues. He served in this position in 1989–1990.

In response to the Columbus quincentenary in 1992, Kee-Kah-Wah-Un-Ga wrote his seminal book "*Being Indian Is . . .*" In this book Kee-Kah-Wah-Un-Ga used his gifts for writing and humor to educate readers regarding the challenges of Indian people in the twentieth century.

Kee-Kah-Wah-Un-Ga traveled to Europe, South America, Canada, Australia, and throughout the United States—over 1 million miles—in an effort to promote the cause of justice and equality for all indigenous people of the Western Hemisphere. It was his goal to enlighten the international audience and reshape national and international perceptions regarding minority populations.

Kee-Kah-Wah-Un-Ga and his wife, Cathy, had six children, all of whom shared his dedication for the betterment and understanding of indigenous peoples. He and his family hosted all-night prayer services to promote peace in the midst of religious prosecution affecting American Indians. In his final days, Kee-Kah-Wah-Un-Ga worked tirelessly to advocate for the introduction of legislation to protect the religious freedom rights of Native Americans. In large part due to his efforts, the Senate introduced and passed Senate Bill 1021, the Native American Free Exercise of Religion Act of 1993.

Kee-Kah-Wah-Un-Ga, died on June 28, 1993. At his funeral, mourners remembered him as a man with a big heart.

Early Life

Kee-Kah-Wah-Un-Ga was born in Winnebago, Nebraska, on January 12, 1937, but spent most of his childhood in Minnesota and Wisconsin. As a youth, he attended Neillsville Mission School in Wisconsin and Haskell Indian School in Lawrence, Kansas. As a young man, Kee-Kah-Wah-Un-Ga was taught by his elders that a true Indian leader is the servant of his people. It was while at these schools that he discovered his gift for writing, a skill that he would use throughout his life for the betterment of Native people.

In 1954, Kee-Kah-Wah-Un-Ga joined the U.S. Army and served as a Green Beret in Berlin, Germany. Upon receiving his honorable discharge in 1959, he pursued an education at a time when many universities were still refusing entry to Native American students. Kee-Kah-Wah-Un-Ga attended Northwestern College in Orange City, Iowa, the University of Nebraska, Omaha, Nebraska, and Peru State College in Nebraska.

Leadership

Kee-Kah-Wah-Un-Ga was a prayer chief and roadman of the Native American church of North America. The prayer chief or roadman is the leader of the all-night peyote ceremony or peyote meeting. The term *roadman* comes from the "peyote road," represented on the ceremonial peyote altar by a line. Kee-Kah-Wah-Un-Ga encouraged the use of peyote as a sacrament within the Native American church and stated that

we call it Peyote, but more often, because of what it does for us, we call it our Medicine. My people have an old story about this herb. They talk about its power. They say that this particular herb is the most powerful of all the plants because God endowed it with his love and compassion. He [the Creator] put those qualities into this lowly herb so that when we eat it we can feel that the love that God is—I emphasize the love that God is, not that God has—is physically inside us. From there it overflows in compassion for human beings and all other kinds of creatures. It enables us to treat one another tenderly, and with joy, love, and respect.

Kee-Kah-Wah-Un-Ga survived life in a mission school, a BIA boarding school, and a tour of duty in postwar Berlin as a Green Beret. He knew well the sting of discrimination, racial prejudice, homelessness, and harassment. It was from these experiences that Kee-Kah-Wah-Un-Ga drew his strength to fight for justice for Native American people. He sought to promote and protect Indian sovereignty; economic, spiritual, and educational equality; and a move toward self-determination and self-governance.

Kee-Kah-Wah-Un-Ga was elected tribal chairman of the Winnebago Nation and was the winner of the prestigious World Peace Prize in 1993. He was a founding trustee and the spiritual adviser for the American Indian Ritual Object Repatriation Foundation and served on the governing board of over fifteen national Native American organizations.

Kee-Kah-Wah-Un-Ga was writing his autobiography at the time of his death. It was completed in 1996 by his friend and Smithsonian Fellow Jay C. Fikes with a title that was one of Kee-Kah-Wah-Un-Ga 's favorite self-descriptions: *Your Humble Serpent*. This title captures the humor of this much-loved man. The book also captures his passionate zeal for Native American justice, freedom, and humanity. Walter Echo-Hawk, noted attorney for the Native American Relief Fund, wrote in the book's afterword that "*Your Humble Serpent*, gives us a role model comparable to Nelson Mandela, Martin Luther King, Jr., Chief Joseph and Chief Seattle."

Your Humble Serpent traces Kee-Kah-Wah-Un-Ga's childhood years on the Winnebago reservation through the all-too-common Indian experience of alcohol abuse and ultimately his spiritual and political awakening in the early 1970s when he became the national leader of the American Indian Movement (AIM). His leadership skills were evident during the historic confrontations following the 1972 Indian march on Washington known as the Trail of Broken Treaties, the 1972 Indian occupation of the Washington, D.C., BIA office building, and the occupation of Wounded Knee in 1973. His last fight was the struggle with the U.S. Supreme Court that resulted in President Clinton's signing into law the American Indian Religious Freedom Act of 1994, landmark legislation safeguarding the use of peyote as a sacrament by members of the Native American church.

Kee-Kah-Wah-Un-Ga died in the early morning hours of June 28, 1993. The day after his death, he was publicly mourned in the U.S. Senate in a statement read by Senator Inouye. At that time, the Senate ordered that a speech recently given by Kee-Kah-Wah-Un-Ga be entered into the *Congressional Record*. Kee-Kah-Wah-Un-Ga was described by the eminent religious historian Huston Smith as the "Dalai Lama of Native Americans."

Further Reading

American Indian Culture and Research Journal 21 (2): 1997.

American Indian Ritual Object Repatriation Foundation: Founding Trustee: Reuben A. Snake, Jr.: http:// www.repatriation foundation. org/snakev.html.

Champagne, Duane, ed. *The Native North American Almanac: A Reference Work on Native North Americans in the United States and Canada*. 1994. Detroit: Gale Research.

Fikes, Jay C. Reuben Snake. *Your Humble Serpent: Indian Visionary and Activist*. 1997. Sante Fe, N. Mex.: Clear Hight Publishers.

Klein, Barry T. *Reference Encyclopedia of the American Indian*. 2000. Nyack, N.Y.: Todd Publications.

In Memory of Reuben A. Snake, Jr.: http://www.narf.org/nill/resources/ nlr/nlr20a.htm.

Reuben Snake: Your Humble Serpent: http://www.islandnet.com/~millenia/s nake.html.

Statement of Ruben A. Snake: http://para-noia.lycaeum.org/war.on.drugs/de-bate/peyote.speech.

Kenekuk

Full Name at Birth: Kenekuk, Pakaka, or Kanakuk

Birth: ca. 1790

Death: ca. 1852

Education: no formal education

Leadership Position: Kickapoo prophet and leading chief of the Vermilion band of Kickapoo Indians

Summary

Kenekuk was a religious prophet and leading chief of the Vermilion band of Kickapoo Indians who taught a syncretic religion that blended Christianity with traditional Kickapoo religion. The new religion combined elements of Catholic, Protestant, and traditional Kickapoo religious beliefs. Opposed to violence, Kenekuk advocated agriculture and the formation of self-sufficient Indian farming communities. He preached nonviolent accommodation and instructed his followers to maintain friendly relations with the young United States.

Early Life

Little is known of Kenekuk's early years. It is believed that he was born around 1790 and spent his early life on the Wabash and Vermilion rivers on either side of the Illinois-Indiana border. In his early life, Kenekuk became addicted to alcohol and allegedly killed an uncle while drunk. As a result of the killing, he was cast out by his people. Following his expulsion, Kenekuk traveled to various white settlements in Indiana and Illinois, where he met a Catholic priest who took him in and instructed him in Christianity. The priest told Kenekuk that if he brought Christian teachings back to his people, they would forgive him for the murder of his uncle. Kenekuk did return to his people, but like the Shawnee prophet before him, he claimed he had a vision that contained a message from the Great Spirit for the Indian people and for the Kickapoo in particular. Kenekuk's vision encouraged accommodation to U.S. culture and land demands and included a new religion that combined Christian ideas with traditional Indian concepts. By his mid-twenties, he had become the leader of the Vermilion band of the Kickapoo tribe.

Leadership

Following the War of 1812, a great wave of white settlers moved into Illinois and Indiana to claim homesteads and lands promised to American soldiers by the U.S. government for war service. To make room, government agents began to relocate the Indians who lived in the area to new lands, west of the Mississippi River.

In the face of this pressure, Kenekuk, a brilliant prophet and tribal leader, emerged among the peaceful Vermilion Kickapoo. Kenekuk had been exposed to alcohol at an early age and allegedly had murdered an uncle while drunk. Expelled by his tribe, Kenekuk traveled to various white settlements in Indiana and Illinois, where he lived on the edge of both societies. In one of the white settlements, Kenekuk met a Catholic priest who took him in and instructed him in Christianity. The priest told Kenekuk that if he brought Christian teachings back to his people, they would forgive him for the murder of his uncle. Kenekuk, now claiming to have received a vision from the Great Spirit, worked to create a new moral and religious community for his followers.

The new syncretic religion Kenekuk introduced combined elements of Catholic, Protestant, and traditional Kickapoo religious beliefs. He advocated agriculture and the formation of self-sufficient Indian farming communities. The new religion banned alcohol, and Kenekuk instructed his followers to maintain friendly relations with the young United States. As a result of his teachings, his followers developed a self-contained, peaceful, religious moral community that tried to preserve its land and identity from the onslaught of the encroaching white settlers and the demands of the U.S. government.

It appears in retrospect that Kenekuk may have been inspired by the Delaware and Shawnee prophets before him, as much of their messages resonate in his teachings. Kenekuk told his followers to live peacefully with each other, stay away from alcohol, and give up superstitious practices such as the singing of traditional medicine songs and carrying of the medicine bag. He also encouraged the Kickapoo warriors to stop painting their bodies, give up the warpath, and take up farming, which traditionally had been women's work. Kenekuk religion included a diagram of the path from earth to heaven that was similar to the map of the soul that had been developed by the Delaware prophet. According to Kenekuk's diagram, the Indians had traveled along the prescribed path and had now reached a turning point in their spiritual development. To continue on their journey, they were told that they must throw away their medicine bags, not to steal, not to tell lies, and not to quarrel. Only by following these rules could the Indians continue on the straight path that would lead them to heaven. Kenekuk was much more than an imitator, however. Unlike the Delaware and Shawnee prophets, Kenekuk believed that the Indians and the whites must live together in peace. He is believed to have said that "every red and white man is my brother and I desire to be united with them in friendship and for this reason I am afraid of nothing."

Kenekuk is one of the most interesting and unusual of the Indian spiritual leaders. Although he did not want to give up the traditional Indian way of life, he was intelligent and perceptive enough to understand that eventually the Indian people would be pushed from their lands if they did not take the hand of the white man. He was a spiritual person who believed that peace and nonviolence was the true message given by the Great Spirit. Kenekuk also knew that the Christian missionaries could help his people receive the annuities (money, supplies and trade goods) promised by the government in return for Kickapoo lands. He therefore played a diplomatic game with the missionaries. His followers went to the Christian church, confessed their sins, and held Sunday services to appease the missionaries. At the same time, they sang their traditional Kickapoo songs, refused to learn English, and interpreted the Christian practices in their uniquely Indian way.

Kenekuk dreamed of a better life for his people, and his spiritual vision led to a happier life for his people on this earth. However, to attain this life, Kenekuk and his disciples were required to observe a strict regimen of fasting, a rejection of all white technology, and return to the traditional Kickapoo lifestyle in which the individual lived close to nature. Kenekuk promised his followers that by seeking a return to traditional Kickapoo lifeways, each would have his reward in a holy place free of torment and American settlers.

The War of 1812 left the Indian tribes in the Great Lakes region in a state of disarray and destitution. In 1819, the Kickapoo ceded half of the present-day state of Illinois to the U.S. government. By means of their passive resistance, however, the Kickapoo defined the removal requirements of the 1819 treaties and were allowed to remain in their homelands. In 1822, Kenekuk's community chose not to participate in the Black Hawk war in hopes that they would be allowed to regain parts of Illinois. Failing this, Kenekuk continued to try to avoid the removal of his people from Illinois to present-day Kansas. In the spring of 1834, Kenekuk led his band of 350 from their Vermilion River homeland toward the west. Kenekuk died around 1852, possibly of smallpox.

Further Reading

Ballantine, Betty, and Ian Ballantine, eds. *The Native Americans: An Illustrated History.* 1993. Atlanta: Turner Publishing.

Champagne, Duane, ed. *The Native North American Almanac.* 1994. Detroit: Gale Publishing.

Gibson, Arrell M. *The American Indian.* 1969. Lexington, Mass.: D. C. Heath.

Hirschfelder, Arlene, and Paulette Molin. *The Encyclopedia of Native American Religions*. 1992. New York: Facts on File.

Kickapoo History: http://www.dickshovel.com/kick.html.

Walker, Paul R. *Spiritual Leaders: American Indian Lives*. 1994. New York: Facts on File.

Washburn, Wilcomb E. *Handbook of North American Indians, Vol. 4*. 1988. Washington, D.C.: Smithsonian Institution.

Keseruk

Full Name at Birth: Keseruk
Birth: ca. 1812, place of birth not recorded
Death: ca. 1890, place of death not recorded
Education: no formal education
Leadership Position: Inuit shaman

Summary

Keseruk was an Inuit *tun'-gha-lik* or shaman of the West Arctic Coast who flourished in the late nineteenth century. The Inuit are frequently misidentified as Eskimos. Shamans among the Inuit possessed specialized supernatural power. Some were *a-klu-kai'-lin-úk*, "the one who knows everything," and some, such as Keseruk, were possessed by the special power of Raven. In the creation legend of the Inuit, Raven Father waved his wings four times over the clay images on earth to endow them with life. When the power of Raven came into Keseruk's body, he became *a-klu-kai'-lin-úk* and was able to see into the future and predict future events that would affect his people. Under the power of Raven, Keseruk was able to communicate with Tun'-run-ai'-yuk (the one Inuit God). Because of this power, Keseruk was highly respected as a person of great power and wisdom and was regarded as possessing the highest authority within the village group. All questions of religion and the mysteries of the invisible world were referred to him for resolution.

Early Life

There is no recorded history of Keseruk's early life. In keeping with Inuit custom, Keseruk was given the name of a deceased relative at his birth. As he grew to puberty, he would have been assigned a number of errands or jobs or light work that were also intended to help the young child acquire hunting and survival skills. Keseruk would have been rewarded for his work with small gifts, which he was expected to respect and use wisely. Inuit children were reported as being mischievous in a respectful way and delighted in playing practical jokes on one another.

Keseruk would have become aware of possessing shamanistic powers by the occurrence of some powerful unexplained circumstance or event in his early life. Having noted the event, he would have sought out the assistance of an elder shaman who had the power to interpret for the supernatural. Once the nature of the power had been ascertained, Keseruk would have been introduced to the village as a shaman. One recorded event by a noted shaman recalled that he was made aware of his power through a series of dreams and finding that he had been transported to different locations when he awoke.

Leadership

Keseruk was a shaman or mystic of exceptional skills. In one of his public performances, he asked the people in attendance to make him a birch bow and two arrows. The arrows were used to discern the location of game animals. The ceremony is reported as follows:

> He would say, "Little persons coming now—both have bow and arrow." Nobody can see them but Keseruk. . . . When he says those little persons have come, some people put Keseruk on top of a caribou skin, tie his feet together at the ankles, tie his hands tight behind him, tie his knees, and then pull the rope around his neck and under his knees and tie it. . . .
>
> By the time Keseruk couldn't move, these people took drums and started to sing . . . Keseruk says, "When the little persons come, they will take my body and use it—when they start to speak, through me, you must put the lamp out." Then they can hear Keseruk clapping his hands, and patting his feet on the floor, saying "ooi, ooi." Then they hear him let the bowstring go, but that arrow never hits the side of the house. "Now my arrow has gone to the head of that creek over there—now it gets to the Noatak River—now it is some place else—"
>
> After those arrows went a long way, they were turning around and coming back.

The people inspected the arrows after they had returned because they provided answers to specific questions. If Keseruk wanted to know about the availability of game animals on the Noatak River, for instance, the arrows would come back painted with blood and caribou hair.

Keseruk called on his Raven powers to solve his most challenging feats of "far seeing," or forecasting the future. He would call on Raven, who would enter and possess his body. Raven would then speak through Keseruk and direct him to carry out special ceremonies such as singing specific songs or conducting specific rituals or dances. Once the proper requirements had been met, Raven would reveal to Keseruk what the future held for the Inuit people. This included the availability of sea mammals, land animals, prediction of the weather and answers to specific questions.

There is no recorded record of Keseruk's death.

Further Reading

Champagne, Duane, ed. *The Native North American Almanac: A Reference Work on Native North Americans in the United States and Canada*. 1994. Detroit: Gale Research.

Dictionary of Indians of North America. 1978. St. Clair Shores, Mich.: Scholarly Press.

Hirschfelder, Arlene, and Paulette Molin. *The Encyclopedia of Native American Religions*. 1992. New York: Facts on File.

Lyon, William S. *Encyclopedia of Native American Shamanism: Sacred Ceremonies of North America*. 1998. Denver: ABC-CLIO.

Nelson, Edward William. *The Eskimo About Bering Strait*. 1971. New York: Johnson Reprint Corporation.

Kicking Bear

Full Name at Birth: Kicking Bear (Mato Anahtaka)
Birth: ca. 1846
Death: 1904, near Manderson, South Dakota
Education: no formal education
Leadership Position: medicine man and Lakota Ghost Dance leader

Summary

Born about 1846, Kicking Bear was a medicine man and a Lakota warrior. He was the nephew of the renowned Hunkpapa Sioux leader Sitting Bull and a contemporary of Crazy Horse, the noted Oglala-Brule Sioux leader. He served as a band chief among his wife's Miniconjou Sioux and fought at the battles of Rosebud, Little Bighorn, and Slim Buttes during the War for the Black Hills of 1876 and 1877. Along with Short Bull,* the Brule Sioux holy man and Ghost Dance prophet, Kicking Bear openly urged a campaign of warfare against the white man.

Kicking Bear was a leading proponent of the Ghost Dance religious movement practiced in the late 1800s in the belief that it would restore the Sioux people and their deceased ancestors to a rapidly disappearing way of life. Kicking Bear and Short Bull fashioned a "ghost shirt" which, they said, was impenetrable armor against the white men's bullets. The U.S. Army stopped the movement with the Wounded Knee Massacre in December 1890. Following the war, Kicking Bear settled on the Cheyenne River Reservation in present-day South Dakota.

An 1896 photo by William Dinwidie of Kicking Bear (Mato Anahtaka), the Lakota medicine man Ghost Dance leader. National Anthropological Archives, Smithsonian Institution.

Early Life

Kicking Bear was an Oglala Sioux by birth but joined the Miniconjou Sioux through marriage and became a band chief. Both the Oglala and the Miniconjou belong to the Lakota Nation.

There are no recorded histories of the early life of Kicking Bear. Because of his stature as a medicine man and band chief on the Miniconjou Sioux, it is reasonable to assume that he was raised in the traditional ways of a Lakota youth. While a young boy, he would have studied the Native life under the direction of a paternal uncle and learned to ride, hunt, and raid against traditional Lakota enemies.

While still a young boy, Kicking Bear would have participated in a vision quest where he would have been taken by his uncle or a medicine person to an isolated spot to fast and pray for a vision. In the vision, he would have been shown a spirit person, animal, or force that guided him and supported him for the remainder of his life.

Kicking Bear became a medicine man among the Sioux people, as well as a warrior. He distinguished himself in several battles to protect Lakota land during the War for the Black Hills (1876–1877), including the battle against Colonel George Armstrong Custer at Little Big Horn Creek.

Leadership

In the late 1800s, Indian people were experiencing increased pressure to abandon their traditional lifeways and surrender their remaining lands to the federal government. Indian people, it was believed, should be separated from contact with westward-moving whites and placed on reservations far from the trails and railroads that moved whites west. The federal government supported a policy of eradication of the great buffalo herds that supported the traditional life, culture, religion, and existence of these people. Army troops increasingly were used to concentrate Indian people on smaller and smaller parcels of land. Despondent and in search for a return to the past, Indian religious leaders sought a new messiah.

In the winter of 1889–1890, Kicking Bear and his brother-in-law, Short Bull, of the Rosebud Reservation, plus nine other Sioux delegates, traveled to Nevada by train to visit the Paiute spiritual leader Wovoka* and witness a new religion known as the Ghost Dance and to learn about Wovoka's teachings firsthand. Wovoka told them of the world to come where the earth would be replenished and the Indian dead would return to life.

In October 1890, Kicking Bear was invited by his uncle Sitting Bull to come to the Standing Rock Reservation in North Dakota to demonstrate what he had learned in his visit with Wovoka. In the intervening period, Short Bull and Kicking Bear, had added a new element to the Ghost Dance religion. According to Short Bull and Kicking Bear, they had been given the design of a Ghost Dance shirt in a dream. The shirt would be impervious to the white man's bullets. Although skeptical, especially about Kicking Bear's claim that the Ghost Dance shirts would repel the white man's bullets, Sitting Bull requested the medicine man teach his followers the Ghost Dance. Kicking Bear quickly became the leader of the Ghost Dance among his people and under his leadership the Ghost Dancers wore the new ghost shirts they believed would protect them from enemy bullets.

White officials became alarmed at the rising popularity of the new dance and the wearing of the Ghost Dance shirt. Agents and missionaries who had already banned other traditional religions that they regarded as heathenistic or potentially militant targeted the dance for repression. Fearing Kicking Bear's growing following, Indian policemen were sent to arrest him; however, they failed to carry out the orders. Kicking Bear's followers believed that his spiritual power had prevented the arrest, and his following grew. Federal troops were now requested to stop the dancing.

In early December 1890, Kicking Bear and other adherents fled to the Stronghold, an area in the Badlands of South Dakota on the Pine Ridge Reservation, and invited Sitting Bull to join them. Fearing that Sitting Bull would join the Ghost Dancers, James McLaughlin, the government agent at Standing Rock who feared the leader's influence, ordered Sitting Bull's arrest. Sitting Bull was murdered on December 15, 1890, when fighting broke out between his followers and the tribal policemen sent to carry out McLaughlin's order.

Following Sitting Bull's death, events escalated. The Miniconjou leader, Big Foot of Cheyenne River, who now feared for the safety of his people, led his followers to seek protection from the Lakota leader Red Cloud at the Pine Ridge Reservation. Mistakenly believing that Big Foot and his band were en route to participate in the Ghost Dance at the stronghold, Big Foot's band was intercepted by the military and taken to Wounded Knee Creek in South Dakota. On December 29, 1890, after a gun reportedly discharged, troops of the U.S. Seventh Cavalry opened fire and massacred more than two hundred men, women, and children of Big Foot's band. Now under relentless pressure and also in fear of their lives, Kicking Bear and other Ghost Dancers surrendered to General Nelson Miles in January 1891. Kicking Bear was incarcerated at Fort Sheridan in Illinois.

In 1891 Kicking Bear's sentence was commuted providing he join Buffalo Bill Cody for two years to travel abroad with his Wild West show. One of their stops was Washington, D.C., where a model of Kicking Bear's body was made by Smithsonian Institution representatives. Photographs of Kicking Bear were also taken. The Ghost Dance leader returned home in November 1892. He later moved his family to a remote area along Wounded Knee Creek that became Manderson, South Dakota. Kicking Bear died in 1904 at the age of fifty-eight. His Ghost Dance shirt was collected by James Mooney at the Cheyenne River Agency, Dakota Territory, in 1869 and was donated to the Smithsonian Institution in Washington, D.C.

Further Reading

Axelrod, Alan. *Chronicle of the Indian Wars: From Colonial Times to Wounded Knee*. 1993. Englewood Cliffs, N.J.: Prentice Hall.

Ballantine, Betty, ed. *The Native Americans: An Illustrated History*. 1993. New York: Turner Publishing.

Hirschfelder, Arlene, and Paulette Molin. *The Encyclopedia of Native American Religions*. 1992. New York: Facts on File.

Kicking Bear: http://www.artsednet.getty. edu/ArtsEdNet/Resources/Maps/battle.html.

Kicking Bear: http://www.pbs.org/weta/ thewest/wpages/wpgs680/68_06.html.

Lakota Dance Ghost Dance Apostles: http://www2.memes.com/artworks/lakota.html.

Waldman, Carl. *Who Was Who in Native American History*. 1990. New York: Facts on File.

Washburn, Wilcomb E. *Handbook of North American Indians, Vol. 4*. 1988. Washington, D.C.: Smithsonian Institution.

John King

Full Name at Birth: John King

Birth: ca. 1901, place of birth not recorded

Death: date and place of death not recorded

Education: no formal education

Leadership Position: Chippewa shaking tent shaman

Summary

John King was a Chippewa shaking tent shaman (*jizikiwinini*) who flourished in the early twentieth century. In 1924, anthropologist Robert Ritzenthaler visited with John King and observed a shaking tent healing ceremony performed on a twenty-five-year-old man who had been diagnosed with incipient tuberculosis during his army physical. After the diagnosis, the man spent six weeks in a tuberculosis sanatorium and then returned to his home for treatment by King. Because Ritzenthaler had provided the transportation for the patient to and from the sanatorium, he was allowed to observe what was normally a restricted ceremony.

Early Life

Little is known of John King's early life. Because he became a prominent shaman, it is safe to assume that he had a traditional Chippewa boy's life. By the age of three or four, a Chippewa boy was familiar with a bow and arrow and could hit birds and small animals with a blunt-tip arrow. By the age of six or seven, he could manage simple traps and had graduated to hunting small game with sharp-pointed arrows. John would have been instructed in the use of these weapons by his father and uncle, whom he would accompany on hunting trips. By the age of fifteen, King hunted alone and participated in his first vision quest. During the vision quest experience, the male elders instructed John to separate from the tribe and go to a remote spot, to receive a visit from one or more supernatural powers who would reveal to him his future. It was not uncommon for a youth to receive no supernatural visit on his first vision quest attempt but would fast and return alone to "cry for vision."

The normal fast was for four days, but many boys fasted for as long as eight days. Once King received his vision, he turned away from the normal life and devoted himself to intimacy with the supernatural. He was required to maintain secrecy of his vision and to devote himself to lifelong self-discipline. It was believed that if a youth talked about his vision he would offend the power giver and he would forfeit the vision.

Leadership

John King was a Chippewa shaman who practiced the shaking tent, or *jizikiwinini* ceremony. This ceremony was considered to be one of the most important rituals in the yearly cycle of harvesting, healing, and ritual activities of the Chippewa people. Through the shaking tent ceremony the shaman was able to communicate with the animal spirits as well as the masters of the spirits of the animals who controlled the procreation of the animals necessary for the survival of the Chippewa people.

John King was most noted for using the shaking tent ceremony to affect cures for members of his tribe. In preparation for such a cure a tribal member would approach John King or one of his assistants and ask that a shaking tent ceremony be held. If King felt capable of curing the individual he would instruct that a shaking-tent lodge or *jiziken* be constructed. The lodge would be a small, conically shaped structure with an animal hide covering. Younger men would act as apprentices to King in the construction of the lodge. Once constructed, King would enter the lodge and the lodge would begin shaking very slowly. The shaking served as a signal for one of the ceremonial assistants to begin drumming. Women shaking rattles accompanied the drumming. The shaking might continue slowly or increase to a rapid pace. The faster the shaking occurred, the more powerful the spirit presence was. It was during this period that King diagnosed the illness and spoke with the spirit of the shaking tent to see if a cure could be prescribed. The spirit spoke only to King and he rarely allowed others to observe the ceremony. The drumming, shaking of rattles, and shaking of the tent continued for a period of time during which the spirit gave instructions that King was to pass on to the person undergoing the

healing ceremony. Once the instructions were given, the ceremony was brought to a close. If the person undergoing the healing ceremony followed the instructions given to him by the spirit of the shaking tent, through John King, that person would be cured.

Further Reading

Champagne, Duane, ed. *The Native North American Almanac: A Reference Work on Native North Americans in the United States and Canada.* 1994. Detroit: Gale Research.

Dictionary of Indians of North America. 1978. St. Clair Shores, Mich.: Scholarly Press.

Hirschfelder, Arlene, and Paulette Molin. *The Encyclopedia of Native American Religions.* 1992. New York: Facts on File.

Landes, Ruth. *Ojibwa Religion and the Mide'wiwin.* 1969. Madison: University of Wisconsin Press.

Lyon, William S. *Encyclopedia of Native American Shamanism: Sacred Ceremonies of North America.* 1998. Denver: ABC-CLIO.

Susan La Flesche Picotte

Full Name at Birth: Susan La Flesche

Birth: 1865 in a tipi on the Omaha Indian Reservation in present-day Nebraska

Death: September 18, 1915; buried in Bancroft, Nebraska

Education: attended the Elizabeth Institute for Young Ladies in New Jersey, 1879–1882; the Hampton Institute in Virginia, 1884–1886; and the Women's Medical College of Pennsylvania, 1888–1889

Leadership position: Omaha healer and physician

Summary

La Flesche was the daughter of the Omaha chief Joseph La Flesche (Inshtamaza, or "Iron") and a mixed-blood Iowa Indian woman, Mary Gale

(Hinnuaganun). She was born in Nebraska and studied with both Presbyterian and Quaker missionaries. She attended the Elizabeth Institute for Young Ladies in New Jersey, the Hampton Institute in

Dr. Susan La Flesche Picotte. Nebraska State Historical Society.

Virginia, and the Women's Medical College of Pennsylvania.

La Flesche has been recognized as the first female Indian physician, although this label reflects a narrow Western definition of medicine. La Flesche received her medical degree from the Women's Medical College of Pennsylvania in 1889, where she graduated at the top of her class. She spent her internship at the Woman's Hospital in Philadelphia. In the late 1800s, La Flesche served as the government reservation doctor for the Omaha, a Siouan-speaking Nation living in Nebraska, seeing hundreds of patients and helping treat diseases chronic to Indian reservations such as tuberculosis, influenza, cholera, conjunctivitis, and typhoid. La Flesche drove a horse and buggy to visit patients who could not come to her office, finally resigning due to health reasons. Beginning in 1891, La Flesche served as the medical missionary to her tribe, sponsored by the Women's National Indian Association, and became a temperance speaker.

In 1894, La Flesche married Henri Picotte, a mixed French-Sioux, and they began a practice for both Indians and whites in Bancroft, Nebraska. Following her husband's death in 1905, La Flesche worked as a missionary at the Blackbird Hills Presbyterian Church while continuing her medical practice.

Susan La Flesche and her sister, Suzette, were noted Indian activists and used their boarding school education to champion Indian rights, lecturing, and lobbying in the halls of Congress. La Flesche lobbied for the eradication of tuberculosis and the prohibition of alcohol on reservations. She also supported individual ownership of land, taking a very controversial stance of allowing individual Omaha Indian people to sell and lease their property free from government supervision.

Early Life

La Flesche was born on the Omaha Indian Reservation in 1865 and studied with Christian missionaries at the government schools she attended. Her father, Joseph La Flesche, the chief of the Omaha tribe, believed that the education of Indian people was the key to success in America. La Flesche studied at the Elizabeth Institute for Young Ladies in Elizabeth, New Jersey, and graduated from Hampton Institute in Hampton, Virginia. Susan and her sister, Suzette, used their boarding school education in the non-Indian world to champion Indian issues. They lectured and lobbied for Indian rights in the U.S. Congress; their brother, Francis, became one of the first Indian anthropologists.

Leadership

La Flesche was born in the present-day state of Nebraska and studied with both Presbyterian and Quaker missionaries. From 1879 to 1882, she attended the Elizabeth Institute for Young Ladies in New Jersey; from 1884 to 1886, the Hampton Institute in Virginia; and in 1888–1889, the Women's Medical College of Pennsylvania. La Flesche received her medical degree from the Women's Medical College of Pennsylvania in 1889, graduating at the top of her class. She spent her internship at the Woman's Hospital in Philadelphia. From August 1889 to October 1893, she served as the government reservation doctor for the Omaha, seeing hundreds of patients in her office and visiting by horse and buggy those patients who could not come to her office. It is said that La Flesche "rode on horseback from reservation to reservation, from family to family, treating the sick . . . by the time of her death, she had treated every member of the Omaha Nation." Starting in 1891, La Flesche also served as the medical missionary to her tribe sponsored by the Women's National Indian Association.

In 1894, La Flesche married Henri Picotte, a mixed French-Sioux, and began a practice for both Indians and whites in Bancroft, Nebraska. After her husband's death in 1905, she worked as a missionary at the Blackbird Hills Presbyterian Church in addition to her medical practice, and in 1906, she moved to Walthill, Nebraska.

Beginning in 1910, she and her sister, Suzette, traveled to Washington, D.C., to champion Indian rights, lecturing and lobbying Congress against government regulations that made it difficult for tribal members to lease their lands and receive payment. They also lobbied for the eradication of tuberculosis and the prohibition of alcohol on reservations. Susan La Flesche supported individual ownership of land, allowing Omahas to sell and lease their property free from government supervision. She was a political liaison for her people with the federal government and active in the temperance movement. During this time, she worked for the government's Office of Indian Affairs. Throughout her life, La Flesche worked for improved health care for the Omaha people. Extensive correspondence has been preserved that documents her communication with the commissioner of Indian affairs, as well as local newspaper accounts of her community achievements in Walthill, Nebraska.

Susan La Flesche Picotte, M.D., by Benson Tong, provides an intimate portrait of La Flesche's life and focuses on her cultural mediations as she moved between two culturally irreconcilable worlds: that of her Omaha life in the West and the world of college, medical training, and politics in the East. Tong reveals that La Flesche never abandoned her Omaha heritage. The daughter of an Omaha chief, she was inculcated with a sense of tribal responsibility early on, and later she used her education and abilities to work for progressive reforms for her people.

Prior to her death, La Flesche adopted Christianity and became a missionary of the Omaha Blackbird Hills Presbyterian Church. She moved to the newly established town of Walthill, where she organized a county medical society and headed the local board of health. In 1913, Picotte set up a hospital on the Omaha Reservation. The hospital was named for her after her death in 1915.

Further Reading

Calloway, Colin G. *First Peoples: A Documentary Survey of American Indian History.* 1999. New York: St. Martin's.

Champagne, Duane, ed. *The Native North American Almanac: A Reference Work on Native North Americans in the United States and Canada.* 1994. Detroit: Gale Research.

"If you knew the conditions . . .": Health Care to Native Americans: http://www.nlm.nih.gov/exhibition/if_you_knew/if_you_knew_12.html.

Picotte, Susan La Flesche (1865–1915): http://www.worldbook.com/fun/whm/html/whm071.html.

Tong, Benson. *Susan La Flesche Picotte, M.D.* 1999. Norman: University of Oklahoma Press.

Waldman, Carl. *Who Was Who in Native American History.* 1990. New York: Facts on File.

Woman Spirit: http://www.meyna.com/omaha.html.

John (Fire) Lame Deer

Full Name at Birth: Lame Deer

Birth: Rosebud Reservation in present-day South Dakota; date of birth unknown

Death: 1976 on the Rosebud Lakota Reservation in South Dakota

Education: attended the Rosebud Reservation Indian day school for eight years

Leadership Position: Lakota holy man

Summary

Lame Deer was born at the beginning of the twentieth century on the Rosebud Reservation in South Dakota. He was a Lakota holy man, and perhaps a *heyoka*, or sacred clown, whose spiritual powers came from the *wakinyan*, or thunder beings. He participated in the Sioux vision quest, Sun Dance and healing rituals. He was also known under the name John Fire.

Lame Deer was a full-blooded Sioux and with the help of several Lakota holy men became a medicine man. Lame Deer also explored other religions, including several Christian denominations and the Native American church. Besides healing with herbs and conducting *yuwipi* ceremonies (a nighttime curing ceremony conducted in a darkened room) and other sacred ceremonies, one of Lame Deer's vision foretold that he would train twenty-four medicine men prior to his death. In 1972, when he told his life story, *Lame Deer, Seeker of Visions*, to Richard Erdoes, who coauthored the book, he had taught eighteen of the twenty-four medicine men.

Lame Deer was the father of Archie Fire Lame Deer, another Lakota holy man. Prior to his death in 1976, Lame Deer told of his life as a young man, "running around, drinking, getting into and running away from trouble." He said, "I had a thirst for women. . . . I believe that being a medicine man [*wichasha wakan*, holy man] is a state of mind. . . . You know I'm no better or wiser than other men. That vision never leaves me."

In *Lame Deer, Seeker of Visions*, Lame Deer explains many spiritual things, symbols, and ceremonies in the same strong, characteristic, earthy fashion that was the hallmark of his life. His book explains his interpretation and practice of the *hanblechia* (vision quest), *yuwipi* (little ant-stones, tied-up man), *initi* (sweat lodge), and the Sun Dance, and the heyoka (the backward clown) ceremonies.

Lame Deer died in 1976 on the Rosebud Lakota reservation in South Dakota.

Early Life

Lame Deer was born in a log cabin on the Rosebud Reservation in present-day South Dakota just shortly after the turn of the twentieth century. His mother was Sally Red Blanket, and his father was Wawi-YohiYa who later became known as Silas Fire. As is common in Lakota culture, Lame Deer spent a great deal of time with his grandparents, developing as strong a relationship with them as well as with his parents.

When Lame Deer was about six years of age, the Bureau of Indian Affairs (BIA) instructed his family to send him to school, and pressures on his traditional way of life began. In keeping with the government's policy of assimilation, Lame Deer attended a government day school on the Rosebud Reservation for eight years. He resisted the challenges to the Lakota culture and teachings of his parents and grandparents and was constantly in trouble with school officials.

When Lame Deer was sixteen, he went to a hilltop pit for his first vision quest. After fasting and being alone for four days and four nights, his great-grandfather, Tahca Ushte (Lame Deer), the Minneconjou chief who had been shot and killed in a battle with General Nelson Miles, appeared before him. From his vision, Lame Deer understood that he was to take his great-grandfather's name. The vision also foretold that he would become a great medicine man who would teach and heal many people.

Leadership

Lame Deer was a Lakota holy man who lived during the most difficult period in the history of Native American people of the American Great Plains. The period was characterized by the constant threat of military attacks aimed at exterminating Indian tribes and complete destruction and loss of cultural identity.

Lame Deer was born a full-blood Lakota in the early 1900s. He was raised in a traditional Lakota family but was eventually forced to attend a BIA boarding school where he witnessed firsthand the government's policy of destruction of Indian culture through education and forced assimilation. Lame Deer experienced wide exposure to the white man's world as a rodeo clown, bootlegger, tribal policeman, soldier, potato picker, shepherd, square dance caller, and sign painter, and he was imprisoned in a white man's jail. He investigated several Christian religions as well as the Native American church but returned to his calling as a medicine man, at which time he stated, "I have my hands full just clinging to our old Sioux ways—singing the ancient songs correctly, conducting a sweat-lodge ceremony as it should be, making our old beliefs as pure, as clear and true as I possibly can, making them stay alive, saving them from extinction. This is a big enough task for an old man."

Lame Deer became a medicine man with the help of three prominent Lakota holy men—Chest, Thunderhawk, and Good Lance—and the remainder of his life was guided by a vision acquired during the traditional vision quest experience. In his book *Lame Deer, Seeker of Visions* Lame Deer gives a firsthand account of the vision quest he had to experience to make the transition from boy to man. The vision quest is a ritual in which a young man or woman seeks to establish communication with the spirit world. The young person is sometimes accompanied to a secluded area by a tribal elder or medicine person. After they sing songs, chant prayers, and pray individually, the attendant leaves. The young person is then left alone for a period of time, often as long as four days, to seek a vision. During this period, the youth fasts and undergoes sleep and other sensory deprivations to facilitate the vision process. Individuals blessed during a vision quest sometimes receive names, objects, songs, dances, or spiritual helpers such as an animal, bird, or other being. This spirit or power helper can be called on throughout the remainder of that person's life for help and guidance.

Lame Deer went through many experiences before realizing his full potential as a medicine man. In his autobiography, Lame Deer tells of his wild life as a young man, running around, drinking, and getting into and running away from trouble. He views all of this as a learning experience, however, and states that "a medicine man shouldn't be a saint. He should experience and feel all the ups and downs, the despair and joy, the magic and the reality, the courage and the fear of his people."

In a discussion with Richard Erdoes, the coauthor of *Lame Deer, Seeker of Visions*, Lame Deer explained that white men had made life difficult for themselves. He believed that white men had changed themselves by living such a regimented life of careers, goals, and habits that they were trapped in the materialistic world. At the time of his death, he believed that men were moving back toward the natural part of life however, living life as Indians did. This was because the original spirit and wisdom is present within each man, and they would soon come around and abandon their materialistic quest.

Late in his life, Lame Deer stated that his vision never left him. One demanding requirement placed on him by the vision was that he was responsible for training twenty-four medicine men. In 1972, at the time he and Erdoes penned his autobiography, he had completed the training of eighteen of the required twenty-four.

Lame Deer died several years later on the Rosebud Lakota Reservation in South Dakota; his son Archie Fire Lame Deer, also a Lakota holy man, carries on his spiritual work.

Further Reading

Beck, Peggy V., Anna Lee Walters, and Nia Francisco. *The Sacred Ways of Knowledge, Sources of Life*. 1990. Flagstaff, Ariz.: Northland Publishing.

Champagne, Duane, ed. *The Native North American Almanac: A Reference Work on Native North Americans in the United States and Canada*. 1994. Detroit: Gale Research.

Erdoes, Richard, and John (Fire) Lame Deer. *Lame Deer, Seeker of Visions*. 1972. New York: Simon & Schuster.

Gill, Sam D. *Native American Religions: An Introduction*. 1982. Belmont, Calif.: Wadsworth.

Hirschfelder, Arlene, and Paulette Molin. *The Encyclopedia of Native American Religions*. 1992. New York: Facts on File.

Review: Lame Deer, Seeker of Visions: http://nativenet.uthscsa.edu/archive/nl/9211/0027.html.

Talking to the Owls and Butterflies: John (Fire) Lame Deer, Richard Erdoes: http://www.colostate.edu/Depts/WritingCenter/assignments/co300/99–00/sutton/port1/sum/pop1j.htm.

White Buffalo Calf Woman: http://indy4.fdl.cc.mn.us/~isk/arvol/lamedeer.html.

Low Horn

Full Name at Birth: Atsitsi ("Screech Owl")
Birth: ca. 1822; place of birth unknown
Death: June 1899 near Serviceberry Creek, Namaka Colony, Alberta, Canada
Education: no formal education
Leadership Position: Blackfoot healer

Summary

Low Horn shared the distinction of being one of the three most powerful Blackfoot healers of his generation. The other two were Black Eagle and a medicine woman, *Kitsin'iki*. Like most other prairie Indians, the Blackfoot, who lived in the present-day states of Montana and the Dakotas and the province of Alberta, were a very proud and religious people. Their religious cosmology closely resembled that of other Plains Indian people and recognized that spirits were present in the sun (*Natos*), the moon (*Kokomi-kisum*), and also the mountains, forests, streams, as well as all animals. The most important of their religious practices is the Sun Dance (*okan*), an elaborate ceremonial performance in which fasting, self-torture, and self-mutilation were practiced. The Sun Dance played a large part in Blackfoot life and was generally held in July. The Sun Dance was held so that men who had made a pledge to the Creator could fulfill the pledge and ensure prosperity for the Blackfoot Nation.

Early Life

Low Horn was born around 1822. At birth he was given the name of Atsitsi (Screech Owl). At the age of thirteen, while the Blackfoot tribe was assembled in camp for their annual Sun Dance, Screech Owl completed a successful vision quest. He traveled alone to the top of a hill carrying only a robe and his pipe. He remained there for three days without food or water, gazing toward the rising sun and praying that a spirit helper would appear. On the third night, a storm swept across the prairie, thunder sounded, and lightning struck the hill where Screech Owl was fasting. It was during this experience that he acquired the song of the thunder spirit. For the remainder of his life, Screech Owl could call on the songs of the thunder whenever he needed help. Shortly after this experience, he also acquired the holy songs of the Sparrow Hawk. Sparrow Hawk appeared to him in a dream and said, "I give you my power. In battle you must wear two feathers from my wings and you'll never be beaten." On another occasion, a large jackrabbit appeared to him and told him, "Because you saved my life, you'll be a leader of your people. You'll escape many dangers." Screech Owl also acquired the power of *kaina-sk'na*, or mouse, which was considered to be a source of great supernatural power.

A Blackfoot warrior was considered fortunate if he acquired one spiritual helper in his lifetime, but Screech Owl had acquired the holy songs of the sparrow hawk, rabbit's power, the power of thunder, and mouse's supernatural power. At the age of fourteen, he began to use his medicine powers as a warrior.

Leadership

Low Horn was a great medicine man who had not only inherited the powers of the Blackfoot warrior but had gained his own spiritual helpers as well.

Low Horn had great powers of stealth and became wealthy through his ability to acquire horses from Blackfoot enemies. His powers seemed to make him immune from danger, and he fearlessly entered enemy camps undetected and captured prized buffalo ponies or racehorses. Wearing his sparrow hawk feathers as instructed by his spirit helper and quietly chanting his holy songs, he moved through enemy encampments like a shadow, "leaving his enemies angry and afoot." It was reported that he gave away all the horses he had taken."

Low Horn died in 1846 in a battle against the Cree Indians. It was reported that when the Cree stripped him of his clothing, they found that he was wearing Spanish mail. The Cree, fearing Low Horn's supernatural powers, chopped his body into small pieces and began to burn them. As they placed parts of his body in the fire, a burning ember popped from the fire and a huge bear arose from the spot where the ember had landed, and the bear killed five of the Cree Indians.

Using his supernatural powers, Low Horn was reincarnated into the body of a young Blackfoot boy named Only Person Who Had a Different Gun. At the age of six, Different Gun and a Blackfoot party came upon a Blackfoot woman named Deer Old Woman, the widow of the deceased Low Horn. Different Gun recognized her as his former wife and told a playmate that "she was my sweetheart when I was young." On the following day,

they crossed the battle site where Low Horn had been killed. Different Gun began to cry and told his father, "I'm crying because this is the place where I was attacked and killed by the Crees. I am Low Horn." The Blackfoot elders were slow to believe Different Gun, so he instructed them to go to two different locations where they would find a whip and a skinning knife that he had hidden prior to his death. The items, though deteriorated, were located exactly where Different Gun had said they would be. "Different Gun was again named Low Horn."

In the 1870s Low Horn began visiting with the medicine men of the tribe and gradually learned their ways. He added the white-headed eagle's power to the array of powers inherited from the former Low Horn and became a renowned healer. One of his most famous healings took place in December 1891, when he cured a Blackfoot warrior named Steel who had been shot in the back and given up for dead by white physicians. The vast majority of healers had no cure for gunshot wounds. "Using four of his most sacred paints and the power of the mouse inherited from the Blackfoot Low Horn, he performed his rituals. Once the evil [bullet] had been removed Low Horn said that Steele would recover." Twelve days later, the wounded man was strong enough to ride a horse to Low Horn's village for further treatment. Steel lived for another fifty years.

Low Horn continued to seek spiritual visions even after he had been forced to remove to the Blackfoot Reserve. During one vision, he was instructed to "never sleep in a white man's bed." In 1899 he fell asleep while sitting on a bed, thus breaking the spirit taboo. He died later that year at the age of fifty-three.

Further Reading

Blood Indians: http://www.newadvent.org/cathen/02603a.htm.

Dempsey, Hugh A. *The Amazing Death of Calf Shirt and Other Blackfoot Stories*. 1996. Norman: University of Oklahoma Press.

Hirschfelder, Arlene, and Paulette Molin. *The Encyclopedia of Native American Religions*. 1992. New York: Facts on File.

Lyon, William S. *Encyclopedia of Native American Shamanism: Sacred Ceremonies of North America*. 1998. Denver: ABC-CLIO.

Mamanti

Full Name at Birth: Mamanti or Maman'te ("Sky Walker")

Birth: date and place of birth unknown

Death: 1875; died a prisoner at Fort Marion in Florida

Education: no formal education

Leadership Position: Kiowa medicine man

Summary

History is silent regarding the life of Mamanti until 1871, when he emerged as a Kiowa medicine man whose influence on leading chiefs of the Kiowa Nation resulted in increased attention by the federal government and the U.S. military. The Kiowa raids led by these famous Kiowa chiefs, at the behest of Mamanti, led to the Texas Red River Wars and the ultimate defeat and reservation confinement of the last remaining Kiowa warriors.

In 1871, Mamanti and other Kiowa leaders, including Santanta, Satank, and Big Tree, laid a trap along the Butterfield Southern stage route between Fort Belknap and Fort Richardson in north-central Texas. Mamanti had been given a dream of an attack on a large wagon train and had advised the chiefs that they would be successful in ambushing an important white man, following which the attacks on the Kiowa would be halted. Now led by Mamanti, the Kiowa laid a trap and awaited the wagon train that he had seen in his vision. What appeared, however, was a small army ambulance wagon, and Mamanti's dream had foretold of a much larger target. He and the Kiowa leader attacked the Warren wagon train that followed along shortly after, killing seven of the twelve defenders and plundering the wagons. General William Tecumseh Sherman on learning of the attack on the wagon train, ordered increased efforts against Kiowa and Comanche militants, resulting in the Red River War of 1874–1875.

Following the Red River Wars and the 1874 battle at Adobe Walls in the Texas Panhandle, Mamanti surrendered and was among those selected by Kicking Bird, the New Kiowa leader, for imprisonment at Fort Marion in present-day Florida. Kicking Bird was the leader of the peace faction and was allowed to select the most dangerous of the Kiowa to be separated out to prevent further warfare. Mamanti, upon learning that Kicking Bird had sealed his fate, reportedly prayed for the death of Kicking Bird, who died within a week. Mamanti died in Florida in July 1875, supposedly immediately after learning of the death of Kicking Bird.

Early Life

There is no recorded history of Mamanti's early life. He was born in the early 1800s into the Kiowa tribe, a Nation that migrated often. By the time of Mamanti's birth, the Kiowa were living in the Black Hills of present-day eastern Wyoming. Early in his life, the Kiowa migrated again, pushed out from the Black Hills by the Lakota and Cheyenne. Mamanti's formative years were spent south of the Arkansas River in present-day Kansas and northern Oklahoma.

The Kiowa were among the first Indian Nations to acquire the horse, and they developed elaborate religious and cultural ceremonies. Mamanti would have been exposed very early in his life to the practice of the Sun Dance ceremony, the keeping of sacred medicine bundles, and the Kiowa warrior societies. The Sun Dance is one of the best-known religious ceremonies conducted by Native American and was practiced in some form by almost all tribal groups of the Great Plains regions, including the Kiowa. The Sun Dance has many variations. However, for most tribes, the sacred ceremony is held to pray for the renewal of the people and the earth, to give thanks, to fulfill a vow, and to protect the people from danger or illness. The Sun Dance was also an important social event for the tribes concerned. It traditionally brought scattered tribal bands together during the summer for social as well as religious activities. The annual Sun Dance period was a time for courting, renewing friendships, exchanging information, visiting relatives, and holding traditional games.

Leadership

In February 1871, Mamanti moved into the recorded history of Indian-white relations in the American West. He led a small raiding party to Young County in north-central Texas and killed four Negro men a couple of miles west on the road to Fort Belknap. Mamanti retold the story about the tough fight the men had put up and how one had almost refused to die. The Negro man, Britt Johnson, was well known to the Kiowa for his "bad habit of coming alone into Indian camps, haggling, threatening, offering inadequate ransom for captives, and stealing back captives."

Later in 1871, Mamanti and other Kiowa leaders, including Satank, Adoltay, Eagle Heart, Big Bow, and Fast Bear, laid a trap along the Butterfield Southern Route between Fort Belknap and Fort Richardson. Mamanti had had a dream in which he was told to lead an attack on a large wagon train in which an important white man was traveling. As the Indian force lay in wait, they allowed a small army ambulance wagon train to pass by because of Mamanti's prophecy that a much larger wagon train would follow. They attacked the Warren wagon train that followed and killed seven of the twelve defenders. Unknown to the Indians, General William Tecumseh Sherman had been riding in the ambulance train and, upon learning of the attack on the Warren wagon train, ordered increased efforts against Kiowa and Comanche militants, resulting in the Red River Wars.

In July 1874, Mamanti was once again raiding into the Lost Valley of Young County in north-central Texas. On July 12, he rode with Lone Wolf in a fight against the Texas Rangers in which Mamanti rode in full view of the Texans who, although they fired at him, could not wound him. Pressure now began to mount, however, and Mamanti and other Kiowa militants joined with Quanah

Parker* of the Comanche in the Lalano Estacado (Staked Plains) of Texas. Mamanti's band suffered the loss of most of their horses and possessions at the hands of troops under Colonel Ranald S. Mackenzie at the Battle of Palo Duro Canyon in September 1874.

In February 1875, Mamanti, Lone Wolf, Red Otter, Dohasan, Poor Buffalo, and 68 other warriors, as well as 180 women and children, came to Fort Sill with all their horses, mules, and livestock. The war was over. The so-called Lords of the Southern Plains—the Kiowa and Comanche—had been conquered. The fates of the participants varied. Kicking Bird of the Kiowa peace faction was given the task of selecting those for deportation to Fort Marion in present-day St. Augustine, Florida. Mamanti was among those sent to Florida, where the military deported warriors whom they considered dangerous. Kicking Bird died mysteriously soon afterward, and the Kiowa believed that Mamanti had prayed Kicking Bird to death. The army surgeon at Fort Sill recorded the cause as "poisoned by strychnine." Legend says that right after learning of Kicking Bird's death, Mamanti willed himself to die because he had used his magical powers to kill Kicking Bird. Mamanti died at St. Francis barracks on July 29, 1875.

In June 1875, just prior to his death, Mamanti made a speech that was forwarded to Washington:

We are termed by all the white people as a very lazy class of men, not willing to do anything for our own support. It is not so. We have been taken away from our wives and children, relatives and friends, shackled and sent down to this place to remain. We do not know how long. We are willing to show that we are not too lazy to support ourselves. If there is anything "Washington" wishes us to do tell us what it is and "Washington" will see how willingly we will do it. . . . There are a great many Indians at Fort Sill and in that county, who have done more bad work than we have, and why should they be allowed to go free and be happy with their families? Yet we are sent down here [St. Francis barracks in St. Augustine, Florida] as prisoners to live in these dark cells. This is not right. Tell "Washington" to give us our women and children and send us to a country where we can live and work like white men.

Further Reading:

Capps, Benjamin. *The Warren Wagontrain Raid: The First Complete Account of an Historic Indian Attack and Its Aftermath.* 1974. New York: Dial Press.

Haseloff, Cynthia. *The Kiowa Verdict: A Western Story.* 1997. Farmington Hills, Mich.: Thorndike Press: http://www.readwesterns.com/kiowa_verdict_excerpts.htm.

Stanley, F. *Santanta and the Kiowas.* 1968. Borger, Tex.: Jim Hess Printers.

Waldman, Carl. *Who Was Who in Native American History.* 1990. New York: Facts on File.

Mabel McKay

Full Name at Birth: Mabel
Birth: January 12, 1907, in Nice, California
Death: May 31, 1993, in Santa Rosa, California

Education: attended two or possible three years of elementary school at an un-named Indian boarding school

Leadership Position: Cache Creek Pomo medicine woman and basket maker

Summary

Mabel McKay was a well-known Pomo medicine woman and a world-renowned basket weaver of the Cache Creek Pomo people. While much attention has been given to McKay's baskets, it must be understood that her basket making cannot be separated from her dreams, for it was through them that she learned to weave and heal.

McKay was trained in basket making by a spirit that visited her in her dreams beginning when she was a young girl. She spent her life healing, making baskets, and teaching others how the spirit speaks through dreams, how the spirit heals, and how the spirit demands to be heard. It was through her dreams, cures, and stories that she kept her culture alive. McKay's basketry and healing were known throughout the world. Pope John Paul II made it a point to seek her out when he visited the Bay Area, as did many other religious leaders.

McKay's baskets are highly prized by collectors and are described by Gregg Sarris as being "beautiful, stunning coiled baskets in different shapes and designs: feather baskets, unlike anything seen before, made from the bright yellow feathers of the meadowlark, the metallic green feathers found on a mallard duck's neck, and the orange breast feathers of the robin." Some of her baskets are so small that a magnifying glass must be used to see the small intricate weaves and designs.

McKay was married twice. Her first husband was a Wintun man by the name of Charles McKay from near Redding, California. She had a son and a number of grandchildren. She resided in Santa Rosa, California, until her death on May 31, 1993.

Early Life

McKay was not given a Pomo traditional blessing and name at birth because the traditional roundhouse where these ceremonies were carried out was closed by the time she was born.

During McKay's early life, her grandmother, Old Grandma Sarah Taylor, cared for her. Taylor thought that McKay was unusually quiet. She noted that McKay was observant, however, and that her eyes darted about all the time; otherwise, she lay still and was rather solemn. McKay appears to have been an inquisitive child, and it was all that Taylor could do to keep her from exploring too far. On one such occasion, McKay swallowed some kerosene, and a non-Indian doctor had to be called in to pump her stomach.

Following the kerosene incident, McKay seemed to waste away. She lost weight, almost to the point of emaciation. Her disposition took on a sharp edge, and people began to think that something was seriously wrong with the child. Most people blamed her strange development on the kerosene.

Grandma Taylor knew differently. She recognized early on that McKay was going to have special powers. Taylor had seen McKay go into "trance like" states and heard her talking in her sleep. On one occasion, she saw McKay chase away a would-be poisoner carrying a tainted piece of meat.

Things did not improve, however. As McKay grew through her childhood years, she was singled out for rude stares, unkind comments, and stories of being under the influence of a curse or snake poison. All of the talk and speculation was false. Grandma Taylor's sleep was often cut short when McKay screamed out in her sleep. She was beginning her life's calling as a "dreamer." McKay did not know when she started dreaming, only that she was very little. The dream spirit gave her things to do. "I put these things to you, and you have to sort them out." 'You have to learn many bad things so you know what to do when the time comes." "That's why people say I'm poison."

Taylor, with McKay in tow, relocated to the Cortina Rancheria in Colusa County, California, to live among the Wintun people who were reported as being friendly and took in strangers. They left the Rumsey Rancheria and went to live among the Wintun.

These were exciting times for McKay. There were dances going on, celebrations, and people coming from everywhere. Taylor took McKay into the roundhouse even though it was against the Wintun traditions. A *moki*—a man who enforced decorum and obedience to the rules—saw that McKay had been brought in. On the fourth night of the dance, the *moki* threw hot coals throughout the roundhouse, filling it with smoke. McKay cried out for her grandma, but the *moki* came up behind her and pressed a hot coal into her shoulder, much like a branding iron.

The next day there was no mark on the child. McKay was still a sickly child, however. A Wintun woman, Mary Wright, came to Taylor and told her to take McKay back to the roundhouse. There were only a few people present, and Wright instructed Taylor to take McKay to the center pole, a sacred place. Wright offered one of her beautiful hand-woven baskets to the pole and prepared a feast. She offered these things for McKay and said that she would grow up to be very special.

Some time later Taylor sold the fourteen-year-old McKay to a sixty-two-year-old Calousa man to be his wife. Over the objections of McKay's natural mother, she took McKay to live with the man.

Leadership

McKay is known for her basket making as much as for her healing abilities. The two are actually intertwined, however. She began basket making at a very early age and displayed an amazing ability to handle willow rods, cattail cane, sedge toots, and redbud bark. She began by making small, intricately designed coiled basketry without ever having seen a design. Grandma Taylor recognized the beauty and uniqueness of McKay's baskets and suggested that she sell them to visitors. McKay told Taylor that in her dreams, the spirit told her that she was not to do that.

McKay continued to suffer from her childhood sickness, and she remained frail and thin. Taylor took her to a number of doctors. Eventually, through a diet of Chinese herbs and other foodstuffs that they found in a Chinese health book and after talking with a Chinese man, McKay put on weight; in fact, she became fat.

McKay was in her teens by this time and was receiving visions and dreaming several times a day. She was enrolled in elementary school long enough to learn the alphabet, spell and write her name, and do simple math problems.

She could not concentrate on school lessons, however, because the spirit was all around her, speaking with her, and when she fell asleep, the spirit spoke to her in her dreams. On one occasion, when McKay was fifteen or sixteen years, two spirits appeared to her in the form of a man and a woman, both of whom spoke the Wintun language. The man spoke with her and challenged her to leave her grandmother and follow him. When McKay refused, the woman in the dream told McKay that the man was actually a doctor and had forecast that McKay would be a doctor as well. When McKay returned to her home, she told Grandma Taylor about the visit. Taylor told McKay that she already knew about it and the person who had appeared was a spirit healer, a doctor. Grandma Taylor told McKay that her destiny was to become a doctor and that her basket making was part of her healing power. She said, "What do you think I am training you for? Doctors can do many things. Already you can do special things. Look at your baskets. Each one is a miracle."

Mabel collected sedge and other materials for her baskets as well as herbs for her healing along the banks of Dry Creek near present-day Healdsburg, in northern California.

The making of the baskets was spiritual for McKay, and her baskets are known today for their exquisite style, beauty, and healing power. When asked about weaving baskets she said, "Well, the same thing. Spirit show me everything. Each basket has Dream. . . . I have rules for that."

One of McKay's close friends was a woman by the name of Essie Parrish, who was a Pomo woman about the same age as McKay. Parrish was a powerful healer in her on right and had the ability to cast spells on other people. McKay was trained as a traditional dreamer and sucking doctor. She drew out "poisons," both material and ethereal, from afflicted persons by sucking on the affected area. She used an elderberry clapper and a cocoon rattle when singing her power songs.

Further Reading

Dancin' on Sacred Land: The Putah-Cache Bioregion Project: http://wdsroot.ucdavis.edu/clients/pcbr/where/doslpres.html.

Lyon, William S. *Encyclopedia of Native American Shamanism: Sacred Ceremonies of North America.* 1998. Denver: ABC-CLIO.

McNamee, Gregory "Native Voices," *Tucson Weekly.* March 9–15, 1995. http://www.tucsonweekly.com/tw/03–09–95/review2.htm.

Native American Medicine: http://www.alternativetherapies.com/select/past/45c.html.

Sarris, Gregg. *Mabel McKay: Weaving the Dream.* 1994. Berkeley: University of California Press.

Ruby Modesto

Full Name at Birth: Nesha ("Woman of Mystery")
Birth: 1913, on the Martinez Reservation, California
Death: April 7, 1980, on the Martinez Reservation, California
Education: began school at age ten; no other information available
Leadership Position: Cahuilla medicine woman

Summary

Ruby Modesto was born on the Martinez Reservation in the Coachella Valley of present-day California. At the age of ten, she received her life's calling, to be a Cahuilla *pul*, or medicine woman. As a *pul*, Ruby specialized in healing individuals possessed by demons. Ruby claimed that because of her unusual powers, she cast out demons with the power and assistance of the Creator. Ruby also had an extensive knowledge of herbs and plants and used them in her healing ceremonies. Respected for her knowledge of Desert Cahuilla culture and traditions, Ruby taught Cahuilla language on the reservation and was a guest lecturer at colleges in the area. She also served as an information to anthropologist Guy Mount.

Early Life

Ruby Modesto was raised in a traditional Cahuilla family steeped in the tradition of shamanism. Family members, who were *puvulam* or shamans, included her father, grandfather, great-grandfather, and a number of uncles. Her grandfather, Francisco, was a clan chief, or *net*, who held the responsibility of preserving the clan's history, culture, ceremonies, and songs. Francisco was also in charge of the ceremonial chamber used for meditation and councils, and at a young age he taught Ruby about Umnáah, the Creator of the Cahuilla. Her grandfather was also a powerful medicine man or shaman, called a *pul*. A *pul* possessed the power to dream and to heal. Ruby was also in close contact with her Uncle Charlie, a powerful *pul*. In Cahuilla society, *puls* were almost always men; however, it was believed that Umnáah gave selected people the power to become a *pul* while still in the womb. Ruby was once such person.

Ruby received a power ally, or helper, at the age of ten through a process of deep dreaming, as opposed to the traditional manner of using datura or jimsonweed for a vision-inducing trance state. Although Ruby experienced her dream and obtained her power helper at a young age, she did not come into her full power as a *pul* until she was a grown woman, following the death of her mother.

Leadership

Ruby Modesto was born on the Martinez Reservation in the Coachella Valley of present-day California. Her mother was a Serrano Indian from the Morongo Reservation, and her father was Desert Cahuilla from the Coachella Valley. Her father was a member of the Dog Clan, and therefore Ruby was a member as well. The Dog Clan was one of the extended family groups that formed the basis of Cahuilla social structure and received its name because the men were good hunters, like dogs, and always brought home something to eat. Modesto grew up learning the traditional ways of her father's people and did not speak English or attend school until after she was ten years of age. At the age of ten, Ruby also received the calling for her life and her dream helper, *Ahswit*, the eagle. As a youngster, she dreamed to such a deep level that her soul became lost in her dream. She required the help of her Uncle Charlie, a shaman, to end the coma-like state she had been in for several days. In Ruby's words:

> I Dreamed to the 13th level. The way you do this is by remembering to tell yourself to go to sleep in your 1st level ordinary dream. You consciously tell yourself to lay down and go to sleep. Then you dream a second dream. This is the 2nd level and the prerequisite for real

Dreaming . . . During Dreaming the soul goes out of the body, so you have to be careful.

When I dreamed to the 13th level that first time, I was young and didn't know how to get back. Usually I only dream to the 2nd or 3rd levels. But that time I kept having different dreams and falling asleep and going to another dream level. That was where I met my helper, *Ahswit*, the eagle. (Walker, 120)

Ruby's mother took her to the Moravian church on the Martinez Reservation, where she was a practicing Christian for many years. As she matured and was drawn more and more into the world of Cahuilla shamanism, she realized that she had to make a choice. Christianity taught that a *pul* gets power from the devil, and Ruby did not believe that. Eventually she chose to be a *pul* rather than pursue Christianity.

Puls were considered to be the most powerful force visible to Cahuilla people. They had the power to heal, kill, or make a person sick and could manipulate a person against his or her own will. As a *pul*, Ruby chose the path of good over evil and specialized in healing individuals possessed by demons. Ruby claimed that because of her unusual powers, she could see demons through spiritual vision and cast them out with the power of *Ahswit* and Umnáah. Ruby also had an extensive knowledge of herbs and plants and used them in her healing ceremonies. Ruby believed, as did many other Indian people, that plants and animals had spirits and that she could induce the spirits to aid her in her curing rituals.

Ruby married David Modesto and had three children. After that time, she walked in two worlds—one as a wife and mother and another as a healer. She considered her husband as her companion but considered herself bound spiritually to Umnáah and her calling as a healer.

In 1976, Ruby became a consultant to an anthropology student named Guy Mount. She taught him the ways of a *pul* as well as Desert Cahuilla traditions, stories, history, and medicinal herbs used by southern California Indians during childbirth. Their friendship resulted in collaboration on a book titled *Not for Innocent Ears: Spiritual Traditions of a Desert Cahuilla Medicine Woman*, which she considered to be a doorway into a magical world of spiritual powers. Ruby believed that some non-Indians would benefit from her experiences but recognized that most white people would not understand and accept her stories. "Very few white people know how to See," she explained, "nor are they willing to learn" (Walker, 123–24).

Further Readings

Hirschfelder, Arlene, and Paulette Molin. *The Encyclopedia of Native American Religions*. 1992. New York: Facts on File.

Modesto, Ruby. *Not for Innocent Ears: Spiritual Traditions of a Desert Cahuilla Medicine Woman*. 1994. New York: Facts on File.

Walker, Paul Robert. *American Indian Lives: Spiritual Leaders*. 1994. New York: Facts on File.

Mon'Hin Thin Ge

Full Name at Birth: Mon'Hin Thin Ge
Birth: ca. 1800, place unknown
Death: late 1800s, place unknown

Education: no formal schooling

Leadership Position: Omaha spiritualist and keeper of the Sacred Tent of War

Summary

Mon'Hin Thin Ge was an Omaha spiritualist who flourished during the historical period when Indian Nations of the Great Plains region prospered. The Omaha adopted the horse when it was reintroduced by the Spanish in the late 1700s, and they developed several traits shared by other Plains tribes. Part of each year they ranged over wide areas of the Plains in search of the huge buffalo herds and lived in hide tepees when on the hunt. They fought against traditional Indian enemies, particularly the Lakota, who encroached on their hunting areas.

The Omaha developed a complex social structure that included age-graded societies (members advanced from one society to another with age cohorts), clubs, and secret organizations open to only a select few tribal members. Other societies were open to everyone in the tribe. Membership in tribal organizations included the knowledge of esoteric ritual, symbolism, song, and dance. Membership in restricted organizations also determined the individual tribal member's ranking and prestige within the tribe.

The sacred beliefs of the Omaha focused on three Sacred Tents: the tent set apart for the Sacred Pole, the Sacred Tent of War, and the Sacred Tent of the White Buffalo. Mon'Hin Thin Ge was the last keeper of the Omaha's Tent: of War. In 1884 he turned over the contents of the Tent to ethnologists Alice Fletcher and Francis La Flesche for placement in the Peabody Museum at Harvard University. In 1888, the contents of another Sacred Tent, the Omaha Sacred Pole, were turned over to the Peabody Museum by their keeper, Shu'Denaci.

Early Life

There is no record of Mon'Hin Thin Ge's early years. Born into the Omaha Nation in the early 1800s, he would have lived in the eastern Great Plains region in what today is northeast Nebraska. The Omaha people believe in a strong relationship between man and the visible powers of the heavens and in the interdependence of all forms of life. Accordingly, on the eighth day following his birth, Mon'Hin Thin Ge would have undergone a ceremony in which an Omaha priest would have asked supplication to the powers of the heavens, the air, and the earth for the safety of Mon'Hin Thin Ge as he traveled a rugged road stretching over the stages of infancy, youth, manhood, and old age.

Upon reaching puberty, Mon'Hin Thin Ge went through a No' zhi zho ceremony, which translates literally as "to stand sleeping." This ceremony was a vision quest ceremony and one of the most significant in his life. For four days and nights, Mon'Hin Thin Ge fasted and prayed in an effort to enter into a personal relationship with the mysterious powers of the universe. He uttered a prayer called Wako' da giko ("to weep from loss") and prayed for supernatural aid. In keeping with Omaha belief, Mon'Hin Thin Ge never related the details of his vision; however, it dictated the role he was to serve among his people: that of the keeper of the Sacred War Tent.

Leadership

Mon'Hin Thin Ge was born when the Omaha were a powerful Indian Nation. They warred with their traditional enemy, the Lakota, over rights to hunting areas, yet a smallpox epidemic brought to the Omaha by white traders in 1802 had a far more devastating impact on the Omaha people. The population dropped from approximately 3,500, to fewer than 300.

The Nation and its leadership were experiencing other pressures as well. The U.S. federal government relocation policy of the 1830s terminated Indian ownership of lands east of the Mississippi River, and the Omaha were forced west. In 1854, at the time the original Indian Territory was reorganized, the Omaha ceded all their lands west of the Missouri River to the United States, and they were settled on "The Village of the 'Make-Believe' White Men," the Omaha Reservation in Nebraska. In 1865, the Omaha were forced to cede the northern part of that reservation to the federal government as Civil War reparations and for the relocation and settlement of the Winnebago Nation.

The changing conditions among the Omaha people brought about by warfare, disease, and relocation caused knowledge of the ceremonies connected with the Omaha Sacred Tents, the heart of their religious tradition, nearly to die out. The tribal societies, song, dance, and ritual were maintained by only a few elder traditionalists. With his advancing age, Mon'Hin Thin Ge feared that his increasing feebleness would cause him to abuse or misuse the sacred objects and that the Omaha would suffer punishment as a result. Because of these fears, he agreed to relinquish the contents of the Sacred Tent of War, which included an ancient cedar tree and other venerated objects, to ethnologists Alice Fletcher and Francis La Flesche. In so doing, Mon'Hin Thin Ge stated,

These sacred articles have been in the keeping of my family for many generations; no one knows how long. My sons have chosen a path different from that of their fathers. I had thought to have these articles buried with me but if you will place them where they will be safe and where my children can look on them when they wish to think of the past and of the way their fathers walked, I give them into your keeping. Should there come a time when I might crave to see once more these things that have been my fathers, I would like to be permitted to do so. I know that the members of my family are willing that I should do this thing, and no others have a right to question my action. There are men in the tribe who will say hard things of me because or this act but I think it best to do so as I am doing.

Fletcher and La Flesche wrote about Mon'Hin Thin Ge and the other Omaha holy men and the sacred objects entrusted to their care in *The Omaha Tribe*.

In 1989, the sacred pole, the most venerated of all Omaha religious manifestations, was returned to the Omaha tribe. Other objects including those from the Sacred Tent of War have also been returned by the Peabody Museum.

Further Reading

Champagne, Duane, ed. *The Native North American Almanac: A Reference Work on Native North Americans in the United States and Canada*. 1994. Detroit: Gale Research.

Fletcher, Alice C., and Francis La Flesche. *The Omaha Tribe*. 1911. Washington, D.C.: Smithsonian Institution.

Hirschfelder, Arlene, and Paulette Molin. *The Encyclopedia of Native American Religions: An Introduction*. 1992. New York: Facts on File.

Native Peoples of the Plains: The Return of the Sacred Pole: http://twist.lib.uiowa.edu/plainsind/spole.html.

Ridington, Robin, and Dennis Hastings. *Blessings for a Long Time: The Sacred Pole of the Omaha Tribe*. 1997. Lincoln: University of Nebraska Press.

Thornton, Russell. *American Indian Holocaust and Survival: A Population History Since 1492*. 1987. Norman: University of Oklahoma Press.

Waldman, Carl, and Molly Braun. *Encyclopedia of Native American Tribes*. 1988. New York: Facts on File.

Mountain Wolf Woman

Full Name at Birth: Mountain Wolf Woman

Birth: April 1884 at her grandfather's home on the East Fork River in Wisconsin

Death: November 9, 1960, at Black River Falls, Wisconsin

Education: attended a government school for Indians in Tomah, Wisconsin, from ages nine to eleven, and the Lutheran Mission School at Wittenberg, Wisconsin, for an unspecified but short period of time

Leadership Position: Winnebago spiritual leader

Summary

Mountain Wolf Woman was a Winnebago healer whose life included participation in three religions; she was steeped in the traditional cosmology of the Winnebago religion; she accepted Christianity and was baptized while attending a Lutheran mission school; and she found in the peyote religion a deep sense of spiritual identification and fulfillment that sustained her throughout her life.

Early Life

Si´ga´xunuga was born into the Thunder Clan of the Winnebago Nation, her father's clan. When she was quite young, she became very ill, and it was feared that she might die. Her mother visited an old Indian woman healer and gave Si´ga´xunuga over to her to be healed. The old woman's name was Wolf Woman, and she treated Si´ga´xunuga and told her

Mountain Wolf Woman. With the permission of the Jackson County Historical Society of Wisconsin, Black River Falls, WI 54615.

that she would live a long life. The woman then gave Si´ga´xunuga her healing powers and a new holy name, Xeháchwinga. She said that it meant "to make a home in a bluff or a mountain, as the wolf does." Translated into English her name became Mountain Wolf Woman.

Xeháchwinga and her family relocated frequently, living in Winnebago villages along the Mississippi and the Missouri rivers, particularly in Nebraska, and Wisconsin. She had three brothers—Crashing Thunder, Strikes Standing, and Big Winnebago—and four sisters—White Thunder, Bald Eagle, Hak´sigaga, and Distant Flashes Standing. Her childhood ended abruptly when she was taken from the Lutheran mission school to participate in a marriage arranged by her brothers against her wishes but in keeping with Winnebago tradition. She vowed that her children would choose their own spouses.

Leadership

Mountain Wolf Woman was a Winnebago religious practitioner who was immersed in three religious traditions; the medicine lodge, Christianity, and peyotism. She was introduced to the traditional Winnebago cosmology by her father, who told her and her sisters that following a successful deer hunt, they were to express thanks to the spirit of the animal by offering tobacco to the animals, trees, stars, and moon, thus nurturing the favor of beings in return for the gift of meat. They concluded the ritual by fasting, and the Winnebago girls experienced humility and learned the importance of gratitude for gifts generously given and gratefully returned. Mountain Wolf Woman left her first husband because of his extreme jealousy and married Bad Soldier, a member of the Bear or Soldier clan.

Mountain Wolf Woman and her husband learned of peyote among the Nebraska Winnebago in the spring of 1908.

At the urging of her sister, she used peyote medicinally to ease the pain of the birth of her third child. Following an easy birth, she realized its medicinal benefits and became a follower. They also used peyote with Oglala Lakota people in Martin, South Dakota, where she was adopted by a family who had lost a daughter. She recalled that "every Saturday we used to have a peyote meeting. We had a gunny-sack full of peyote and that is why we were able to have meetings every Saturday. . . . There were all kinds of Winnebago, Nebraskans and a lot of Wisconsin Indians. It was very pleasant" (Stewart, 160–61).

Mountain Wolf Woman observed both the Half-Moon and Cross-Fire versions of the peyote ceremony. The Half-Moon version is so named for the crescent-shaped altar on which the chief peyote button rests. The Cross-Fire peyote ceremony comes from the Big Moon ceremony and uses a larger horseshoe-shaped altar. Both ceremonies emphasized the divine role of peyote and its power to teach and heal; both opposed the use of liquor and believed that peyote destroyed the taste for it; and in both peyote was eaten to concentrate and to learn, not for the purpose of achieving visions.

It was while attending a peyote meeting that she experienced a vision that was to change her life. Mountain Wolf Woman had eaten perhaps twenty peyote buttons and was meditating. In her dream, the world was black, the clouds came whirling, and the ground kept caving in. People were running, stumbling, and rolling over and over. She thought to herself, "Where are they fleeing? Nowhere on this earth is there any place to run to. There is not any place for life. . . . Jesus is the only place to flee to. . . . Then I see Jesus standing there. I saw that he had one hand raised high. The right hand, high in the air." She felt that she was to pray, and when she did, she was transformed into an angel. She wanted to fly away but could not because her time on earth was not yet completed. Following this experience, she realized that the peyote religion was holy.

Following her vision, Mountain Wolf Woman became a peyote practitioner. She and her fellow peyotist put up tepees, and people came from great distances as her reputation as a peyote leader spread. She traveled to Nebraska and held peyote ceremonies that lasted for days. Mountain Wolf Woman and her followers were not welcomed everywhere, and peyote ceremonies were often disrupted by those who saw it as the work of the devil. She persisted, however, to preach that it was a holy religion that embraced Jesus Christ and would heal the Indian people of their addiction to alcohol and other bad behaviors. She sometimes converted those who came to disrupt the peyote meetings.

In addition to being a peyote practitioner, Mountain Wolf Woman obtained the knowledge of traditional Winnebago healing from her grandfather, Náqiwankwa´xo´piniga, who was a traditional medicine man. Náqiwankwa´xo´piniga feared that the knowledge of Winnebago healing was going to disappear at his death; however, because of Mountain Wolf Woman's special calling, he passed on his knowledge to her. With this power and knowledge, she became a Winnebago medicine woman and practiced traditional medicine cures throughout her life.

Mountain Wolf Woman's deepest belief was in the peyote religion, for it was through peyote that she had seen Jesus. She remained a peyote practitioner until the end of her life and financed a meeting in 1958 to commemorate the fiftieth anniversary of peyote's introduction in Wisconsin. Mountain Wolf Woman died on November 9, 1960, a short time before her life story was published as *Mountain Wolf Woman: Sister of Crashing Thunder*, edited by her adopted niece Nancy Oestreich Lurie. Her family included eleven children, three of whom had died, and at least thirty-eight grandchildren and nine great great-grandchildren.

Further Readings

Calloway, Colin G. *First Peoples: A Documentary Survey of American Indian History*. 1999. New York: St. Martin's Press.

Champagne, Duane, ed. *The Native North American Almanac*. 1994. Detroit: Gale Research.

Hirschfelder, Arlene, and Paulette Molin. *The Encyclopedia of Native American Religions*. 1992. New York: Facts on File.

Hittman, Michael. *Wovoka and the Ghost Dance*. 1990. Ashland, Ohio: Book Masters.

Lurie, Nancy. *Mountain Wolf Woman: Sister of Crashing Thunder: The Autobiography of a Winnebago Indian*. 1961. Ann Arbor: University of Michigan Press.

Mountain Wolf Woman: Sister of Crashing Thunder: http://www.press.umich.edu/titles/06109.html.

Stewart, Omer C. *Peyote Religion: A History*. 1990. Norman: University of Oklahoma Press.

Nakaidoklini

Full Name at Birth: Nakaidoklini (Nakaydoklunni, Nocadelklinny, Nockay-Delklinne, Nock-ay-det-klinne, Babbyduclone, Bardudeclenny, Bobby-ti-klen-ni)

Birth: date and place of birth unknown, but described by a physician in 1875 as being approximately fifty years old

Death: August 30, 1881, at Cibicu Creek, Arizona

Education: no formal education

Leadership Position: White Mountain Apache medicine man and tribal chief

Summary

Nakaidoklini was a White Mountain Apache medicine man and tribal chief who preached a religion that some historians view as a precursor to the Ghost Dance religion taught by the Paiute prophet Wovoka.* In 1881, Nakaidoklini preached the resurrection of the dead and a return to the days when the Apache controlled their traditional homelands free from Euro-American contact. He instructed followers of his religion to bring about the Apache revitalization and invoke the spirits by means of a dance, anticipating Wovoka's Ghost Dance.

Nakaidoklini's message of the Apache return to power spread fears of an Indian uprising in the Southwest and resulted in an increase in military troops under the leadership of Colonel Eugene Asa Carr. The August 30, 1881, arrest, shooting, and death of Nakaidoklini led to the Battle of Cibicu Creek, where Colonel Carr's command suffered heavy casualties. Colonel Carr and his detachment barely escaped annihilation by a large number of Apache attackers, many of whom had participated in the hunting down and arrest of Nakaidoklini.

Early Life

There are no written records of Nakaidoklini's early years. Because of his later stature as a White Mountain medicine man, it can be safely assumed that he was a full-blood Apache raised in the Apache traditional homelands known as Apacheria, present-day Arizona. Nakaidoklini and his contemporaries experienced the invasion of Apacheria when gold was discovered in California in 1848 and then in their homelands in 1852. The Apache were militarily inclined, having previously been at war with the Spanish and with Mexico. They viewed Euro-Americans as another power attempting to subvert their way of life, to capture, sell, or enslave Apache men, women, and children; and ultimately to kill them or remove them from their traditional homes. Nakaidoklini's role as a medicine man who encouraged a revitalization of Apache lifeways and the destruction of the white interlopers reflects this tension.

Leadership

Nakaidoklini was a prophet among the White Mountain band of Apache who lived on the White Mountain Indian Reservation in present-day Arizona. He flourished as a prophet in 1881 when he introduced a new dance that had been given to him by the Creator. If performed as instructed by Nakaidoklini, the new dance was believed to have the power to return life to the dead. During the dance performance, Nakaidoklini was instructed to stand at the center of the dancers; both men and women were then to arrange themselves in files, as spokes in a wheel facing him. Nakaidoklini was instructed to bless the participants with a sacred pollen called hoddentin that was made from the tule plant or cattail rush. John G. Bourke, an army officer who later fought against the Apache, stated that Nakaidoklini "drilled the savages in a particular dance, the like of which had never been seen among them."

In June 1881, Nakaidoklini announced that he would return two chiefs to life after he had received gifts of horses, saddles, blankets, cattle, and food to complete the resurrections. His followers complied, and he held the dance near his home in August 1881. When the two chiefs did not rise from the dead, Nakaidoklini announced that "the spirits had notified him that the dead warriors could not return to the country until the whites had left it." He announced that the whites must leave by the time of the annual corn harvest, which was held in August or September.

Colonel Carr, the commander at Fort Apache, received a report of the prophet and the growing support for his new religion. On August 4 and 5, Nakaidoklini held large dances near Fort Apache to give the military and civilian personnel an opportunity to see how popular the dance had become. White miners and settlers saw the religion of Nakaidoklini as dangerous and conducive to rebellion. Colonel Carr now feared that Nakaidoklini was fomenting an Indian insurrection and attempted to lure him to the agency. The attempt failed. On August 10, the Apache Indian agent Jo-

seph Tiffany wired Colonel Carr and stated that he had been informed that the Indians had said that if the dead did not rise up, it was because of the continuing white presence and that "the whites must go." On August 13, Colonel Carr received a telegram from Major General Orlando Bolivar Wilcox, the top commander in the Military Department of Arizona. General Wilcox directed him to arrest Nakaidoklini "if you deem it necessary, to prevent trouble."

On August 30, Colonel Carr and a detachment of seventy-nine U.S. cavalry, twenty-three White Mountain Apache scouts, and nine civilians moved into Apacheria to seek out and arrest Nakaidoklini, who was believed to be hiding at Cibicu Creek in present-day Arizona. Anxious to avoid a full-scale Indian war and believing Nakaidoklini to be the instigator of the current unrest, Agent Tiffany gave instructions to "have Nakaidoklini arrested or killed, or both." Colonel Carr's Apache scouts were successful in locating Nakaidoklini's camp and during a surprise attack Colonel Carr was successful in arresting Nakaidoklini.

Once Colonel Carr had Nakaidoklini in custody, he instructed his troops to set up camp outside the Apache village. About one hundred followers of Nakaidoklini then attacked the encampment. During the battle, Nakaidoklini was killed. The exact details of his death are unclear. The trumpeter William O. Benites claims that Nakaidoklini had been wounded, and he killed him with a shot in the neck. Lieutenant Wallis O. Clark informed a newspaper reporter that soldiers found Nakaidoklini alive "after firing the shots into him" and that they killed the medicine man by crushing his skull with rifles. Colonel Carr's Apache scouts, now fearing for their lives, mutinied, killing an army captain. This action then precipitated the battle of Cibicu Creek on August 31. Colonel Carr's command suffered heavy losses following this engagement. He and his troops retreated to Fort Apache, where they were again attacked by Nakaidoklini's followers.

The killing of Nakaidoklini prompted additional uprising by the Apache, and the U.S. Army continued to pursue its policy of capturing and concentrating the Apache Indian people on Indian reservations. The Apache resisted as long as possible, and the Apache wars continued until August 1886.

Further Reading

Apache Nightmare: http://library.ncsu.edu/marion/AJW-8598.

Apache Wars:http://www.historychannel tours.com/tours/thc/apache wrsov. html.

Axelrod, Alan. *Chronicle of the Indian Wars from Colonial Times to Wounded Knee.* 1993. Englewood Cliffs, NJ: Prentice Hall.

Hirschfelder, Arlene, and Paulette Molin. *The Encyclopedia of Native American Religions.* 1992. New York: Facts on File.

Waldman, Carl. *Who Was Who in Native American History.* 1990. New York: Facts on File.

Washburn, Wilcomb E. 1988. *Handbook of North American Indians, Vol. 4.* Washington, D.C.: Smithsonian Institution.

Neolin (Delaware Prophet) ("The Enlightened One")

Full Name at Birth: Neolin (Delaware Prophet) ("The Enlightened One")

Birth: ca. 1720; place unknown

Death: date and place unknown

Education: no formal education

Leadership Position: Delaware (Lenape) spiritual leader

Summary

Neolin was an important eighteenth-century American Indian prophet who claimed that he communicated with the Master of Life, who had given him a message for all Indians to bring about a united Indian country. He told Indian people to return to traditional ways and abandon all customs that came from whites. Additionally, they were to abstain from the alcoholic beverages that had contributed to their diminished numbers and cultural destruction. He told the people that the Great Spirit would assist them in their struggles against their enemies and in recovering their losses. Pontiac, an important Ottawa leader, recognized the pan-Indian following that the Prophet had gathered and supported his teachings as a means of forming a multitribal military alliance that Pontiac believed could push the English out of Indian Territory in the Great Lakes region.

Early Life

As with many other religious leaders of the early American period, very little is known of Neolin's early life. The first recorded histories begin in 1762 when he was living in the village of Tuscarawas on the Muskingum River in present-day Ohio. He traveled among Native people with a message he had received from the Great Spirit and delivered a message to the Indian people of the Old Northwest that sought to restore balance and harmony to a world that had become chaotic.

Leadership

Neolin rose to prominence as a Prophet during the early 1760s, a time of turmoil and uncertainty for Indian people in the Great Lakes region of the present-day United States. The French and Indian War had concluded in December 1759, and the English now threatened trade, military, and diplomatic domination over Indian people. The French had transferred their claims east of the Mississippi River to the British, and the British had gained a monopoly over the fur trade south of the Great Lakes. The British now controlled the distribution of trade goods such as guns, cloth, and other manufactured goods that the Indians had become dependent on. They also threatened to establish military control over the Ohio and Great Lakes region by occupying the old French forts, including the important fort at Detroit. The Indians were rapidly becoming disillusioned with the authoritarian, repressive policy adopted by the victorious British regime, and a prominent Ottawa chief by the name of Pontiac hoped for the return of the French to help drive the British from their lands.

Neolin was the spiritual answer for those determined to fight the English. He had communicated with the Great Spirit in one of several ways. Some oral histories state that Neolin died and visited heaven, where he was given a message for regaining the spiritual and political salvation of the Indian people. Neolin claimed that he had been led by a beautiful woman wearing snow-white clothing to meet the Master of Life, who had given him a message for all Indians to bring about a united Indian country.

The Master of Life told Neolin that Indian people must return to traditional ways and abandon all customs that came from whites. Still another history says that Neolin had a vision in which he was given a message to deliver to Indian people. During his vision, he received instructions that Indian people were to abandon the customs adopted from the whites and were to return to Native traditions. Additionally, they were to abstain from the alcoholic beverages that had contributed to their diminished numbers and cultural destruction.

In his preachments, Neolin combined Native traditions and Christian revivalism. He told the Indian people that because they had given up the traditions and lifestyle of their ancestors and traded and accepted the goods of the Europeans, their path to heaven was blocked. Concepts of heaven and the strong emphasis on personal salvation were included in his message and were probably borrowed from the Christian religion. Neolin called on Indians to join in a united rejection of all Europeans as well as their trade goods so they could once again enjoy a happy and prosperous life. He told his people they should not fight among themselves, to act as brothers to one another, and to give up drinking alcohol. To emphasize the loss of Indian lands, the Master of Life gave Neolin a special map, drawn on animal skin that showed the lands that Indian people had lost to the Europeans. The map was reproduced and distributed among Indian people to serve a reminder of his spiritual teachings and the perfidy of the white man.

Neolin's message had reached as far west as the Illinois country by 1763, where an important chief of the Ottawa Nation, Pontiac, was among those who adopted his teachings. His ideas were nativist and had considerable power of their own. The message of rejection of the British resonated well with Pontiac, and he began to see the possibility of transforming the resentment of the British by the Ottawa, Chippewa, and Potawatomi into action. Pontiac believed that with Neolin's followers and with the aid of the French still present in the area, it might be possible to defeat British military power at Detroit and perhaps drive the British out of the Great Lakes region altogether. The potential of Pontiac's movement built on the spiritual revitalization offered by the Delaware Prophet and a growing widespread Indian desire to drive the British from their lands.

Neolin's message spread to other tribal groups in the region and influenced them to unite with Pontiac against the British. Pontiac was genuinely inspired by Neolin's message but changed the message to meet his military needs. Neolin's teaching prohibited the use of European trade goods; however, Pontiac believed that the Indians should use guns to drive the British from their lands. On May 9, 1763, Pontiac himself led the attack on Fort Detroit and signaled the beginning of an American Indian protest that would ultimately include attacks on all British forts west of Niagara. The siege lasted six months and included almost a thousand Indian warriors. In October 1763, Pontiac received word that the war between the British and the French was officially ended. Without the French allies, Pontiac could no longer sustain the siege and on October 30 withdrew his men into present-day Illinois.

Little more was written about Neolin in the aftermath of the siege on Fort Detroit and in 1765 the Delaware Prophet disappeared from the pages of recorded history. His message did not die, however. Other famous prophets such as Tenskwatawa,* the Shawnee Prophet, would resurrect Neolin's message of rejection of European trade goods and creation of a pan-Indian alliance.

Further Reading

Ballantine, Betty, and Ian Ballantine, eds. *The Native Americans: An Illustrated History*. 1993. Atlanta: Turner Publishing.

Calloway, Colin G. *First Peoples: A Documentary Survey of American Indian History*. 1999. New York: St. Martin's Press.

Hirschfelder, Arlene, and Paulette Molin. *The Encyclopedia of Native American Religions*. 1992. New York: Facts on File.

Trigger, Bruce G., and Wilcomb E. Washburn. eds. *The Cambridge History of the Native Peoples of the Americas, Vol. 1, North America Part 1*. 1996. Cambridge: Cambridge University Press.

Washburn, Wilcomb E. *Handbook of North American Indians, Vol. 4*. Washington, D.C.: Smithsonian Institution.

Weslager, C. A. *The Delaware Indians: A History*. 1990. New Brunswick, N.J.: Rutgers University Press.

Ne-sha-pa-na-cumin (Charles Journeycake)

Full Name at Birth: Ne-sha-pa-na-cumin

Birth: December 16, 1817, on the Upper Sandusky River in Ohio

Death: January 3, 1894; buried near Alluwe, Oklahoma

Education: no record of formal education

Leadership Position: mixed Delaware Baptist preacher and principal chief of the Delaware Nation

Summary

Ne-sha-pa-na-cumin was born on the upper Sandusky River in present-day Ohio, the son of Chief Solomon Journeycake and his Delaware-French wife, Sally Williams Journeycake. In 1827, Ne-sha-pa-na-cumin was among the members of the Delaware Nation who were removed from their homelands to be relocated to the present-day state of Kansas, then part of the newly designated Indian Territory. The federal government encouraged tribal groups to cede their homelands voluntarily and move west to avoid further contact and conflict with the westward spread of the American nation. The new Indian Territory was to be established as their homeland, "for as long as the rivers flow and the grasses grow," free from contact with the land-hungry Anglo-Americans.

Ne-sha-pa-na-cumin was baptized in the Indian Territory in 1833 and became the first Delaware west of the Mississippi River to be converted to Christianity. In 1866, a treaty allowed the Kansas Delaware to become U.S. citizens and remain in Kansas or retain their tribal affiliation and remove to the Cherokee Nation as the Registered Delaware. Those who chose to remove to the Cherokee Nation were paid $1 an acre for their lands. By this time, Ne-sha-pa-na-cumin had been chosen as a subchief of the Delaware Nation, and he and three other Delaware leaders signed the document for removal of the Delaware. The sum of $157,000 was held in trust for the Delaware by the federal government, and interest on the capital was to be paid in annual annuities.

On January 21, 1890, six prominent Delaware empowered Chief Ne-sha-pa-na-cumin to act as the tribe's agent or attorney-in-fact in negotiations with the U.S. government to obtain additional funds due them. He was chosen as principal chief of the Delaware, upsetting many of the Delaware traditionalists who did not regard him as their principal chief because he had been appointed at the behest of U.S. Indian agent Fielding Johnson, who claimed that he had recommended Ne-sha-pa-na-cumin for the position of subchief, not principal chief.

In addition to being a remarkable spiritual leader, Ne-sha-pa-na-cumin was an astute political leader of his people. He was a negotiator and signatory on U.S. Treaties with the Delaware in 1854, 1861, and 1866. In the 1890s, Ne-sha-pa-na-cumin pursued a court case through the U.S. Supreme Court and helped win a Delaware claim against the Cherokees and the federal government for compensation from land sales to white settlers in both Kansas and the Indian Territory. Following Ne-sha-pa-na-cumin's death in 1894, no elections were held to name a successor.

Early Life

Ne-sha-pa-na-cumin was born on the upper Sandusky River in present-day Ohio, the son of Chief Solomon Journeycake and his Delaware-French wife, Sally Williams Journeycake, and was educated in both Indian and white customs. His mother served as an interpreter for Methodist missionaries among the nearby Wyandot Nation. She converted to Christianity in 1827 and died on February 6, 1859, at the approximate age of seventy-six. In 1827, Ne-sha-pa-na-cumin, along with the remainder of the Delaware nation, was removed from his homeland and began the long removal journey to Kansas. Ne-sha-pa-na-cumin was baptized in the Indian Territory in 1833.

Leadership

Ne-sha-pa-na-cumin was a mixed Delaware trapper, guide, preacher, and tribal leader who became a Baptist at the age of sixteen. He worked as a trapper and a guide and on one occasion was asked by a group of Delaware hunters to lead them on a hunting expedition because of his reputation of leading successful expeditions. Ne-sha-pa-na-cumin agreed to the request but insisted that the Indians attend prayers at camp every night and morning and spend the Sabbath in rest and religious exercises. The men not only kept their promises to be present at prayers, but also participated in singing hymns and listened while Ne-sha-pa-na-cumin read the scriptures to them.

Ne-sha-pa-na-cumin was one of many devout Christians among the modernist Delaware. The term *modernist*, as opposed to *traditionalist*, is used to identify those Delaware who were in favor of voluntary removal west of the Mississippi River. Ne-sha-pa-na-cumin was one such modernist and is known to have preached from the pulpit for as long as an hour and a half at one time. He was a devout Christian and exerted a strong influence on improving the moral behavior of the Delaware and in teaching temperance. He was also one of the charter members of the Baptist mission in Kansas.

During the 1830s, many Delaware voluntarily relocated west of the Mississippi River to what was originally the northern part of the Indian Territory, present-day Kansas. In the 1860s, the Kansas Delaware were again being pressured by white settlers to relocate. Ne-sha-pa-na-cumin, now a subchief of the Delaware Nation, was among the tribal leaders who negotiated with the federal government for a new homeland among the Cherokee in a severely shrunken Indian Territory, the present-day state of Oklahoma. He and his Delaware-French wife, Jane Sosha, had twin daughters Adeline and Emeline, who attended the Baptist mission school about four miles northeast of Edwardsville, Indiana. By 1869, they had settled on a former Cherokee holding in present-day northeastern Oklahoma, where Ne-sha-pa-na-cumin worked as a preacher and farmer. He was recognized as a remarkable spiritual and political leader. An eloquent Christian minister and statesman, he personally baptized the man who had murdered his brother.

Ne-sha-pa-na-cumin's life and reputation were beset by problems internal to the Delaware Nation. In 1861, Kock-a-to-wha, the chief of the Turkey band of Delaware, died. The U.S. Indian agent, Fielding Johnson, recommended that Ne-sha-pa-na-cumin be named as his successor. Ne-sha-pa-na-cumin, however, was of the Wolf band. Nevertheless, he was unanimously confirmed as the new chief, which broke the traditional practice of succession from within clan lines. Agent Johnson claimed that he had recommended Ne-sha-pa-na-cumin only as a subchief; however, the damage was done, and the U.S. influence further divided a nation already split along modernist and traditional lines.

By the 1860s, the Kansas Delaware were again being pressured by white settlers and the U.S. government to relocate. In 1861, Ne-sha-pa-na-cumin and three other Delaware leaders signed a treaty with the Delawares that resulted in the second removal of the Delaware Nation. It is claimed, and probably correctly, that the Delaware did not have legal representation during the treaty discussions and that two of the signers were illiterate. The document itself was drafted by the Department of the Interior, and government lawyers phrased it. Ne-sha-pa-na-cumin was coerced into signing the removal agreement through assurances "that it was in their best interest to do so."

In the 1890s, Ne-sha-pa-na-cumin helped win a Delaware claim against the Cherokees and the federal government for compensation from land sales to white settlers in both Kansas and the Indian Territory. On January 21, 1890, six prominent Delaware leaders empowered Chief Ne-sha-pa-na-cumin to act as the tribe's agent or attorney-in-fact in negotiations with the U.S. government to obtain funds due them for unpaid lands in Kansas, and for timber, ponies, and cattle illicitly taken by white settlers. Following the court victory, the federal government held $900,000 in a trust account for the Delaware. The interest on the capital was paid in annuities, and Delaware families gathered twice a year on Ne-sha-pa-na-cumin's property on Lightning Creek near present-day Alluwe, Oklahoma, where government representatives disbursed the interest payments.

Ne-sha-pa-na-cumin was a remarkable spiritual and political leader and fathered a written constitution guaranteeing freedom and rights for members of the Delaware Nation. Agent Johnson stated in his letter recommending Ne-sha-pa-na-cumin for the position of subchief that he was "one of the most intelligent Indians belonging to the tribe, honest and upright in his dealings deservedly popular with all classes and . . . is beyond the reach of bribery and would look after and protect the interests of the people and particularly the industrial and moral interests of the tribe." Ne-sha-pa-na-cumin was the last chief of the Delaware Indians and was a man of integrity, having a reputation for high moral conduct.

Ne-sha-pa-na-cumin married Jane Sosha, a Delaware woman, in 1837 and they had fourteen children. He died on January 3, 1894, and was buried near Alluwe, Oklahoma. Besides his work as a minister and tribal chief, Ne-sha-pa-na-cumin translated religious tracts and at least one hymnal.

Further Reading

Articles of agreement between the United States and the chiefs and councilors of the Delaware Indians, July 4, 1886. http://digital.library.okstate.edu/kappler/treaties/del0937.htm.

Hirschfelder, Arlene, and Paulette Molin. *The Encyclopedia of Native American Religions.* 1992. New York: Facts on File.

Indian Tribes of Washington County: The Delaware: http://ourworld.compuserve.com/homepages/meadorman/indian.htm.

Love Made Manifest by: Edward M. Cook: 14 Biographies That Constitute "An Aristocracy of Unselfish Service": http://www.vgsales.com/bios.html.

Marks in Time: Delaware Treaty History: Treaty of 1854: http://members.tripod.com/~lenapelady/deltreaty1854.html.

Roark, Harry M. *Charles Journeycake: Indian Statesman and Christian Leader.* 1970. Dallas: Taylor Publishing Company.

Treaty with the Delawares, 1861: http://digital.library.okstate.edu/kappler/treaties/del0814.htm.

Waldman, Carl. *Who Was Who in Native American History*. 1990. New York: Facts on File.

Weslager, C. A., *The Delaware Indian Westward Migration with the Texts of Two Manuscripts (1821–22) Responding to General Lewis Cass's Inquiries About Lanape Culture and Language*. 1978. Wilmington, Del.: Middle Atlantic Press.

Weslager, C. A. *The Delaware Indians: A History*. 1971. New Brunswick, N.J.: Rutgers University Press.

Samson Occum

Full Name at Birth: Occom, Ocum ("On the Other Side")

Birth: 1723, in New London, Connecticut

Death: 1792, in New Stockbridge, New York

Education: attended Moor's Indian Charity School in Connecticut in the mid-1700s

Leadership Position: Mohegan Christian convert; first Indian to preach in England

Summary

Occum was a famous Mohegan Christian Indian who became the first formally trained and ordained Christian Indian minister. He was known as "minister to all the tribes of New England" and "the great Indian man who takes care of Indians." Occum was converted to Christianity in 1741 by Reverend Eleazor Wheelock and educated in Wheelock's family, studying English, Latin, Greek, and Hebrew. In 1749 he moved to Long Island, where he married Mary Montauk, by whom he had ten children. In 1759, Occum was ordained by the Presbyterian church and began serving as minister to the Montauks.

Occum recruited Indian youths on behalf of Reverend Eleazor Wheelock for Moor's Indian Charity School. In 1765, he traveled to England as Wheelock's representative, staying for more than two years, making numerous appearances, and raising considerable funds. In 1769 Moor's Indian Charity School was moved from Connecticut to New Hampshire and chartered as Dartmouth College. Occum soon became disillusioned with Wheelock's new emphasis on educating white missionaries for work with Indian Nations rather than educating the Indians themselves. As a result, Occum began preaching among the Mahicans, Montauks, Narragansets, and other Algonquian peoples in eastern New York. After traveling and preaching throughout southern New England, he helped organize an effort to relocate Indians from Long Island to a religious colony northeast of present-day Syracuse, New York, named Brotherton. The colony of Brotherton became home to a mix of Indians from throughout New England and Long Island. A few years later, Occum established an Indian school to teach children reading and writing.

Early Life

Little is known about Occum's early life. He was born in New London, Connecticut, and was the first student of Eleazor Wheelock, a Christian missionary. Occum himself became a Christian

Mr. Occom's Addreſs

TO

HIS

INDIAN BRETHREN.

On the Day that MOSES PAUL, an Indian, was executed at NEW-HAVEN, on the 2d of SEPTEMBER, 1772,
for the Murder of MOSES COOK.

I.

MY kindred Indians, pray attend and hear,
With great attention and with godly fear;
This day I warn you of that curſed ſin,
That poor, deſpiſed Indians wallow in.

II.

'Tis drunkenneſs, this is the ſin you know,
Has been and is poor Indians overthrow;
'Twas drunkenneſs that was the leading cauſe,
That made poor Moſes break God's righteous Laws.

III.

When drunk he other evil courſes took,
Thus harried on, he murdered Moſes Cook;
Poor Moſes Paul muſt now be hang'd this day,
For wilful murder in a drunken fray.

IV.

A dreadful wo pronounc'd by God on high,
To all that in this ſin do lie;
O deviliſh beaſtly luſt, accurſed ſin,
Has almoſt ſtript us all of every thing.

V.

We've nothing valuable or to our praiſe,
And well may other nations on us gaze;
We have no money, credit or a name,
But what this ſin does turn to our great ſhame.

VI.

Mean are our houſes, and we are kept low,
And almoſt naked, ſhivering we go;
Pinch'd for food and almoſt ſtarv'd we are,
And many times put up with ſtinking fare.

VII.

Our little children hovering round us weep,
Moſt ſtarv'd to death we've nought for them to eat;
All this diſtreſs is juſtly on us come,
For the accurſed uſe we make of rum.

VIII.

A ſhocking, dreadful ſight we often ſee,
Our children young and tender, drunkards be;
More ſhocking yet and awful to behold,
Our women will get drunk both young and old.

IX.

Behold a drunkard in a drunken fit,
Incapable to go, ſtand, ſpeak, or ſit;
Deform'd in ſoul and every other part,
Affecting ſight! enough to melt one's heart.

X.

Sometimes he laughs, and then a hideous yell,
That almoſt equals the poor damn'd in hell;
When drown'd in drink we know not what we do,
We are deſpiſed and ſcorn'd and cheated too.

XI.

On level with the beaſts and far below
Are we when with ſtrong drink we reeling go;
Below the devils when in this ſin we run,
A drunken devil I never heard of one.

XII.

My kindred Indians, I intreat you all,
In this vile ſin never again to fall;
Fly to the blood of CHRIST, for that alone
Can for this ſin and all your ſins atone.

XIII.

Though Moſes Paul is here alive and well,
This night his ſoul muſt be in heaven or hell;
O! do take warning by this awful ſight,
And to a JESUS make a ſpeedy flight!

XIV.

You have no leaſe of your ſhort time you know,
To hell this night you may be forc'd to go;
Oh! do embrace an offer'd CHRIST to-day,
And get a ſealed pardon while you may.

XV.

Behold a loving JESUS, ſee him cry,
With earneſtneſs of ſoul, "Why will ye die?"
My kindred Indians, come juſt as you be,
Then Chriſt and his ſalvation you ſhall ſee.

XVI.

If you go on and ſtill reject Chriſt's call,
'Twill be too late, his curſe will on you fall;
The Judge will doom you to that dreadful place,
In hell, where you ſhall never ſee his face.

Samson Occum's 1772 address to his Indian brethren. Courtesy, American Antiquarian Society.

convert at the age of eighteen. He studied under the tutelage of Wheelock, and when he finished his studies, he became a schoolteacher for a short period of time. It is believed that his mother had worked for Wheelock, and it was through Wheelock's interest in her son that he became a student at Wheelock's charity school.

Occum married Mary Montauk, and in 1759 the Presbyterian church ordained him a minister. While a young man, Occum traveled to England and was the first Indian person to preach in England.

Leadership

When Occum completed his studies under Eleazor Wheelock, he devoted his life to teaching and converting the Indian people to Christianity. Occum was licensed as a Presbyterian minister in Connecticut and ordained in 1759 by the Suffolk presbytery of Long Island. His first parish was among the Montauk Indians, and among his duties was the recruitment of Indian youth for Wheelock's Moor's Indian Charity School. In 1765, Occum traveled to England, where he stayed for two years as Wheelock's representative, preaching and fund raising. He succeeded in raising over £12,000 from wealthy nobles and royals like the earl of Dartmouth and King George. Using the funds raised by Occum, Wheelock moved his Indian school to Hanover, New Hampshire, where it was established as Dartmouth College. When Occum returned to New England, he left Wheelock's ministry because Wheelock had changed his emphasis to training white missionaries to convert Indian people. Occum believed that Indian ministers should be trained to teach and minister to the Indians directly. Regarding Wheelock's change in emphasis, Occum

stated, "Your having so many White Scholars and so few or no Indian Scholars, gives me great Discouragement."

Occum continued to teach and preach among Native Nations from 1768 to 1784. Following the Revolutionary War, he became a minister and teacher to an Algonquian-speaking community of Indian people in eastern New York called Brotherton, made up of several Indian tribes that had accepted Christianity. He was also instrumental in resettling remnants of New England tribes, who became known as the Brotherton Indians.

In 1772, Occom published his *Sermon Preached at the Execution of Moses Paul*, the first example of a literate American Indian, who controlled the publication as well as the public presentation of his speech. The sermon, an indictment of non-Natives for supplying alcohol to American Indians, was popular in its day, going through multiple printings. Occum served as a minister to Brotherton Indians from 1784 until his death in 1792 at New Stockbridge, New York.

Further Reading

Champagne, Duane, ed. *The Native North American Almanac: A Reference Work on Native North Americans in the United States and Canada*. 1994. Detroit: Gale Research.

Hirschfelder, Arlene, and Paulette Molin. *The Encyclopedia of Native American Religions: An Introduction*. 1992. New York: Facts on File.

Mohegan Heroes: http://www.mohegan.nsn.us/tribe/s220content.html.

Preaching to the Indians: http://www.lihistory. com/3/hs326.htm.

Waldman, Carl. *Who Was Who in Native American History*. 1990. New York: Facts on File.

Molly Ockett

Full Name at Birth: Singing Bird (Marie Agathe)
Birth: ca. 1744, near the mouth of the Saco River in present-day New England
Death: August 2, 1816, in Andover, Maine
Education: no formal education
Leadership Position: Abenaki healing woman

Summary

Molly Ockett was a Pigwacket Abenaki healing woman who flourished in the mid- to late 1700s and traveled throughout the upper Androscoggin and Connecticut rivers in the western part of the present-day state of Maine. Referred to as "Androscoggin Valley's Florence Nightingale," her life has been the topic of legend, romance, and mystery. Ockett learned the healing art from her mother, who was killed while Ockett was in her teenage years. She knew the healing properties of roots, barks, berries, and herbs that grew in Wabanaki country. Ockett collected her healing medicines and provided for herself as she been taught by family members. She knew how to create medical potions, salves, and poultices. Once her home village of Pigwacket had been taken over by land-hungry American colonists, Ockett used her herbal remedies whenever and wherever there was a need, treating both Indian and non-Indian patients. For many years, Ockett was the only doctor in the area. Ockett was known to be a fine hunter and used this skill for survival. She traded meat and skins for food, cloth, and other useful goods.

Ockett was married to Captain John Sussup in 1776. Captain Sussup served with the French in 1755 and with the Americans during the Revolutionary War. For several years, she also shared her life with Sabbatis, a Pigwacket Indian man. Sabbatis was very fond of liquor, however, and Ockett eventually parted company with him.

It is believed that Ockett had children by both men. She had a daughter who was sometimes called Molly Sussup. Sussup attended school at Bethel and, like her mother, spoke fluent English. She married a Penobscot Indian man. A son, John Sussup, was born around 1768, and it is believed that Ockett gave birth to another daughter in 1769. In 1798, Ockett treated another of her sons, Paweel, for wounds received in a fight, and another daughter is believed to have married a white man and was living in Derby, Vermont, in 1800. Ockett died in 1816 and was buried in a cemetery in the town of Andover, Maine.

Early Life

Marie Agathe was born in the early 1740s when her parents were camped with their people, the Abenaki, during their summer harvest festival. She was born in the ancient homeland of the Pigwackets. (The name Pigwacket means "the cleared place.") Ockett was given an Abenaki name at birth, but it was soon replaced with the Christian name Marie Agathe, which, because of the pronunciation, was changed to Marie Ockett. In 1744, during the colonial wars, the

Ockett family relocated near Plymouth Country in Massachusetts, where she learned to speak the English language and learned English customs and religious beliefs. Following the colonial war, she and two female companions were held as hostages and were sent to live with English families in Boston. Ockett survived this period of loneliness and alienation and adapted well to life in the home of a Boston judge and his wife. After several years in captivity, Ockett was returned to her people, who had reclaimed their traditional lands at Pigwacket. Ockett found that she had retained the Abenaki language and was fluent in English as well. Both languages would serve her well throughout the remainder of her life.

In 1755, war began between the French and English. A bounty was placed on Indian scalps, and at the age of fifteen, Ockett hid in the bushes during a raid on her home village by Rogers' Rangers, a band of frontiersmen led by Major Robert Rogers. Ockett told a friend of escaping with her family to Canada, where the trail was littered with the skeletons of her people. Ockett's mother and father were killed during this period, and in 1762 Ockett and the few remaining Pigwackets returned to their homeland, only to find it inhabited by white settlers. Ockett and her people built a new village in the vicinity of their old village and adjusted to the presence of the newcomers. They prepared items for trade such as crafts, furs, and tanned hides, for which they received flour, corn, peas, tobacco, sugar, rum, and ammunition.

Leadership

Ockett was born during a tumultuous time in the history of the Abenaki. The French and English seemed to be in a constant state of war. American colonists joined in the revolution against France. France fought a colonial war against England. And both were followed by the American Revolutionary War. All were fought in the homelands of the Wabanaki. The Pigwacket band into which Ockett was born initially attempted to remain neutral, but later her family sided with the French. During the French and Indian War, Ockett's small family band sought safety among the English because they had not fared well under French protection. Ockett and her family left their homeland and went to live under the shadow of English settlers in Plymouth County. It was during this time that Ockett's curiosity led her to learn the English language as well as English customs and religious beliefs. A year after the war's end, Ockett's family was allowed to return; however, Ockett and two companions were held hostage to ensure that the Pigwacket would not turn against the English. Ockett was taken into the home of a Boston judge, where she learned the skills and behavior of a proper English girl. Ockett was miserable and lonely, and longed to return to her family. After approximately one year in captivity and now ten years old, Ockett and her friends were released into the keeping of Wabanaki hunters. Their return home took at least an additional year.

It is unclear who mentored Ockett as she grew into young womanhood and learned her healing arts. While in her early teens, Ockett spent much of her time along the Androscoggin River, where she learned the land, its plants, and their healing secrets. She collected her healing medicines and provided for herself as her ancestors had taught her. Molly was a fine hunter and was described as having a large frame and features. She shared generously with those around her: "When she made a large kill near a settlement she would seek help from the locals in dragging the kill out and shared generously with her assistants."

As the white population increased, Ockett used the skills that she had learned while in captivity and generally got along well with her new white neighbors. She dressed and spoke almost identical to English women. One writer describes her normal dress as a "long one piece dress to her ankles, sleeves cut half way to wrists, fringed at hemline and sleeves, leather band around her forehead with a single white feather in the back." When she searched the forests for her healing medicines, she dressed in the fashion common to Indians and wore a pointed cap, which would have been appropriate for an Abenaki woman of that period. When Ockett was in the Fryeburg vicinity, she camped in a cavelike rock shelter near the base of Jockey Cap Mountain. She kept a birch bark camp at Bethel on the north side of the Androscoggin River. At Andover, she was known for her beautiful baskets and other small crafts that she sold to the locals. Molly's responsibilities as a healer led her to established camp sites at Andover, Massachusetts; Rumford, Maine; Canton, Ohio; Minot, Maine; Paris Hill, Maine; Bethel, Minnesota; and North Conway, Fryeburg, Maine. Ockett claimed the lands of these towns as belonging to her by birthright.

In 1816 Molly was camped on Lake Molechunkamunk (Upper Richardson Lake) twenty miles north of Andover, Maine, with Wabanaki chief Metallak and his small band, when she became ill. She was approximately eighty years old. Metallak brought Ockett to Andover, and Captain Thomas Bragg took over her care. At her request, Bragg made her a wigwam in a stand of pines near his house, and each day he visited her, gave her a meal, and rekindled her fire. Just before her death, she asked to be carried out of her camp and placed on the ground under the sky. She was content that she had lived an honorable life and was beginning her journey to heaven.

Ockett died a ward of the state and was buried in an unmarked grave in Woodland Cemetery in Andover, Maine, where she died. Sometime after her death, a headstone was placed on her grave. The stone reads: "Molly Ockett Baptized Mary Agatha, died in the Christian Faith, August 2d, A.D., 1816. The Last of the Pigwackets."

Further Reading

Lyon, William S. *Encyclopedia of Native American Shamanism: Sacred Ceremonies of North America*. 1998. Denver: ABC-CLIO.

McBride, Bunny. *Women of the Dawn*. 1999. Lincoln: University of Nebraska Press.

Molly Ockett: The Last of the Androscoggins: http://www.avcnet.org/ne-do-ba/bio_moly.html.

Molly Ockett Middle School Survey April 2000: http://www.msad72. k12.me. us/molly.html.

Open Door

See Tenskwatawa

Págits

Full Name at Birth: Págits ("Little Fish")
Birth: date and place unknown
Death: date and place unknown
Education: no formal education
Leadership Position: Northern Ute shaman

Summary

In 1914 a Ute Indian man by the name of Fred Maft served as an interpreter to the anthropologist Frances Densmore, who interviewed the Ute shaman Págits. It is from this interview that we gain an insight into Págit's life and the practice of Ute shamanism.

Among the Ute, there were two methods of treating the sick, both of which included a dependence on supernatural aid. In one method, that practiced by Págits, no material support paraphernalia was employed. In the other method, it was customary to administer herbs or other remedies. Págits explained the distinction between the two methods by saying that a shaman, when treating a sick person, acted under the guidance and directions from his supernatural adviser, given him during the time the healing ceremony was taking place. A doctor, on the other hand, was required to state first the source and authority by which he acquired his power. This often emanated from a long-past vision, usually of a bird or animal. Págits said that shamans did not buy songs from other people but possessed the ability to secure songs in a supernatural manner. Doctors, on the other hand, were accustomed to buying and selling songs, the older doctors frequently transferring songs to younger men.

Págits was entirely independent of material assistance during his healing, not using a rattle or wearing amulets or charms when treating the sick, as was custom among the doctors. Págits said that after seeing and questioning a sick person, he could tell whether he could cure him. When asked if he would treat a case in which he felt unsure if he could cure the person, he stated that he had never done so and replied, "We believe that if a doctor begins on a case which he is not sure he can cure he will certainly fail."

Págits said that he treated the sick under the tutelage of a "little green man" and that many other shaman were under the same guidance. He first saw the little green man when he was a boy and continued to see him throughout his lifetime. Sacred songs were an important part of Págits' healing ritual and he began receiving his songs in about 1911.

Págits' specialty was the treatment of acute pain, and he said that he could cure pain in any part of the body. Págits said that he took from the patient's body a "strange something," sucking it out through the skin. He took the extracted object from his mouth and showed it to all the people. As soon as the substance was removed from the patient's body, the patient began to recover.

Págits said that it often took two or three weeks to cure a sick person, singing at first every evening and then less often as the condition of the patient improved. If the patient was extremely ill, Págits sang two hours at a time and would continue his singing until daylight.

Early Life

When he was born, Pagitsh was given the birth name of Págits. Over time the pronunciation was changed to Pagitsh, and ultimately to Teddy Pageets. His original name, Págits, meant "Little Fish." Págits knew early in his life that he was destined to become a shaman because a little green man visited him when he was about twelve years of age. At that time, he was in the mountains and fell asleep. He then heard the little green man singing these songs and learned them in this manner. Págits said that "when a man hears a song in a dream he sings aloud in his sleep and remembers the song after he wakes."

Págits continued to be visited by this healing spirit at intervals thereafter. Little else is known of his early life. He was interviewed in 1911 and was a practicing shaman at that time, having been given healing songs about three years earlier.

Leadership

Págits was a Northern Ute shaman who treated the sick with the assistance of a spirit helper and the singing of sacred songs. His power came from a class of spirits called *pitukupi*, who have generally been described as little green men. Págits special-

ized in the treatment of acute pain, and he claimed that he could cure pain in any part of the body. He once stated, "I always tell the person that he will get well because I *know it is true*"; also, "If the sick person does not think I can cure him I do not talk about it; I just cure him and prove it."

People who asked Págits to perform a healing "brought with them a stick about 18 inches long, painted green and forked at the end." This was his particular token. Págits doctored only at night and during his heating rituals used no paraphernalia such as drums or rattles; but rather simply sang a series of healing songs. The anthropologist Francis Densmore recorded nine of Págits' songs that were subsequently published by the Smithsonian Institution in an anthology, *Northern Ute Music*.

Regarding his spirit helper, the "little green man," Págits said, "the little man was green from head to foot and carried a bow and arrow. In disposition he was good to those he liked, and especially favored medicine men. Throughout his treatments the little green man stayed outside the tent, and he could see him and hear what he said, every phase of the treatment being according to his direction." Págits' treatment consisted of removing a disease object from the patient's body by singing and sucking on the area that was affected. Prior to the sucking, however, Págits reported that he usually had to sing five times before removing the diseased object. When the object was removed, Págits would take it from his mouth and display it to the audience. Págits informed Densmore, "As soon as this substance was removed from the patient's body he began to recover. Sometimes this substance is one of the little green man's arrows, which he has shot into the person's body. In shape this 'strange something' was said to be like a carrot and one or two inches in length. In was red in color, like blood. The arrows were always of the same kind, differing only in size." Págits reported that he usually had to sing five times before removing the disease object.

Further Reading

Densmore, Frances. *Northern Ute Music*. 1922. Washington, D.C.: Government Printing Office, Smithsonian Institution Bureau of American Ethnology.

Lyon, William S. *Encyclopedia of Native American Shamanism: Sacred Ceremonies of North America*. 1998. Denver: ABC-CLIO.

Music from the Smithsonian: http://www2.bitstream.net/~dtrohr/Music%20Minnesota.htm.

Quanah Parker

Full Name at Birth: Kwaina

Birth: ca. 1850

Death: February 23, 1911, near Lawton, Oklahoma

Education: no formal education

Leadership Position: Comanche tribal and spiritual leader

Summary

Quanah Parker was a war chief of the Comanche Nation and one of the most important roadmen, or leaders, in the early peyote religion in Indian Territory (present-day Oklahoma). He fought for the right of Indian people to practice the peyote religion at a time when the religion was increasingly threatened by government efforts to make its use illegal. Later in his life, Parker became a judge on the Court of Indian Offenses. Parker made numerous trips to Washington, D.C., where he participated in Theodore Roosevelt's inaugural events and lobbied for rights for Indian people.

Early Life

Parker was born between 1845 and 1850. His father was Peta Nocona (also referred to as Noconi, meaning "Wanderer"), chief of the Quahada (or Kwahadi) band of Comanche Indians. Quanah Parker took the surname of his

Comanche tribal and spiritual leader Quanah Parker, c. 1885. Courtesy of Panhandle-Plains Historical Museum, Canyon, Texas.

mother, Cynthia Ann Parker, a white woman who had been captured along with her brother John at about nine years of age in late May 1836. They were captured during a Comanche raid on a Navasota River settlement in present-day Limestone County, Texas. She later became one of Nocona's wives. Her brother, John Parker, who was six years of age at the time of their capture, grew to be a Comanche warrior.

Cynthia Ann Parker was recaptured by a rancher, Charles Goodnight, and returned to white society in 1860. Following her recapture, she asked repeatedly to be returned to the Comanche, but was never allowed to do so. She died in 1864 at her brother's home in Anderson County, Texas.

While in his teens, Parker was left without parents. Following the death of his father in about 1866 or 1867, he was raised by his grandfather, who trained him in the arts of hunting, warring, racing horses, and making or repairing weapons. In Comanche society, it was customary for grandfathers to teach the boys to make their own shields, bows, and arrows. Grandfathers were also charged with the responsibility of instilling in young boys the belief that their prestige and place in society were based on war and the hunt. Grandfathers encouraged competition for leadership and taught that courage and generosity earned respect in Comanche society.

Parker excelled under his grandfather's instruction and rose rapidly to commanding influence, rising to leadership as a successful warrior.

Leadership

Quanah Parker grew to manhood at a time when continuous warfare and European-introduced disease were taking a heavy toll on all Indians. As he matured, he became a war leader to claim and maintain control of Comanche hunting and warring. In 1868, as Indian people throughout the West were being forced onto small Indian reservations, Parker was one of the Comanche who still raided Mexican as well as Texan settlements. Throughout the 1870s, he led numerous attacks against the U.S. Army and the Texas Rangers. He participated in the attack on Adobe Walls in 1874 and the Red River War 1874–1875. He and his band escaped capture longer than most of the other Comanche bands and lived freely on the Great Plains. Parker viewed treaties with the U.S. government as anathema to Native people's interests, and as a Comanche leader he refused to sign the Treaty of Medicine Lodge, which reduced Comanche land holdings.

In the 1870s, new high-powered, long-range rifles and increasing numbers of buffalo hunters and homesteaders were systematically killing buffalo and destroying the way of life for Plains Indians. The transcontinental railroad now moved army troops rapidly, and the telegraph helped report the location of Parker and his warriors. In 1875, Parker and his warriors turned themselves in, defeated not by the U.S. Army but by hunters with repeating rifles and technology that was beyond their grasp. They were among the last American Indians to roam freely over the southern Plains.

Upon his surrender, Parker quickly adapted to the assimilationist ways and set about establishing a new way of life for his people—a way that would combine Comanche and Anglo-American ways. He encouraged the pursuit of education and sent three of his children to Carlisle Indian School. Parker also encouraged other Indian people to educate their children in the white man's schools.

Parker became a war chief among the Kwahadi band of the Comanche by approximately 1867. He was also one of the most important roadmen, or leaders, in the early peyote religion in Indian Territory (present-day Oklahoma). Peyote is a spineless cactus and was originally one of the offerings made to the gods in Aztec temples, where the buttons of this small hallucinogenic cactus plant were ritually consumed. Peyote flourished in other regions of Mexico and in South Texas. The Comanche frequented South Texas and were reportedly using peyote in the early 1800s. Since Parker was born just before 1850, it is reasonable to assume that he was familiar with peyote throughout his lifetime and perhaps used it in his power quest (a quest often including fasting and isolation to acquire a spiritual helper). Parker obtained his power through mystic visitations, a dream phenomenon, or hallucinatory experience.

Parker's involvement with peyote began in 1884 after he became seriously ill from a wound or ailment. Peyotists successfully used the plant to treat him, and when he recovered, he attributed his cure to peyote. This made him a convert to the peyote religion, and he entered upon a lifelong pursuit to spread the practice of the peyote religion, among Native peoples. His position as a respected and influential chief contributed to the spread of peyotism by attracting followers to his beliefs. He defended Native use of peyote against powerful opponents and incorporated some Christian elements into the religion. Parker is reported to have said, "The White man goes into his church house and talks about Jesus, but the Indian goes into his tipi and talks to Jesus."

Parker fought for the right of Indian people to practice the peyote religion at a time when the religion was increasingly threatened by government efforts to make the use of peyote illegal. He and other peyotists successfully defended their right to the religious use of peyote before the Medical Committee of the Oklahoma State Constitutional Convention in 1907 where they convinced the committee that peyote was not harmful and was a sacrament necessary in their Indian religious service.

In 1866, Parker was awarded one of three judgeships on the Courts of Indian Offenses, which were established to replace traditional sources of law and authority on Indian reservations. These courts prohibited many traditional cultural and religious practices and also designated tribal leaders to sign leases of tribal lands. Federal officials approved his appointment even though he practiced polygamy, a traditional Comanche practice that the court hoped to eradicate. Parker remained a judge until 1898, at which time he was dismissed for adding a new wife to his family.

Parker was the chief representative for the Comanche people in the allotment of tribal lands under the Dawes Act of 1887, which divided up tribal domains into individual plots of 160 acres or less. He used his position to represent his people and assist them in obtaining lease money from cattlemen for the use of their allotments.

Parker became a successful businessman who built a large house and ranch in Texas. He owned a large herd of cattle but still refused to cut his hair or comply with the government's rule forbidding polygamy. He made numerous trips to Washington, D.C., where he participated in Theodore Roosevelt's inaugural events and lobbied against the trespass of Texas cattle ranchers on Comanche land.

Parker often hosted influential leaders at his home, and the Texas town of Quanah was named in his honor. He became a friend of President Theodore Roosevelt, who visited Parker in his Texas home in 1906 and went on a hunting trip with him.

Prior to Parker's death, he appealed to have his mother's remains returned from East Texas to her former Indian home on the Red River. He said that she had loved Indian life and had never wanted to go back to the white people. On December 4, 1910, he reburied his mother's remains on the Comanche reservation. The Comanche chief and roadman died near Lawton, Oklahoma, on February 23, 1911.

Further Reading

Ballantine, Betty, and Ian Ballantine, eds. *The Native Americans: An Illustrated History*. 1993. Atlanta: Turner Publishing.

Calloway, Colin G. *First Peoples: A Documentary Survey of American Indian History*. 1999. New York: St. Martin's Press.

Champagne, Duane, ed. *The Native North American Almanac*. 1994. Detroit: Gale Research.

Hirschfelder, Arlene, and Paulette Molin. *The Encyclopedia of Native American Religions*. 1992. New York: Facts on File.

Neeley, Bill. *The Last Comanche Chief: The Life and Times of Quanah Parker*. 1995. New York: Wiley.

Quanah Parker: http://www.stainblue.com/quanahparker.html.

Quanah Parker—A Texas Legend: http://www.lnstar.com/mall/texasinfo/quanah.html.

Trigger, Bruce G., and Wilcomb E. Washburn, eds. *The Cambridge History of the Native Peoples of the Americas. Vol. 1, North America Part 2*. 1996. Cambridge: Cambridge University Press.

Vecsey, Christopher, ed. *Handbook of American Indian Religious Freedom*. 1993. New York: Crossroad Publishing Company.

Essie Parrish

Full Name at Birth: Pewoya

Birth: ca. 1898 on the Haupt Ranch in Sonoma County, present-day California

Death: 1979 on the Kashaya Reservation in Sonoma County, California

Education: no record of formal education; taught at the Kashaya Reservation school

Leadership Position: California Kashaya Pomo shaman

Awards, Achievements: worked with Robert Oswalt, a University of California Berkeley scholar and linguist, to compile a Kashaya Pomo dictionary

Summary

Parrish was a Kashaya Indian woman sucking shaman who was born at the close of the 19th century. She was the last of four spiritual leaders believed to have been sent to guide and instruct the Kashaya Pomo people.

Little is known of Parrish's early life other than she began "dreaming" at a very early age, perhaps as young as six years old. Indian dreamers, women and men, were endowed with powerful spiritual powers and were called on to diagnose causes and cures for sickness. In their dreams, the

A 1960 photo of the Kashaya Pomo shaman Essie Parish preparing acron meal. Courtesy of the Phoebe Apperson Hearst Museum of Anthropology and the Regents of the University of California, Pomo Photo Collection, 15-19 554.

"dreamer" was given instructions to prescribe either a ceremony or medicine that would cure an ailing person. Among the Pomo people, the sucking shaman was the most powerful.

Parrish described her experience as a sucking shaman as follows:

Way inside the sick person lying there, there is something. If you put tissue over something, you could see through it. That's just the way I see it inside. I see what happens there, and I feel it with my hand. I don't place my hand myself; it feels like someone—the disease—is pulling with a string. And then it touches it. I use my hand and a rattle, and let the voice of the rattle tell me what is happening in the person's body. I also sometimes use a feather, sweeping it gently though a person's energy body feeling for the intrusion.

Once the intrusion had been located, she used the powers that had been given her to remove it:

After a long time . . . I noticed that I had something in my throat to suck pains out with. . . . That power is always near me. But other people can't see it. I alone can see it. . . . When I take it out you can't see it. You can't see it with your bare eyes, but I see it. Whenever I send it away, I see what the disease is.

Parrish was not only a religious leader but a political leader and a scholar as well. She collaborated with Robert Oswalt, linguist from the University of California, and compiled a Kashaya dictionary as well as Kashaya texts where many of the Kashaya legends and Parrish's personal experiences are recorded. She also consulted with scholars at the Lowie Museum at the University of California at Berkeley on Pomo basketry and the use of native California plants by the Kashaya Pomo. In 1967, Parrish met Robert Kennedy when he came to the Kashaya Reservation during his presidential campaign, and presented him with a sacred basket that she had woven.

Parrish was the mother of thirteen children. Her daughter Violet Chappell notes, "Mom was one of a kind. She could do anything. Play the piano, the accordion, the harmonica. She could cook. People used to come from the cities just to get her pies. She didn't believe in the word can't. And, above all else, she taught us to be proud, how great it was to be Indian and know who we are."

Parrish has been called the most important California Indian of the twentieth century.

Early Life

Parrish was born in 1898 on the Haupt Ranch in Sonoma County, California, the daughter of Emily Colder and John Pinola. In her own words, she was born "on the rancheria in an old shack between the redwood trees and the acorn trees." Her maternal grandmother, Rosie Jarvis, raised her. Parrish began dreaming in her early childhood and was only six years old when her people, the Kashaya Pomo who live at Stewart's Point in northwestern Sonoma County, acknowledged her as their dreamer. She treated her first patient at age nine.

Leadership

Parrish was born in present-day Sonoma County, California, where many of the Kashaya Pomo resided until the federal government purchased a forty-two-acre ranch, five miles west on Skaggs Springs Road, and established the Kashaya Indian Reservation. Parrish began dreaming in her early childhood, and it is reported that she treated her first patient when she was nine years old. In 1943, after the death of Annie Jarvis, her predecessor as tribal leader, Parrish became the official religious leader, or dreamer, of the Kashaya people. In this context, the term *dreamer* can be translated to mean visionary, doctor, or healer, but also included the duties of religious priest and prophet. Now recognized as the tribal leader, she doctored the sick and directed all religious activity within the tribe, including the making of costumes for the numerous religious ceremonies. Parrish used her religious and tribal knowledge to bind the Kashaya people together at a time when tremendous pressure was being exerted to terminate Indian tribes. As a result of her efforts, the Kashaya Pomo are viewed by many authorities as the most knowledgeable band among the Pomo groups regarding traditional religious and historical issues.

Parrish married a Point Arena Pomo, Sidney Parrish. She lived in Graton and Windsor, in Sonoma County, but always considered the Kashaya Reservation her home. She raised children, and it became her mission to educate the Kashaya children in the Indian language, culture, and laws. She not only taught in the reservation school, but compiled a Kashaya Pomo dictionary. Her spiritual gifts, particularly the ability to prophesy and interpret dreams, drew scholars to her. Parrish became a consultant to the most noted anthropologists of the time, Alfred Kroeber and Samuel Barrett. She made more than two dozen films on various aspects of Pomo culture, including films on her dream dances and doctoring. A documentary on her life won a Cannes Film Festival award in 1969. Parrish was in great demand as a speaker, relating her dream visions and teaching the history of her people.

In the late 1960s and early 1970s, Parrish became an activist for Indian land restoration and took a leading role in persuading the federal government to grant a portion of the former CIA listening facility near Forestville, California, for an Indian education center, known as Ya Ka Ama, which means "our land" in Kashaya.

Parrish died in 1979 and is buried at the Kashaya Indian Reservation.

Further Reading

Bataille, Gretchen M., ed. *Native American Women: A Biographical Dictionary*. 1993. New York: Garland Publishing.

Essie Parrish: http://www.pressdemocrat.com/extras/top50/parrish.html.

Hirschfelder, Arlene, and Paulette Molin. *The Encyclopedia of Native American Religions*. 1992. New York: Facts on File.

Lyon, William S. *Encyclopedia of Native American Shamanism: Sacred Ceremonies of North America*. 1998. Denver: ABC-CLIO.

Passaconaway

Full Name at Birth: Papisseconewa (derived from Papoeis, "a child," and Kunnaway, "bear cub" or "son of the bear"

Birth: ca. 1555

Death: ca 1665

Education: no formal education

Leadership Position: Pennacook *powah* (medicine man)

Summary

Passaconaway lived in the village of Pennacook along the Merrimack River near present-day Concord, New Hampshire. Around 1619, as the result of European-introduced disease and a decimating population decline, the Indian people who lived along the Merrimack united under a grand sachem (leader) named Passaconaway, which means "bear cub," or "son of the bear." The new formation was known as the Penacook Confederacy or Pawtuckett Confederacy.

Using his diplomatic skill, Passaconaway consolidated his leadership and was the most powerful sachem of southern New Hampshire when the colonists arrived. At one time during his reign, the Confederacy numbered over three thousand and was capable of putting over five hundred men into battle.

Under his rule, the Penacook Confederacy defended their territory against the Mohawk Nation (a member of the Iroquois Confederation), who were expanding west to increase their fur trade territory. The Penacook also resisted white encroachment into their homelands and made periodic raids against white settlers, who were now claiming Pennacook lands. In 1742, colonial soldiers retaliated and moved on Passaconaway's village, capturing his wife and son. Passaconaway protested to Massachusetts officials and ultimately gained their release.

Passaconaway was considered by his people to be a *powah*, or medicine man who began his career as a spiritual leader prior to becoming a political leader. It was said by his people that he possessed great spiritual power and could "make water burn and trees dance; that he could turn himself into a flame; that he could raise a green leaf in the middle of winter and bring a living snake from the skin of a dead snake; to have shamanistic powers as well as political wisdom; he reportedly had visions about the British conquest of his people" (Siclis).

In 1644, Passaconaway, fearing the death and destruction of his people, formally submitted to British authority and encouraged a policy of peaceful trade relations. Following his death in the mid-1600s, his son Wannalancet succeeded him.

Early Life

Little is known of Passaconaway's early life. It is believed that he was born between 1555 and 1573 and in keeping with Pennacook custom, on his reaching maturity, was given a name that encapsulated his most pronounced characteristics. "It is said that to have received the name 'Papisseconewa' which is derived from Papoeis—a child—and Kunnaway—bear—he must have been a powerful, fierce and gigantic youth" (Siclis). It also appears that Passaconaway understood very early the effect of his magical powers and is reported as having performed public feats "to the wonderment and awe" of his Indian and non-Indian audience. English

traders who witnessed several of his magic tricks stated that Passaconaway swam across the Merrimack River under water at a place where it was far too wide to cross in one breath. It was explained that "after entering the water on the farther side, a mist was cast before the spectators' eyes and he was not again seen until he stepped out upon the bank in front of the wondering beholders." On another occasion Passaconaway placed a bowl of water before him. "The usual incantation then followed, in the midst of which a black cloud hovered over the assembled company and suddenly a sharp clap of thunder rent the air. To the amazement of the spectators, a solid piece of ice floated in the bowl; this trick was performed in the middle of summer." Non-Indian observers stated that this "doubtless was done by the agility of Satan, his [Passaconaway's] magical consort" (Siclis).

Leadership

The man we know today as Passaconaway was born between 1555 and 1573 and upon reaching maturity was given a name based on his most visible and defining characteristics. He received the name Papisseconewa, meaning "bear cub" or "son of bear," indicating that he commanded great physical and spiritual power. He was also assigned the position title of *Bashaba*, given to a person who was considered to be more powerful than the tribal sachem or chief.

At the time that the Pilgrims landed at Plymouth Rock in 1620, Passaconaway was flourishing as the most powerful medicine person of his generation, and was one of several medicine men summoned to Plymouth to drive out the English. It is believed that he was probably the recognized leader of this group and he stated "that the Great Spirit whispered to him then, 'Peace, peace with the whites. You and your people are powerless against them.' . . . I made war upon them, my young men were struck down before me, when no one was near them." Following this disappointment, Passaconaway returned to Pennacook, aware now that he could not destroy the invaders by his magical powers, nor could his warriors successfully contend against the miraculous fire and thunder of the intruders. Passaconaway recognized the superiority of the English technology; rather than fighting against them, he decided to attempt to establish a peaceful trade relationship that would be beneficial to the Pennacook people.

One of the earliest of Passaconaway's transactions with the English is said to have been his signing of the famous Wheelwright Deed of 1629, which became the basis for granting several townships in the state of New Hampshire. While many charged that the deed was a forgery, including the Reverend N. Bouton, editor of the *Provincial Papers of New Hampshire*, the deed was recorded in the office of Recorder of Deeds at Exeter, New Hampshire. The deed certifies "that Passaconaway, for certain valuable considerations, sells to John Wheelwright and his associates a tract of land extending from the then [1629] Massachusetts line thirty miles into the country, and from the Piscataqua to the Merrimac, reserving the hunting and fishing rights to his people." Passaconaway signed the deed, as did several noted tribal leaders. A provision in the deed stipulated that Passaconaway would receive "one coat of trucking cloth a year" for "every township within the aforesaid limits or tract of land that hereafter shall be settled." It was Passaconaway's understanding of the agreement that the Pennacook would not have to vacate the lands they had sold but rather that the whites would come to live with his people and thus provide protection against their enemy, the Mohawk.

Despite having signed the Wheelwright deed, Passaconaway distrusted the sincerity of whites and seems never fully to have overcome that feeling. During the spring of 1647, an apostle identified only as "Apostle Eliot" came to the Pennacook at Pawtucket to preach Christianity to the confederated tribes gathered there. Pennacook came to the conclusion that a religion that tolerated the behavior exhibited by the English merited only contempt. Before Eliot arrived, Passaconaway took his family and departed for his homeland. He left word for Eliot that he "was afraid the English would kill him." During the next few years, Passaconaway became deeply interested in religion, however, and in 1648 he was found eagerly listening to the Apostle Eliot. After a period of time, Passaconaway accepted the new religion for himself and his family and urged that his tribesmen do the same.

Little is heard of Passaconaway between 1648 and 1660. During the 1660 fishing season, Passaconaway, now over one hundred years old, summoned all the subject tribes of the Pennacook for his farewell address:

Hearken to the words of your father. I am an old oak that has withstood the storms of more than a hundred winters. Leaves and branches have been stripped from me by the winds and frosts—my eyes are dim—my limbs totter—I must soon fall! But when young and sturdy, when my bow—no young man of the Pennacook could bend it—when my arrow would pierce a deer at an hundred yards—and I could bury my hatchet in a sapling to the eye—no wigwam had so many furs—no pole so many scalps as Passaconaway's! Then I delighted in war. The whoop of the Pennacook was heard upon the Mohawk—and no voice so loud as Passaconaway's. The scalps upon the pole of my wigwam told the story of Mohawk suffering.

The English came, they seized our lands; I sat me down at Pennacook. They followed upon my footsteps; I made war upon them, but they fought with fire and thunder; my young men were swept down before me, when no one was near them. I tried sorcery against them, but they still increased and prevailed over me and mine, and I gave place to them and retired to my beautiful island of Natticook. I that can make the dry leaf turn green and live again—I that can take the rattlesnake in my palm as I would a worm, without harm—I who have had communion with the Great Spirit dreaming and awake—I am powerless before the Pale Faces.

The oak will soon break before the whirlwind—it shivers and shakes even now; soon its trunk will be prostrate—the ant and worm will sport upon it. Then think, my children, of what I say; I commune with the Great Spirit. He whispers me now—"Tell your people, Peace, Peace, is the only hope of your race. I have given fire and thunder to the pale faces for weapons—I have made them plentier than the leaves of the forest, and still shall they increase! These meadows they shall turn with the plow—these forests shall fall by the ax—the pale faces shall live upon your hunting grounds, and make their villages upon your fishing places!" The Great Spirit says this, and it must be so! We are few and powerless before them! We must bend before the storm! The wind blows hard! The old oak trembles! Its branches are gone! Its sap is frozen! It bends! It falls! Peace, Peace, with the white men—is the command of the Great Spirit—and the wish—the last wish—of Passaconaway.

Further Reading

Passaconaway. Table of Contents: http://www.sidis.net/PassContents.htm.

Siclis, Boris. *Passaconaway in the White Mountains.* 1916. Boston: Badger Publications.

Waldman, Carl, and Molly Braun. *Encyclopedia of Native American Tribes.* 1988. New York: Facts on File.

Walker, Paul Robert. *American Indian Lives: Spiritual Leaders.* 1994. New York: Facts on File.

Piapot

Full Name at Birth: birth name unknown

Birth: 1816

Death: 1902

Education: no formal education

Leadership Position: Cree medicine man and war chief

Summary

Piapot was a Plains Cree medicine man and war chief and the brother-in-law of Little Pine, a noted Cree leader. Little is recorded of Piapot's early life other than that he was captured by a Sioux Indian war party and freed by a Cree war party fourteen years later. The knowledge he learned of the Sioux people during his captivity propelled Piapot into an early selection as tribal chief.

Piapot and his band hunted the buffalo and were noted for their bravado as raiders and horse thieves. Piapot believed strongly in the protection of the Cree hunting grounds and resented the encroachment of buffalo hunters and enactment of laws that attempted to restrict his people's ability to maintain their traditional way of life. In the mid-1800s, Piapot was a proponent of peaceful negotiation as a way to resolve differences, however, and he believed that peaceful coexistence was possible.

The Blackfoot Indians were traditional enemies of the Cree, vying for the dwindling buffalo herds, and warfare frequently erupted between the two nations. In 1870, Piapot and his warriors, some seven hundred strong, suffered a major defeat at the hands of the Blackfoot. Piapot's idea was that a combined Cree and Assiniboine force would attack a small band of Blackfoot on the Belly River, near present-day Waterton Lakes in Alberta, and deliver such a decisive blow that other Blackfoot would fear to venture into their hunting area. The combined force penetrated as far south as the Red Deer River in present-day Calgary, whereupon they came upon what they believed to be a small, poorly armed, isolated village. They attacked. Piapot and the other leaders had no way of knowing that a large number of Blackfoot, all heavily armed, were located at a village just a short distance away. The Cree and Assiniboine had only flintlocks and bows and arrows, which were no match for the repeating rifles of the Blackfoot. Between two hundred and three hundred Cree and Assiniboine were killed that day. It was the last major battle between the Cree and the Blackfoot tribes.

In 1875, Piapot reluctantly signed Canadian Treaty No. 5, ceding lands in the Qu'Appelle Valley of Manitoba, and then

Piapot in a studio photograph taken about 1885. Brock, J. A./National Archives of Canada-PA-18 2240.

moved his band west to what is now Saskatchewan. Soon, however, Piapot understood that the Canadian government had negotiated a fraudulent treaty, and he became active in attempting to amend the treaty or stand in the way of its enforcement.

In 1885 Piapot exercised his role as a Sun Dance chief and called for a Sun Dance (outlawed by the Canadian government) in an attempt to gain spiritual assistance from the Great Spirit. Among the Cree, the Sun Dance was the most sacred and difficult vow to fulfill and the one most likely to bring about the desired results. The *nipakwe-cimuwn*, or "thirsting dance," lasted for several days and was the most solemn of all Cree ceremonies. Because of the Sun Dance, Canadian officials deposed Piapot in an attempt to undercut his authority. His band continued to honor his authority, however.

Early Life

Piapot was born in present-day eastern Saskatchewan to an Assiniboine father and a Cree mother. While he was young, both of his parents died as the result of one of many smallpox epidemics that ravaged the Plains Indian Nations in the early 1800s. Following his parents' death, Piapot lived with his grandmother until he was taken captive by a Sioux war party.

Piapot lived with the Sioux for fourteen years until he was ultimately freed by a Plains Cree war party. When he returned to the Cree, he was given the name Piapot (*payepot*), which translates "one who knows the secret to the Sioux" or "hole in the Sioux." The knowledge he obtained from the Sioux helped him to become a Cree war chief at the age of twenty-four. He was the leader of the Young Dog band who in the eyes of the Canadian government were notorious raiders and horse thieves. Piapot's band hunted the buffalo, and they resented the incursion of the Canadian government into their hunting territory.

Because Piapot was taken captive at an early age, it is impossible to know if he participated fully in the male puberty rites that were traditional for Cree boys. In his later life, Piapot became a Sun Dance chief, so it is reasonable to assume that he underwent one or more vision quests at some point early in life. Upon reaching the age of puberty, a Cree boy and his father would go to a secluded location to fast and pray for a visit by the spirit powers, *atayohkanak*. After the father offered up a pipe in prayer to the Great Spirit, he left the boy alone. The boy would remain alone for a number of days praying, fast-

ing, and performing any other types of activity that he felt might hasten the appearance of a vision. When a spirit helper appeared, it became the boy's *pawakan*, his supernatural guardian or spirit helper.

Leadership

Piapot flourished at a time of tremendous change for Plains Indians. A boundary line had been drawn by the U.S. and Canadian government that placed Piapot and his people under the oppressive hand of Canada and the Canadian Mounted Police.

The Cree Indians were a horse-mounted, mobile, buffalo-hunting society that recognized access to traditional hunting areas in both Canada and the United States to the exclusion of all other tribes. Anyone, Indian or white, trespassing on Cree lands was subject to punishment for trespass. The two governments attempted to restrict border crossings (called raiding). Both governments also began a process of negotiating (often by force) treaties with the individual Indian Nations in an attempt to remove them to reservations (in the United States) and reserves (in Canada). Piapot grew to the position of chief of the Cree Nation during this period and counseled peace as opposed to extinction.

In the summer of 1874, Canadian officials began to negotiate a treaty, officially known as Treaty Four, with the Cree. Chief Piapot had not been informed about the provisions of the treaty and was disappointed when he saw the document. Later, when he was asked to sign the treaty, he requested additional items to protect the hunting rights of the Cree people. The treaty officials did not give Piapot an outright refusal, and he believed his requests had been granted. Piapot later refused to accept the treaty terms because the provisions were not included. In 1875, however, he finally signed Canadian Treaty Number Five, ceding lands in Qu'Appele Valley.

In 1879, as professional hunters and railroad workers decimated the buffalo population, Cree Indian bands from Canada were forced to follow herds south into the United States or face starvation. The Canadian government rejected a demand by the Cree chiefs for contiguous reserves, and in 1882 Piapot and his warriors pulled up survey stakes along a thirty-mile stretch of the Canadian Pacific Railway west of Moose Jaw, Saskatchewan. The next year at Maple Creek, Saskatchewan, Piapot had his band erect their tepees directly in the path of track-laying crews. The North West Mounted Police knocked down their tepees and drove the Indians away in a show of force.

In 1882, Piapot complained to Commissioner Irving of the North West Mounted Police that a Cree Indian, Little Fisher, had been arrested for horse stealing and sentenced to nine months in prison. Just three months earlier, three Indian raiders who had stolen horses from the Cree had served only fourteen days for the same crime. Piapot stated that the police were quick to arrest Cree, but those who stole from the Cree appeared to get away unharmed. Piapot stated, "You deter our young men from stealing horses from their enemies by threatening to put them in jail, and now that we are starving, what are we to do?" The official warned the Cree against stealing from ranchers or white settlers. However, he stated, "If other tribes were stealing horses from them, why could they not simple steal them back?" Piapot jumped up and said, "You hear what the white chief says. He tells you that you can go to steal horses from Indians and that he will not punish you. Now, young men, you can do as you like, I won't interfere with you, either to encourage you or discourage you."

In 1882 when Canadian officials were trying to get Piapot to remove to the reserve, he asked that the removal be postponed until after the annual religious festivals. When the commissioner refused, Piapot tore down his treaty flag, took the peace medal from around his neck, passed them both to the interpreter, and walked out of the council. Piapot was a leader who never gave up. He was peaceful in his negotiations, but determined to fight for what was best for his people. Piapot died in 1902, just before the Canadian government deposed him as chief for calling for a Sun Dance religious ceremony.

Further Reading

Braroe, Niels Winther. *Indian and White: Self-Image and Interaction in a Canadian Plains Community*. 1975. Stanford: Stanford University Press.

Champagne, Duane, ed. *The Native North American Almanac: A Reference Work on Native North Americans in the United States and Canada*. 1994. Detroit: Facts on File.

Dempsey, Hugh A. *Big Bear: The End of Freedom*. 1984. Lincoln: University of Nebraska Press.

Milloy, John Sheridan. *The Plains Cree*. 1988. Winnipeg: University of Manitoba Press.

Powerful Images: Piapot: http://www.museumswest.org/exhibit/piapot.htm.

Treaty Biographies: Piapot: http://www.otc.ca/piapotbio.html.

Waldman, Carl, and Molly Braun. *Encyclopedia of Native American Tribes*. 1988. New York: Facts on File.

Popé (Popay)

Full Name at Birth: Popé or Popay

Birth: Although Popé's date and place of birth are unknown, he is believed to have been fifty or sixty at the time of the Great Pueblo Revolt of 1680, placing his birth between about 1620 and 1630.

Death: ca. 1690

Education: no formal education

Leadership Position: Tewa Pueblo spiritual leader

Summary

Popé was an important spiritual leader of the Tewa Pueblo of San Juan in the upper Rio Grande region of present-day New Mexico. In August 1680, he formed a military alliance among the various Pueblo tribes and led a successful rebellion against the Spanish, which was known as the Pueblo Revolt. In the first few days of the revolt, approximately 400 Spanish men, women, and children were killed, including 21 priests. Approximately 250 Indians were killed. Popé and his followers then set about to remove all signs of Spanish presence and influence. Spanish churches and homes were burned, European livestock was slaughtered, and fruit trees were pulled up by the roots. In a cleansing ceremony, Popé ordered baptized Indians washed with yucca suds to nullify the Christian baptism. Following the revolt, the Pueblo Indians were free to practice their traditional culture and religion.

It should be noted that the word *pueblo* more accurately describes a building type than a specific Native tribe. The Pueblo Indians, as they came to be recognized, occupied twelve villages on the southern edge of Black Mesa, Arizona, and twenty-seven villages in New Mexico.

Early Life

There is no recorded history of Popé's early life; however, some conclusions can be drawn from his fierce devotion to his Native religion and protection of Tewa culture in his later life. Popé was most likely raised in the traditional Tewa way. He would have belonged to a patrilineal moiety (male-based side of a tribal group) of the Tewa Pueblo, which was closely associated with the religious ceremonials that ensured the survival of the pueblo people. As a young boy, he would have been an observer of the elaborate ceremonies conducted by pueblo priests dedicated to supernatural spirit beings called *kachinas* (powerful spirits whose function it is to ensure rain, crops, and continuity of pueblo life). At about age twelve, he and other youth in his age cohort would have been initiated into the kachina society and instructed in their place in Tewa cosmology. The remainder of his life would have been spent in carrying out annual prescribed rituals to ensure that balance was maintained between the summer and winter solstices. The Tewa people believed that proper observance of these ceremonies would ensure that they would survive in the harsh desert environment found in the southwestern part of what would become the United States. The name Popé meant "ripe plantings" in English and associated Popé with the summer moiety, charged with conducting ceremonials that ensured the fertilization and growth of plants. The summer moiety was also associated with the female, life-giving, nurturing side of existence. From the time of his initiation into the *kachina* society, Popé was charged with the responsibility to protect life. As his later life proves, this was a duty he approached with the utmost seriousness.

Leadership

Popé, an important medicine man of the San Juan Pueblo, resisted Spanish colonization and attempts to destroy the Tewa religious beliefs. He was known for his fierce resistance to Christianity and for clinging with bitter determination to the religion of the *kiva* (man's ceremonial chamber).

The Spanish colony of New Mexico was founded on Pueblo Indian land in 1598. Indian people were forced to pay the Spanish taxes in the form of labor, crops, and cloth, and Spanish solders also raped and abused the pueblo women. European diseases and famine had drastically reduced the pueblo numbers from as many as 100,000 prior to European contact, to approximately 17,000 by the late 1600s. More destructive to pueblo life was the Catholic church's quest for Christian converts. Conversion called for the abandonment and destruction of Indian religious beliefs and rituals. The priests believed that destruction of *kachina* masks and other sacred objects in the *kivas* would break the pueblo people's will and that they would then abandon their religion. Aided by the Spanish soldiers from the nearby presidio, they raided the *kivas* and publicly burned masks and sacred objects. Rather than giving up their traditional religion, however, the Indians

clung to their faith and practiced their beliefs in secrecy.

The Franciscan priests recognized Popé as an important religious leader, and he often clashed with them because of his attempts to keep the traditional Indian faith alive. The friars regarded him as a dangerous troublemaker, and there is evidence that he had been punished several times for his stubborn adherence to the *kachina* rituals that were central to the pueblo religion. He was captured and flogged by Spanish authorities on at least three occasions and wore on his back the scars from the beatings that became a symbol of resistance to his people.

Popé suggested as early as 1668 that the time had come for the Pueblo Indian people to unite and drive the Spaniards from their homelands. He realized, however, that the pueblos had never engaged in large-scale coordinated warfare and that a planned revolt would require a great deal of planning and persuasion. In 1675, Spanish authorities arrested Popé and a number of other Pueblo medicine men who refused to convert to Christianity. Upon his release, Popé went to the Taos Pueblo, where he began organizing the rebellion and covertly enlisting recruits. He spent a great deal of time in one of the Taos *kivas*, communing with a figure that he identified as a Pueblo war god. Popé preached that the *kachina* spirit had ordered him to restore the traditional way of life of his people. A number of pueblo towns pledged allegiance to his cause.

Over the next five years, with the help of other pueblo religious leaders, Popé formed an alliance that would eventually include some seventeen thousand pueblo people living in more than two dozen independent towns spread out over several hundred miles. Making matters even more difficult, the various pueblo peoples spoke at least six different languages and countless dialects.

By 1680, an alliance formed, and August 13 was agreed on as the day of the uprising. Lacking a common calendar system, however, a coordinating effort to commence the revolt was needed. Swift runners carrying knotted cords that indicated the number of days until the revolt went from pueblo to pueblo. As the runners reached a village, a smoke signal went up as a sign that the leaders understood the date of the attack and were prepared to move against the Spanish. Popé feared spies among his alliance, however, and took strict precautions to prevent the Spanish from learning of the coming rebellion. A death sentence was decreed for anyone who disclosed the planned assault. The governor of the Tewa Pueblo at San Juan, Popé's son-in-law, was suspected of being a spy and was stoned to death as a warning to any other potential betrayers. Despite Popé's best efforts, word of the planned revolt leaked, but Popé advanced the date. On August 10, the Pueblo Revolt began. From the various pueblo towns, the Indian people fell upon the Spanish and the missions at the same time. After a number of successful small engagements, the large Indian force moved on to Santa Fe in present-day New Mexico. They set fire to the churches, seizing and destroying religious images just as the Spanish had done in the Indian *kivas*. Ultimately, they left thirty-four pueblo villages destroyed. The Pueblo Revolt resulted in the killing of over 400 Spanish colonists and 21 Franciscan missionaries. The remaining Spanish retreated south to El Paso, in present-day western Texas. Over 250 Indian people died as well.

With the expulsion of the Spaniards, the Indians set about to remove all traces of Spanish rule. Popé oversaw the destruction of all Spanish property and cultural institutions. European livestock was slaughtered and fruit trees pulled up. Churches were burned to the ground. Indians who had been baptized by Catholic priests were washed with suds from the yucca plant to "cleanse" their spirits, or in some cases the people waded into the river to wash away the taint of baptism.

Following the successful revolt, Popé chose to live in Santa Fe. By the time of his death in 1690, the alliance of the region's Indians had dissolved in the face of drought and attacks by Apache and Ute bands. By 1692, Santa Fe was once again under Spanish control.

Further Reading

Ballantine, Betty, and Ian Ballantine, eds. *The Native Americans: An Illustrated History.* 1993. Atlanta: Turner Publishing.

Calloway, Colin G. *First Peoples: A Documentary Survey of American Indian History.* 1999. New York: St. Martin's Press.

Champagne, Duane, ed. *The Native North American Almanac.* 1994. Detroit: Gale Research.

Hirschfelder, Arlene, and Paulette Molin. *The Encyclopedia of Native American Religions.* 1992. New York: Facts on File.

People in the West: Popé: http://www.pbs.org/weta/thewest/wpages/wpgs400/w4pope.html.

Popé: http://cbs.infoplease.com/ce5/CE041710.html.

Silverberg, Robert. *The Pueblo Revolt.* 1970. New York: Weybright and Talley.

Trigger, Bruce G., and Wilcomb E. Washburn, eds. *The Cambridge History of the Native Peoples of the Americas, Vol. 1, North America Part 1.* 1996. Cambridge: Cambridge University Press.

Washburn, Wilcomb E. *Handbook of North American Indians, Vol. 4.* Washington, D.C.: Smithsonian Institution.

Porcupine

Full Name at Birth: Porcupine, Hishkowits ("The Messiah Preacher")

Birth: ca. 1847; place of birth unknown

Death: 1929, in the upper Rosebud Valley, Montana

Education: no formal education

Leadership Position: Cheyenne shaman and tribal chief, Ghost Dance priest

Summary

Porcupine was a renowned Cheyenne shaman, born around 1847, and was recognized as the principal moral and religious leader of the Cheyenne for forty years. When he spoke, all others listened because of his wisdom and knowledge of Indian social relations and spiritual matters. In addition to possessing sacred knowledge, he was a chief and spokesman for his people. In 1867, Porcupine became known for devising and implementing a plan to derail a Union Pacific Railroad train. He was spokesman in four Cheyenne treaty councils and on one occasion met with President William Henry Harrison on a trip to Washington, D.C.

In November 1889 Porcupine visited with the Paiute Indians at Walker Lake, Nevada, where he spent the winter learning the Ghost Dance from its founder, Wovoka.* Upon his return home, Porcupine introduced the religion to the Northern Cheyenne leaders over a five-day council period. He then went on to become a Ghost Dance leader among the Cheyenne people.

Photographer Gill W. De Lancy took this portrait of Porcupine (Hishkowits), the Cheyenne shaman, in Washington, D.C., August 1907. National Anthropological Archives, Smithsonian Institution.

Early Life

Porcupine was born in 1848. His father was White Weed, an Arikara Indian, and his mother was a Lakota woman. He grew up among the Lakota but married a Cheyenne woman and then lived the majority of his life among the Northern Cheyenne.

While little is recorded of his early life, it can be surmised that Porcupine grew to manhood during a period when the Lakota were a proud and powerful people, living as horse-mounted buffalo hunters in present-day North and South Dakota, eastern Wyoming, and Montana. As a young boy, Porcupine would have participated in a traditional vision quest, where he would have been taken by his uncle or a medicine person to an isolated spot, where he would have fasted and prayed for a vision. In the vision, he would have been shown a spirit person, animal, or force that guided him and supported him for the remainder of his life. Porcupine may have participated in more than one vision quest, and it is probable that he received his calling as a shaman during one of these experiences.

Leadership

In the late summer of 1867, Porcupine was among a group of Cheyenne warriors who wrecked a freight train of the Union Pacific Railroad near present North Platte, Nebraska. It appears that Porcupine and his companion, Red Wolf, planned the attack after having successfully derailed a smaller railroad handcar. Joined by other Cheyenne warriors, they took levers, pulled the spikes holding the rails, then bent the rails up into the air. When the train reached the broken rails, Porcupine recalled, "The locomotive jumped into the air and the cars all came together." The following morning, Porcupine and his men plundered and then burned the wrecked train after scattering the contents over the prairie.

Porcupine also rode with Morning Star and Little Wolf's band of Cheyenne in 1878 when they bolted from the Southern Cheyenne Reservation and led thousands of U.S. soldiers on a month-long fruitless chase across Kansas and Nebraska. Porcupine was captured later and tried for the murder of a Kansas frontiersman but was not convicted.

Porcupine was equally well known for his leadership in the Ghost Dance religion that swept the Great Plains in the late 1800s. The Ghost Dance was based on a vision that Wovoka received while ill with a severe fever in December 1888. While in a feverish state, Wovoka received a vision, heard a "great noise," then lost consciousness. When he revived, he announced that he had been taken to the other world where he had seen the Creator and all of the Indian people who had died before. The old were made young again. Everyone was well fed, dancing, and blissfully happy. The Creator instructed Wovoka to return to the earth and tell the people that they must be good and love one another. Indian people were to cooperate with the white people and live in peace without warfare until the time that the Creator would remove all white people from the earth. Indian people were to abstain from alcohol and were instructed not to fight, steal, or lie.

Of the Ghost Dance experience, Porcupine reported, "I and my people have been living in ignorance until I went and found out the truth [from Wovoka]. All the whites and Indians are brothers, I was told there. I never knew this before." Porcupine was arrested at the turn of the century and sentenced to hard labor at Fort Keogh, Montana, for continuing to encourage and practice the Ghost Dance after it had been forbidden by the U.S. government.

Porcupine was a famous shaman and healer in his own right. During his healing ceremonies, he used a braid of sweet grass, which he burned on a coal; a sacred rattle, which he passed through the smoke for purification; and a medicine root. Porcupine owned numerous sacred songs, three of which were sung as he began doctoring the patient. Sweet grass was again burned, a sacred pipe was smoked, and medicine was given to the patient. Porcupine sang five more healing songs, and then the poison that had affected the patient was sucked from his or her body. A medicinal tea was administered, after which Porcupine bit off a piece of the medicine root, chewed it, and spat it on certain parts of the patient's body. The rattle was passed through the smoke again, and seven different songs were sung. The pipe was smoked again, and Porcupine then mixed medicine with deer fat and rubbed the mixture on his hands, held them over the fire, and placed his hands on the part of the body where the pain was concentrated. The rattle was again held over the smoke, and nine different songs were sung, which completed the healing ritual. The patient then rested peacefully. Porcupine died in 1929 somewhere in the upper Rosebud Valley in present-day Montana.

See also Wovoka.

Further Reading

Grinnell, George Bird. *The Cheyenne Indians: Their History and Ways of Life.* 1962. New York: Cooper Square Publishers.

Grinnell, George Bird. *The Fighting Cheyennes.* 1915. Norman: University of Oklahoma Press.

Hirschfelder, Arlene, and Paulette Molin. *The Encyclopedia of Native American Religions.* 1992. New York: Facts on File.

Lyon, William S. *Encyclopedia of Native American Shamanism: Sacred Ceremonies of North America.* 1998. Denver: ABC-CLIO.

Marquis, Thomas B. *The Cheyennes of Montana.* 1978. Algonac, Mich.: Reference Publications.

Pretty-Shield

Full Name at Birth: Pretty-Shield

Birth: ca. 1857, near the Missouri River

Death: date and place not recorded

Education: no formal education

Leadership Position: Mountain Crow medicine woman

Summary

Among the Crow people, there was a belief that sacred possession, including medicine privileges, could be bestowed on both men and women and that either could participate equally in ceremonial activity.

Pretty-Shield was a Crow medicine woman who flourished in the late 1800s. She received her medicine power while in mourning over the death of "a beautiful baby girl." Following the child's death, Pretty-Shield slept little and fasted, eating only enough to keep herself alive, hoping for a vision that not only would help her but would help others as well. One morning while in a medicine dream state, Pretty-Shield saw a spirit woman who instructed her to perform a series of spiritual rituals. After she had done as told, Pretty-Shield entered a beautiful white lodge with a war eagle at the head. The war eagle became one of her spiritual helpers, as did the powerful little people, the ants.

Early Life

Pretty-Shield was named on the fourth day of her life, as was customary among the Crow people. Her name came from her paternal grandfather, Little-Boy-Strikes-with-a-Lance, and was associated with a medicine shield that he owned. Pretty-Shield recalled that "my grand-father's shield was handsome; and it was big medicine." She was the fourth child to be born of Crazy-Sister-in-Law, her father, and Kills-in-the-Night, her mother.

Pretty-Shield went to live with her maternal aunt, Strikes-with-an-Axe, a River Crow, when she was three years old. Her aunt had lost two girls to Lakota war parties and Pretty-Shield went to live with her to "heal her heart." Her aunt's lodge (home) was large, and Pretty-Shield recalled that the separation from her natural family was not difficult because the Crow people visited often. Pretty-Shield also enjoyed the migratory patterns of the Crow people, who moved as part of their traditional lifeways. As a young girl Pretty-Shield enjoyed games and recalled, "Once several of us girls made ourselves a play village with our tiny teepees. Of course our children were dolls, and our horses dogs, and yet we managed to make our village look very real. . . . We had great fun."

When Pretty-Shield was thirteen years old and in keeping with the custom of the Crow, she was promised by her father as a wife to a Crow warrior, Goes-Ahead. Pretty-Shield regarded herself as a promised woman from that time onward, and at age sixteen Goes-Ahead took her as his wife. Goes-Ahead was already married to Pretty-Shield's sister Standing-Medicine-Rock, and when Pretty-Shield's younger sister, Two Scalps, became sixteen years old, she too married Goes-Ahead. Thus there were three lodges, three sisters, all married to Goes-Ahead. This marriage pattern was not uncommon. Among the Crow, a man who had given the father the bride-price for the eldest of several sisters had the right to marry the younger girls as they came of age. Despite the father-arranged marriage and three sisters being married to one man, women were not chattel property and as a rule were not coerced into marrying men they found repulsive. Pretty-Shield was the only wife to bear Goes-Ahead children. The young age at which she and her sisters were married were uncommon only in that Crow girls often married prior to their first menses and were sometimes teased if they were not married by that time.

Before turning seventeen, Pretty-Shield became ill with smallpox, the disease that killed tens of thousands of Indian people, including her father. She was healed through the efforts of a Crow medicine man, Sharp-Skin.

Leadership

In 1931, Pretty-Shield, about seventy-four years old, told her life story to author Frank Linderman through an interpreter and the use of sign language. She told of Crow Indian life before the white man came and the buffalo were hunted to extension. Her account of the female side of native life was among the first recorded. Pretty-Shield recalled the traditional lifeways of her people before European contact and spoke about many Crow customs, including those related to childhood, courtship, marriage, and childbirth.

Pretty-Shield became a "wise one" or medicine woman in part through the spiritual assistance she reviewed in a vision while mourning the death of a baby daughter. After assuming the role, Pretty-Shield, like her grandfather, possessed the right to name children. A member of a respected family, her clan, the Sore-Lip or Burned-Mouth, was also prominent and produced many Crow leaders, including the great Crow leader Chief Plenty-Coups.

Pretty-Shield's story was published in 1932 as *Red Mother* and later as *Pretty-Shield: Medicine Woman of the Crows*. It includes an account of her medicine dream, or vision and her subsequent spiritual help from ants. Pretty-Shield outlived all but one of her children and raised two families of grandchildren. Her husband, Goes-Ahead, and her uncle, Half-Yellow-Face, were both scouts for Custer and survived the Battle of the Little Big Horn. Pretty-Shield's memory of their account of the historic confrontation is included in her book. When Linderman interviewed her, she was raising grandchildren and trying to cope with the changes introduced among her people. Pretty-Shield recalls the changes forced on her and her people when "white men began to fence the plains so that we could not travel. We began to stay in one place she said, and to grow lazy and sicker all the time. Our men had fought hard against our enemies, holding them back from our beautiful country by their bravery; but now with everything else going wrong, we began to be whipped by weak foolishness. Our men, our leaders, began to drink the white man's whiskey, letting it do their thinking."

Pretty-Shield recalled her grandmother's talk about the hard lives the Crow had lived before the introduction of the horse and decided that horses had changed everything for the better: "There was always fat meat, glad singing, and much dancing in our villages." Pretty-Shield said that the Crow believed for a long time that the buffalo would come again to us, but they did not. "Nothing, we found nothing, and then, hungry, they stared at the empty plains, as though dreaming."

Further Reading

Ballantine, Betty, and Ian Ballantine, eds. *The Native American: An Illustrated History*. 1993. Atlanta: Turner Publishing.

Calloway, Colin G. *First Peoples: A Documentary Survey of American Indian History*. 1999. New York: St. Martin's.

Hirschfelder, Arlene, and Paulette Molin. *The Encyclopedia of Native American Religions*. 1992. New York: Facts on File.

Linderman, Frank B. *Pretty-Shield: Medicine Woman of the Crows*. 1972. Lincoln: University of Nebraska Press.

Rainbow

See John Trehero

Rolling Thunder

Full Name at Birth: Rolling Thunder

Birth: 1915 in the Cherokee Nation, present-day state of Oklahoma

Death: date and place unknown

Education: no formal education recorded

Leadership Position: spiritual leader of the Cherokee and Shoshone tribes

Summary

Rolling Thunder is an American Indian spiritual leader and philosopher of the contemporary era who offers a philosophical or religious basis for contemporary ecological thought. His view is fundamental to understanding Native American belief systems. He is recognized as the guardian of a wealth of spiritual knowledge that has been passed down to him through countless generations of spiritual leaders. His knowledge includes the power to cure disease, heal wounds, find and use medicinal herbs, perform exorcisms, and communicate with other medicine people through mental telepathy.

Rolling Thunder explains the Indian's view of chaos through ecological imbalance as follows:

> When you have pollution in one place, it spreads all over. It spreads just as arthritis or cancer spreads in the body. The earth is sick now because the earth is being mistreated, and some of the problems that may occur, some of the natural disasters that might happen in the near future are only the natural readjustments that have to take place to throw off sickness. A lot of things are on this land that don't belong here. . . . It's very important for people to realize this. The earth is a living organism, the body of a higher individual who has a will and wants to be well, who is at times less healthy or more healthy, physically and mentally. People should treat their own bodies with respect. It's the same thing with the earth. Too many people don't know that when they harm the earth they harm themselves, nor do the realize that when they harm themselves they harm the earth. . . . It begins with respect for the Great Spirit, and the Great Spirit is the life that is in all things—all the creatures and the plants and even the rocks and the minerals. All things—and I mean all things—have their own will and their own way, their own purpose; this is what is to be respected.

Early Life

We have no written record of Rolling Thunder's early life other than that given his biographer, Doug Boyd. Rolling Thunder told Boyd that he received his spiritual healing calling by birth; other medicine people receive their calling through the vision quest process. He explains that

> when our young people are twelve or thirteen years old, they go out and pray on the high mountain at certain sacred places while an older person waits at the foot of the mountain. They go up there with no clothes, just a blanket, no food or water, for as long as three days. If they drop off to sleep, they wake up praying. Then there comes a time when they have a vision showing them what they're supposed to do. They won't know the meaning of it, most likely, so they come on down to the base of the mountain they tell the older person; then they go together to the medicine man and tell of the vision again, and the medicine man looks into it. Next they have the name ceremonies and decide what the meaning of this dream is and how it's interpreted. That person then gets a feeling and a name, and they know their purpose in life.

Leadership

Rolling Thunder retired from the Southern Pacific Railroad in 1981 after having been a brakeman for thirty-five years. When he was not on duty with the railroad, he was a medicine man traveling around healing a growing circle of people and tribes. One example of a healing ceremony was told to his biographer Doug Boyd.

In 1982, Rolling Thunder received a request to heal a woman who suffered from multiple sclerosis. The woman, who was part Cherokee, had numbness in her legs and would often fall uncontrollably. She also suffered from depression. Rolling Thunder agreed to meet with the woman but could not agree to help her until he got permission from the Great Spirit. Once the spirit had empowered him, he requested that the woman be brought to him, and he announced that he would perform a healing ceremony. He then asked the people who were present to hold hands and form a circle. He and the woman moved to the middle of the circle. Rolling Thunder then performed the ceremony as given to him by the Great Spirit. He acknowledged that he did not have the power to completely cure her of multiple sclerosis but he healed her immediate symptoms, made her walk better, and lifted her from her depressed state.

Rolling Thunder is highly respected for his healing power and is a close associate of other powerful medicine men, such as Peter Mitten (Mohawk) and Mad Bear Anderson (Tuscarora).

Further Reading

American Indian Prophecies: A Brief History of the Future of America: http://www.texfiles.com/features/prophecies.html.

Boyd, Doug. *Rolling Thunder*. 1979. New York. Random House.

Nicholson, Shirley, ed. Student Summaries of Chapters in Shamanism: http://www.mwsc.edu/~mullins/250s98/shmnbk.htm.

Juan de Jesus Romero (Deer Bird)

Full Name at Birth: Juan de Jesus Romero (Deer Bird)
Birth: 1874
Death: July 30, 1978, at Taos Pueblo, New Mexico
Education: no formal education
Leadership Position: Taos *cacique* (religious leader)

Summary

Romero was the *cacique*, or religious leader, of the Taos people at their pueblo in present-day New Mexico. This is a hereditary leadership position and the *cacique* is responsible for preservation of the tribe's spiritual life. The *cacique* is charged with the responsibility of knowing and carrying out the complex ritual and ceremony that has preserved the continuity of the Taos Indians since their emergence from the underworld, which they believe took place at the sacred Blue Lake (Maxolo). They revere Blue Lake as a sacred site where the world was created, and the site therefore has great religious and symbolic significance in Taos Pueblo culture. Ceremonies acknowledging the creation of the world and of man were annually celebrated by the Taos community at Blue Lake.

The Taos, who number about 1,800, have lived around Blue Lake since the fourteenth century, however, President Theodore Roosevelt appropriated the

In December 1970, Juan Jesus de Romero (center) watches as President Nixon signs a bill granting title to Blue Lake to the people of Taos Pueblo. © Bettmann/Corbis.

land in 1906 for the Carson National Forest, and the Taos people had been allowed to occupy it only on a permit basis. The Taos people had long complained of incursions by tourists and hunters and refused cash compensation for the land.

In 1906, Romero began a personal campaign for the return of the ancestral lands surrounding Blue Lake. Initially, he met with little success in this endeavor, but vowed to keep up pressure on the government. Forty-five years passed before the tribe filed a lawsuit against the government for the area including the lake and the land. In 1965, the government offered $297,684.67 for over 500,000 acres surrounding Blue Lake and also, in exchange, a larger parcel of land in and around what is known as the town of Taos. This offer was rejected by the Taos people in favor of their original

claim. The National Council of Churches recognized the significance of preserving Blue Lake as a place of worship that had been in use for longer than the great cathedrals of Europe and supported the Taos people in their fight.

Romero was adamant that the lake be returned, and he traveled to Washington, D.C. in 1970 to plead his case before President Richard M. Nixon.

The restoration legislation (House of Representatives Bill 471), was held up in the Senate even though it passed the House of Representatives several times. This was done primarily because of the powerful opposition of New Mexico Senator Clinton P. Anderson.

In July 1970, President Nixon issued a strong endorsement of pending Blue Lake restoration legislation and shortly after, the measure passed the Senate. Blue Lake and its surrounding wilderness were returned to the Taos people.

Early Life

Romero was born into the Taos Tribe of Pueblo Indians who inhabit the northernmost of the nineteen native pueblos or villages still in existence in New Mexico today. They are the direct descendants from the great Anasazi Indian culture that flourished in the Four Corners area of the southwest where Utah, Arizona, Colorado, and New Mexico join. Romero was born into a small tribe in the remote mountains of northern New Mexico in 1874 in a simple mud and straw house. He belonged to the hereditary family from which the tribe had traditionally drawn its most important members. From his clan came the *cacique*, the highest authority in both religious and secular affairs. Unable to read or write, this young man would himself become a *cacique* and would lead his people to an extraordinary victory against the U.S. government.

Leadership

Romero was the hereditary *cacique* or head man of Taos Pueblo as well as its spiritual leader. At age ninety, he traveled to Washington, D.C., to address the Senate and the president of the United States in an attempt to have the Taos sacred Blue Lake and adjacent lands returned to his people.

When President Theodore Roosevelt created the Carson National Forest in 1906, he carved away thousands of acres of land belonging to the Taos Pueblo people and directed that the Taos Blue Lake and its surrounding acreage be included in the national forest, thereby turning over control and use of the Blue Lake region to the U.S. Forest Service. In 1906, Romero began his personal campaign for the return of the ancestral lands surrounding Blue Lake that had been expropriated from his people, a campaign that would last until 1970.

For years, he met with little success in this endeavor, but vowed to keep up pressure on the government. The Taos believe that Blue Lake is a sacred site where the world was created, and therefore it has great religious and symbolic significance in Taos Pueblo culture. Ceremonies acknowledging the creation of the world and of man are annually celebrated by the Taos community at Blue Lake.

Forty-five years passed before the tribe filed a lawsuit against the government for the area including the lake and the land. In 1965 the government offered $297,684.67 for over 500,000 acres surrounding Blue Lake and also offered an exchange—a larger parcel of land in and around what is the present-day town of Taos. The tribe rejected these offers in favor of their original claim. The National Council of Churches recognized the significance of preserving Blue Lake and issued a statement that "recognizing the religious rights and freedom of the Taos Pueblo Indians, is vitally important to all Indian tribes as well as to all American citizens."

Romero was insistent that the lake be returned, and he traveled to Washington, D.C., in 1970 to present his case before the Senate and President Richard M. Nixon. His efforts and those of the National Council of Churches and the National Committee for the Restoration of the Blue Lake Lands proved successful; President Nixon issued a strong endorsement of pending Blue Lake restoration legislation in July 1970. A motion was put before the U.S. Senate and passed, with seventy senators for and twelve against, for the return of Blue Lake to the Taos along with 48,000 acres of surrounding land. Nixon signed the bill in 1971, and Blue Lake was again within the Taos domain. After the return of the lake, Romero said, "Now when I die, I will die at peace." He died in 1978 at the age of 104. Romero had been hospitalized in early June 1978 and was discharged from Presbyterian Hospital in Albuquerque just days before his death. For his lifelong efforts in the fight for Blue Lake, Romero won the prestigious Indian Council Fire Award in 1974.

Further Reading

Cassidy, James J., Jr. *Through Indian Eyes.* 1995. Pleasantville, N.Y.: Reader's Digest Association.

Champagne, Duane, ed. *The Native North American Almanac: A Reference Work on Native North Americans in the United States and Canada.* 1994. Detroit: Gale Research.

Gordon-McCutchan, R. C. *The Taos Indians and the Battle for Blue Lake.* 1991. Santa Fe: Red Crane Books.

Hirschfelder, Arlene, and Paulette Molin. *The Encyclopedia of Native American Religions.* 1992. New York: Facts on File.

Taos Blue Lake Collection Papers: http://libweb.princeton.edu/libraries/firestone/rbsc/finding_aids/taosbluelake/taosbluelake_1.html.

Taos Indians Thankful for Blue Lake Vote: http://members.aol.com/chloe5/news-7.html.

Sanapia

Full Name at Birth: Sanapia

Birth: spring 1895, at Fort Sill, Oklahoma

Death: 1968

Education: Cache Creek Mission School, Oklahoma, 1902–1909

Leadership Position: Comanche medicine woman

Summary

Sanapia was a medicine woman of great significance to the Comanche people. She was born in 1895 in Fort Sill, Oklahoma, where her family had traveled to draw government rations. She attended Cache Creek Mission School in southern Oklahoma for seven years and then began four years of training to become an Eagle Doctor—a medicine person spiritually assisted by the eagle. As an Eagle Doctor, Sanapia acquired a position of high prestige and social power among the Comanche. In addition to using herbal medicines, Sanapia obtained healing power from her spiritual helper, the eagle, and through her medicine songs. Her medicine practice included treatment of a ghost sickness, a feared condition believed to derive from the patient's contact with ghosts. Sanapia was recognized for her high degree of success in treating individuals with the ghost sickness and was a highly respected member of Comanche society.

Early Life

Sanapia was born at Fort Sill, Oklahoma, in the spring of 1895. Her father was Comanche, and her mother was Comanche-Arapaho. She was the sixth in a family of eleven children. Her maternal grandmother was instrumental in rearing Sanapia, as is customary among the traditional matrilineal Comanche people. Of great significance to her later calling as a medicine woman, both her mother and her mother's older brother were Eagle Doctors. Sanapia's uncle was an influential leader among the Comanche peyotists, and her grandfather was a peyotist as well. Sanapia thus grew up in a highly charged religious atmosphere. Her father was a Christian; her uncle and grandfather were peyotists, and her mother an Eagle Doctor. The Comanche people also participated in the Great Plains vision quest ritual for the acquiring of guardian spirits. During her early life, Sanapia was exposed to the teachings of each of these religions, and she successfully combined elements of the four separate cosmologies into her own calling as a medicine woman. She attended the Cache Creek Mission School in southern Oklahoma for seven years and then began four years of training to become an Eagle Doctor, a medicine person spiritually assisted by the eagle.

Leadership

While attending Cache Creek Mission School, Sanapia spent her summer vacations with her mother in Chandler Creek, Oklahoma. During one such vacation, her mother offered to train her in the skills and knowledge necessary to become an Eagle Doctor. Pressure from her mother and maternal grandmother overcame Sanapia's initial reluctance, and she began her instruction at age thirteen. Sanapia left school when she was fourteen years old, and by the time she was seventeen, she had completed the Eagle Doctor instruction. Although she possessed all of the skills, knowledge, and powers necessary, in keeping with religious restrictions, she was unable to begin her doctoring until after menopause. During her training period, she was closely observed by her mother, maternal uncle, maternal grand-

mother, and paternal grandfather, each of whom had to give their final approval through a blessing ceremony. In addition to studying medicine plants and the diagnosis and treatment of illnesses, she was instructed in the proper religious taboos and the conduct of doctors. She acquired many of her healing skills when she assisted her teachers, her mother, and uncle as they treated patients.

Sanapia was married three times. The names of her husbands are not recorded, and she referred to only her second spouse as her husband. Her oldest brother, who by Comanche tradition had the prerogative of giving his sister away in marriage, arranged the first marriage. She had a son by her first husband, whom she left at her mother's urging, and a son and a daughter by her second husband, who died in the early 1930s. She married a third time after 1945.

Following the death of her second husband, Sanapia was devastated and depressed. Sanapia referred to these years as the time when she was roughing it out. It was during this period that she first employed her healing skills. One of her sisters approached her and asked her to doctor her child. Reluctant to test her abilities, Sanapia recalled that her mother had instructed her during her training that she could not refuse treatment to anyone. She healed the child and thus began her Eagle Doctor practice.

Besides using herbal medicines, Sanapia obtained healing power from her spiritual helper, the eagle, and through her medicine songs. Sanapia kept her botanical and nonbotanical medicines in a medicine box that only she was allowed to touch. The medicine kit was considered potentially very dangerous if handled by the wrong person. Included in her pharmacopeia were white otter fur used to treat infants; porcupine quills used in the treatment of children; a medicine bone used for wounds, infections, boils, and pains, and a medicine feather (the tail feather from a golden eagle) that she employed in every case she doctored. Among all of the medicines she carried, the eagle feather was the one most revered. Tallow or rendered beef fat, called Indian lard, was used as a general-purpose salve, which was especially effective in the treatment of severe burns. Red paint, which she obtained by grinding and powdering dark red clay, was used in all of her blessing ceremonies.

Sanapia's medicine practice included treatment of ghost sickness, a condition believed to derive from the patient's contact with ghosts. Many Comanche were terrified by ghosts, and Sanapia considered herself to be an expert on the causation and behavior of ghosts. She believed that ghosts were the spirits of deceased persons who had led evil lives and were therefore doomed to wander the earth forever. Ghosts were thought to be jealous of the living and therefore a threat to be dealt with. Particularly worrisome was the ghost's ability to deform his victims by causing paralysis in various parts of the body and contortions of the facial muscles.

Ghosts were believed to be present between sunset and sunrise and to prey on individuals who traveled alone. Ghosts also appeared during daylight hours as a whirlwind. Eagle Doctors, because of their possession of ghost medicine, had greater power than ghosts and thus had the ability to control the behavior of ghosts and cure the illnesses that they caused. Sanapia treated the ghost sickness by applying her mouth to the patient's face in an attempt to suck the ghost-injected illness from the individual. She also applied liquid medicines to the affected area. During the next phase of the treatment process, Sanapia sang her medicine songs and drew her eagle feather over the afflicted area. Sanapia was recognized for her high degree of success in treating individuals with the ghost sickness, as well as her power to protect the Comanche society as a whole from attacks by ghosts.

In the late 1960s, Sanapia was the last surviving Eagle Doctor and was considering passing on her spiritual knowledge and power to one of her children, possibly her eldest son or one of her grandchildren. She believed that the eagle medicine that she practiced would ultimately die as the Comanche people became more and more acculturated. Sanapia died in 1968, and no known successor has emerged to continue as an Eagle Doctor. As an Eagle Doctor, Sanapia acquired a position of high prestige and social power among the Comanche people and held a status in her society equal to a man.

Further Reading

Hirschfelder, Arlene, and Paulette Molin. *The Encyclopedia of Native American Religions.* 1992. New York: Facts on File.

Jones, David E. *Sanapia: Comanche Medicine Woman.* 1972. Prospect Heights, Ill.: Waveland Press.

Shoniagizik

Full Name at Birth: Shoniagizik ("Sky Money"), Zhoniiá Gishig, also John Mink
Birth: ca. 1850, near Rice Lake, in present-day Wisconsin

Death: 1943; place not recorded

Education: no formal education

Leadership Position: Ojibwa Midewiwin priest

Summary

Shoniagizik was a Midewiwin priest, a Drum Dance society leader, and an Ojibwa medicine man who lived among his people on the Lac Courte Oreilles Reservation in the present-day state of Wisconsin. In Ojibwa society, the roles of shaman and priest were merged together and the position required a great deal of codified esoteric knowledge. In keeping with this dual role, Shoniagizik was a physician, obstetrician, pharmacologist, psychiatrist, homeopath, bonesetter, and surgeon. He was a master of the healing arts, and the position carried both prestige and a certain authority.

Shoniagizik's knowledge of the sacred art of healing and his authority to practice it came through dreams. The treatment he used for healing varied according to the nature and source of the illness, which he determined with the aid of his spirit helpers. He had a wide knowledge of an extensive native pharmacopoeia. He had medicines to stop bleeding, reduce fever, and ease colic.

The second office held by Shoniagizik was that of ceremonial leader in both the *midewiwin*, or Medicine Lodge society, and the Drum Dance society. The purpose of the *midewiwin* society was to prolong life. The society also combined moral teachings and a code of conduct with the use of plants and herbs with which to heal diseases. The Drum Dance society was a quasi-social society centering about a number of highly decorated sacred drums. The drums were regarded and treated as sacred living beings, and their ritual care included protecting the drums from touching the bare ground, maintaining a light next to them at night, and maintaining appropriate behavior in their presence. As a shaman and ceremonial leader, Shoniagizik's services were in demand at every point in the Nation's life.

Shoniagizik was married four times and had many children and grandchildren. Toward the end of his life, he provided information about his religious practices to anthropologists Joseph B. Casagrande and Robert Ritzenthaler, who wrote an account of his life, "John Mink, Obijwa Informant," in *In the Company of Man*.

Early Life

Shoniagizik related the experiences of his early years to Joseph Casagrande, an anthropologist conducting fieldwork among the Ojibwa in the early 1930s. Shoniagizik recalled,

> I was born in the time of the ripening strawberries when my people were camped near Rice Lake [in present-day Wisconsin]. My mother's mother helped at my birth and . . . my father killed a deer for a feast. . . . I remember the taste of my mother's milk. It tasted rich and good like bear fat. When I was able to eat wild rice and venison and blueberries, I stopped nursing. Except when unavailable, the rice was as pervasive as bread is today.

Shoniagizik stressed that tribes migrating to the western Great Lakes region made wild rice their basic foodstuff. Shoniagizik continued,

John Mink (Shoniagizik). Courtesy of the Milwaukee Public Museum.

I remember being tied up on my cradleboard and watching the bright charms that hung from the hood. My mother put my umbilical cord in a little black bag when it fell off and hung it from the hood. When I got off the cradleboard, I got my first moccasins and they had holes cut in the soles to help me walk. I was small and frisky and everyone liked me and laughed at me. My first toys were a little toboggan and a little bow and arrow with which I killed squirrels and chipmunks. . . . I fasted all the time when I was young. In the early morning I would paint my face with charcoal and go off into the woods without eating. The spirits came to me in my dreams as I fasted and gave me the power to kill and game and to cure peo-ple. They taught me songs and charms and how to suck the disease from sick people and made medicines.

Leadership

As a spiritual leader of the Ojibwa Nation, Shoniagizik, more than any other on the Lac Courte Oreilles Ojibwa Reservation, strove to preserve the traditions and customs of Ojibwa life. As the foremost priest in the *midewiwin* society, he had in his custody a birch bark scroll consisting of four separate panels on which pictographs and other mnemonic devices depicting Ojibwa history were engraved. Each of the scroll's four panels embodied the collected memory of the ceremonial and cultural history of the Ojibwa required for membership in the *midewiwin* society.

Shoniagizik fasted many times as a youngster and received his spiritual power to heal, and he learned many sacred songs and medicines as the result of trances and dreams. It is said that "everyone at Courte Oreilles seemed to know Shoniagizik. Some called him a medicine man, priest, and friend, while others called him a sorcerer, pagan and scoundrel. But all agreed that his knowledge of the old ways was unsurpassed by any of the 1700 Ojibwa on the reservation." Shoniagizik had prescriptions to start or stop menstruation and to induce the flow of milk in a new mother. It is said that his favorite medicine was learned from his paternal grandfather and was used to bring on labor: "The expectant mother drank the portion from a birchbark vessel on the inside of which the image of a snake was etched with the heat at the place on the rim from which the woman drank. As the liquid was drained, the figure of the snake was revealed and the child thereby frightened from its mother's womb." The most dramatic therapy he practiced was performed in a shamanistic trance during which he magically sucked a diseased substance out of the body of the patient. This treatment was used primarily to treat those who were the victims of sorcery.

Shoniagizik met his first wife at La Pointe, in present-day Wisconsin, where the government made annual annuity payments to the tribe. They were attracted to each other and wanted to become man and wife. They lived with her family for awhile, and later made their own home. Shoniagizik described his wife as being a good worker, and they were happy together. She died in childbirth after they had been married five years. Two years later, he remarried. His second wife was from the Whooping Crane Clan and had been married before and had two girls and a boy. They lived together for about ten years. All together he had four wives and many children. His last wife, "Little Girl," died in 1931. Following her death Shoniagizik lived alone near the Couderay River in present-day Wisconsin, in a house he had occupied for more than half a century.

When Shoniagizik died in 1943, his death marked the passing of a way of life. He was one of the last of the Ojibwa who followed the traditional cultural and spiritual lifeways passed down to him by his elders and his spiritual helpers.

Further Reading

Casagrande, Joseph B., ed. *In the Company of Man: Twenty Portraits by Anthropologists*. 1960. New York: Harper & Brothers.

Hirschfelder, Arlene, and Paulette Molin. *The Encyclopedia of Native American Religions*. 1992. New York: Facts on File.

Vennum, Thomas. *Wild Rice and the Ojibwa People*. 1988. St. Paul: Minnesota Historical Society Press.

Short Bull

Full Name at Birth: Short Bull (Tatanka Ptecela)

Birth: ca. 1845

Death: 1924

Education: no formal education

Leadership Position: Brule Sioux holy man and Ghost Dance prophet

Summary

Short Bull was a Brule Sioux holy man who was an apostle of the Ghost Dance religion of 1890. He was born in the mid-1800s and was a member of Chief Lip's band of Lakota who were located on Pass Creek between Rosebud and Pine Ridge in Dakota Territory. Short Bull is best known as a Ghost Dance prophet. He also achieved prominence as a warrior at the Battle of the Little Big Horn and in other intertribal wars.

Short Bull was one of the delegates chosen by Lakota leaders in 1889 to visit Wovoka,* the Paiute holy man, to listen to and study the Ghost Dance religion that promised a new life for Native peoples. Short Bull became a staunch believer in the new religion. He returned to his people and delivered the message of world renewal and regeneration promised by Wovoka and the Ghost Dance.

In December 1890, the furor created by the Ghost Dance culminated in tragedy in Dakota Territory. Government agents feared that the Ghost Dance signaled a new round of Indian wars and attempted to suppress the new religion and arrest those who continued to practice the Dance. Although warned to stop practicing the new faith by government authorities, Short Bull and his followers persisted. Short Bull advised his followers to continue dancing and not to fear the soldiers who opposed them because their sacred Ghost Dance shirt, which he had seen in a dream, would protect them. On December 28, 1890, the reconstructed U.S. Seventh Cavalry massacred more than two hundred men, women, and children of Big Foot's band of Miniconjou Sioux at Wounded Knee in South Dakota.

Short Bull was arrested in 1891. Rather than go to prison he joined Wil-

Photographer Richard Throssel took this portrait of the Sioux holy man Short Bull (Tatanka Ptecela) in December 1905. National Anthropological Archives, Smithsonian Institution.

liam "Buffalo Bill" Cody's Wild West show and toured Europe and the United States. In his final years, he joined the Congregational church.

Early Life

Short Bull was born in 1845 along the Niobrara River in what is now Nebraska, at a time when extreme pressure was being exerted on Indian people to abandon their traditional lifeways and relocate onto government Indian reservations. Government hunters and private entrepreneurs had decimated the great buffalo herds, which sustained the Great Plains Indian way of life. Indian people looked to their religious leaders for advice and survival.

There are no recorded histories of his early life; however, it is known that he was the brother-in-law of the Lakota Ghost Dance leader and medicine man Kicking Bear.* Short Bull was one of the delegates Lakota leaders chose to visit Wovoka, the

Paiute holy man, in 1889 to listen to and study the Ghost Dance religion, which promised a new life for Native peoples. Short Bull and Kicking Bear visited Wovoka at an encampment near Walker Lake in present-day Nevada and were converted to the new religion.

Leadership

Short Bull was one of the delegates Lakota leaders chose from the Pine Ridge Reservation to visit Wovoka, the Paiute holy man, to learn of his new religious teachings firsthand. In 1889, Short Bull traveled to Nevada with his brother-in-law, Kicking Bear, and other Lakota emissaries. After meeting with Wovoka, Short Bull became a staunch believer in the new religion. He returned to his people and began teaching the sacred beliefs and songs of the visionary movement known as the Ghost Dance. The dance movement promised deliverance from the encroaching white horde, and its popularity and practice spread rapidly among the Plains Indian Nations.

Government officials misunderstood the importance of the Ghost Dance. Although it was a religious revitalization religion for the Indian people, they interpreted the movement as a call for new Indian warfare. In October 1890, federal troops issued orders for Indian people to stop practicing the Ghost Dance, and additional federal troops were dispatched to South Dakota to enforce the orders. With the appearance of the troops, Short Bull led his Ghost Dancer followers from the Rosebud Reservation to what he proclaimed was a sacred tree at Pass Creek. From there, he led his followers along the White River to an area of the badlands known as the Stronghold. Although warned to stop practicing the new faith by government authorities, Short Bull per-

sisted and advised his followers to continue dancing. He prophesied the date of a new world to come when the Indian dead would be returned to life, the buffalo restored, and the whites would vanish from the earth. Short Bull told his followers not to fear the soldiers who opposed them because the new sacred Ghost Dance shirt that he had been shown in a dream would protect them.

James McLaughlin, the government agent at the Standing Rock Reservation, feared the implications of the Ghost Dance shirt and feared that Sitting Bull, the Hunkpapa Sioux holy man, and his followers would join Short Bull and the Ghost Dancers. Sitting Bull was not a follower of the Ghost Dance but had resisted government efforts to impose Christianity and civilization on his people. Sitting Bull was murdered on December 15, 1890, when fighting erupted between his followers and the tribal policemen sent to carry out McLaughlan's orders to arrest the holy man. When Big Foot, the Miniconjou Sioux leader, learned of Sitting Bull's murder, he led a band of Lakota, including Ghost Dancers, to seek protection on the Pine Ridge Reservation. Federal troops intercepted Big Foot on December 28, 1890, and on December 29 massacred more than two hundred men, women, and children of Big Foot's band at Wounded Knee in South Dakota. Following the massacre, the remaining Lakota Ghost Dancers surrendered to General Nelson A. Miles. In January 1891, Short Bull, Kicking Bear, and other adherents were imprisoned at Fort Sheridan, Illinois, to serve a two-year sentence. In the spring of 1891, the government agreed to Buffalo Bill Cody's request that the prisoners be released to him and be allowed to travel abroad with his Wild West show. Short Bull toured with Cody's show in Europe and the United

States over the next two years. In 1893 Buffalo Bill Cody used Short Bull as an actor and a consultant in making a film that re-enacted the 1890 massacre at Wounded Knee. In the final years of his life, Short Bull joined the Congregational church.

See also Kicking Bear; Wovoka.

Further Reading

Axelrod, Alan. *Chronicle of the Indian Wars from Colonial Times to Wounded Knee.* 1993. Englewood, N.J.: Prentice-Hall.

Cassidy, James J., Jr. *Through Indian Eye: The Untold Story of Native American Peoples.* 1995. Pleasantville, N.Y.: Reader's Digest Association.

Hirschfelder, Arlene, and Paulette Molin. 1992. *The Encyclopedia of Native American Religions.* 1992. New York: Facts on File.

Short Bull: http://www.olc.edu/shortbull/ shortbull.html.

Waldman, Carl. *Who Was Who in Native American History.* 1990. New York: Facts on File.

Sitting Bull (Haná cha-thí ak)

Full Name at Birth: Bítaye ("Captor")

Birth: ca. 1854, place unknown; described as being about age thirty-six in September 1890

Death: 1932 in Carlton, Oklahoma

Education: no formal education

Leadership Position: Arapaho Ghost Dance apostle

Summary

Sitting Bull (Haná cha-thí ak), the Arapaho Ghost Dance apostle, should not be confused with the more famous Hunkpapa Sioux principal chief Sitting Bull (Tatanka Yotanka), although the two flourished during the same historical period (1870–1890).

In late 1889 Sitting Bull (Haná cha-thí ak) was a member of a larger group of medicine men who traveled to Nevada to meet Wovoka,* the Paiute messiah. The delegation included Arapaho, Shoshoni, Lakota, and Cheyenne emissaries, including the Brule Sioux holy man Short Bull* and the Lakota medicine man Kicking Bear.* Sitting Bull interviewed the Paiute messiah himself to learn the whole truth of Wovoka's prophetic message that promised Indian world renewal and regeneration. Following a five-day conference, during which Wovoka entered into a trance state on at least one occasion, Sitting Bull and the other medicine men returned to Wyoming, arriving in March 1890.

Sitting Bull believed the teachings of Wovoka and became a leading Ghost Dance apostle among the Arapaho people. He became a highly respected prophet and was regarded almost in the same light as the messiah Wovoka himself, although his specific instructions to his followers were somewhat different.

Wovoka told his followers that Indian people were to cooperate with the white people and live in peace without warfare until the time that the Creator would remove all white people from the earth. Indian people were to abstain from alcohol and were instructed not to fight, steal, or lie. Wovoka was given a number of powers that included weather control, invulnerability to weapons, political responsibility, and prophecies. He was also given a sacred Ghost Dance to be performed for four successive nights, and the last night they were to keep up the dance until the morning of the fifth day. Wovoka told his followers that if they practiced the Ghost Dance religion, the white people would be swallowed up, and Indian people, alive and dead, would be reunited on a regenerated earth that was forever free from death, disease, and all the other miseries that had recently been experienced by Indian people.

Sitting Bull taught that the new earth would be preceded by a wall of fire, which would drive the whites across the ocean to their original lands, while the Indians would be enabled by means of sacred eagle feathers to survive the flames. When the expulsion of the whites had been accomplished, a rain continuing for twelve days would extinguish the fire. As in Wovoka's teachings Indian people, alive and dead, would then be reunited on a regenerated earth that was forever free from death, disease, and misery.

Early Life

There is little written history of Sitting Bull's early life. The author James Mooney states in *The Ghost-Dance Religion and the Sioux Outbreak of 1890* that when he was a boy, Sitting Bull was known as Bítaye ("Captor"), but upon reaching manhood, his name was changed to Haná cha-thí ak ("Sitting Bull"). Sitting Bull told Mooney that he was originally a southern Arapaho, but in 1876 he joined with the northern branch of the tribe living in Wyoming. Sitting Bull was described as being "a full-blood Arapaho, although rather light in complexion and color of eyes. He was about 5 ft. 8 in. tall,

dignified but plain in his bearing, with a particularly winning smile. Sitting Bull spoke only his native language, but could converse with ease in the universal sign language of the [Great] [P]lains [Indians]." The sign language referred to was a common sign language developed among the various Native tribes, as well as white traders and trappers, to converse and conduct business. Sitting Bull later used this same sign language to instruct his Ghost Dance disciples among the Caddo, Wichita, and Kiowa who could not speak his Siouan language.

Leadership

Sitting Bull was a highly respected medicine man and Ghost Dance prophet, not only among his people, the Arapaho, but among the Kiowa, Caddo, and Wichita as well. Many Indian men and women wanted to touch the holy man and would come into his tepee and rub their hands on him and cry. Unlike many other medicine men, Sitting Bull made no demands for service or presents and rejected all claims that he had ever done so. When asked about the Ghost Dance religion, Sitting Bull said that he had seen Wovoka, the man whom Jesus had helped or inspired. Sitting Bull did not view himself as an exalted individual but danced and sang like the humblest person present. He believed in the visions of Wovoka and was largely sincere in his teachings. Sitting Bull truly believed that he was giving his people a better religion than they had before and taught this followers precepts that if faithfully carried out would bring them into a better world.

Sitting Bull's teachings differed somewhat from Wovoka's as the result of a dream that he had had. Wovoka had been given a sacred Ghost Dance to be performed for four successive days and nights and if practiced religiously would ultimately bring about a new world that would be absent the white menace and free from death, disease, and all of the other miseries that had visited upon Indian people. Sitting Bull taught that the new earth would be preceded by a wall of fire that would drive the whites back across the ocean, while the Indians would be enabled by means of sacred eagle feathers to survive the flames. When the expulsion of the whites had been accomplished, a rain would cleanse the earth, and, as in Wovoka's teachings Indian people, alive and dead would be reunited on a regenerated earth that was forever free from death, disease, and misery.

In late 1890, Sitting Bull's popularity as a Ghost Dance apostle grew. At a Ghost Dance held on the South Canadian river, about two miles below the Indian agency at Darlington, Oklahoma, it was estimated that approximately three thousand Indians were present, including nearly all of the Arapaho and Cheyenne, as well as a number of Caddo, Wichita, and Kiowa. Many of the participants experienced Ghost Dance trances at this gathering through the medium of Sitting Bull. One participant reported that Sitting Bull had hypnotized him with the eagle feather and the motion of his hands, and while in this unconscious state, he saw his dead brother but awoke just as he was about to speak to him.

Sitting Bull played a controversial role in the selling of Indian lands and as a result came under criticism from many tribal members. In 1890, a U.S. government treaty commission approached the Arapaho leadership for the sale of their reservation lands. The great majority of the Arapaho opposed the land sale; Sitting Bull, however, advised the leaders to sell the land for what they could get, as

the people had need of the money. Sitting Bull reassured the tribal leaders that the Ghost Dance messiah would come and restore the land to them. Based on Sitting Bull's recommendation, Chief Left Hand signed the agreement in the face of threats from those opposed to it. This incident shows how strongly Sitting Bull and the other Arapaho believed in the new doctrine.

As the religious movement spread, it took on features unique to individual groups. Initially, the Ghost Dance was to be held frequently in small dances at each camp at irregular intervals. Wovoka soon instructed his followers to change to larger dances participated in by several camps together at regular intervals of six weeks, each dance continuing for five consecutive days. The change was opposed by Sitting Bull and some others. When the Ghost Dance reached the Lakota, they added the wearing of a Ghost Dance shirt to the religion. The shirt would be impervious to the white man's bullets. The Ghost Dance shirt frightened Indian agents and government officials, who now saw Indian warriors performing a strange new war dance that was supposed to result in the disappearance of whites and the return of the buffalo. The wearing of the Ghost Dance shirt thus transformed Wovoka's religious movement into a warrior movement. In 1890, the United States outlawed the practice of the Ghost Dance on Indian reservations. Tensions intensified between the Lakota and the soldiers as Indian people continued to participate in the Ghost Dance ritual out of sight of the army.

On December 29, 1890, remnants of Custer's 7th Cavalry massacred more than two hundred men, women, and children of Big Foot's band of Miniconjou Sioux at Wounded Knee in

South Dakota. It was erroneously believed that Big Foot and his followers were en route to join Ghost Dancers who had left the Cheyenne River Reservation to carry out the teachings of Wovoka. In fact, Big Foot was en route to the Pine Ridge Reservation to encourage the Indian people to return to their reservation.

In October 1892, Sitting Bull and other tribal delegates once again visited the home of Wovoka. Sitting Bull found the Ghost Dance messiah lying down, his face covered with a blanket, and singing to himself. When questioned regarding the Ghost Dance, Wovoka told Sitting Bull that he (Wovoka) "had preached to them and had given them a new dance, but that some of them, especially the Sioux, had twisted things and made trouble."

Wovoka advised the Indian delegation to return home and tell the people to stop practicing the Ghost Dance.

Sitting Bull lost influence as a result of the 1890 massacre at Wounded Knee and because the land lost by treaty based on his recommendation was never restored to the Arapaho people.

See also Wovoka.

Further Reading

Hirschfelder, Arlene, and Paulette Molin. *The Encyclopedia of Native American Religions.* 1992. New York: Facts on File.

Michael Hittman. *Wovoka and the Ghost Dance.* 1990. Carson City: Grace Dangberg Foundation.

Mooney, James. *The Ghost-Dance Religion and the Sioux Outbreak of 1890.* 1991. Lincoln: University of Nebraska Press.

Skanyadariyoh

See Handsome Lake

Skolaskin (or Kolaskin)

Full Name at Birth: Skolaskin or Kolaskin

Birth: ca. 1839 in the Sanpoil village of Sinakialt on the Columbia River in the Pacific Northwest

Death: March 30, 1922, on his land allotment near Snukéilt in Washington State

Education: no formal education

Leadership Position: Sanpoil dreamer-prophet

Summary

Skolaskin was a nineteenth-century dreamer-prophet from the Sanpoil tribe in the Pacific Northwest's Columbia Plateau region. He received his dream, or divine message, from the Giver of Life while recovering from a near-death injury. His message combined elements of Christianity with traditional tribal beliefs and emphasized adherence to traditional dress and lifeways. He instructed his followers to return to traditional subsistence patterns of gathering and fishing and the adoption on an austere religious life. Despite his peaceful message, federal authorities suppressed him and his followers. Skolaskin was imprisoned at the military prison on Alcatraz Island between 1889 and 1892 for subverting reservation discipline, but returned to the Colville Reservation following his release and continued to criticize both private land ownership and Christianity.

Early Life

Skolaskin was raised with three younger half-brothers, a full brother, and a sister in Sinakialt, a small Sanpoil village on the Columbia River. He and his family probably shared a mat home (a house made from tule reeds)with four or five other families, most of whom would have been relatives of his father. It is believed that Skolaskin acquired a minor spirit helper in his youth and participated in the daily village activities of gathering subsistence and playing games.

As a young man, Skolaskin suffered a disorder that crippled at least one of his legs and required him to place his hands on his knees or to use a staff when he walked. The exact cause of this crippling cannot be identified with certainty because of conflicting accounts attributing the injury to a horse-related injury, the possibility of rheumatism, or possible revenge wrought by a vengeful husband. It is known that his convalescence was extensive, possibly as long as two years. This event was pivotal in shaping Skolaskin's life as a prophet, for his illness and recovery appear to be the basis for a religious experience whereby he visited the spirit world. Skolaskin claimed to have been near death when he visited the other world and returned with instructions from Quilentsuten, "the Spirit who made us," to teach to the people. Bent over, with his hands on his knees, Skolaskin

preached his vision or dream and founded the Dreamer religion.

Leadership

Skolaskin received his call to become a dreamer-prophet at a propitious time. In the mid-nineteenth century, the Native American people in the Pacific Northwest were experiencing great physical and cultural devastation. White gold miners and settlers were continuing to spread northward in great numbers, threatening the independence of the Sanpoil people. European-introduced diseases decimated the tribal populations, and in 1872, the area experienced a great earthquake. Taken together, these cataclysmic events indicated to the Native people that their world had become spiritually and physically unbalanced. It was in this world of chaos that Skolaskin received his religious instruction and preached the message of his dream. Some say that Skolaskin actually forecast the earthquake and had said, "The land is going to shake. Buildings will fall down. People will go out of their heads" (Ruby and Brown, 144). Following the earthquake, very much in evidence in the Sanipol homeland, Skolaskin developed a control over the people as if hypnotized. For instance on May 16, 1889, the Spokane Falls *Mourning Review* carried a story describing Skolaskin's career and "How He Frightened His People and Became an Absolute Monarch in Washington" (Ruby and Brown 144–145.)

The Native people were fearful of Skolaskin and in awe of his warnings. He constantly reminded them of his recovery from near death, the dreams and revelations that he had received, and his prophetic powers, all of which he claimed that Quilentsuten, the Creator, had given him. Skolaskin told people that they would go to hell if they did not turn from drinking, stealing, and committing adultery, among other sinful ways. Sunday was to be observed as a day of rest during which no one was to work. Gambling, a Sanpoil tradition, was banned, and people were admonished to be friendly and kind to one another. Sexual licentiousness was not to be tolerated; a return to puritanical virtues was required. While some of the banned practices, particularly gambling, were difficult to give up, his followers vowed to heed his teachings and promised to follow the dream from the Giver of Life.

Skolaskin's claim to be a prophet was not without challenge, however, and he recognized that control over his followers was imperative if he was going to be successful in driving the white people out of Sanpoil lands. To safeguard his people and keep them true to the Dreamer religion, he found it necessary to form a guard force to prevent outside influence from eroding his authority and help maintain control of the people. Skolaskin controlled his followers by maintaining a culture of fear and hope. Those who opposed or challenged his leadership were faced with what they considered to be the very real threat that Skolaskin would turn them into an inanimate object such as a rock or tree.

The continuing government encroachments gave credence to Skolaskin's teachings and made his people more willing to heed his words. Skolaskin did understand that they were sorely outnumbered. In August 1872, the Washington territorial superintendent of Indian affairs, R. H. Milroy, met Skolaskin and informed him that the Indians were like leaves in winter against whites who were as numerous as the sands of the shore.

It is unclear how or where Skolaskin received his message and motivation, but around the year 1873 he proposed building an ark to save his followers from a cataclysmic flood that he predicted. Numerous Native prophets had preached the destruction of the physical world inhabited by whites and a regeneration of a pure Native world. Skolaskin had ample opportunity to hear their stories as well as stories, from missionaries or other whites. Skolaskin had undoubtedly heard the story of Noah, the ark, and the great biblical flood. The rain never came, however, and the ark was never built. Skolaskin did use the opportunity to build a church.

Skolaskin rejected the government's land grab and assimilation programs and often ran into disfavor with the government over issues of law and order on the reservation. Because of Skolaskin's influence and control over his followers, General John Gibbon suggested that it would be better if Skolaskin were to be sent to "some distant point where he can no longer exercise his pernicious influence over his followers in interfering with the designs of the Government" (Ruby and Brown 178). On October 30, 1889, Acting Secretary of the Interior George Chandler recommended that Skolaskin be brought under military control because he was "a most dangerous and turbulent element among the Indians." Less than one month later, on November 21, 1889, Skolaskin was arrested and incarcerated without benefit of a trial in the military prison on Alcatraz Island, where he remained a prisoner until June 22, 1892.

Upon his return to his people, Skolaskin found that drastic changes had taken place on the reservation. He condemned the Indians who had opened up more than 1.5 million acres of Indian land to white settlement. His church was still intact, however. Two of his disciple chiefs, Umtosoolow and Skmoautkin, had kept his ministry alive. By the turn of the century, various forms of the Dreamer faith, often called the Longhouse or Feather religion, had spread across the Northwest and south into California. The religion provided a sanctuary for the protection of Native values and a vehicle for the preservation of Native leadership. Skolaskin and many of his followers converted to Roman Catholicism, and by the 1980s, only a few traditionalist still clung to hopes for a revitalization of the kind once envisioned by Skolaskin.

Further Reading

Hirschfelder, Arlene, and Paulette Molin. *The Encyclopedia of Native American Religions.* 1992. New York: Facts on File.

Ruby, Robert H., and John H. Brown. *Dreamer-Prophets of the Columbia Plateau: Smohalla and Skolaskin.* 1989. Norman: University of Oklahoma Press.

Trigger, Bruce G., and Wilcomb E. Washburn, eds. *The Cambridge History of the Native Peoples of the Americas, Vol. 1: North America, Part 2.* 1996. Cambridge: Cambridge University Press.

John Slocum

Full Name at Birth: Squ-sacht-un

Birth: ca. 1840, near Puget Sound, Washington; flourished in the 1880s

Death: ca. 1896–1898; place of death unknown

Education: no formal education

Leadership Position: Nisqually Shaker Religion prophet and medicine man

Summary

John Slocum was a Native American prophet in the Puget Sound area who founded Tschadam, the Indian Shaker religion.

In the fall of 1881 John Slocum "died" as the result of an accident that occurred while he was working as a logger in the forests around Puget Sound in present-day Washington State. It is reported that his neck was broken in a logging accident, and while in a death state, he was transported to the gates of the Christian heaven. Slocum announced that while he was in heaven, he met an angel who sent him back to earth with a message telling how Indian people could survive the trauma of reservation life. Indian people, he was told, must stop drinking, gambling, and relying on Indian shamanism for their healing. Slocum's new teachings were unique in that they combined traditional Native spirituality with both Protestant and Roman Catholic influences. Also in keeping with Christian teachings, Slocum taught that God's son, Jesus Christ, lived on earth and would return again. Indian people were instructed to pray every morning and evening and before meals and to attend regular church services. If they followed these teachings, Slocum stated, God would give them a great and unique religion to help them. He taught that God was good and all-powerful, and that he would help Indian people who avoided sin and prayed to him regularly. Slocum's teaching closely resembled that of Christian missionaries who had visited the Puget Sound area.

In 1882, Slocum became seriously ill for a second time. His wife, Mary Johnson Slocum, found him near death, and as she approached her husband's bed, she began shaking uncontrollably. Slocum's health soon improved, and his recovery was attributed to Mary Slocum's shaking, interpreted as a sign of divine powers. Shaking then became an important part of the new religion. The religion was named the Shaker Religion after the shaking or twitching motion participants experienced while healing or "brushing off" their sins while in a meditative state.

The Shaker church was formally organized as an association on June 7, 1892, at Mud Bay, Washington, and incorporated as the Shaker church on June 20, 1910, at Olympia, Washington.

Early Life

Little is known about John Slocum's early life. Where he was born or when he died is unknown. Slocum is described as being a very ordinary man, about 5 feet 8 inches tall. His head had been flattened at birth in keeping with the traditional practice of the Nisqually people. It was believed that a flattened head was a sign of beauty. He was soft-spoken and humble. John married Mary Johnson, and they had thirteen children; only two lived to adulthood. Slocum supported his family by working in a logging operation in the forests around his home. In the late fall of 1881, when John Slocum was about forty years old, he was seriously injured, possibly suffering a broken neck, which would change the lives of thousands of Indian people.

Leadership

John Slocum was a religious prophet and a medicine man. He was a member of the Squaxin Band of the Nisqually Indians of Mud Bay in the present-day state of Washington. Slocum lived an unremarkable life until 1881, when it is said that he rose up from the dead following a serious logging accident. Slocum returned with a message for his people that they must live moral, upright lives and reject evils such as alcohol and Indian shamanism. Slocum was also given healing powers and achieved importance as the founder of the Indian Shaker church.

In the fall of 1881, John Slocum was gravely injured while working as a logger in the Puget Sound area of present-day Washington State. One eyewitness reported that Slocum suffered a broken neck. Slocum, believed to be dead, was carried back to his house, where his family washed and dressed his body for burial. His body was then covered with a white sheet. After a few hours, Slocum began to move beneath the sheet. As his family and other mourners watched, he pulled the sheet away, moved his head from side to side, and sat up. Slocum arose, walked outside, removed his clothing, washed with clean water, and wrapped himself in a clean sheet. He then instructed that his burial clothing be destroyed.

On June 25, 1893, James Wickersham, the attorney for the Shaker church, recorded Slocum's personal deposition regarding the incidents surrounding his death and rebirth, as well as the prophetic insights that led to the founding of the Shaker religion. Slocum believed that he in fact had died because he said he "saw a shining light—a great light—trying my soul. I looked and saw my body had no soul—looked at my own body—it was dead." Slocum returned and spoke to an assemblage of his friends, saying, "when I die, do not cry." At that point he died a second time. "Angels told me to look back and see my body. I did, and saw it lying down." According to the Shaker prophet, his "soul left his body and went up to judgement place of God." The prophet reported that "he spoke to angels who told him to go back and turn alive again on earth because his work on earth had not been completed." Slocum also stated, regarding his rebirth, "When I came alive, I tell my friend, good things in heaven. God is kind to us. If you all try hard and help me, we will be better men on earth." Through the Spirit the Indians learned to help themselves or others in sickness, by kneeling in prayer and asking for help to cure, and if we do not learn to help him, we generally lose him." Slocum taught that "the single most important element of practice in the Shaker faith was healing through the power of the Holy Spirit, which was broadly defined to mean working through prayer to restore the health and balance of everyone and everything."

The Shaker religion arose at a time of great religious and cultural turmoil, when Native people were faced with increased pressure to surrender traditional lands and be confined to Indian reservations. Following his "rebirth," Slocum continued to experience trances in which he received divine messages on how Indian people could survive the trauma of reservation life. The *Tschadam* or the Indian Shaker religion combined the traditional guardian spirit religion of the Nisqually people with Protestant and Roman Catholic in-

fluences. It has also been suggested that elements of the Shaker religion came from the earlier Ghost Dance movement in the Plateau area. This religion was based on the belief that by dancing like the dead in the other world, Indians could renew their worlds and bring about the return of the dead.

As Slocum attracted more followers, the religion attracted a good deal of opposition from missionaries and Indian agents. Slocum and his followers, especially among the Squaxin, Skokomish, Nisqually, and Chehalis tribes, were imprisoned regularly by white officials for inciting resistance to assimilation programs. Later, when it was recognized that the Shaker religion had a beneficial social influence on the Native people, the objection of government and church officials became less vocal.

The element of "the shake," and thus the name of the religion, developed out of a later incident in John Slocum's life. In 1882, about a year after his resurrection, Slocum became ill again and was expected to die. Faced with what appeared to be John's impending death, his wife, Mary, became hysterical. She approached his prostrate body trembling uncontrollably. When her "shaking had passed it was observed that John Slocum had recovered somewhat. Slocum's health continue to improve and was attributed to the shake, which was understood as a manifestation of God's divine power. Thus, the shake became a basic element in Shaker services, which continues to this day.

The Shaker church was legally constituted in 1892 and incorporated under Washington State law in 1910. The Indian Shaker religion is still practiced today among coastal Indians of British Columbia (Canada), Washington, Oregon, and northwestern California.

Further Reading

Calloway, Colin G. *First Peoples: A Documentary Survey of American Indian History.* 1999. New York: St. Martin's.

Champagne, Duane, ed. *The Native North American Almanac: A Reference Work on Native North Americans in the United States and Canada.* 1994. Detroit: Gale Research.

Gibson, Arrell Morgan. *The American Indian: Prehistory to the Present.* 1980. Lexington, Mass.: D. C. Heath.

Hirschfelder, Arlene, and Paulette Molin. *The Encyclopedia of Native American Religions.* 1992. New York: Facts on File.

Trafzer, Clifford E. *American Indian Prophets.* 1986. Newcastle, Calif.: Sierra Oaks Publishing Co.

Trigger, Bruce G., and Wilcomb E. Washburn. *The Cambridge History of the Native Peoples of the Americas. Vol. 1: North America, Part 2.* 1996. Cambridge: Cambridge University Press.

Waldman, Carl. *Who Was Who in Native American History.* 1990. New York: Facts On File.

Walker, Paul Robert. *American Indian Lives: Spiritual Leaders.* 1994. New York: Facts on File.

Redbird Smith

Full Name at Birth: Redbird (Red Bird) Smith

Birth: July 19, 1850, near Fort Smith, Arkansas

Death: 1918

Education: no formal education

Leadership Position: Keetoowah Cherokee nativistic movement leader and principal chief of the Cherokee Nation

Summary

Redbird Smith was an advocate for the restoration of religious and cultural traditions among his people and led a resistance movement against policies of the U.S. government to redistribute Indian lands. He and a number of colleagues revived the Keetoowah (Keetoway, Kituhwa) Society to protect Indian sovereignty. The society was an ancient religious group that perpetuated a strong interest in Cherokee culture and religion. Redbird Smith was one of the primary leaders in the revival movement.

Early Life

Redbird Smith was born on July 19, 1850, during the Cherokee forced removal from Arkansas to the Cherokee Nation in Indian Territory, present-day Oklahoma. The family settled in the Illinois district of the Cherokee Nation, and Redbird grew up among the western Cherokee people. Redbird's father, Pig Smith, was a traditionalist full-blood Cherokee. His mother, Lizzy Hildebrand, was the mixed-blood daughter of a German miller and a full-blood Cherokee woman from the Wolf Clan. Pig Smith, Redbird's father, acquired the name "Pig Smith" from working with pig iron in his trade as a blacksmith. Pig Smith also served in the Cherokee government.

In 1859, when Redbird Smith was nine years old, traditional Cherokee, fighting for preservation of Cherokee land and culture, formed the Keetoowah

Society (from *kituwha*, the Cherokee word for "key"). The organization held secret meetings at night; thus, it was given the name Nighthawk Keetoowah Society. Redbird Smith's family were active participants and leaders in the movement.

In some Cherokee clans, it was customary for a father to select a spiritual adviser for each of his male children. Creek Sam, a Natchez visionary, was selected to instruct, educate, and guide Redbird Smith.

Leadership

Following the 1830 Indian Removal Act, the federal government had designated large areas of western land to be reserved for removed tribes. This land was designated as Indian Territory and was primarily in the present-day state of Oklahoma. The land was to be protected from white encroachment and was to become a separate Indian state. As more and more settlers moved westward, however, they demanded that the federal government abrogate the treaty relationship with individual Indian Nations and open the lands to white settlement. In 1887, Congress passed the Dawes Act (also known as the Allotment Act), which broke up tribal estates and forced fee simple title upon Indian land holders, the remaining lands to be made available for sale and opened for white settlement. The Five Civilized Tribes, including the Cherokee, were exempt from this initial land theft. In 1893, the federal government removed the exemption protecting the Cherokee and in 1902 Congress passed the Cherokee Land Allotment Act, which provided for the abolishment of Indian Territory and the allotment of lands belonging to the Cherokee Nation. For many Indian people, no word for *allotment* existed and was analogous to religious, cultural and political extinction.

In response to the General Allotment Act and the Cherokee Land Allotment Act, conservative members of the Cherokee Nation revived the Nighthawk Keetoowah Society, which established a committee under Redbird Smith to resist allotment. Redbird Smith and the Nighthawks claimed that the society was a religious organization and refused to recognize the right of the U.S. government to allot tribal lands. The society urged nonviolent passive resistance and the revival of old town-square grounds modeled on nineteenth-century Cherokee ceremonial centers.

In 1902, the Indian office arrested Redbird Smith and other members of the Nighthawk Keetoowah Society in an effort to break up the resistance movement. Fearing further government reprisals, society members withdrew from tribal political participation and turned to the traditional religion of their people to sustain them. Redbird Smith established a ceremonial ground, now named for him, in his home community in 1902, and over twenty others emerged in other settlements within a year.

In 1907, Indian Territory became the state of Oklahoma. Smith's activism did not end, however. He recruited leaders and members from the other Five Civilized Tribes (Choctaw, Creek, Seminole, and Chickasaw) and in 1912 formed the Four Mothers Society to carry on the battle. The Four Mothers Society committed itself through collective action to preserving and advocating for political and legal rights of Indian tribes seeking alternatives to the allotment process. It raised modest sums to send delegations to Washington to protest the actions of the federal government and urge that the

Cherokee be permitted to return to their religion and tribal customs, including communal ownership of land. Redbird Smith of the Cherokee and Chitto Harjo of the Creek continued to oppose the dissolution of Indian Territory and the allotment of Indian lands long after both events had occurred.

Redbird Smith's leadership contributed to the survival of Cherokee sacred ways that otherwise would have been lost. He was elected to the office of principal chief of the Cherokee Nation in 1908 and died in 1918.

Further Reading

Champagne, Duane, ed. *The Native North American Almanac: A Reference Work on Native North Americans in the United States and Canada*. 1994. Detroit: Gale Research.

Gibson, Arrell Morgan. *The American Indian: Prehistory to the Present*. 1980. Lexington, Mass.: D. C. Heath and Company.

Hirschfelder, Arlene, and Paulette Molin. *The Encyclopedia of Native American Religions*. 1992. New York: Facts on File.

Redbird Smith: http://www.louisville.edu/k-12/camden/conroy/redbird.html.

Trigger, Bruce G., and Wilcomb E. Washburn. *The Cambridge History of the Native Peoples of the Americas. Vol. 1: North America, Part 2*. 1996. Cambridge: Cambridge University Press.

Waldman, Carl. *Who Was Who in Native American History*. 1990. New York: Facts on File.

Washburn, Wilcomb E. 1988. *Handbook of North American Indians, Vol. 4*. Washington, D.C.: Smithsonian Institution.

Smohalla

Full Name at Birth: Wak-Wei, or Kuk-Kia

Birth: ca. 1815–1820 in the village of Wallula on the Columbia River

Death: 1907, Yakima Indian Reservation, Washington State

Education: no formal education

Leadership Position: Wanapam dreamer-prophet

Summary

Smohalla was a member of the Wanapam Indian tribe that lived along the upper Columbia River in present-day eastern Washington State. He attained his medicine and power through the vision quest ritual, as well as two death and rebirth experiences where he traveled in death to receive instructions from the Great Spirit. In his rebirth form he advocated the preservation of traditional subsistence: fishing and gathering, a return to traditional lifeways. The Dreamer religion was given to Smohalla by the Great Spirit to counteract the death, disease, and influence of the Christian religion on Indian people.

Early Life

Smohalla was born between 1815 and 1820 in the area of present-day Wallula, Washington. He belonged to the small Shahaptian-speaking Wanapam tribe that lived in the Bid Bend area of the Columbia River, an area rich in salmon and fur-bearing animals. In keeping with Wanapam traditions, Smohalla would have numerous names during his lifetime.

At the time of his birth, he was given the name Wak-wei or Kuk-kia. This name, which means, "arising from the dust of the Earth Mother," would have great significance in his later life when he spoke of the need to protect mother earth and not to desecrate or what the Creator had given to his people. He later became known as Smohalla, Smowhalla, Shmoqula, Smuxale, or smo x El. These names were given to him after he rose to prominence as a prophet and are interpreted as "dreamer" or "preacher." Still another name associated with Smohalla was Waipshwa, or "Rock Carrier."

Leadership

Smohalla was a member of the Wanapam Indian tribe that lived along the upper Columbia River in present-day eastern Washington State. He left this area around 1850 after a dispute with Peopeomoxmox, a local Wallawalla chief, over a tryst between Smohalla and Peopeomoxmox's youngest wife. Following a severe flogging and public humiliation, Smohalla left the Wallula area and moved to P'na Village, also in present-day Washington State. Smohalla also came into conflict with the influential Wallawalla chief Homily (Homli), who feared Smohalla's rising importance as a medicine person, and Moses, a Sinkiuse chief who believed that Smohalla was making strong medicine against his life.

Smohalla attained his medicine and power through the vision quest ritual, whicht was traditional for youth of the Wanapam tribe. It was during one such quest atop La Lac, a sacred mountain known for successful vision quests, that Smohalla received the ability to communicate with various animals. By communicating with the animals he could predict the death of a tribesman, good or bad

times, and good places for hunting and fishing. During his vision quest, he was also given special songs and symbols associated with his special powers.

As he matured as a prophet, religious truths and instruction came to Smohalla in dreams—thus, the name of his religion: Dreamer religion. In one such revelation from the Great Spirit, he gained as many as 120 power songs and rituals. Among the teachings received was the repudiation of U.S. culture, including alcohol and agricultural practices. Smohalla has been credited with the following oft-mentioned quotations that can be traced to his childhood name Wak-wei, or Kuk-kia, which means, "arising from the dust of the Earth Mother: You ask me to plough the ground! Shall I take a knife and tear my mother's bosom? Then when I die she will not take me to her bosom to rest. You ask me to dig for stone! Shall I dig under her skin for her bones? Then when I die I can not enter her body to be born again. You ask me to cut grass and make hay and sell it, and be rich like white men, but how dare I cut off my mother's hair? Smohalla also prophesied that the Indian people would be resurrected and whites would be banished from their lands.

In addition to the power received through the vision quest and dreams, Smohalla is believed to have had two death and rebirth experiences where he traveled in death to receive instructions from the Great Spirit. In the resurrection experience, he brought back a message that to the Wanapam had the ring of authenticity. Another version of Smohalla's communication with the Great Spirit comes from Wanapam elders and descendents of Smohalla, who argued that his communication with the Creator is said to have occurred while he was mourning the loss of a beloved child.

Smohalla began to preach his revitalization doctrine about 1850. His preaching, which emphasized a return to tribal traditions and beliefs, was a combination of nativist sentiment, rejection of white culture, and resistance to the U.S. government and Christianity. The Dreamer religion focused on the belief in an impending destruction and renewal of the world, during which the dead would return. He rejected the government's assimilation program and advocated an end to sales of "mother earth." Smohalla advocated the preservation of traditional subsistence: fishing and gathering and the adoption of an ascetic religious life.

His popularity came at a time when the Indian population of the region was declining due to disease and land losses to U.S. settlers. Smohalla blamed the suffering and death from diseases directly on the white intruders in Wanapam homelands. Smohalla blamed the Reverend Dr. Marcus Whitman, whom the Indians killed in 1847, for poisoning the air by releasing disease from a bottle that Whitman brought from the East in 1843, thus causing the death of Indian people, including his own daughter and granddaughter.

The rapid spread of Smohalla's following, believed to be approximately two thousand in 1854, is believed to have materially contributed to the formation of a confederation of tribes in the region against white expansion during the Yakima War of 1855–1856. The war was fought by a coalition of tribes opposed to the assault on their land and traditional cultures and the confinement of Indian people to small reservations.

Smohalla spread his message throughout the area of present-day Oregon and Washington State and had many converts, including Old Joseph, a former Christian and influential chief among the Nez Percé nation. One of the best known of a series of prophets in the area, Smohalla's teachings also influenced a number of later prophets who preached messages of resistance, revitalization, and cultural survival. He is credited with having revived the Washani creed, an earlier Native medicine religion, and the Washat ceremonial dance that gave form to the Washani creed, while introducing other features from his dreams or visions.

Despite government opposition and interference, Smohalla practiced his religion until the end of his life. After his death in 1907, he was succeeded by his son Yoyouni (also Yo-onan) and then by his nephew, Puck Hyah Toot, who carried the Dreamer religion into the twentieth century.

Further Reading

Ballantine, Betty, and Ian Ballantine, eds. 1993. *The Native Americans: An Illustrated History.* Atlanta: Turner Publishing.

Champagne, Duane, ed. *The Native North American Almanac.* 1994. Detroit: Gale Research.

Hirschfelder, Arlene, and Paulette Molin. *The Encyclopedia of Native American Religions.* 1992. New York: Facts on File.

Ruby, Robert H., and John A. Brown. *Dreamer-Prophets of the Columbia Plateau: Smohalla and Skolaskin.* 1989. Norman: University of Oklahoma Press.

Thornton, Russell. *We Shall Live Again: The 1870 and 1890 Ghost Dance Movements as Demographic Revitalization.* 1986. Cambridge: Cambridge University Press.

Trigger, Bruce G., and Wilcomb E. Washburn, eds. *The Cambridge History of the Native Peoples of the Americas. Vol. 1, North America, Part 1.* 1996. Cambridge: University of Cambridge Press.

Washburn, Wilcomb E. *Handbook of North American Indians, Vol. 4.* 1988. Washington, D.C.: Smithsonian Institution.

Reuben A. Snake, Jr.

See Kee-Kah-Wah-Un-Ga

Stone Forehead

Full Name at Birth: Hohonaíviuhk (also known as "Man Who Walks with His Toes Turned Out" and "Medicine Arrow")
Birth: ca. 1795; place unknown
Death: 1876; place unknown
Education: no formal education
Leadership Position: Cheyenne holy man

Summary

Stone Forehead was a venerated Cheyenne holy man who served as keeper of the Sacred Arrows of the Cheyenne Nation from 1849 until his death in 1876. The Sacred Arrows, the most sacred possession of the Cheyenne people, united the Cheyenne as one people and represented male power. Two of the arrows are man arrows, and two are buffalo arrows. The Sacred Arrows are treated as living human beings and are considered to be the living manifestation of spiritual power. The four arrows were first bestowed upon the great Cheyenne prophet Sweet Medicine,* by the Supreme Being, Maheo, at Noaha-vose, the sacred mountain.

When Stone Forehead served as keeper of the Sacred Arrows, the Cheyenne people and their traditional way of life came under increasing attack from the influx of invaders to their territory as Americans moved west. Stone Forehead was a pipe carrier as well as the leader of Cheyenne war parties. A pipe carrier was a follower of the traditional Indian religion and used a prayer pipe as a physical representation of that following. During this period, Stone Forehead assumed other tribal leadership roles including that of head chief of the Cheyenne Nation. He possessed the power to see into the future and foretold the death of Lieutenant Colonel George Armstrong Custer at the Battle of the Little Big Horn. He also possessed the power to call to him his spirit helper, from whom he sought advice and information.

Early Life

There are no written records of Stone Forehead's early life. We do know that he was a full-blood Cheyenne, steeped in the traditional ways of a Cheyenne youth. Stone Forehead was a member of the Ivistsinih´pay, or Aorta, band of the Cheyenne Nation and was noted for possessing extraordinary spiritual powers. The name of his wife is unrecorded. It is known that he had three sons: Black Hairy Dog, Tall Wolf, and Fox Tail.

Stone Forehead was born in approximately 1795 and grew to manhood at a time when extreme pressure was being exerted on Indian people to surrender their traditional lands and relocate to Indian reservations. Stone Forehead grew to fill a dichotomous role among the Cheyenne people: that of a pipe carrier (peacemaker) and war party leader. The contradiction evident in these cultural traditions reflects the tumultuous times in which he grew to maturity and power.

Leadership

Stone Forehead was a tribal chief, a war party leader, and a highly respected Cheyenne holy man who served as keeper of the Sacred Arrows of the Cheyenne Nation from 1849 until his death in 1876. Stone Forehead was a member of the Ivistsinih´pay, or Aorta, band and was noted for possessing extraordinary spiritual powers. He could call to him his *maiyu* (spiritual helpers), and he could converse with the spirit world. In one demonstration of his connection to the spirit world, Stone Forehead's spirit helper would call out, "Make a light!" and after the fire had blazed up Stone Forehead had disappeared, although his rattle could be seen and heard moving alone through the air, as if shaken by a person. On other occasions, Stone Forehead would demonstrate his spiritual power by dancing through the camp, carrying a pole in one hand and a drum in the other. He then threw the drum in the air, and it would fly a long way, then suddenly turn and fly back, coming to the end on the pole where the drum would then slide down the pole into Stone Forehead's hand.

Stone Forehead demonstrated his connection with the spirit world in other ceremonies as well. One such ceremony was performed when many people were present. Traditional singers were invited into Stone Forehead's lodge, where he then unwrapped his sacred bundle that contained personal power items given to him in dreams or during vision quests. As Stone Forehead opened his medicine bundle, the singers changed their spiritual songs, and the fire was permitted to die out, until the lodge was dark. Before the fire was out and before he began to call for his spirit helpers, Stone Forehead was tied with four bowstrings. Each finger of each hand was tied separately to the next finger, in a hard knot, and the ends of the bowstrings were tied together on each hand, then bound behind his back so that his hands were tightly secured. His feet were tied together in the same manner, each toe being tied to the next one in a hard knot, and the feet bound together by the bowstrings. Once he had been tied securely, Stone Forehead was placed at the back of the lodge and tied to one of the lodge-poles.

After the fire had gone out, Stone Forehead's spirit helpers would enter the lodge, which would begin to shake as if by a strong wind. The poles creaked and bent, and suddenly in the lodge, a voice, or voices, could be heard talking to Stone Forehead. The spirit helper had been called, perhaps to be asked where the buffalo were or where the Cheyenne enemies were. The spirit helpers could also assist in locating missing people or even to tell where lost horses might be found. After Stone Forehead's spirit helpers had gone and a light had again been made, he was found to be untied and the bowstrings used to bind him were lying in the door. It was believed that his spirit helpers had untied him.

During the period when Stone Forehead served as keeper of the Sacred Arrows, the Cheyenne people and their traditional way of life came increasingly under attack by the federal government to surrender their homelands. In 1851, Stone Forehead was one of the signers of the Treaty of Fort Laramie. Approximately 10,000 Cheyenne, Sioux, Crow, Arapaho, Assiniboine, Gros Ventre, and Arikara Indians met with U.S. officials at Horse Creek near Fort Laramie in Wyoming Territory. The treaty included provisions establishing territorial boundaries and rights of way as well as pledges of peace and friendship between the U.S. government and the Native Nations. The Plains Indians defined their territories and promised to stop further hostile acts. In return, the United States pledged to protect the tribes from trespass and depredations by American citizens and to pay compensation for any damages suffered. The United States also promised the tribes an annual distribution of annuity goods for a ten-year period. Failure of the United States to comply with its obligation under the Treaty of Fort Laramie precipitated twenty-two years of intermittent war that culminated in the Battle of the Little Big Horn in 1876. Stone Forehead eventually concluded that peace could be possible only if the white invaders were driven out of Indian lands.

In 1869, Lieutenant Colonel George Armstrong Custer smoked the sacred pipe with Stone Forehead and other Cheyenne in the Sacred Arrow lodge and promised not to fight against them. Stone Forehead warned Custer that the outcome of treachery would be the death of him and his entire command. Stone Forehead then put ashes from the pipe bowl on Custer's boots and warned Custer that Maheo, the Creator, would destroy him if he went against the words spoken while smoking the pipe. The Cheyenne people remembered Stone Forehead's prophetic warning after Custer and the Seventh Cavalry were defeated at Battle of Little Big Horn in 1876. Stone Forehead died among the Cheyenne people in 1876 in an undisclosed location.

Further Reading

Grinnell George Bird. *The Cheyenne Indians: Their History and Ways of Life*. Vol. 2. 1962. New York: Cooper Square Publishers, Inc.

Grinnell, George Bird. *The Fighting Cheyennes*. 1956. Norman: University of Oklahoma Press.

Hirschfelder, Arlene, and Paulette Molin. *The Encyclopedia of Native American Religions*. 1992. New York: Facts On File.

Suwi

Full Name at Birth: Suwi (Sam Clam)
Birth: date and place not recorded
Death: date and place not recorded
Education: no formal education
Leadership Position: Cocopa Ghost doctor

Summary

Suwi was a noted Cocopa ghost doctor and healer in the early twentieth century. The Cocopa are a Yuman-speaking tribe located near present-day Somerton, Arizona, during Suwi's lifetime. Suwi diagnosed a patient's illness by laying the palm of his left hand on the area of the person's body where the pain was located. If there was motion in the outer joint of Suwi's little finger, he knew that a cure was possible; in addition, his mouth would water. If Suwi's mouth became dry, he would advise the person to contact another healer because he knew that he would be unable to effect a cure.

Early Life

Very little is recorded of Suwi's early life. We do know, however, that it was not typical of a Cocopa youth. Most Cocopa male children would participate in a vision quest at about the age of twelve. The youth would travel alone to a secluded place known for its sacred qualities. The youth would fast for three or four days, awaiting a vision. Suwi received his first power dream at the age of ten, but at the time he did not recognize the significance and did not understand that he was called to become a shaman. Over the next few years, Suwi dreamed of animal spirit helpers—Horned Owl, Turtle, Spider, *Kamuyum* (hairy person), *Sumalitup* (chief of winds and clouds), and *Mistau*—all of whom taught him power songs. At first he told no one of his powers. But after conferring with a shaman who interpreted his dreams, he began to treat members of his family. A short time later, he began his life's calling as a tribal healer.

Leadership

Suwi, whose English name was Sam Clam, was a Cocopa ghost doctor (not to be confused with the Ghost Dance religion) who flourished during the early part of the twentieth century. Suwi was particularly adept at treating illnesses caused by soul loss. The Cocopa people believed, as did many other Indian people, that the soul departed the body at the time of an individual's death. They believed that communications (carried out by shamans and ghost doctors) could intervene and entice or plead with the soul spirit to return to the body, and thus the person would return from the dead. Suwi was known to be able to return the deceased person's soul spirit, and thus his or her life, within a matter of hours. Suwi had the power to project his own soul ahead of the soul of the patient to intercept on the road to the other world. Although Suwi sent his own soul out of his body, he remained conscious and active. Suwi would also blow sacred tobacco smoke to the southeast, the direction the lost soul had taken toward *Inbawhela*, the Land of the Dead. The use of sacred tobacco and smoke from a fire kept burning within the healing room caused the ghost who had stolen the soul to release it. Suwi would then revive the patient by blowing tobacco over his body as the soul reentered the body.

Suwi was capable of attaining heightened states of consciousness where he could "see everything that happened, even what other shaman were doing." He could see what ordinary people could not see. Suwi also used datura, or jimson weed, to obtain gambling medicine for his people's stick-guessing game known as *peon*. Datura was a poisonous plant used only under the direction of a shaman. Too much datura could result in death. Suwi would ingest datura about six hours before the gambling started. During the game, the spirit of datura would tell Suwi how many sticks were being held by the opposing players.

Further Reading

Lyon, William S. *Encyclopedia of Native American Shamanism: Sacred Ceremonies of North America*. 1998. Denver: ABC-CLIO.

Sturtevant, William C. *Handbook of North American Indians*. Vol. 8. 1978. Washington, D.C.: Smithsonian Institution.

Waldman, Carl, and Molly Braun. *Encyclopedia of Native American Tribes*. 1988. New York: Facts on File.

Sweet Medicine

Full Name at Birth: Sweet Medicine, Mut´ si-í ú iv ("the Prophet"), Nizhevoss ("Eagle's Nest")

Birth: date and place unknown; flourished ca. 1775–1790

Death: date and place unknown

Education: no formal education

Leadership Position: Cheyenne prophet and cultural hero

Summary

It is believed that the Cheyenne Nation originally lived in present-day south-central Canada. In the mid-1700s, as the result of increasing warfare and colonial expansion, the Cheyenne were forced to migrate west and eventually established their new homes on the Great Plains areas of present-day Montana and the Dakotas. Once settled, the Cheyenne quickly adapted to the Plains culture and adopted some Plains tribes' religious practices such as the Sun Dance and sacred bundles into their own religious cosmology.

The Cheyenne were granted their sacred laws and covenant with the Creator through a prophet by the name of Sweet Medicine, who received the law directly from the Creator. Sweet Medicine received his powers and spiritual instructions for the Cheyenne people while in a lodge on Noaha-Vose, the Cheyenne's most sacred mountain, in present-day South Dakota. Based on the Creator's teachings, Sweet Medicine instructed the Cheyenne to form a council representing the ten traditional Cheyenne bands and four chiefs to represent the four sacred directions.

Sweet Medicine was instructed by the Creator to give the Cheyenne a sacred bundle, composed of four sacred arrows and a particular version of the Sun Dance to be practiced by the Cheyenne people. Sweet Medicine also taught the Cheyenne a dance that renewed the relationship between the Cheyenne Nation and the Creator. Sweet Medicine told the Cheyenne people that to continue the covenant relationship now established with the Creator, they must uphold the sacred law and ceremonies, and in return the Creator would protect the Cheyenne Nation from physical and cultural destruction.

Early Life

Little is known of Sweet Medicine's early life. According to Cheyenne legend, it is said that while he was yet a baby, his parents died. Following their death, Sweet Medicine was raised by a very poor, old woman who had only scraps of a buffalo robe with which to cover him. As he grew older, he became a strange, inquisitive, and mischievous young man. Because of his activities, some of the Cheyenne people resented and distrusted him.

In his early life, Sweet Medicine was given special powers by the Creator and could perform wonderful feats. One such power concerned his relationship with the buffalo, the provider of fool and shelter for the Cheyenne people. During a period of prolonged starvation, Sweet Medicine used his power to draw the buffalo back to the people.

As a youth, Sweet Medicine journeyed to a sacred lodge located on Noaha-Vose, Bear Butte, in the Black Hills of South Dakota. While in the sacred lodge, the chief person, or Creator, spoke to him and gave him advice regarding his role in life as a Cheyenne prophet. Sweet Medicine was also given four sacred medicine arrows, telling him to take them back to the tribe. The Creator instructed him. "Take these Arrows with you and guard them carefully. They will be of great help to you for a long time. You will keep them until they are no longer a help—until they are of no more use to you." Sweet Medicine was then given a coyote's skin in which to wrap the arrows. The arrows were feathered with eagle feathers. In his hair he wore an eagle feather from the eagle that had given the feather for the arrows. It is believed that these events took place somewhere around the year 1775.

Leadership

Sweet Medicine, or Mut´ si-í ú iv, is one of the most venerated prophets of the Cheyenne people. Originally he was called Nizhevoss or Eagle's Nest. Because of his own power and his relationship to the tribe, the people named him Sweet Medicine or Sweet Root. The sweet root is the plant used to increase the flow of a mother's milk after childbirth. Sweet Medicine's teaching is seen as the spiritual milk by which the Cheyenne have grown in wisdom. His greatest gift to the People was Mahuts, the Sacred Arrows.

According to Cheyenne oral history, Sweet Medicine met with the Creator and four sacred people in a lodge on Noaha-Vose, the most sacred area of the Black Hills. It was here that Sweet Medicine received his spiritual teachings and gifts of immense sacred power, including the gift of the Sun Dance celebrated so that the Cheyenne people might yearly renew the world, its game, and their relationship with the Creator.

Following his pilgrimage to Noaha-Vose, Sweet Medicine began instructing the Cheyenne people in the sacred laws and ceremonies that the Creator had given him. The greatest and most holy gifts that Sweet Medicine brought to the people were the Four Sacred Arrows and the Sacred Arrow Dance. Sweet Medicine told the people that the Four Sacred Arrows were uniquely sacred objects because they shared the supreme power of the Creator himself. The Sacred Arrows, he said, are "the channels through which the Creator's supernatural life flows into Cheyenne lives." The Creator told Sweet Medicine that the loss of the arrows would mark the final scattering of the Cheyenne Nation, an event that Sweet Medicine later prophesied himself.

Sweet Medicine is said to have remained among the Cheyenne people for "four lifetimes," aging through the seasons of each year and then becoming young again each spring. During the four lifetimes, he taught the people many rituals, sacred ceremonies, beliefs, and skills. He taught the people how to tan skins, make clothing, and dress buffalo robes. He taught them how to make pipes from the leg bone of a deer and how to dry a certain plant and smoke it in their pipes.

Sweet Medicine served as the first keeper of the Sacred Arrows, and also founded the Kit Fox, Elk-Horn Scrapers, and other societies. These societies were age-graded societies that had specific responsibilities in times of war, in the hunt, and in daily tribal life. The governing body of the Cheyenne Nation that Sweet Medicine founded became the Council of Forty-Four.

Prior to his death, Sweet Medicine foretold the future of Indian people. He spoke of the increasing influence of the horse, conflict among Native Nations, as well as the coming of the white man and the effect on the Cheyenne people. He said that "a time is coming when you will meet other people. You will fight with them and kill each other. Each tribe will want the other tribe's land, and you will be fighting always." Pointing to the south, he said, "Far away in that direction is another kind of buffalo [the horse]. It has long hair on its neck and a tail that drags on the ground. It has a round hoof. . . . You will ride this animal." "The buffalo will disappear," he said, and "[w]hen the buffalo are gone, the next animal you

eat will be spotted (the cow). . . . And soon you will find among you a people with hair all over their faces. Their skin will be white. When that time comes, they will control you. The white people will be all over the land and at last you will disappear."

Sweet Medicine died in the summer when he was still a young man. No year is given for his death. After Sweet Medicine's passing, the keepers of the sacred arrow bundle have been venerated as men who share the holiness of the Prophet himself.

Further Reading

Cassidy, James J., Jr., ed., *Through Indian Eyes: The Untold Story of Native American Peoples.* 1995. Pleasantville, N.Y.: Reader's Digest Association.

Champagne, Duane, ed. *Native North American Almanac: A Reference Work on Native North Americans in the United States and Canada.* 1994. Detroit: Gale Research.

Hirschfelder, Arlene, and Paulette Molin. *The Encyclopedia of Native American Religions.* 1992. New York: Facts on File.

Powell, Peter J. *Sweet Medicine: The Continuing Role of the Sacred Arrows, the Sun Dance, and the Sacred Buffalo Hat in Northern Cheyenne History.* 1969. Norman: University of Oklahoma Press.

Tatan' ka ohi' tika

See Brave Buffalo

Tavibo (Northern Paiute-White Man)

Full Name at Birth: Numu-tibóó; Tavibo is Northern Paiute for "White Man"
Birth: ca. 1835 near Walker Lake in present-day Esmeralda County, Nevada
Death: ca. 1915, Mason Valley, Nevada
Education: no formal education
Leadership Position: Paiute religious leader

Summary

A dreamer-prophet leader of the Paiute community, Tavibo was a well-known shaman and visionary who was said to have the power to affect the weather. He was also said to be bulletproof.

Tavibo insisted that the only real world was the dream world and that the spirits of the dead talked freely to the chosen, such as himself. It was in one such revelation that Tavibo was instructed to have his followers attain a state of trance by dancing a traditional circle dance that would be the centerpiece of both the Ghost Dance religion of 1870 and the Ghost Dance religion of 1890. Although Tavibo is often credited with being the founder of the Ghost Dance Religion of 1870, whether or not this claim is true is unclear. It is clear, however, that he was associated with that religion, and his teachings had a strong influence on his son Wovoka,* who founded the Ghost Dance religion of 1890.

Early Life

There are no written recordings of Tavibo's early life. It is believed that he was a shaman to his people even as a young man. Therefore, we can surmise that he was in all likelihood raised in a traditional Paiute village of his time.

The ecosystem of the Southwest and Great Basin homeland of Tavibo's people would have made life challenging. The high desert environment would have demanded much of Tavibo and his people. Villages would have been small, consisting of family and extended-kin clans or bands. Food and water would have been gathered daily and closely husbanded, as would materials for clothing and shelter.

Among the Paiute, there had always been a strong belief in communicating with the Great Spirit to ensure success in the food quest and to maintain the precarious balance with nature. In the mid-1800s, as Tavibo came to maturity, Americans were crossing Paiute homelands in large numbers, destroying and straining the limited ecosystem. In times of crisis such as this, it was not uncommon for a prophet to receive a message of deliverance from the Great Spirit. Tavibo was one such visionary who experienced a number of dreams or visions that provided hope and guidance for the Paiute people.

Leadership

Tavibo was a Paiute shaman who had a close relationship with the supernatural powers of nature and the Creator. He practiced hand magic (healing by placing a hand on the infected area) and spoke of the spirit world to come. Tavibo taught about a time in the now-arid Southwest and Great Basin region when all of the land was green with grass and rich with game. That was a long time before the invasion of the strangers who were gaunt and hungry. It was a pleasant world where the Paiute were a happy race. They never quarreled and never drew bows in fight. Their women were faithful and good to look upon. Tavibo acknowledged that the world had been full of wars and killing but counseled his people that peace was better than war.

Like many other Native Americans in the Great Basin, Tavibo, born in approximately 1835, is reported to have initially been friendly to fur trappers and emigrants. It is believed that Tavibo belonged to a Paiute band led by Hadsapoke "Red Horse, to Yurdy's band led by Wahi "fox" on the Carson River, or possibly the band led by Chief Winnemucca (Itonadu) at Pyramid Lake.

In all probability, Tavibo fought against American encroachment on Great Basin lands in the Pyramid Lake War of 1860, the Bannock War of 1878, or the Owens Valley War of 1863. He may have fought in one or all of these engagements.

Described as a good talker, Tavibo was also said to have possessed boohoo or "power" and on at least one occasion was accused of being a witch because he treated a woman who subsequently died. His son, Wovoka, also said that Tavibo's magic made him bulletproof. In his later life, some reported that Tavibo was wild, quarrelsome, and unprincipled. This is most likely attributable to the illegal encroachments on Paiute land.

Following the intense pressure and destruction brought about by white migration during the California gold rush of 1849, Tavibo experienced a series of visions concerning the destiny of all Indians and the white invaders. In 1870, after a period of solitude in the mountains, he received a vision from the Great Spirit. The white invaders would be destroyed in one great earthquake, he was told. Indians would be spared and would repopulate a restored and prosperous land. Tavibo was appointed as the visionary who was to carry forth this teaching to his people that deliverance was at hand. Returning to preach his message, he was ridiculed and gained only a few converts. Tavibo journeyed back to the mountain, where he received a second vision. He returned to his people and prophesied that the coming earthquake would kill not just whites but all humans. After a given period of time, however (some reported three days), Indians would be returned to life and would live in a restored land of plenty. Failing to gather the following that he expected, Tavibo later claimed a third revelation. He related to his people that the Great Spirit would punish their lack of faith in him and that only Indians who believe Tavibo would be resurrected. Those Indians who doubted, along with whites, would be sentenced to eternal punishment. For a time, Tavibo's message generated interest among the Paiute, Bannock, Shoshone, and Ute, but his failed prophecies led to an eventual decline in followers. He died before his following reached an appreciable size.

Tavibo was living in the Walker River area of Nevada in the late 1800s and no doubt participated in the 1870 Ghost Dance religion, a revitalization movement that began at the Walker River Reservation in 1869. In one of Tavibo's revelations, he was instructed to have his followers attain a state of trance by dancing a traditional round or circle dance. This was an important part of the 1870 Ghost Dance religion. His son, Wovoka, carried on and refined his beliefs and practices, which became the foundation on which Wovoka would build the influential Ghost Dance of 1890. Tavibo's wife, Tiya, died two or three years after him.

See also Wovoka.

Further Reading

Bailey, Paul. *Ghost Dance Messiah*. 1970. Los Angeles: Westernlore Press.

Cassidy, James J., Jr. *Through Indian Eyes: The Untold Story of Native American Peoples*. 1995. Pleasantville, N.Y.: Reader's Digest Association.

Champagne, Duane, ed. *The Native North American Almanac*. 1994. Detroit: Gale Publishing.

Gibson, Arrell M. *The American Indian*. 1969. Lexington, Mass.: D. C. Heath.

Hirschfelder, Arlene, and Paulette Molin. *The Encyclopedia of Native American Religions*. 1992. New York: Facts on File.

Hittman, Michael. *Wovoka and the Ghost Dance*. 1990. Carson City: Grace Danberg Foundation.

Waldman, Carl. *Who Was Who in Native American History*. 1990. New York: Facts on File.

Washburn, Wilcomb E. *Handbook of North American Indians: History of Indian-White Relations, Vol. 4.* 1988. Washington, D.C.: Smithsonian Institution.

Kateri (Catherine) Tekakwitha

Full Name at Birth: Tekakwitha; the Lily of the Mohawks; La Sainte Sauvagesse ("Indian Saint")

Birth: 1656 at Gandaouague, now Auriesville, N.Y., near present-day Albany

Death: April 17, 1680, at the Mission of the Sault at Kahnawake, near Montreal, Canada

Education: educated as a Catholic nun at the Christian mission at Kahnawake near Montreal, Canada

Summary

Kateri Tekakwitha, whom many Catholics call "Lily of the Mohawks," was the daughter of a full-blood non-Indian Mohawk chief and a Christianized Algonquian captive. She was born in 1656 near present-day Auriesville, New York, on the south side of the Mohawk River. She lost her family to smallpox when she was about four years old and was herself disfigured by the disease. The disease left her face pockmarked and weakened her eyes so that she could not bear bright light.

Kateri witnessed Christianity firsthand when Fathers Fréman, Bruyas, and Pierron stayed in her uncle's lodge while seeking to establish missions among the Nations of the Iroquois League. Kateri converted to Christianity in the 1670s and was baptized in 1676 at the age of twenty by Jacques de Lamberville, a Jesuit missionary. Following the baptism, Lamberville gave her the Christian name Catherine. Conversion to Christianity brought Kateri ridicule and harassment from tribal members, including close relatives, making her an outcast among her people. In 1677, she fled her village with some visiting Christianized Oneida Indians and settled near a Christian Mohawk community, Kahnawake, outside present-day Montreal. She hoped to establish a convent on Heron Island.

Kateri became a nun and with two other women dedicated themselves to Christianity and chastity. They practiced a number of penances including walking barefoot in ice and snow, burning their feet with a hot brand, putting coals and burning cinders between their toes, self-flagellation, fasting, and sleeping on beds of thorns. The self-mortifications took their toll; at age twenty-four, Kateri Tekakwitha died.

It is said that when Kateri died, a miracle occurred: the pockmarks on her face suddenly disappeared. She was buried near the La Chine Rapids between La Prairie Mission and Caughnawaga. People visiting her tomb have claimed to experience visions and to be cured of illnesses. Kateri's divine intervention is

The Congregation of American Sisters (Lakota) was inspired by the life of Kateri Tekakwitha. This photo appeared in an 1890 edition of *Sina Sapa Wocekine Taehyanpaha*, a Catholic Lakota-language newspaper published on the Devil's Lake Reservation at St. Michaels, North Dakota. Marquete University Archives.

also credited with saving several Jesuits from certain death when a windstorm destroyed the mission church at Kahnawake.

Kateri became a candidate for sainthood in the Roman Catholic church in 1884. Approximately five hundred Indian people representing thirty-five tribes from the United States and Canada made a pilgrimage to Rome, Italy, and made a presentation to Pope John Paul II asking for beatification of Kateri Tekakwitha. In 1943, the Roman Catholic church acknowledged Tekakwitha's holiness and declared her "venerable," and in 1980, she was declared "blessed." Kateri was declared venerable in 1934, the first American Indian to be beatified.

Early Life

According to her hagiographers (biographers of saints), the Jesuits Pierre Cholenec and Claude Chauchetiére, Tekakwitha "did what all Iroquois girls did" as a young girl. She was gentle, patient, chaste, innocent, and well behaved. She helped gather firewood, worked in the corn fields, and became skilled at decorative crafts. "She arrayed herself in typical Iroquois finery and engaged in other vanities." She was known among her people for her industry and her skill in manufacturing wampum. The word *wampum* comes from *wampumpeag*, an Algonquian word meaning "strings of white beads." The Mohawk used wampum in their religious and civil ceremonies.

Kateri's father was a traditional Mohawk chief, and her mother was an Algonquian Indian who had been captured by the Mohawk. The Jesuits at Trois Riviéres had missionized her mother. Kateri's parents died when she was four years old, and she grew up with her aunts and an uncle in the village of Caughnawaga, near present-day Fonda, New York. Her uncle (whose name is not recorded) was considered to be one of the most powerful men in the village and was vehemently opposed to Christianity. When Tekakwitha reached marriageable age, her relatives began pressuring her to marry. At one point, they arranged a marriage, but when the intended bridegroom came into the longhouse and seated himself next to Kateri (which would have bound the marriage ceremony), she left the lodge and hid in the fields.

Kateri met the Jesuit fathers Frémin, Bruyas, and Pierron missionaries around 1667. Several years later the Jesuit missionary Jacques de Lamberville visited Tekakwitha's lodge and found her eager to hear more about the Christian religion. He baptized her in 1676.

Leadership

Kateri lost her father, mother, and an infant brother to smallpox in 1660. She was raised by an uncle who was a traditional Mohawk chief, as her father had been. Kateri was herself disfigured by the smallpox disease; her face was severely scarred. The disease also weakened her eyes so that she could not bear bright light. Her eye problems and other ailments often kept Kateri confined to her Mohawk longhouse. (A longhouse was the traditional housing style among the Mohawk; several families related through the female lineage shared the same structure.)

The Jesuit fathers Fréman, Bruyas, and Pierron visited Kateri's village in the 1670s, and she was baptized at the age of twenty by Jacques de Lamberville, a Jesuit missionary. Her uncle and other family members strongly opposed her conversion, and her religion caused her ridicule and made her an outcast among her people. A traditional Mohawk marriage was arranged without Kateri's knowledge or consent and at the age of twenty, Kateri fled her village in a canoe with some visiting Christianized Oneida Indians. Kateri found refuge in Kahnawake, or Caughnawaga, a Christian Mohawk community near Montreal where she found meaning and hope in the church. Kateri was determined to embrace the Christian religion and modeled her life on that of the local nuns. She pledged herself to a life of perpetual chastity for the sake of Jesus Christ.

Kateri hoped to establish a convent on Heron Island, Canada, modeled on a convent she had visited in Montreal. The church authorities rejected her plan; however, they did accept her vow of chastity and accepted her into the order of nuns. Kateri devoted the remainder of her life to the church and developed what some called an almost fanatical devotion and commitment to helping others.

A number of miracles or divine interventions have been attributed to Kateri, including the account that when she died in 1680, scars from her childhood case of smallpox disappeared. Kateri's divine intervention is credited with having saved several Jesuits from certain death when a windstorm caused the mission church at Kahnawake to collapse around them. In 1693, a man by the name of André Merlot credited Kateri with healing an inflammation of his eyes after he made a novena to Kateri. He rubbed his eyes with a solution of water and earth from Kateri's grave and ashes from her clothing. Colombiére, canon of the Cathedral of Québec, testified in 1696 that "his appeal to Tekakwitha relieved him of a slow fever, against which all remedies had been tried in vain, and of a diarrhea, which even [known medicines] could not cure."

In 1884, Kateri became a candidate for canonization by the Roman Catholic church. In 1943, Pope Pius XII declared her venerable; in 1980, she was beatified by Pope John Paul II, the second step toward sainthood. Kateri was the first American Indian person to be beatified and is currently a candidate for canonization by the Roman Catholic Church.

Kateri was buried near the La Chine Rapids between La Prairie Mission and Caughnawaga. The Jesuits have a shire to her at her first home near Auriesville, New York; the Franciscans maintain a shire at her second home near Fonda, New York. She is also honored at the present-day Kahnawake Reserve in Quebec.

Further Reading

Calloway, Colin G. *First Peoples: A Documentary Survey of American Indian History.* 1999. New York: St. Martin's.

Champagne, Duane, ed. *The Native North American Almanac: A Reference Work on Native North Americans in the United States and Canada.* 1994. Detroit: Gale Research.

Hirschfelder, Arlene, and Paulette Molin. *The Encyclopedia of Native American Religions.* 1992. New York: Facts on File.

Kateri Tekakwitha: http://www. ukans.edu/kansas/wn/kateri.html.

The Life of the Blessed Kateri Tekakwitha: http://www.bluecloud.org/kateri.html.

Shoemaker, Nancy. *Negotiators of Change: Historical Perspectives on Native American Women.* 1995. New York: Routledge.

Waldman, Carl. *Who Was Who in Native American History.* 1990. New York: Facts on File.

Washburn, Wilcomb E. *Handbook of North American Indians, Vol. 4.* 1988. Washington, D.C.: Smithsonian Institution.

Tenskwatawa ("Open Door")

Full Name at Birth: Lalawethika

Birth: 1775 in the village of Pique, on the Mad River near present-day Springfield, Ohio

Death: November 1837 in present-day Kansas City, Kansas

Education: no formal education

Leadership Position: Shawnee spiritual leader

Summary

In the first decade of the nineteenth century, Tenskwatawa emerged as an important spiritual leader in the Ohio River and Mississippi River valleys. He preached that the Master of Life had selected him to spread a new religion among the Shawnee people. His teachings promised a revitalization of Shawnee culture that required Indian people to give up alcohol, refuse intermarriage, reject Christianity, lay down European-made trade goods, and return to traditional Shawnee customs. While many Indians rejected his message, hundreds flocked to join Tenskwatawa and his brother Tecumseh at Prophetstown on the Tippecanoe River in Indiana.

Early Life

Tenskwatawa was born in early 1775 in a Shawnee settlement known as Old Piqua (near the present-day city of Springfield, Ohio) in the Ohio River Valley. His father was a Shawnee war chief, and his mother was a Cherokee-Creek woman. A triplet with two brothers, he grew up without his parents, as his father had died before his birth at the Battle of Point Pleasant in October 1774. His mother either returned to her people or accompanied the Shawnee west when they left Ohio in 1779. In his early life, he was known as Lalawethika ("the rattle" or "noisemaker"). An addiction to alcohol acquired in adolescence increased his boasting and earned the disdain of other tribal members. During childhood, he also lost the sight in his right eye in a hunting accident. It is believed that Tenskwatawa took a wife and fathered several children.

Leadership

Better known as the Shawnee Prophet, Tenskwatawa was a holy man whose religious movement was used by his brother Tecumseh to forge an intertribal, pan-Indian confederacy prior to the War of 1812. The brothers envisioned a vast Indian confederacy strong enough to keep the colonists from expanding any farther west. Tenskwatawa's influence began to grow with other Indians, and he and Tecumseh traveled extensively among tribes from Wisconsin to Florida, spreading the message. In August 1794, he participated in tribal opposition to "Mad" Anthony Wayne's legions at the Battle of Fallen Timbers.

In February 1806, Tenskwatawa became ill and was believed to have died. Before his funeral arrangements were completed, he revived and told the people assembled that the Master of Life had sent two young men to carry his soul to the spirit world, where he was shown the past and future. He described paradise as a rich country with plenty of game and fish and fine hunting grounds and cornfields, where the spirits of good Shawnee would go. Tenskwatawa also described the fiery torture that would await the souls of evil-doers. As a result of his journey, he vowed to give up his sinful ways and quit drinking. His name was changed from Lalawethika to Tenskwatawa to symbolize leading his people through the "open door" to paradise. In the months to follow, Tenskwatawa had additional visions that urged personal and social repentance and showed the way to healing through ritual and ceremony and the recovery of lost spiritual power. Based on his instructions from the Master of Life, Tenskwatawa developed his religious doctrines, which he taught to fellow Shawnee and then to members of other tribal groups. In late November 1805, Tenskwatawa met with Shawnee, Ottawa, Seneca, and Wyandot delegations at Wapakoneta on the Auglaize River to expound on his religion. He declared that his sole purpose was to reclaim Indian people from bad habits and have them live in peace with everyone. He denounced a number of practices, including the drinking of alcohol, intertribal violence, polygamous marriages, and promiscuity.

Tenskwatawa's beliefs were essentially nativistic. His followers were encouraged to return to the communal life of their ancestors and abandon white technology. He promoted claims that he could cure sickness and prevent death and warned that opposing him meant opposing the Master of Life. Those who did so would be suspected of witchcraft. Challenged by Indiana governor William Henry Harrison to prove that he was a prophet, Tenskwatawa stated that he could "cause the sun to stand still." Tenskwatawa promptly did as much by accurately predicting the total eclipse of the sun on June 16, 1806. After this public display of his power, thousands of Indian people quickly became believers and hastened to join the new religion.

From 1805 to 1809, Tenskwatawa dominated the pan-Indian movement that now included his brother Tecumseh, attracting adherents to Greenville, Ohio, then to Prophetstown on the Wabash. After the Treaty of Fort Wayne, at which the Indians ceded over 3 million acres of land in Indiana and Illinois to the United States in 1809, Tenskwatawa's followers shifted their focus to Tecumseh's political-military strategy. At the heart of Tecumseh's military strategy was the formation of a pan-Indian military alliance that would include tribes from the Great Lakes south to the Gulf of Mexico and would serve as a blockade to further European westward expansion. Concerned with the growing following of Tenskwatawa and Tecumseh, William Henry Harrison understood the danger such an alliance would have. Harrison, aware that Tecumseh had journeyed south to recruit southern Indians into the alliance, also concluded that an attack against Tenskwatawa's village would more likely be successful in Tecumseh's absence. On November 7, 1811, an American army of some 1,000 men, led by General William Harrison, prepared to launch a preemptive strike against the Prophet's village.

Prior to departing on his recruiting journey south, Tecumseh had advised Tenskwatawa not to be drawn into a premature military confrontation with Harrison's numerically superior force. Tecumseh was aware that a large Indian alliance would be necessary to defeat the Americans. Tenskwatawa, who knew of Harrison's invasion plan, and the size of the invasion force, decided to meet the Americans in combat despite his brother's warning. Rather than waiting for the Americans to attack, Tenskwatawa launched an offensive action. Prior to going into battle, however, Tenskwatawa performed various rituals designed to make his warriors immortal and invincible while rendering the American troops confused and impotent. He told his followers that the Americans' rifles would not fire. Heavy dew filled the area the night prior to the attack; Harrison ordered his soldiers to sleep with their rifles under their blankets, thus keeping the primer cords dry. When Tenskwatawa's warriors attacked the village, an alarm was sounded, the rifles fired, and Harrison's men prevailed. Tenskwatawa's magic had failed, and his followers now denounced him as a fraud. His followers retreated to Prophetstown, joined with their families, deserted Prophetstown, and returned to their individual villages.

The Indian defeat at the Battle of Tippecanoe was devastating to Tenskwatawa's religious movement because he had assured his followers of victory. Tenskwatawa's movement ended with his flight to Canada in 1813. In 1832, Tenskwatawa posed for the artist George Catlin, who portrayed him in traditional garments and wearing symbols of his religious movement. The Shawnee Prophet died in November 1837 and was buried in what is now Kansas City, Kansas.

Further Readings

Ballantine, Betty, and Ian Ballantine, eds. *The Native Americans: An Illustrated History*. 1993. Atlanta: Turner Publishing.

Calloway, Colin G. *First Peoples: A Documentary Survey of American Indian History*. 1999. New York: St. Martin's Press.

Champagne, Duane, ed. *The Native North American Almanac*. 1994. Detroit: Gale Research.

Hirschfelder, Arlene, and Paulette Molin. *The Encyclopedia of Native American Religions*. 1992. New York: Facts on File.

Snow, Dean R. *The Iroquois*. 1996. Cambridge, Mass.: Blackwell Publishers.

Tenskwatawa (The Prophet): http://www.npg.si.edu/col/native/tensk.html.

Tenskwatawa (Open Door): http://www.newagepage.com/miracle/NOV/nov24.html.

Trigger, Bruce G., and Wilcomb E. Washburn, eds. *The Cambridge History of the Native Peoples of the Americas. Vol. 1, North America, Part 1*. 1996. Cambridge: Cambridge University Press.

Washburn, Wilcomb E. *Handbook of North American Indians, Vol. 4*. 1988. Washington, D.C.: Smithsonian Institution.

Albert Thomas

Full Name at Birth: Albert Thomas

Birth: date and place unknown

Death: date and place unknown

Education: no formal education

Leadership Position: Achomawi (Pit River)/Wintu shaman

Summary

Thomas was a highly respected shaman throughout northern California around the turn of the twentieth century. Half Wintu and half Achomawi, he was raised among the Achomawi, but once he achieved his status as a healing shaman, he traveled widely among the Wintu, with whom he conversed in English or in *nomsus* (a language shared by many western groups).

Thomas regularly sought guardian spirits by swimming at power pools (sacred springs that were believed to be visited and used by sacred spirits; in some cases, the spirits lived in the pools) "even when it was icy cold." Wintu power spots called *sauel* are visited by shamans or novices to acquire guardian spirits. Quite often the *sauel* is a deep pool. The shaman dives into the pool in an attempt to reach the bottom; this is known as *memtuli sauel*, or "water-swimming sacred-places." Sometimes a shaman finds a charm stone at the bottom of the pool, which then becomes his talisman. In instances where the *sauel* is not deep enough for diving, the guarding spirit comes to the shaman through dreaming.

Thomas was respected by other shamans, and it was reported that in the Wintu area, no jealousy was felt toward him. His most prominent rival, a shaman by the name of Charles Klutchie, held him in high esteem, and they were sometimes described as partners. It is unclear if a partnership existed, but an agreement existed that mediated against conflict between the two powerful men.

Early Life

The little we know of Thomas's early life was obtained from several sources, recorded by Sarah Fan, passed to the anthropologist Cora Du Bois, and was published as *Wintu Ethnography* in 1935. Thomas was half Achomawi (contemporarily known as Pit River Indians) and Wintu. He was raised among the Achomawi people but received his spirit helpers in Wintu areas. Thomas became a shaman during his adult life, so we may surmise that he spent his early years in the same manner as other Achomawi youth.

The Achomawi were located in the vicinity of the present California-Oregon border. They were a fishing people who used five different kinds of nets. Thomas' uncles and father would have taught him the fishing skills early in his life. Thomas would have accompanied his mother and along with other youth would have harvested acorns that were then pulverized with mortar and pestle, bleached with hot water on a bed of sand, and made into mush or bread. He would have also helped harvest pinole, which were seeds gathered from several species of grasses and plants such as the sage.

Leadership

Sarah Fan, the granddaughter of two Indian shamans and cousin to four others, provides a keen insight into the world of the shaman and the powers possessed by Thomas. Fan begins by stating that she did not see why anyone would want to become doctors (shamans). They had to starve themselves and had a very hard time acquiring spiritual helpers. This often involved prolonged journeys to numerous sacred places, to tops of mountains, down into the depths of caves, and dancing and dancing "as if

crazy." Out of a large number of novices attempting to become shamans, only a small number successfully complete the ordeal. Once they had done this, those who failed "tell them how to be good, how to talk well. They promise them feathers. They blow acorn meal over them. Maybe they will give them red-headed woodpeckers' heads. After that they all go to a sacred place to swim."

Fan did not know if Thomas had any shamans in his family line. He became a shaman in his adult years after he was married and had three children. Thomas participated in the ordeal of seeking shaman power as described by Fan. He then made a vow to take care of the shaman power and to obey the spirit. "If a spirit told him not to eat, he wouldn't. If it told him to eat something he didn't want, he would." It was reported that he visited the water power pool, *sauel* often, seeking additional power.

Shamans often had assistants. Fan stated that "you need another doctor to help you be a doctor. If another doctor gives you some poison and you run it in your ear or you head, then you get to be a doctor quickly without dancing." One of Thomas's assistants during the early part of his career reported:

We stayed together two months that summer. I used to go around and interpret for him [i.e., tell the audience what Thomas was saying during trance]. I went as far south as Vina. The first time that the lizard spirit came to him I couldn't understand very well what he said, so he told me to call the "old white mans's" spirit. Then a white man's spirit came to him and he began talking in English. That summer, I used to see Thomas draw fire with his hands from a lamp and light his pipe with it. I saw him do it often. He said it was electricity which drew the fire. Once I saw him lift a blazing piece of live oak. He didn't even scorch his shirt or hair. He does this best when he has the lizard spirit. But he can do it only when he is in a trance.

Other than the belief in shamanism, the Achomawi held no strictly religious ceremony and offered no prayers to any deity. They did pray to a supernatural power for assistance in hunting and in war. They were expected to display good moral conduct, which consisted of forbidding incest, killing without just cause, or stealing more than had been stolen from them. As a people, they were expected to practice kindness and hospitality. There is no recorded information regarding the death of Albert Thomas.

Further Reading

The Achomawi: http://curtis-collection.com/tribe%20data/achamawi.html.

Du Bois, Cora. *Wintu Ethnography.* 1935. Berkeley: University of California Press.

Lyon, William S. *Encyclopedia of Native American Shamanism: Sacred Ceremonies of North America.* 1998. Denver: ABC-CLIO.

Toohoolhoolzote

Full Name at Birth: Toohoolhoolzote, Toohulhulsote, Too-hool-hool-suit, or Tulhulhutsut.

Birth: ca. 1810

Death: September 30, 1877, at the Battle of Bear Paw Mountain in present-day Montana

Education: no formal education

Leadership Position: Nez Percé dreamer priest

Summary

Toohoolhoolzote was a Nez Percé dreamer-priest and leader of his people who lived near the mouth of the Salmon River in present-day Idaho. He began to preach his revitalization religion about 1860, at a time when non-Indian traders discovered gold while prospecting on the Nez Percé Reservation in Idaho.

Nez Percé chiefs signed the Stevens Treaty with the United States in 1855 in an attempt to live in peace with the settlers and to remain neutral during the Plateau Indian War of 1855–1858. Promises were made that the United States would never again ask for Nez Percé lands. In 1860, however, prospectors and settlers flooded onto Nez Percé treaty lands. In 1863, the government responded by writing a new treaty reducing the reservation to one-tenth its original size. In return, it promised agricultural implements, mills, schools, churches, and other tools of civilization. Toohoolhoolzote's beliefs, similar to those of the dreamer-prophet Smohalla, led to his refusal to sign the "Thief's" Treaty of 1863. Many other Nez Percé followed his lead, and they came to be known as the "non-treaty Nez Percé." The miners and settlers offered the government a fait accompli (they had occupied the Nez Percé land), and the Senate acquiesced and ratified the treaty.

In 1876, Toohoolhoolzote was appointed spokesman for all of the lower Nez Percé bands. At the Lapwai Council held in 1877, General Oliver Howard announced that the nontreaty Nez Percé would have to give up their most priced possession, the Wallowa valley (the Nez Percé traditional homelands), or be removed by force. Toohoolhoolzote refused to do so and was arrested for inciting others to disobey Howard's order. He was released from the guardhouse in time to join Chef Joseph (the younger) and some eight hundred Nez Percé who were fleeing.

Religious truths and instruction came to Toohoolhoolzote in dreams—thus, the name of his religion, the Dreamer religion. Among the teachings received was the repudiation of the white culture, including alcohol and agricultural practices. Toohoolhoolzote's preaching, which emphasized a return to Nez Percé traditions and cultural beliefs, was a combination of nativist sentiment, rejection of white culture, and resistance to the U.S. government and Christianity. He rejected the government's assimilation program and advocated an end to sales of "mother earth." He advocated the preservation of traditional subsistence: fishing and gathering and the adoption of an ascetic religious life.

Early Life

There is no recorded history of the early years of Toohoolhoolzote's life. He was a full-blood Indian of the Nez Percé Nation and lived in peace with the United States for most of his life. The Nez Percé had been in contact with white Americans since the Lewis and Clark expedition of 1803–1806 and prided themselves as having never fired a shot in anger against the white people. In his early years, Toohoolhoolzote was an active supporter of the tribe's longstanding peace with whites.

Leadership

Toohoolhoolzote was a Nez Percé dreamer-priest and leader of his people, who lived near the mouth of the Salmon River in present-day Idaho. He shared the teachings of Chief Joseph, who believed that "Indians were of the earth and grew up in its bosom." There were two Nez Percé chiefs by the name of Chief Joseph, the elder (ca. 1790s–1871), Chief Joseph, and the son, Chief Joseph the younger (1840–1904). Both shared the strong connection with Mother Earth and the belief that the earth could not be sold and should not be plowed for agricultural purposes.

Toohoolhoolzote was possibly influenced by the Wanapam spiritual leader Smohalla,* who flourished as a dreamer-prophet along the Columbia River in present-day eastern Washington State in the 1850s. Both men received their religious instruction through dreams—thus, the name of the religion, the Dreamer religion. Among the teachings received was the repudiation of the white culture, especially agricultural practices. Toohoolhoolzote believed that the earth was mother and nurse, was sacred to his affections, and was too sacred to be valued by or sold for silver or gold. To plow into the earth was the same as to cut into one's mother's breast.

In addition to the power received through vision quests and dreams, Toohoolhoolzote is believed to have had a death and rebirth experience where he traveled in death to receive instructions from the Great Spirit. In the resurrection experience, he brought back a message that to the Nez Percé had the ring of authenticity. Toohoolhoolzote began to preach his revitalization doctrine about 1860. His preaching emphasized a return to tribal religion and cultural traditions and beliefs, the rejection of white culture, and resistance to the U.S. government and Christianity. The Dreamer religion focused on the belief in an impending destruction and renewal of the world, during which the dead would return to life. Toohoolhoolzote also advocated the preservation of traditional subsistence: fishing and gathering.

Toohoolhoolzote was appointed by the U.S. government as a spokesman to represent the Lower Nez Percé bands at a council with army officer General Oliver Howard. During an 1877 meeting with General Howard, Toohoolhoolzote gave his reasons for not agreeing to sell or relinquish the land. He stated that the earth was his mother and a part of himself. Toohoolhoolzote said that people should subsist on the earth's natural bounty without disturbing it. He also stated that the earth could not be sold. An argument arose between Toohoolhoolzote and Howard. "The earth is my body," Toohoolhoolzote said, "and I never gave up the earth." Howard described Toohoolhoolzote as "the cross-grained growler" and had him arrested. Toohoolhoolzote, outraged by his imprisonment, talked of war and persuaded many of the young men that they should fight rather than be driven from the land where they were born. Howard released Toohoolhoolzote only after tempers had subsided and a number of Indian people who opposed the ceding of Nez Percé lands agreed to go to a reservation. When they agreed to the treaty terms, Toohoolhoolzote was released. The last words he said to Howard were that the whites were "trifling with the laws of the earth."

General Howard, a one-armed Civil War veteran, declared that the Nez Percé who had not signed the 1863 treaty must now come onto the reservation or be moved there by force. They were given until April 1, 1877, to complete the move. Howard threatened a cavalry attack on the nontreaty holdouts onto the reservation. Chief Joseph the younger, now the tribal chief, believed that military resistance was futile and reluctantly led his people toward Idaho. Toohoolhoolzote, now released from the guardhouse, joined Chef Joseph and some eight hundred Nez Percé who fled east. Violence soon broke out, leading to the Nez Percé war of 1876. Fighting off Howard's troops, the Nez Percé crossed the Bitterroot Mountains into Montana, where they hoped to find assistance from the Crow Nation. They rested at the Big Hole River, but Colonel John Gibbon attacked in a surprise dawn assault. With American troops at their backs and the Crow now scouting for the U.S. Army, the Nez Percé decided to head for Canada. In rapid retreat, they passed through the newly created Yellowstone Park and defeated General Samuel Sturgis's cavalry at Canyon Creek. Thirty miles from the Canadian border, they halted in exhaustion, having traveled some 1,700 miles. Carrying out a policy of relentless pursuit, General Nelson Miles and six hundred men attacked the Nez Percé and forced the surrender of Chief Joseph and 150 followers. Toohoolhoolzote died in the fighting.

Further Reading

Calloway, Colin G. *First Peoples: A Documentary Survey of American Indian History.* 1999. New York: St. Martin's.

Champagne, Duane, ed. *Chronology of Native North American History.* 1994. Detroit: Gale Research.

Hirschfelder, Arlene and Paulette Molin. *The Encyclopedia of Native American Religions*. 1992. New York: Facts on File.

Historical Figures: http://www.geocities.com/RodeoDrive/3077/favppl.html.

Trafzer, Clifford, ed. *American Indian Prophets*. 1986. Newcastle, Calif.: Sierra Oaks Publishing Co.

Waldman, Carl. *Who Was Who in Native American History*. 1990. New York: Facts on File.

Toypurina (Regina Josefa Toypurina)

Full Name at Birth: Toypurina

Birth: ca. 1760 in the area of present-day Long Beach, California; flourished in the 1780s

Death: May 22, 1799, at Mission San Juan Bautista, California

Education: no formal education

Leadership Position: Gabrielino religious leader-shaman

Summary

Toypurina was a female Gabrielino religious leader who was considered to have supernatural powers by her people. Among the Gabrielino, women could acquire considerable power, and Toypurina was considered to be a powerful female shaman. In 1785, she and the neophyte (newly converted Christian) Nicolas Jo'se plotted a rebellion against the San Gabriel Mission near present-day Los Angeles. On October 25, 1785, she and a group of warriors from surrounding rancherias sneaked over the adobe parapet of Mission San Gabriel Arc´angel. The plans for the rebellion had been discovered in advance, however, and Toypurina and her followers were arrested. On January 4, 1786, Governor Don Pedro Fages ordered that Nicolas Jo'se and the two of the rebellion leaders should be locked in irons and be sent to the San Diego Presidio. Toypurina was to remain in secure custody at the San Gabriel mission. Most of the other participating Indians were publicly administered fifteen to twenty lashes each in a display meant to discredit Toypurina's claim to power. Toypurina was ultimately pardoned and was deported to San Carlos Mission in northern California, where she later married Manuel Montero, a native of La Puebla de los Angeles. The first of her four children, Cesario Antonio Montero, was baptized at Mission San Luis Obispo. Toypurina died at Mission San Juan Bautista on May 22, 1799.

Early Life

Little is written about Toypurina's early life other than that she was a daughter of a Gabrielino Indian chief. As a child, she most likely grew up in or near the Gabrielino village of Pavunga, near present-day Long Beach, California. Following the normative behavior of Gabrielino girls, she would have been taught modesty in all things and was expected to show deference to her elders. She was taught that she was never to pass between adults or to interrupt their conversation. Reaching puberty would have been an occasion for joy and happiness for Toypurina. At this time, she underwent a purification ceremony that included sweat bathing (purification through sweating) for three consecutive days. During this period, her aunt or her sisters attended her and certain dietary restrictions were observed. At this important time of her life, Toypurina was honored by dancing and singing, and she was formally presented to Gabrielino society as a marriageable woman. During the ceremony, a sand painting was prepared depicting certain cosmological supernatural events and beings, the significance of which foretold her place, role, and function in the overall scheme of Gabrielino creation and religious cosmology. It is possible that her future as a medicine woman was made known to her at this time.

Leadership

Toypurina was a Gabrielino religious leader who was reputed and feared as the wisest shaman among the Gabrielino. Her magic and incantations held supreme rule over their minds, and her power was feared and respected. So great was her power that the Gabrielino believed she could kill the Spanish by merely wishing it to be so. Among the Gabrielino, shamans served mainly their own village and possessed the ability to cause as well as cure illness. They also served as diviners, guardians of the village sacred bundle, locator of lost items, and collectors of poisons used on arrows, and they could be called on to make rain.

A shaman obtained her power directly from the supernatural through dreams or visions, often caused by the ingestion of datura. California Indian people used datura, also known as jimsonweed, extensively in religious ceremonies. A shaman under its spell could see things hidden from ordinary view and could see into the future. Shamans often used datura as an anaesthetic during the setting of bones and surgery. While under the influence of datura, a power helper with energizing power, such as an animal, would appear to the shaman and henceforth would be her power aid.

In 1785, Toypurina, along with the neophyte Nicolas Jo'se, plotted a rebellion against the San Gabriel Mission near present-day Los Angeles. They convinced Indians of six villages to participate. The fact that she had followers from six villages is indicative of her power, as shamans were usually followed by members of their own village only. It is possible that Jo'se, a new Christian convert living at the San Gabriel mission, organized the rebellion and that the coalition leaders enlisted the aid of Toypurina because of her considerable power.

On the night of October 25, 1785, Toypurina's well-armed war party advanced on the mission. Toypurina was supposed to have killed the soldiers and padres with her magic. Jo'se Maria Pico, a soldier of the guard who understood the Gabrielino dialect, had forewarned the priests and soldiers of the uprising, however, and arrested the insurgents. On November 30, 1785, Governor Fages reported that he had seven Christian Indian and four gentiles in custody, including Toypurina, two pagan chiefs, and Nicolas Jo'se. At the subsequent trial, Toypurina denounced the Spanish for trespassing on and despoiling the Indian's ancestral lands. Jo'se condemned the padres for preventing the practice of traditional Gabrielino religious ceremonies. Most of the Indians received between fifteen and twenty lashes each. Jo'se and the two head men were imprisoned in the presidio at San Diego.

It is reported that when Toypurina was brought before Governor Fages, she stared fiercely at him and kicked aside the proffered stool and stood before the board of inquiry in all her native dignity. "If her looks could kill, her inquisitors would have dropped like autumn leaves."

> She had an arrogant face and almost queenly stance despite her bonds. . . . She admitted that she had ordered Chief Tomasajaquichi to come to the mission rancheria and persuade the Christians not to believe another word of the hated padres, and to trust only in her. She said that she hated the padres for living here on her native soil—for trespassing upon the land of [her] forefathers and despoiling the tribal domain. Her eyes never left the Governor's as she unburdened herself of her deep resentment against the Spaniards. Her real reason for joining and inciting to riot was to be rid of the white men. She came to inspire her people, and not to quail at the sight of Spanish sticks that spit fire and death.

Following a Christian baptism, Toypurina was pardoned and sent to the San Carlos Mission in northern California to be exiled without hope of ever returning to the Gabrielino people. At the time of her conversion, she was twenty-seven years of age. Toypurina had previously been married; however, she obtained a divorce when her husband re-fused to convert to Christianity. On March 7, 1787, she married a Spaniard, Manuel Montero, a native of La Puebla de los Angeles and a soldier of the Royal Presidio at San Carlos de Monterey. She was baptized on March 7, 1787, by Padre Miguel Sanchez and given the name Regina (Queen) Josefa Toypurina.

She died on May 22, 1799 at Mission San Juan Bautista, having led an exemplary Christian life. Fray Jose Manuel de Martiarena buried her the following day in the mission Camp Santo.

Further Reading

Heizer, Robert F. *Handbook of North American Indians.* Vol. 8. 1978. Washington, D.C.: Smithsonian Institution.

Jackson, Robert H., and Edward Castillo. *Indians, Franciscans, and Spanish Colonization: The Impact of the Mission System of California Indians.* 1995. Albuquerque: University of New Mexico Press. Native California. Indian Revolts: http://www.chez.com/bateauxmls/#CHIIIe.

Temple, Thomas Workman II. "Toypurina the Witch and the Indian Uprising at San Gabriel." *Masterkey*, 32, no. 5 (September–October 1958)

Waldman, Carl. *Who Was Who in Native American History.* 1990. New York: Facts on File.

John Trehero ("Rainbow")

Full Name at Birth: Trehero, Truhujo, Treeo
Birth: ca. 1883, place unknown
Death: January 1985 in Wyoming
Education: obtained eighth-grade education at government boarding school and Episcopal mission school
Leadership Position: Shoshone medicine man and Sun Dance chief

Summary

John Trehero was a Shoshone medicine man and Sun Dance chief who reintroduced the Sun Dance on the Crow Reservation in 1941. In 1922, he acquired a hereditary Sun Dance medicine bundle from his mother, who was a descendant of

Chief Yellow Hand, a Sun Dance leader and Shoshone chief.

In 1938 Trehero conducted a Sun Dance at Fort Washakie, in present-day Utah, and it was attended by visiting Crow leaders, including William Big Day. Big Day subsequently invited Trehero to the Crow Reservation, where he reintroduced the Sun Dance in 1941.

During his long life, Trehero trained many medicine men, introduced innovations to the Sun Dance, and healed many people. The Sun Dance is one of the best-known and most spectacular religious ceremonies of native North America. The annual dance period was a time for renewing friendships, exchanging information, visiting relatives, holding traditional games, and conducting council meetings. Among the Shoshone, the Sun Dance was like a church. The participants received their messages through the medicine men. The Sun Dance generally includes sweat lodge purification, the preparation of male pledges by instructors, prolonged fasting, and dancing before a sacred pole.

Besides working as a medicine man, interpreter, and policeman, Trehero hauled wood and coal and owned herds of cattle and sheep for a time.

Photograph of John Trehero in *The Shoshoni-Crow San Dance*, by Fred W. Voget. University of Oklahoma Press.

Early Life

There are few recorded recollections of Trehero's early life. It is believed that when Trehero was about six years old, his father died. His mother died in 1922. Family members who wanted him educated in the white man's school sent him to a government boarding school in White Rock, Utah. Trehero was very unhappy with the regimented boarding school and remained there for less than two years. He then returned to Fort Washakie, Wyoming, where his family en-

rolled him in an Episcopal mission school. At about age nineteen, Trehero completed the eighth grade and dropped out of school. The Reverend John Roberts, the Episcopal minister in charge of the mission school, baptized Trehero at the age of fourteen or fifteen. Although he was a baptized Christian, Trehero was primarily interested in the traditional religious practices of his people. He learned about the Sun Dance and its beliefs from his maternal relatives and participated in the sacred ceremony for the first time when he was eighteen years old.

Leadership

Trehero flourished at a time when a number of influential Indian prophets were vying for religious leadership among the Shoshone people. He acquired a hereditary Sun Dance medicine bundle as well as instructions in the Sun Dance religion from his mother, a descendant of Chief Yellow Hand, a prominent Sun Dance leader among the Shoshone. The medicine bundle was very important to the Shoshone people and held a sacred object or a collection of objects. The objects that were contained in the bundle were sometimes seen in a dream or vision or acquired through inheritance, which was the case for Trehero. Bundles have great powers that benefit people. They may have the power to cure, make the wearer clairvoyant, call game animals, or ensure success in hunting. Bundles are considered to be alive and must be treated with respect and cared for by those who possess the proper qualifications.

Trehero became very influential on the Crow Indian Reservation where he had relatives and lived for about five years. In 1938, Trehero conducted a Sun Dance at Fort Washakie that was attended by visiting Crow leaders, including William Big Day. Big Day came under the religious influence of Trehero and subsequently invited him to the Crow Reservation, where he reintroduced the Sun Dance in 1941. Trehero served as mentor and instructor to Big Day and gained the support of influential Crow leaders. The last nineteenth-century Sun Dance among the Crow is believed to have been held in 1875.

During his long life (102 years), Trehero trained many medicine men and healed people. In 1967, when Trehero was eighty-four years old, he transferred his medicine powers and religious leadership to Thomas Yellowtail, a Crow medicine man and Sun Dance chief. In 1975, at age ninety-two, his blessings were still sought by Crow leaders he had instructed in his earlier life.

The Sun Dance is one of the best-known and misunderstood religious ceremonies conducted by Native American people. It was practiced in some form among the tribal groups of the Great Plains regions, including the Arapaho, Arikara, Blackfeet, Comanche, Crow, Cheyenne, Lakota, Nakota, Dakota, Gros Ventre, Kiowa, Mandan, Plains Creek, Plains Ojibwa, Shoshone, and Ute. The dance has many variations; however, for most tribes, the sacred ceremony is held to pray for the renewal of the people and the earth, give thanks, fulfill a vow, and protect the people from danger or illness.

Among the Crow, the Sun Dance was a prayer for vengeance. A man who was overcome with sorrow at the killing of a kinsman resorted to the Sun Dance as the most effective, if most arduous, means of getting a vision by which he might revenge himself upon the offending tribe.

The Sun Dance was an annual event, with its timing determined by natural events such as when certain berries began to ripen, when the trees were in leaf, or when the buffalo returned. Among the Crow, the performance might lapse for years. It has been reported that between 1830 and 1874, the average interval between successive performances was probably not less than three or four years.

The Sun Dance was also an important social event. It traditionally brought scattered tribal bands together during the summer for social as well as religious activities. The annual Sun Dance period was a time for courting, renewing friendships, exchanging information, visiting relatives, and holding traditional games. The length of the dance gathering varied, but among some groups, the sacred ceremony included four days of preparations, which included sweat lodge purification, the purification of male pledges, and dancing by the participants. The preparations were then followed by four days of rituals.

The Sun Dance ceremony may or not include the piercing of flesh and sun gazing. Piercing includes the insertion of wooden skewers under the muscle on either side of the chest. Leather strips were tied to the skewers and tied to the top of the Sun Dance pole. The participant gazed into the sun and leaned back on the leather tethers until the wooden skewers were pulled through the chest muscle. Sometimes a man had his back pierced with a skewer, to which as many as seven buffalo skulls were attached, and he would drag these through the Sun Dance arena until they were torn loose. Medicine men and their aides assisted all the participants. The Sun Dance reinforced such values as bravery, generosity, fortitude, and honesty.

U.S. and Canadian government agents eventually condemned the Sun Dance and it was officially banned in both countries. Adherents of the religion were forced to discontinue the ceremony or practice it in secret. The Sun Dance, became a punishable offense of the Courts of Indian Offenses, established by the U.S. government in 1883. Penalties for offenders included the withholding of treaty rations and imprisonment. The official ban ended in 1934 when Commissioner of Indian Affairs John Collier issued Circular No. 1970 on Indian religious freedom.

The Sun Dance is said to have ended among the Crow in 1875, the Gros Ventre in 1884, the Kiowa in 1890, and the Lakota bands in 1881–1883.

Modern Sun Dance practitioners continue to pray for the regeneration of the earth, and the continuation of the people, just as their ancestors did at past ceremonies.

Further Reading

Fitzgerald, Michael O., Thomas Yellowtail, and Fred Voget. *Yellowtail, Crow Medicine Man and Sun Dance Chief: An Autobiography*. 1994. Norman: University of Oklahoma Press.

Hirschfelder, Arlene, and Paulette Molin. *The Encyclopedia of Native American Religions*. 1992. New York: Facts on File.

Lowe, Robert H. *The Crow Indians*. 1983. Lincoln: University of Nebraska Press.

Washburn, Wilcomb E. *Handbook of North American Indians, Vol. 4*. 1988. Washington, D.C.: Smithsonian Institution.

Two Wolves

Full Name at Birth: Two-Wolves, "The Prophet"

Birth: date and place unknown; flourished in the early nineteenth century

Death: date and place unknown

Education: no formal education

Leadership Position: Arikara shaman

Summary

Two Wolves was an early-nineteenth-century Arikara shaman who was famous for his ability to foretell the future and seek out information such as the identity of a person who had committed a crime or performed a certain feat.

Two Wolves received the power to "speak with Thunder" as the result of having been caught up in a thunderstorm following a buffalo chase in present-day North or South Dakota. Two Wolves and his companions had completed the hunt when a storm approached. He became separated from his friends and remained out all night and the following day. He was missed that night, and it was believed that he was dead. His relatives mourned for him and set out to search for him once the storm had passed. Two Wolves had been protected by a sacred spirit, however, and survived the storm. The ruling power of the storm Waruhti gave Two Wolves the power to understand the speech of the Thunder-beings. Some time after this experience, Two Wolves began to practice his medicine, and he was much sought after because of his power. In 1903 James Murie, a member of the Skidi band of Pawnee Indians, told George Dorsey, curator of anthropology at the Carnegie Institution of Washington, D.C., that because of his popularity Two Wolves "always had his lodge full" (he was very popular and much sought after for healing).

Early Life

There is no recorded history of Two Wolves' early life. He flourished as a shaman in the late 1800s and early 1900s. From this, we can draw some conclusions.

The Arikara were a hardy Indian tribe that split from the Pawnee tribe about 1832. They, like the Hidatsa and the Mandan, lived in large, permanent earth lodges along the Missouri River in present-day North and South Dakota until 1854, at which time they were forced to relocate along with the Mandan and Gros Ventre to the Fort Berthold Reservation in North Dakota. Two Wolves was almost certainly born and grew to manhood af-

ter the move to Fort Berthold. Prior to that time a young Arikara boy would have participated in a traditional vision quest where he would have sought out an isolated spot to fast and pray for a vision. In the vision, he would have been given a spirit helper that would have guided him and supported him for the remainder of his life. Two Wolves did not receive his power in this traditional vision quest manner but as the result of being isolated during a storm and being visited by Waruhti, the ruling power of the storm.

Leadership

Two Wolves was revered because of his ability to discover the identity of people who transgressed tribal law and custom and his ability to prophesy forthcoming events. He did these things through his ability to understand the speech of the Thunder-beings. George Dorsey, curator of anthropology at the Carnegie Institution in Washington, D.C., with the assistance of James Murie, a member of the Skidi band of Pawnee Indians, recorded a number of displays of Two Wolves' powers, one of which is paraphrased here. Two-Bears, an Indian man, owned a herd of ponies that were being bothered by horses owned by another Indian man, Roving-Coyote. One day, unknown to Roving-Coyote, Two-Bears killed one of Roving-Coyote's horses that continued to harass his herd. Upon finding his pony dead, Roving-Coyote went to Two Wolves to find out who had shot and killed the animal. Two Wolves agreed to perform the ceremony that would divulge the identity of the guilty party. He called all of the men of the village together and sent forth a crier who said, "O people of this village, Two-Wolves wants the man who killed the horse belonging to Roving-Coyote to report to his lodge." This message was repeated over and over again. While the village crier was in the process of making this proclamation, black clouds rose in the sky. Two Wolves said, "Now my father is coming" (meaning his spirit helper). Two Wolves again called for the killer of the pony to identify himself and said that secrecy would do no good. Two-Bears did not believe that Two Wolves could understand the speech of the Thunder-beings, so he remained quiet. Thunder told Two Wolves that Two-Bears was the guilty party. When Two-Bears refused to identify himself, Two Wolves sent for him to come to his lodge. Two Wolves confronted Two-Bears and told him that the Thunder-beings had seen him kill Roving-Coyote's pony. Two-Bears then acknowledged that he had done the deed that he was accused of and said, "Yes, I know now that you are a wonderful man."

It is reported that Two Wolves "lived a long time, doing good work, discovering thieves, and prophesying many wonderful things."

Further Reading

Dorsey, George A. *Traditions of the Arikara*. 1904. Washington, D.C.: The Carnegie Institution of Washington.

Lyon, William S. *Encyclopedia of Native American Shamanism: Sacred Ceremonies of North America*. 1998. Denver: ABC-CLIO.

Wabokieshiek

Full Name at Birth: Wabokieshiek (also known as White Cloud or The Winnebago Prophet)

Birth: ca. 1794; place unknown

Death: ca. 1841; place unknown

Education: no formal education

Leadership Position: Sac (or Sauk), Fox, and Winnebago prophet

Summary

Wabokieshiek served as a prophet to Black Hawk, the chief of the Sac and Fox at a critical time in the formation of the United States. Wabokieshiek interpreted dreams and gave out supernatural advice that called for a resurgence of the Native traditional way of life. Wabokieshiek counseled Black Hawk that he had seen a vision in which Black Hawk would be aided in his struggle with westward-expanding whites by the Great Spirit and an army of ancestral warriors. Wabokieshiek told Black Hawk that all the American war chiefs (General Edmund Gains and Henry Atkinson) were trying to do was scare the Sac and Fox away from their villages. Black Hawk heeded Wabokieshiek's advice and resisted the encroaching army of settlers. The resulting battle is known as the 1832 Black Hawk War, in which the prophet's predictions proved false. The Sac and Fox made a last stand at the Bad Axe River, where over three hundred Indians died. Black Hawk and Wabokieshiek were taken prisoner and confined in Jefferson Barracks (present-day St. Louis, Missouri) and later at Fort Monroe, Virginia. Upon their release from prison in 1834, Wabokieshiek and Black Hawk were taken on a tour of the east coast of the United States as part of an effort to impress Indians with the size and wealth of America and to impress on them the futility of further uprisings. The trip included public appearances and included a visit to Washington, D.C., where they met with President Andrew Jackson. Following his release and the eastern tour, Wabokieshiek lived among the Sac in Iowa until they were relocated to Kansas, then rejoined the Winnebago, among whom he died in obscurity.

Early Life

Very little is known concerning Wabokieshiek's early life. He first appears in written history in the events that led up to and included Black Hawk's War. His mother and father are nowhere mentioned, nor is a wife. It is reported that he had an adopted son; however, the child's name is not recorded, nor are events in his life.

Because of his Winnebago and Sac ancestry, it is reasonable to assume that he was born in the present-day Wisconsin State area. His birth year is approximated at 1794, which would have made him thirty-eight years of age at the time of the Black Hawk War. Wabokieshiek was described as a big man who stood more than six feet tall. It is recorded that his face was full and his eyes set deep. Most of the time, he frowned. He wore his hair long and also had a black mustache, something that few Indians wore. When carrying out his role as a prophet, he held a long pipe that was decorated with duck feathers, beads, and ribbons.

Leadership

Wabokieshiek was an important supporter of Black Hawk, the Sac and Fox leader during the final conflicts for the Old Northwest Territory in the 1830s. Due to his prophetic visions and supernatural abilities Wabokieshiek was given the name Winnebago Prophet. He is also identified in some written histories as White Cloud.

Wabokieshiek was born at a time when Native Americans were experiencing extreme political and military pressure for surrender and removal from the area known as the old Northwest Territory, now known as the Great Lakes region. His homeland was known as Prophet's Village or Prophetstown, situated on the Rock River near the present-day site of Prophetstown, Indiana, at the junction between the Tippecanoe and Mississippi rivers.

Wabokieshiek's hatred of the whites was intense. Although he was described as a man of reckless disposition, a scoundrel, and an evil genius, he kept his followers at peace during the early Winnebago uprising of 1827. By the time of the Black Hawk War five years later, however, he was advocating rebellion.

Wabokieshiek came to Black Hawk in 1832, when the Sac and Fox leader was gathering forces for his return to Saukenuk, a major Sac village in present-day Illinois.

The power that Wabokieshiek wielded among the Sac was impressive. Black Hawk viewed him as a man of great insight and knowledge, and Wabokieshiek quickly became his principal adviser. Wabokieshiek advised Black Hawk never to give up his village "for the whites to plough up the bones of our people." Wabokieshiek told Black Hawk that if the Sac remained in their village the whites would not wage war against them. He advised those who had departed to return and remain at the village. Wabokieshiek said that he would not listen to talk of war, because no white war chief would dare attack the Sac as long as they were at peace. While Wabokieshiek was speaking, however, General Henry Atkinson was en route from Jefferson Barracks with a large body of soldiers with the intention of compelling the surrender of Black Hawk and his people.

Following Wabokieshiek's advice, Black Hawk collected his people, numbering about one thousand men, women, and children, and settled them near their old tribal grounds at Rock Island. Federal officials urged Black Hawk to move across the Mississippi River into Iowa and to abandon their traditional lands forever. Wabokieshiek then told Black Hawk of a vision that he had experienced in which the Great Spirit would help defeat their enemies. He promised that with the aid of certain ceremonies, he could create an army of ancestral warriors who would aid Black Hawk in defeating the U.S. Army. Thereafter, the Indians could reclaim their homelands that were occupied by the United States. Neolin,* the Delaware Prophet (1760–1963), and Tenskwatawa,* the Shawnee Prophet (1806–1811) had made similar prophecies in their people's conflicts with European colonist and settlers.

Wabokieshiek's counsel was not without merit. With Sac ancestry, Wabokieshiek had followers among the Sac as well as the Winnebago. The Sac chief Ne-a-pope was reportedly under Wabokieshiek's influence. Wabokieshiek received wampum and tobacco from the Ottawa, Chippewa, and Potawatomi, committing them to support the Sac in case of war. Wabokieshiek was also successful in enrolling a number of Kickapoo warriors to Black Hawk's cause.

Equally important, Wabokieshiek received reassurance from the British that they were going to send guns, ammunition, provisions, and clothing early in the spring to assist in the Black Hawk War. Black Hawk was informed and said that he was pleased that the British intended to help. Wabokieshiek told Ne-a-pope and Black Hawk that all the different tribes would fight for the Sac if necessary, and the British would support them.

Wabokieshiek believed in his prophecies as well as the promises made by the British. He remained with Black Hawk throughout the Black Hawk War and was at his side when the Indian leader was forced to surrender at Prairie du Chien in present-day Wisconsin on August 27, 1832. Black Hawk later renounced the promises that had been held out to the Sac by Wabokieshiek claiming that they were false. Black Hawk said that the supplies they were promised and the reinforcements they were to have were never received.

Wabokieshiek was imprisoned with Black Hawk in Jefferson Barracks, Missouri, and at Fort Monroe, Virginia. Upon release from prison, he traveled with Black Hawk as a kind of war trophy in the eastern United States, where they met President Andrew Jackson. In his later life, Wabokieshiek lived for a number of years in relative obscurity, first with the Sac and later with the Winnebago.

Further Readings

Axelrod, Alan. *Chronicle of the Indian Wars: From Colonial Times to Wounded Knee.* 1993. Englewood Cliffs, N.J.: Prentice Hall.

Champagne, Duane, ed. *The Native North American Almanac: A Reference Work on Native North Americans in the United*

States and Canada. 1994. Detroit: Gale Research.

Cole, Cyrenus. *I Am a Man, The Indian Black Hawk*. 1938. Iowa City: Iowa State Historical Society.

Donald Jackson. *Ma-ka-tai-me-she-kia-kiak, Black Hawk*. 1955. Urbana. University of Illinois Press.

Jackson, Donald. *Black Hawk: An autobiography*. 1990. Urbana: University of Illinois Press.

Quaife, Milo Milton, ed. *Life of Black Hawk, Ma-Ka-Tai-Me-She-Kia-Kiak*. 1834. Chicago: Lakeside Press.

Waldman, Carl. *Who Was Who in Native American History*. 1990. New York: Facts on File.

Walker, Paul R. *Spiritual Leaders: American Indian Lives*. 1994. New York: Facts on File.

Washburn, Wilcomb E. *Handbook of North American Indians, Vol. 4*. 1988. Washington, D.C.: Smithsonian Institution.

Wassaja (Carlos Montezuma)

Full Name at Birth: Wassaja ("signaling," "beckoning")

Birth: 1867, probably in the Superstition Mountains of present-day central Arizona

Death: January 31, 1923, in a traditional *wickiup* on the Fort McDowell Reservation in present-day Arizona

Education: Carlisle Indian School; University of Illinois, B.S.; Chicago Medical College, M.D., 1889

Leadership Position: Yavapai physician

Summary

Montezuma, whose birth name was Wassaja, meaning "signaling" or "beckoning," was born among the Yavapai Indians in Arizona. As a boy, he was captured by the Pima Indians, who sold him to Carlos Gentile, a white photographer who named him Carlos Montezuma. When Gentile's business was destroyed by fire and he felt that he could no longer care for Wassaja, Gentile delivered him to George Ingalls, a Baptist missionary, who brought the young Montezuma to Urbana, Illinois. William H. Steadman, a Baptist minister, became his guardian.

Montezuma received his schooling in the Chicago area and received his medical degree from Northwestern University's Chicago Medical College in 1889. After an attempt at private medical practice, he was appointed physician-surgeon at the Fort Stevenson Indian School in North

The Future Yavapai physician, Carlos Montezuma (Wassaja), as a young man, c. 1882. Courtesy, Carlos Montezuma collection, Arizona collection, Arizona State University Libraries.

Dakota. Now working for the federal government's Indian Service, Montezuma

practiced medicine on various Indian reservations until his frustration with conditions led him to take a position at Carlisle Indian School in Pennsylvania.

After leaving Carlisle, Montezuma returned to Chicago, where he established a successful private medical practice. His concern and frustration over the substandard medical treatment on Indian reservations soon caused him to turn his attention to activist work for Indian rights. Montezuma advocated the abolition of the Bureau of Indian Affairs and the reservation system and advocated for citizenship for Indian people. Presidents Theodore Roosevelt and Woodrow Wilson were impressed by Montezuma's dedication to the improvement of health services for Indian people and asked him to become the commissioner of Indian affairs. Montezuma refused both presidential invitations. Montezuma died on January 31, 1923, of tuberculosis at the Fort McDowell Reservation in Arizona, where he was born.

Early Life

Wassaja was born in the Superstition Mountains of Arizona among the Southeastern Yavapai Indians. His father's name was Coluyeva, and his mother was Thilgeyah.

In the 1860s, when Wassaja was still young, Anglo-Americans were rapidly encroaching into the world of the Yavapai and other Indian nations of the American Southwest. The streams of non-Indian prospectors and settlers disrupted Native American life, destroying food resources and causing intratribal wars for survival. In 1869, a drought set in in southern Arizona. In 1871, in one of many intratribal clashes between the Pima and the Yavapai, a group of Pima surprised a Yavapai encampment, killing a number of them and capturing others. Wassaja and his two sisters were among those taken captive. The Pima renamed Wassaja Hejelweiikam (Left Alone). He and his sisters were separated, never again to reunite. His sisters were apparently sold to a man who eventually took them to Mexico, where they died. Wassaja did not see any of his family members again, even though his mother attempted to recover her lost children and was killed by army scouts. Wassaja's father was moved to the San Carlos reservation in the 1870s, where he died.

Three Pima men took young captive Wassaja to the village of Adamsville, a small settlement about seven miles from the town of present-day Florence, Arizona, where they met a man by the name of Carlos Gentile, an immigrant from Italy. Gentile purchased Wassaja for $30. On November 17, 1871, Gentile had Wassaja baptized as Carlos Montezuma. The baptismal record listed Montezuma's birth date as 1866. In his later life, Montezuma used 1867 as his date of birth. When hard times fell on Gentile, a Baptist missionary, George Ingalls brought Montezuma to Urbana, Illinois, where a Baptist minister, William H. Steadman, became his guardian.

Leadership

Montezuma was a successful Yavapai physician who was born in present-day Arizona. In 1884 he graduated from the University of Illinois with a bachelor of science degree and received his medical degree from Northwestern University's Chicago Medical College in 1889. After an attempt at private medical practice in Chicago, Montezuma accepted an appointment from the Indian Service as physician-surgeon at the Fort Stevenson Indian School in North Dakota. Between 1889 and 1896, Montezuma worked for the Office of Indian Affairs and practiced medicine at a number of different reservations. His final post was at the Carlisle Indian School Hospital in Pennsylvania.

From 1896 to 1922, Montezuma maintained a successful private medical practice in Chicago. During this period, he also taught courses at various medical schools in Chicago and was offered a teaching position at the College of Physicians and Surgeons in the Postgraduate Medical School. Increasingly, however, Montezuma turned his attention to Indian rights.

Montezuma's experiences working in the reservation health system made him extremely critical of the Indian Service, and he advocated for the abolition of the Bureau of Indian Affairs (BIA) and the Indian reservation system. He was joined in his criticism by many prominent people, including Dr. Charles Eastman,* a noted Lakota physician and writer. Presidents Theodore Roosevelt and Woodrow Wilson invited Montezuma to become the commissioner of Indian affairs. Montezuma refused and continued his calls for the abolition of the BIA.

In 1906, the Yavapai became engaged in a water rights struggle when the city of Phoenix, Arizona, proposed building a dam in the middle of the Fort McDowell Indian reservation. The government proposed to remove the Yavapai to the Pima Salt River Reservation, but the Yavapai refused. Under the leadership of Montezuma, the Yavapai successfully established their ownership of the land and the water on their reservation and defeated the dam proponents. Because of his activist position Montezuma earned a reputation with the BIA as an agitator. He gave lectures in which he criticized the BIA and the reservation system and advocated

citizenship for the Indian people. He was among the first to call for pride in Indianness.

Montezuma was married to a Romanian-American woman, Marie Keller. She was reportedly much younger than he and was described as being "beautiful but demure." Suffering from diabetes and tuberculosis, he returned to his place of birth with his wife in 1922. The next year, on January 31, 1923, he died at the Fort McDowell Reservation, in a *wickiup* (a brush shelter) built especially for him. In the final paragraph of the last article that he wrote in *Wassaja*, Carlos Montezuma wrote, "If the world be against us, let us not be dismayed, let us not be discouraged, let us look up and go ahead, and fight on for freedom and citizenship of our people. If it means death, let us die on the pathway that leads to the emancipation of our race; keeping in our hearts that our children will pass over our graves to victory."

Further Reading

Champagne, Duane, ed. *The Native North American Almanac: A Reference Work on Native North Americans in the United States and Canada*. 1994. Detroit: Gale Research.

"If you knew the conditions . . ." Health Care to Native Americans: http://www.nlm.nih.gov/exhibition/if_you_knew/if_you_knew_10. html.

Iverson, Peter. *Carlos Montezuma and the Changing World of American Indians*. 1982. Albuquerque: University of New Mexico Press.

Papers of Carlos Montezuma, M.D.: http://sun3.lib.uci.edu/~slca/microform/resources/p-q/p_030.htm.

Waldman, Carl. *Who Was Who in Native American History*. 1990. New York: Facts on File.

White Bird

Full Name at Birth: White Bird (Penpenhihi, Peopeo Hihhih, Peopeo Kiskiok Hihih) ("white goose")

Birth: ca. 1807

Death: ca. 1882

Education: no formal education

Leadership Position: Nez Percé medicine man; tribal leader during Nez Percé War of 1877

Summary

White Bird was a Nez Percé medicine man and chief and one of the Nez Percé, along with Chief Joseph (the elder, ca. 1790–1871), who refused to sign the Thief Treaty of 1863 and move to the Lapwai Reservation in Idaho. He originally counseled peace with white settlers, as did Chief Joseph (the younger, ca. 1840–1904), but when tensions mounted in 1877, White Bird joined in calling for war.

In 1877, General Oliver O. Howard, commander of the Northwestern Department, met with Nez Percé chiefs, including White Bird. All agreed to relocate, including Chief Joseph and White Bird. However, on the way to their new home, a skirmish involving young Nez Percé warriors occurred that resulted in the Nez Percé War of 1876. The older Nez Percé tried to keep the peace and deal peaceably with the whites. The younger warriors were hard to control because they were under the influence of liquor sold to them by a white man by the name of Dave Spooner who tended bar in a nearby saloon.

A 100-man cavalry command rushed south from Fort Lapwai, Idaho, to capture the warriors, and on June 17, 1877, they struck the camp of White Bird, in White Bird Canyon (named after the famed medicine man). The Nez Percé repelled the attack with heavy casualties, and the war was on. In October 1877, just forty miles short of the Canadian border, General Miles caught up with the exhausted Nez Percé, who had paused to rest. The chiefs were able to organize a defense, but they lost their primary war leaders Toohoolhoolzote* and Ollakot, Chief Joseph's brother. Chief Joseph urged surrender. White Bird wanted to continue to resist, however, and led some three hundred people to safety by escaping into Canada. Chief Joseph surrendered to General Nelson A. Miles on October 5, 1877.

White Bird was a medicine man, and that is how he lived and how he lost his life. He was of accused of using his medicine power control over Chief Joseph to push the Nez Percé into a devastating war. He was also accused of placing an evil spell on two sons of Hasenahmahkikt, another Nez Percé medicine man. The two boys identified White Bird as the sorcerer on their deathbeds; however, White Bird's medicine was stronger than that of Hasenahmahkikt, and the boys died. Hasenahmahkikt was unable to reverse the spell of the more powerful medicine man, and he killed White Bird.

Early Life

There is no recorded history of White Bird's early life. We do know that he was a medicine man among the Cheyenne people. *Medicine man* (or woman), is a term that is applied to many Native American practitioners and healers who possess spiritual power. Medicine people may possess both good and evil powers, and for this reason they are highly respected and feared. The role of medicine man or woman varies from tribe to tribe, but in all instances they command a great deal of authority and in some cases domination. This was the case with White Bird. He could command spiritual powers, foretell the future, and cast both good and evil spells. White Bird also had the ability to cure diseases caused by spiritual or evil sources. The great Nez Percé Chief Joseph (the younger) was strongly influenced by White Bird and acceded to him when making important decisions.

Leadership

White Bird was a powerful Nez Percé medicine man and the oldest of the five nontreaty Nez Percé chiefs who signed the Stevens Treaty with the United States in 1855 in an attempt to live in peace with white settlers. Promises were made that the United States would never again ask for Nez Percé lands. In 1860, however, prospectors and settlers flooded onto Nez Percé treaty lands. In 1863, the government responded by writing a new treaty, the Thief's Treaty, reducing the reservation to one-tenth its original size. In return, the government promised agricultural implements, mills, schools, churches, and other tools of civilization. Those who refused to sign the treaty, such as White Bird, came to be known as the "non-treaty Nez Percé."

White Bird is described as having been a handsome man, about 5 feet 9 inches tall. He was well proportioned, with a splendid physique and stately bearing. When in council, he assumed the condition of impassability or rigid fixedness and displayed not the slightest emotion. He was mild in temper and in speech and was not an advocate of war. In addition to his position as a venerated medicine man, White Bird boasted a long line of noted warrior ancestry. His status and influence was pronounced, and he held an honored place in all councils.

After the defeat of Lieutenant Colonel George Armstrong Custer at the Little Big Horn in June 1876, the U.S. Army feared other Indian uprisings and ordered that all non-reservation Nez Percé be placed on reservations. In 1877, General Oliver O. Howard, commander of the Northwestern Department, met with Nez Percé chiefs, including White Bird. Howard asked the nontreaty leaders if they would move. Despite surrendering their homeland valley of Wallowa, all agreed to relocate, including White Bird.

On May 15, 1877, the settlers living along the Salmon River in the Wallowa Valley sent a petition to General Howard. The petition was read to White Bird and stated that the residents of Salmon River were sorely annoyed by the presence of a lawless band of Nez Percé Indians. They asked that measures be taken to remove the remaining Nez Percé from their midst speedily and that they be placed on a reservation where some restraint might be imposed. White Bird replied substantially that the problems that had arisen were the result of the white men selling whiskey to Indians, and when the whites and Indians drank, both acted with folly. He had advised his people against drinking and troubling the white settlers but some of it was impossible for him to control. At the Lapwai Council, held in 1877, General Howard announced that the Nez Percé would now have to give up their most priced possession, the Wallowa, or be removed by force. The war leader Toohoolhoolzote refused to do so and was arrested for inciting others to disobey Howard's order.

On June 15, 1877, White Bird was seen riding around his tent on horseback and making sacred circles on the ground, his way of declaring that the Nez Percé had taken up the hatchet (declared a state of war). It was reported that Chief Joseph was under the control of White Bird and was forced by White Bird and other chiefs to accompany them and that when they wanted to surrender, White Bird had driven them before his forces in the direction of the Bitterroot Mountains.

The army responded by rushing a 100–man cavalry command from Fort Lapwai, Idaho, and on June 17, 1877, the unit attacked the camp of White Bird, in White Bird Canyon. The Nez Percé threw back the attackers with heavy casualties, and the war was on. The Nez Percé War continued over 1,700 miles and raged from June 17 to October 5, 1877. Forty miles short of the Canadian border, General Miles caught up with the fleeing Nez Percé. The chiefs were able to organize a defense but lost their war leaders Toohoolhoolzote and Ollakot. Chief Joseph now urged surrender. White Bird wanted to continue to resist and made a dash for safety in Canada, leading some three hundred people to safety.

White Bird was criticized for the advice that he had given to Chief Joseph and was accused of starting the Nez Percé War. It was not uncommon for a medicine man to be put to death if his magic, or power, failed to produce the desired results. There was some speculation that White Bird was killed for this reason.

White Bird lived and died as a medicine man, however, and he was killed by another Nez Percé medicine man, Hasenahmahkikt, who was angry because White Bird had killed his two sons. It is reported that in 1882, one of Hasenahmahkikt's young sons had become gravely ill. He grew worse, and just before dying, his father asked him, "Who are you?" The sick child replied, "Peopeo Hihhih." It was Peopeo Hihhih's (White Bird's) power killing the child, and this power made the boy answer to the father's questions. The boy died. A second son also became ill and died saying the same words when asked, "Who are you?" The father then shot and killed White Bird.

Further Reading

Axelrod, Alan. *Chronicle of the Indian Wars: From Colonial Times to Wounded Knee.* 1993. Englewood Cliffs, N.J.: Prentice Hall.

Ballantine, Betty, and Ian Ballantine, eds. *The Native American: An Illustrated History.* 1993. Atlanta: Turner Publishing.

Brown, Mark H. *The Flight of the Nez Percé.* 1967. New York: G. P. Putnam's Sons.

Champagne, Duane, ed. *The Native North American Almanac: A Reference Work on Native North Americans in the United States and Canada.* 1994. Detroit: Gale Research.

McWhorter, L. V. *Hear Me, My Chiefs! Nez Percé Legend and History.* 1992. Caldwell, Idaho: Caxton Printers.

Waldman, Carl. *Who Was Who in Native American History.* 1990. New York: Facts on File.

Washburn, Wilcomb E. 1988. *Handbook of North American Indians, Vol. 4.* Washington, D.C.: Smithsonian Institution.

White Buffalo Calf Woman

Full Name at Birth: Ptehincalasanwin or Ptesan-Wi; also known as White Buffalo Calf Maiden and White Buffalo Woman

Birth: unknown

Death: unknown

Education: no formal education

Leadership Position: Lakota holy woman

Summary

White Buffalo Calf Woman is the holy person who is credited with giving the Lakota people their most sacred possession, the Buffalo Calf Pipe. White Buffalo Calf Woman made humans relatives of all four-legged and fur-bearing beings and foretold the seven sacred rites for the Lakota people.

Early Life

White Buffalo Calf Woman is a spirit being who appeared to the Lakota people as a full-grown woman. No reference is made to an earlier life or early years.

Leadership

There are numerous oral histories and recordings telling of White Buffalo Calf Woman's visit from the spirit world. They vary only slightly in the tellings. The following history is taken primarily from the voice of Black Elk (Neihardt 3–6), and Ed McGaa (McGaa 3–6) and incorporates other tellings as well.

One summer many, many years ago, the seven sacred council fires of the Lakota Oyate, or Nation, came together and camped. Two hunters of the Itazipcho or Sans Arc band of the Lakota Nation were sent out to scout for buffalo for the people. When the scouts reached the crest of a hill, they saw something to the north, a great distance away. As the image moved closer, they noted that it was a beautiful woman. As she drew closer, they observed a beautiful maiden, dressed in white buckskin, carrying a bundle wrapped in buffalo hide. She appeared to be floating above the ground rather than walking on it. As she moved, she sang out, "Behold me, Behold me, For in a sacred manner I am walking." She sang this out and repeated the song several times as she walked slowly toward them. She was the most beautiful woman the young men had ever seen. She wore a beautifully tanned white buckskin dress embroidered with sacred and magical designs. In her hands she carried a large bundle and a fan of sage leaves. One of the men thought evil thoughts regarding the woman, however, and spoke them to the other scout. His companion told him that this was surely a sacred woman and that he should throw all bad thoughts away. The men approached the woman, who could read their thoughts; she told the evil thinker, "You do not know me, but if you want to do as you think, you may come." As he approached her, they were surrounded by a cloud of white smoke. When the smoke cleared, the beautiful young woman came out of the cloud and all that remained of the man was his skeleton, covered with worms. Some versions state that lightning instantly struck the young man and burned him up, so that only a small heap of black bones remained (Erdoes and

Ortiz 48). Some versions say that his skeleton was covered by snakes.

After emerging from the cloud, White Buffalo Calf Woman instructed the remaining man to return to his camp, gather the leaders, and wait for her. He was instructed to have a large tipi built for her in the center of the Nation. She instructed him further to send runners to the distant bands of the Sioux nations and to bring in the many leaders, the medicine people, and the holy men and holy women. He did all of this. After a period of time, she appeared in the village and went into the tipi where she sang: "With visible breath I am walking. A voice I am sending as I walk. In a sacred manner I am walking. With visible tracks I am walking. In a sacred manner I walk." After entering the tipi, she walked in a clockwise direction, stopping before the leader. White Buffalo Calf Woman took a bundle from her back and removed a pipe and round stone. She then began her sacred teachings. Beginning with the pipe, she explained its meaning and the significance of each of its components. She told the people that the pipestone bowl represented the earth and that the wooden stem represented all the earth's growing things. She said that the buffalo calf carved on the bowl represented the earth and all four-legged creatures and that the pipe's twelve feathers, from the spotted eagle, represented the sky and all winged creatures. Whoever prayed with it would be joined to all other life in the universe. The holy woman also instructed the people regarding the stone, explaining that the seven circles on it stood for the seven sacred rites of the Lakota people. She presented the first rites, the Ghost-Keeping, or Soul-Keeping, ceremony and told them that the remaining six ceremonies

would be made known to them in visions and that the sacred pipe was to be used in each of them.

She sang again, walked in a clockwise direction around the tipi, then went out of the tipi. As she started to leave, she told them to remember how sacred the pipe was and to treat it in a sacred manner, for it would be with the Lakota forever.

The people watched as she walked some distance away from them. As she walked over the ridge of a hill, she sat down. When she rose, she had been transformed into a white buffalo calf. She then walked farther away, bowed to the four sacred quarters of the universe, and disappeared. (Gill and Sullivan 337). White Buffalo Calf Woman's bundle was left with the people, and to this day, a traditional Sioux family, the Keepers of the Sacred Bundle, guards the bundle and its contents on the Sioux reservation (McGaa 3–6). The birth of a white buffalo calf is considered to be a spiritual event with great significance for Lakota people. They pray that White Buffalo Calf Woman will walk among them once again and renew their pride, culture, and spirituality.

Further Reading

Erdoes, Richard, and Alfonso Ortiz. *American Indian Myths and Legends.* 1984. New York: Pantheon Books.

Gill, Sam D., and Irene F. Sullivan. *Dictionary of Native American Mythology.* 1992. New York: Oxford University Press.

Hirschfelder, Arlene, and Paulette Molin. *The Encyclopedia of Native American Religions.* 1992. New York: Facts on File.

McGaa, Ed. *Mother Earth Spirituality: Native American Paths to Healing Ourselves and Our World.* 1989. San Francisco: Harper & Row.

The Story of White Buffalo Calf Woman: http://www.cudenver.edu/~ccambrid/whitebuf.html.

White Buffalo Calf Woman: http://indy4.fdl.cc.mn.us/~isk/arvol/buffpipe.html.

White Bull ("Ice" or "Hail")

Full Name at Birth: Ice
Birth: ca. 1837
Death: July 10, 1921, on the Tongue River Reservation in present-day Montana
Education: no formal education
Leadership Position: Cheyenne holy man

Summary

White Bull was a highly respected medicine man and Sun Dance priest among the Cheyenne people. For the majority of his life, he was a member of the Crazy Dog and the Elk-Horn Societies, highly venerated warrior societies. White Bull was among those in attendance at the Lakota Sun Dance at which Sitting Bull, the Hunkpapa, Lakota, holy man, received his vision foretelling the 1876 defeat of Lieutenant Colonel George Armstrong Custer and the Seventh Cavalry at the Battle of the Little Big Horn.

White Bull railed against the surrender of Native lands and recognized farming as a major threat that would eliminate much of what still remained of Cheyenne traditional culture. He hated the white people for their reckless slaughter of the buffalo. He also feared that white boarding schools would destroy the Indian youth and return useless people to the Indian Nations. White Bull led many war parties in an attempt to stop the westward-moving Americans.

White Bull was a powerful medicine person and was sought after for his ability to heal sickness and foretell future events. He publicly displayed his spiritual powers well into his later years.

The death of White Bull's son, Noisy Walking, changed White Bull's life in a profound manner. Noisy Walking, like a select number of his Cheyenne friends, vowed to participate in the Suicide Warriors Dance, or Dying Dance, before fighting against the enemy. Those who performed this dance promised to fight to the death for the survival of their people. Noisy Walking died in a battle against the U.S. cavalry after having performed the Dying Dance. White Bull was so distraught following Noisy Walking's death that he stopped his warring against the white man and became a scout for General Nelson A. Miles. White Bull's scouting duties included accompanying General Miles against the famous Sioux warrior Lame Deer and his Minneconjou Lakota band in May 1877. White Bull died on July 10, 1921 at the approximate age of eighty-four.

Early Life

Little is known of White Bull's formative years. It is known that during his early years, his name was Ice; a name attributed to his grandfather and his father. White Bull participated in the Cheyenne vision quest ritual at the age of fifteen. The vision quest is still practiced today and is a ritual in which a young man or woman seeks to establish communication with the spirit world. The young person is sometimes accompanied to a secluded area by a tribal elder or medicine person. After they sing songs, chant prayers, and pray individually, the attendant leaves. The young person is then left alone for a period of time, often as long as four days, to seek a vision. During this period, the youth fasts and undergoes sleep and other sensory deprivations to facilitate the vision process. Individuals blessed during a vision quest sometimes receive names, objects, songs, dances, or spiritual helpers such as an animal, bird, or other being. This spirit or power helper can be called on throughout the remainder of that person's life for help and guidance.

Leadership

White Bull was the most famous of the Northern Cheyenne medicine men and Sun Dance priest. Because of his long life, he was in a unique position to assess the cultural and physical destruction that the Northern Cheyenne had suffered as a result of Anglo invasion of Native traditional lands.

White Bull feared the adoption of white technology and agriculture and on one occasion related a prophecy that he had received that said the white boarding schools were also bad. Cheyenne children, he was told, who were taken away to be educated in white-run schools would "never know anything" they would cease being Indian. His biggest fear was that the Cheyenne people would forget the teachings of the Cheyenne prophet Sweet Medicine.* Sweet Medicine had told the Cheyenne people in the mid-1700s that to continue the covenant between the Cheyenne and the Creator, they must uphold the sacred law and ceremonies, and in return, the Creator would protect the Cheyenne Nation from physical and cultural destruction. Adoption of white agriculture and sending Cheyenne children to distant boarding schools was a transgression against the sacred covenant.

As a powerful and mystical medicine person, White Bull could perform many feats that no one could understand. On one occasion (in approximately 1867) White Bull had some tribesmen tie his hands and feet behind his back with rawhide thongs, then double up his body and continue to wrap him with the long strips of rawhide strips around and around about his body. After being so secured, he was placed in a pit that was approximately ten feet deep. A large number of Cheyenne men then got an immense flat stone and placed it over the pit. The observers went away for a period of time. When they returned, they found White Bull sitting untied on top of the flat stone. The rawhide bindings were in the pit with all knots tied as they had been. His escape became knows as "Ice's miracle," and he received the name White Bull a short time later.

White Bull also served as a warrior, chief, and scout during his lifetime. His father, North Left Hand, was said to have been banished from the Cheyenne Nation after being accused of murder by Cheyenne warrior society leaders. During his period of exile, North Left Hand joined the Arapaho people and married an Arapaho woman. White Bull, who was identified as the son of North Left Hand and his Arapaho wife, returned to the Cheyenne people, where he was adopted into membership of the Crazy Dog Society and Elk-horn Scraper societies.

Among the Cheyenne, band and society membership is extremely important. Everyone belongs to a band from the time of birth, and all members are blood related. Societies consist of chosen members that cut across band lines. The Crazy Dog Society (or Crazy-Dogs-Wishing-to-Die) was a warrior society that was added to the military associations about 1836 after the Kiowa and Comanche annihilated the Bow-string Society. Members of the Crazy Dog Society wore distinctive headdress adorned with sections of mountain sheep or buffalo horns and trimmed with weasel skins. A band of red cloth, about four inches in width, was attached across the cap. The bravest members wore a pair of sashes or red cloth that crossed in front and trailed on the ground behind and were known as "sash wearers." Individual war medicines were attached to the sashes. When the Cheyenne went to war, the sash wearers were in the forefront of the battle. When all others had been killed or fled the field of battle, they were expected to make a stand. They dismounted from their horses and placed a staff in a hole in the sash and stood their ground until they were killed or released by another sash wearer. Their song was, "This is the way I sing when I want to die."

White Bull was also a member of the Elk-horn Scraper, or Elk Warrior Society. The Elk-horn Scraper Society consisted of one hundred proven warriors and four virgin maidens. A loose woman among the Cheyenne was without social status, and these maidens honored both the Cheyenne people and the warrior societies by being selected for membership in the society. Members of the Elk-horn Scraper Society protected the virtue of all Cheyenne women.

Warrior societies such as the Crazy Dog and Elk-horn Scraper societies had a wide range of authority. They were considered to be governing officials in such matters as public safety, initiation, and execution of needed charities. They acted regarding personal property and could and did serve as law enforcement agents. They made law, and they enforced it.

White Bull was also a Sun Dance priest. The Sun Dance is one of the best-known religious ceremonies conducted by Native Americans and was practiced in some form by almost all tribal groups of the Great Plains regions, including the Cheyenne, Arapaho, Arikara Blackfeet, Comanche, Crow, Cheyenne, Lakota, and Dakota. The Sun Dance has many variations; however, for most tribes, the sacred ceremony is held to pray for the renewal of the people and the earth, give thanks, fulfill a vow, and protect the people from danger or illness. The Sun Dance was also an important social event for the tribes. It traditionally brought scattered tribal bands together during the summer for social as well as religious activities. The annual Sun Dance period was a time for courting, renewing friendships, exchanging information, visiting relatives, and holding traditional games.

White Bull's life was profoundly affected by the death of his son Noisy Walking. Noisy Walking and other youths vowed to perform a Suicide Warriors Dance, or Dying Dance, before going into battle against the enemy. Those who performed such a dance pledged to die if necessary to prevent harm to the Cheyenne people. Noisy Walking died in battle, protecting his people as he had pledged. White Bull had little desire for war after his son's death and became a scout the following year. The holy man became the first Cheyenne scout under the command of General Nelson A. Miles.

In his later years, White Bull continued to demonstrate his spiritual powers. In 1908 during a Sun Dance, he caused hailstones to fall during the summertime to assist a participant who had collapsed. The name "hail" was given to him at that time. Greatly respected as healer as well as a holy man, White Bull died on July 10, 1921.

Further Reading

Beck, Peggy V., Anna Lee Walters, and Nia Francisco. *The Sacred Ways of Knowledge, Sources of Life*. 1990. Flagstaff: Northland Publishing Co.

Hirschfelder, Arlene, and Paulette Molin. 1992. The Encyclopedia of Native American Religions. 1992. New York: Facts on File.

Hoebel, E. Adamson. *The Cheyennes: Indians of the Great Plains*. 1978. New York: Holt, Rinehart and Winston.

Llewellyn, K. N., and E. Adamson Hoebel. *The Cheyenne Way: Conflict and Case Law in Primitive Jurisprudence*. 1967. Norman: University of Oklahoma Press.

Mails, Thomas E. *Plains Indians: Dog Soldiers, Bear Men and Buffalo Women*. 1985. New York: Bonanza Books.

Marquis, Thomas B. *The Cheyennes of Montana*. 1978. Algonac, Mich.: Reference Publications.

Eleazar Williams

Full Name at Birth: Eleazar Williams

Birth: 1788 near Lake George, New York

Death: August 28, 1858, on the St. Regis Reservation, near Hogansburg, New York

Education: attended an Episcopal School in Long Meadow, Massachusetts, 1800–1812

Leadership Position: Mohawk chief and Episcopal missionary

Summary

Eleazar Williams was a full-blood Mohawk Indian who was born in approximately 1788 near Lake George, New York. When he was twelve years old, his father enrolled him, against his mother's wishes, in an Episcopal school in Long Meadow, Massachusetts, where he studied the Episcopal religion under Nathaniel Ely. Following Ely's death in 1807, Williams continued his studies under Reverend Enoch Hale until 1812. During the War of 1812, Williams became the superintendent-general of the Northern Indian Department. He was wounded at the Battle of Plattsburgh in New York on September 14, 1814. Following the war, Williams lived among the Oneida Indians at Oneida Castle, New York, and convinced the Oneida to sell several hundred acres of their homelands to provide funds for building a church and school. Williams served as an Episcopal catechist while continuing his theological studies with General A. G. Ellis.

Williams worked with the U.S. War Department on a plan to remove the Iroquois people from New York State. The removal plan was officially rejected by the Iroquois Council, however, and eventually faltered. When the plan failed to materialize, Williams was repudiated by the Oneida and lost support from missionary societies.

In 1853, Williams claimed to be the lost dauphin of France, Louis XVII, son of Louis XVI and Marie Antoinette. Williams claimed that Prince de Joinville, son of Louis Philippe assured him of his identity as the dauphin in 1841. Williams also claimed that he had received lashings from a jailer in the Tower of the Temple in Paris. A book, *The Lost Prince*, and an article, "Have We a Bourbon Among Us?" were written by Reverend John Hanson in 1854 in support of Williams's claim. Other authors proved that Williams's claim was groundless. Williams's wife, Mary Jourdain, was also rumored to have ties to French royalty. Williams died on August 28, 1858, on the St. Regis Reservation, near Hogansburg, New York.

Early Life

Williams was a Mohawk Indian and one of thirteen children. His mother's name was Konwatewenteta (Mary Rice Williams), and his Mohawk father was Tehoragwanegen (Thomas Williams). He was born in 1788, probably near Lake George, New York, and grew up on the Caughnawaga (Kahnawake) Reserve outside Montreal, Quebec. When he was twelve years old, Williams was placed in the care of Nathaniel Ely for Episcopal studies. Following Ely's death in 1807, Williams continued his studies under Reverend Enoch Hale from 1809 to 1812.

Leadership

Following his educational training in the Episcopal religion under Nathaniel Ely and Enoch Hale, Williams voiced intentions of becoming a Christian missionary to the Indians. In early 1812, William began his quest to convert Indian members of the Iroquois League to the Episcopal faith and began a missionary tour as an agent of the American Board of Missions. Although Williams had little success in converting the Iroquois people from Catholicism, he did gain their respect and was elected a chief among the Mohawk at Caughnawaga.

Williams returned to Massachusetts at the start of the War of 1812 and received an appointment as superintendent general of the Northern Indian Department in the hope that he could prevent the tribes of the Iroquois League from supporting England. Through his Iroquois contacts, Williams provided valuable information to his superiors, Generals Henry Dearborn and Jacob Brown, concerning British troop movements, and on September 14, 1814 Williams was injured at the Battle of Plattsburgh.

Following the War of 1812, Williams worked among the Oneida at Oneida Castle, New York, and was successful in converting a number of members of this tribe to the Episcopal faith. Williams was also successful in convincing the Oneida to give him a grant of one hundred acres of their land and to sell additional property to the state for the purpose of building a church and a school.

In 1820, a group that included Williams, the Reverend Jedediah Morse, other missionaries, the Ogden Land Company, and the War Department developed a controversial plan to relocate the Iroquois west of Lake Michigan. The group hoped to remove the tribes of the Iroquois league and shape a new Iroquois empire with a single leader. Williams was accused of writing a fictitious speech, supposedly given by an Oneida chief in support of the plan, and forging the signatures of council members. The relocation scheme was rejected by the member tribes of the Iroquois League, Williams's promises to his followers of acquiring large land grants were never realized, nor were his promises to missionary societies of establishing churches and schools, and he lost credibility with both Indians and whites. Having been disavowed by the Oneida people, Williams moved to Wisconsin in 1823 and dropped out of public life.

In 1853, Williams resurfaced and garnered public attention with the claim that he was the lost dauphin of France, Louis

XVII, son of Louis XVI and Marie Antoinette, who supposedly had been killed in the French Revolution. Williams claimed that scars on his arms and legs were the results of lashings by his jailer during his stay in the Tower of the Temple in Paris. Williams gained some believers, including the Reverend John Hanson, who wrote a book, *The Lost Prince*, supporting the story, which was soon proved to be false.

Williams died on August 28, 1858 on the St. Regis Reservation, near Hogansburg, New York. His publications included an Iroquois spelling book in 1813, a prayer book in 1853, and an account of his father's life in 1859.

Further Reading

Waldman, Carl. *Who Was Who in Native American History*. 1990. New York: Facts on File.

Washburn, Wilcomb E. *Handbook of North American Indians, Vol. 4*. 1988. Washington, D.C.: Smithsonian Institution.

Jack Wilson

See Wovoka

Wodziwob ("Gray Hair")

Full Name at Birth: Wodziwob
Birth: ca. 1844
Death: ca. 1918, on Walker River Reservation, Nevada
Education: no formal education
Leadership Position: Paiute Ghost Dance religious leader

Summary

Wodziwob is credited with being the originator of the 1870 Ghost Dance. The movement began when Wodziwob is believed to have visited the spirit world during a trance or temporary death experience and returned to life with sacred teachings given to him by the Creator of Life. Disciples spread his revelation to other Indian groups, and the Ghost Dance religion of 1870 became one of the most widely spread and influential Indian religions of the 1800s. Disciples included Tavibo,* the father of the messianic figure Wovoka,* who founded the 1890 Ghost Dance religion.

Early Life

There are no written records of Wodziwob's early life, however, we can draw from oral histories and cultural tradition to reconstruct his early years. Wodziwob was born into a Paviotso (Southern Paiute) family in the early to mid-1800s and lived in the barren high desert environment of the Great Basin in extreme western Nevada. Because of the harsh environment, his family would have belonged to a small patrilineal blood-related band. Out of necessity, Wodziwob and his family would have spent a great deal of time forging in a subsistence system that required that they be alert to all possible food sources. Wodziwob and his family depended on mobility and flexibility to survive. They practiced an elaborate seasonal cycle and harvested every variety of fish, plant, and animal that was available for their food, clothing, and limited shelter. As a child, Wodziwob would have learned the intricate knowledge required for survival in a harsh desert environment. His grandfather would have taught him how to hunt small animals, the use of the bow and arrow, as well as the worldview and cultural traditions of the Paviotso people.

Leadership

The Ghost Dance religion of 1870 was a dynamic religious revitalization movement started by the Wodziwob in 1869. *Ghost Dance* is a general term that has been used to cover a series of related religious movements that developed between 1869 and 1872 and then again in 1890. The original doctrine of the religion was given to Wodziwob during a near-death or trance experience in 1869. This occurred at the time that the Lake Paiute staged their regular pine nut harvest festival. While in this death or trance state, Wodziwob visited the land of the dead and was told that a ruler was coming to the earth and would bring with him all the spirits of the dead. He would change earth into paradise, bring eternal life for Indian people, and all of the white intruders on Paiute land would be eliminated. While some said that all whites were to burn up and disappear, others said that not all whites would be eliminated, and still others said that there would be no distinction between the races. The single overriding doctrine of the 1870 Ghost Dance movement was the belief in the return of the dead. This was the central focus and persisted throughout

the movement. Wodziwob also emphasized giving up the white man's religion completely.

Preparation for this event required that a person dance with only short rests, bathe daily, and decorate oneself with red, black, and white paint. It was thought that dancing would hasten the approach of the dead. Ghost Dancers were encouraged to dance until they fainted and to dream of the returning dead. In these Ghost Dance dreams, many people reported that they had actually met and talked with dead relatives who were on their way back to join the living. Others saw that everyone in the land of the dead was happy, and they prophesied that the end of the world was near.

The Ghost Dance was a direct response to the social and cultural destruction and deprivations American Indian people experienced following contact with white Americans. As miners and settlers moved west, they crossed Paviotso lands and destroyed the ecological balance that regulated their lives. As a result, the Ghost Dance provided an understandable and attractive alternative and was spread rapidly by prophets, who also modified the dance to fit the spiritual and cultural needs of other Indian Nations. One Ghost Dance prophet, Weneyuga (Frank Spencer), converted the Washo in present-day western Nevada and then traveled to the Paviotso in northeastern California and the Klamath in southern Oregon. They readily adopted Wodziwob's teachings. A modified version of the Ghost Dance known as the Earthlodge religion developed in present-day north-central California among the Wintun and Hill Patwin tribes. The Earthlodge religion emphasized the end of the world more than the return of the dead. Among the Wintun and Patwin, the Ghost Dances were held in semi-subterranean structures to protect the religion's members from the holocaust that they feared would occur at the world's end.

The Earthlodge religion was next carried to the Pomo tribe, north of present-day San Francisco, which developed it into an elaborate dreamer religion known as the Bole Maru. This religion consisted of women dreamers inspired by the Christian God, who taught the revelations of their dreams and preached a highly moralistic code. They rejected the teaching of the impending end of the world and emphasized teachings about the Creator and the afterlife. It also spread to the Shasta Nation in present-day northern California, where it was transformed into the Warmhouse dance. From the Shasta it spread to the Siletz reservation, and from there to the Tolowa of northern California where it inspired the later Shaker religion.

In Oregon, among the Tillamook people, the Ghost Dance became the Southwest Wind Dance. The Tillamook who participated in the Ghost Dance adopted Wodziwob's teachings and believed that if they danced, they would live, and their dead relatives would return. The Southwest Wind Dance included a new belief: that whatever they wished for while dancing would appear the next morning.

In all cases, local dreamers, prophets, and religious leaders became the local authorities even though the religions themselves came from outside the communities and can ultimately be traced to the Ghost Dance introduced by Wodziwob. The modified versions filled the specific needs of individual tribes and were soon accepted into the local religious cosmology, where they were placed into the hands of specialists and authorities on sacred practices.

Wodziwob's teachings came at a time of significance for many Indian Nations. On reservations, the traditional means of attaining prestige and rank had vanished. Young Indians had little to aspire to; there were no wars, no hunting, and no raiding. As the result of white invasion, the traditional tribal economy collapsed, and this collapse precipitated radical changes. The Ghost Dance held out hope because it promised a renewal of the world during which time the dead would return and Indian homelands would be renewed. Wodziwob died on the Walker River Reservation in 1918.

Further Reading

Ballantine, Betty, and Ian Ballantine, eds. *The Native Americans: An Illustrated History*. 1993. Atlanta: Turner Publishing.

Champagne, Duane, ed. *The Native North American Almanac*. 1994. Detroit: Gale Research.

Gill, Sam D., and Irene F. Sullivan. *Dictionary of Native American Mythology*. 1992. New York: Oxford University Press.

Hirschfelder, Arlene, and Paulette Molin. *The Encyclopedia of Native American Religions*. 1992. New York: Facts on File.

Hittman, Michael. *Wovoka and The Ghost Dance*. 1990. Ashland, Ohio: BookMasters.

Ruby, Robert H., and John A. Brown. *Dreamer-Prophets of the Columbia Plateau: Smohalla and Skolaskin*. 1989. Norman: University of Oklahoma Press.

Thornton, Russell. *We Shall Live Again: The 1870 and 1890 Ghost Dance Movements as Demographic Revitalization*. 1986. Cambridge: Cambridge University Press.

Trigger, Bruce G., and Wilcomb E. Washburn, eds. *The Cambridge History of the Native Peoples of the Americas. Vol. 1, North America, Part 2*. 1996. Cambridge: Cambridge University Press.

Washburn, Wilcomb E. *Handbook of North American Indians, Vol. 4*. 1988. Washington, D.C.: Smithsonian Institution.

Wolf Chief

Full Name at Birth: Wolf Chief
Birth: ca. 1830; place unknown
Death: date and place unknown
Education: no formal education
Leadership Position: Hidatsa shaman

Summary

Wolf Chief was a Hidatsa shaman who flourished around the turn of the twentieth century. He was described as wearing elegant regalia and spent his days riding, shooting, and pursuing the village women. He acquired most of his medicine power from his father, Small Ankle, who had received his powers from a shaman named Missouri River. Some of Wolf Chief's medicines included a medicine pipe, two human skulls, a buffalo skull, and a turtle shell. The medicine pipe was approximately twenty inches long, made of hickory, and was a most sacred possession. The keeper of the medicine pipe was regarded as a person of great stature, and Wolf Chief was highly honored to have this responsibility.

Early Life

Little is known of Wolf Chief's early life. He was born into the Prairie Chickens, a clan of the Hidatsa Nation. His biological father was Small Ankles; he had a sister, Buffalo Bird Woman, and his closest clan brother was a youth by the name of Knife.

From early childhood, Hidatsa girls and boys were required to follow a regimented life. They were required to learn their respective roles and duties within the tribe so that there was never a question of how they should conduct themselves in any circumstance. Wolf Chief pointed out that this allowed little opportunity for independent thought or activity. He stated, "I often think how important it was in the olden days to do the same as the others did and there was no way to get out of it. We fasted and we went to war because our fathers did. . . . It was like a deep trail; one had to follow the same path the others before had made and deepened."

All Hidatsa, boys and girls under the age of twelve passed through an age-graded system. Age-graded societies consisted of people of the same sex and approximately the same age. Each group had officers who were identified by body decoration, society regalia, and duties assigned. Each society had a crier who informed the village people of the activities of the society. And each was connected to sacred rituals and possessed strong supernatural power. There were no options for young people; they were required to join the societies. Wolf Chief was reportedly frustrated by the restrictions placed on him and stated that the age-grade requirement was "like a deep trail; one had to follow the same path the others before had made and deepened."

Leadership

Wolf Chief's most prized and important possession was his medicine pipe, which he carried in a sacred bundle. One power the pipe contained was a war medicine. Its proper use protected the user and those in his company from harm during battle. When an enemy approached, Wolf Chief took the pipe out of its sacred bundle and rolled it on the ground toward the enemy. While carrying out this ceremony, he sang a medicine song that had been given to him by his father. This power of the pipe coupled with the ceremony caused the enemy to become frightened and flee.

The two human skulls were equally important. During a drought, the skulls were placed on a bed of pennyroyal, water was sprinkled on them, and songs were sung to bring rain. Pennyroyal, a member of the mint family, was highly regarded because of its sweet smell. Pennyroyal was also placed in water before the skulls and then rubbed on an ailing person to heal him or her.

The buffalo were sacred to the Hidatsa and were an intricate part of the medicine pipe ceremony. When buffalo became scarce and could not be found, the medicine pipe was filled and rubbed with buffalo fat. It was then placed before the skulls, and a sacred song was sung to the buffalo. Wolf Chief, around the age of seventeen, had seen his father perform this latter ceremony:

When the men [making the request] had gone away, my father took down the two skulls and placed them on a cloth; he then took out the medicine-pipe, anointed it with buffalo-fat, laid it on top of the skulls, and sang a mystery song. When he sang he covered himself with the buffalo-robe that had covered the skulls. This he did all night. In the morning he sent me out to call the chiefs and head-men together. They all came, and he said to them, "Yesterday you came and gave many things to my gods [spirits]; so I prayed, and my gods answered me. I had a vision that in four days many buffalo would come. So I now tell you." After two days some men shouted from the housetop, "Buffalo come from the hills! The buffalo come toward the village!" This was the fort Berthold village, and the buffalo were in the hills about five miles away.

On another occasion Wolf Chief saw his father use the skulls to bring rain:

He prayed and sent me for aromatic weed (pennyroyal), and I went to a wet place in the timber to get it. He put this on the ground and on it laid the skulls. About noon, while the people sat there, I went out and made a fire outside and cooked dinner. But my father sat with the buffalo-robe-hairy-side-out-over him, and sang and prayed for rain.

At dinner all ate. Then some old men went out and came back saying, "Black clouds gather. We see them."

My father got up, took water and threw it over the skulls, and walked around them.

In the afternoon clouds came over the village. At night rain fell. The clouds hung overhead until midnight. Then fell a gentle shower, then harder and harder the rain came until the afternoon of the next day.

In the early 1880s, Wolf Chief learned how to write and began bombarding the commissioner of Indian affairs with complaints against the Indian agents assigned to the Hidatsa people. In 1885 he founded the community of Lone Hill. A day school was built there in 1894, a Congregational church in 1912, and a Catholic church in 1919. The small community grew to become the present-day town of Independence, Missouri. In the early 1900s, Wolf Chief opened a reservation store where he sold Indian beads, spangles, "and other gimcracks." The Bureau of Indian Affairs disapproved of his selling these items, and he was allowed to remain in business only after he turned to selling approved items (blankets, cradles, boards, bows, and arrows). Wolf Chief also served as an informant for several anthropologists, including Alfred W. Bowers. There is no recorded information concerning Wolf Chief's death.

Further Reading

Champagne, Duane, ed. *The Native North American Almanac: A Reference Work on Native North Americans in the United States and Canada*. 1994. Detroit: Gale Research.

Dictionary of Indians of North America. 1978. St. Clair Shores, Mich.: Scholarly Press.

Hidatsa: http://emuseum.mnsu.edu/cultural/northamerica/hidatsa.html.

Hirschfelder, Arlene, and Paulette Molin. *The Encyclopedia of Native American Religions*. 1992. New York: Facts on File.

Lyon, William S. *Encyclopedia of Native American Shamanism: Sacred Ceremonies of North America*. 1998. Denver: ABC-CLIO.

Meyer, Roy W. *The Village Indians of the Upper Missouri: The Mandans, Hidatsas, and Arikaras*. 1977. Lincoln: University of Nebraska Press.

Peters, Virginia Bergman. *Women of the Earth Lodges: Tribal Life on the Plains*. 1995. North Haven: The Shoe String Press.

Wovoka (Jack Wilson)

Full Name at Birth: Wovoka or Wuvoka

Birth: ca. 1856 near the Walker River in present-day Esmeralda County, near Yerrington, Nevada

Death: September 29, 1932, in Yerrington, Nevada

Education: no formal education

Leadership Position: Paiute Numu spiritual leader

Summary

Wovoka is credited with founding the Ghost Dance religion of 1890. In December 1888, Wovoka experienced a death and rebirth experience during which the Creator of Life gave him a number of powers that included a sacred dance that he was to teach to his people. The dance became known as the Ghost Dance. Indian people were told that if they obeyed the laws of the Creator of Life, white people would be removed from the earth, and Indian people would be reunited with family and friends in a new world, free from hunger, disease, and war. In 1890, because of cultural misunderstanding and a fear of Indian wars, the Ghost Dance movement was crushed by the remnants of the army's Seventh Cavalry at the 1890 massacre at Wounded Knee Creek.

Early Life

Wovoka was born about 1856 near Walker Lake in present-day Esmeralda County, Nevada. He grew up in the area of Mason Valley, Nevada, near the present Walker Lake Reservation. Wovoka is believed to be the son of Tavibo,* a visionary and founder of the earlier Ghost Dance religion of 1870. As a young person, he was known by the name of Wovoka or Wuvoka, which means "the cutter" in Paiute. He later took the name of his paternal grandfather, Kowhitsaug. On the death of his father, he was taken into the family of a white farmer named David Wilson and was given the name Jack Wilson, by which he was known among local American settlers. Wovoka later worked on Wilson's farm, and when he was in his twenties, he married Tumma, who took the name Mary Wilson.

Leadership

Wovoka's great revelation to his people occurred on January 1, 1889, during an eclipse of the sun, or a time "when the sun died." In December 1888 Wovoka had become ill with a severe fever. While in a feverish state, Wovoka received a vision, heard a "great noise," then lost consciousness. When he revived, he announced that he had been taken to the other world where he had seen the Creator and all of the Indian people who had died before. The old were made young again. Everyone was well fed, dancing, and blissfully happy. The Creator instructed Wovoka to return to the earth and tell the people that they must be good and love one another. Indian people were to cooperate with the white people and live in peace without warfare until the time that the Creator removed all white people from the earth. Indian people were to abstain from alcohol and were instructed not to fight, steal, or lie.

While in the presence of the Creator, Wovoka was given a number of powers, including five songs for weather control, invulnerability to weapons, political responsibility, and prophecies. He was also given a sacred dance that he was to teach to his people. The dance was known

to the Northern Paiute as *nanigukwa*, "dance in a circle." Prior to the dance, the people were to make a feast and prepare enough food for all to eat. The dance was to be performed for four successive nights, and on the last night, they were to keep up the dance until the morning of the fifth day. At that time, they all were to bathe in the river and then disperse to their homes. The people were instructed to do the new dance every six weeks. If the people obeyed these instructions, they would be reunited with family and friends in the other world, where there would be no sickness, old age, or death.

Wovoka's vision became the basis of the Ghost Dance religion, which was based on the belief that there would be a time when all Indian people—the living and the dead—would be reunited on an earth that was spiritually regenerated and forever free from death, disease, and all the other miseries that had recently been experienced by Indian people. Word of the new religion spread quickly among Indian peoples of the Great Basin and Plains regions. Indian people representing over thirty tribes traveled great distances to visit Wovoka and to learn more of his teachings, often returning home filled with messages of hope for their people. Many Indian people who had undergone severe cultural and physical attacks eagerly accepted the teachings of Wovoka. The U.S. Army's scorched earth military policy instituted by Generals Sherman and Sheridan, the destruction of the buffalo, confinement on reservations, and epidemics of strange and lethal diseases set the stage for the acceptance of Wovoka's message of revitalization.

As the religious movement spread, it took on features unique to individual tribes. When the Ghost Dance reached the Lakota they added the wearing of a Ghost

Dance shirt to the religion. The Ghost Dance shirt, it was believed, would be impervious to the white man's bullets. Non-Indians now became alarmed by reports of what they perceived to be warriors performing a strange new war dance that was supposed to result in the disappearance of whites and the return of the buffalo. The wearing of the Ghost Dance shirt thus transformed Wovoka's religious movement into a warrior movement. Government agents and missionaries opposed the Ghost Dance, and in 1890 the army outlawed the practice of the dance on Indian reservations. Tensions intensified between the Lakota and the soldiers as Indian people left the reservations without permission to hunt and to participate in the Ghost Dance ritual out of sight of the army. Sitting Bull,* a revered Lakota spiritual leader, was erroneously blamed for the unrest. He was killed by Indian police in December 1890 when it was believed that he intended to join the Ghost Dancers who had left the Standing Rock Indian reservation. Two weeks later, on December 29, 1890, remnants of Custer's Seventh Cavalry massacred more than two hundred men, women, and children of Big Foot's band of Miniconjou Sioux at Wounded Knee in South Dakota. It was incorrectly believed that Big Foot was en route to join Ghost Dancers who had left the Cheyenne River Reservation to carry out the teachings of Wovoka. In fact, Big Foot was en route to the Pine Ridge Reservation to encourage the Indian people to return to their reservation.

In the aftermath of the events on the Northern Plains, Wovoka continued to receive correspondence from Ghost Dance believers. Wovoka, with the help of a white storekeeper, mailed sacred red ocher, eagle or magpie feathers, Stetson hats, and other clothing he had worn to those who had made requests and who sent money. He also traveled to distant reservations where he served as a shaman and healer. He repeated his message of peace, hard work, and sobriety until his death.

A complex figure, Wovoka was revered by Indians while being denounced as an imposter and a lunatic by the local settlers throughout his life. Wovoka spent the last fifteen years of his life at the Yerrington Indian Colony in Nevada. He died at his home on September 29, 1932.

Further Reading

Ballantine, Betty, and Ian Ballantine, eds. *The Native Americans: An Illustrated History.* 1993. Atlanta: Turner Publishing.

Calloway, Colin G. *First Peoples: A Documentary Survey of American Indian History.* 1999. New York: St. Martin's Press.

Champagne, Duane, ed. *The Native North American Almanac.* 1994. Detroit: Gale Research.

Hirschfelder, Arlene, and Paulette Molin. *The Encyclopedia of Native American Religions.* 1992. New York: Facts on File.

Hittman, Michael. *Wovoka and The Ghost Dance.* 1990. Ashland, Ohio: Book Masters.

People in the West: Wovoka: http://www.pbs.org/weta/thewest/wpages/wpgs400/w4wovoka.html.

Ruby, Robert H., and John A. Brown. *Dreamer-Prophets of the Columbia Plateau: Smohalla and Skolaskin.* 1989. Norman: University of Oklahoma Press.

Thornton, Russell. *We Shall Live Again: The 1870 and 1890 Ghost Dance Movements as Demographic Revitalization.* 1986. Cambridge: Cambridge University Press.

Trigger, Bruce G., and Wilcomb E. Washburn, eds. *The Cambridge History of the Native Peoples of the Americas. Vol. 1, North America, Part 2.* 1996. Cambridge: Cambridge University Press.

Washburn, Wilcomb E. *Handbook of North American Indians, Vol. 4.* 1988. Washington, D.C.: Smithsonian Institution.

Wovoka's Message: http://www.dreamscape.com/morgana/wovomsg.htm.

Allen Wright

Full Name at Birth: Kiliahote, Kilihote ("Let's Kindle a Fire")

Birth: November 28, 1825, in Attala Country, along the Yaknukni River in present-day Mississippi

Death: December 2, 1885, in Oklahoma

Education: attended the Choctaw Nation's Spencer Academy; graduated from Union College, New York, 1852, and from Union Theological Seminary, New York, 1855; recognized for his mastery of English, Greek, Latin, and Hebrew

Leadership Position: Choctaw minister

Summary

Allen Wright, whose birth name was Kiliahote, was a Choctaw minister who served as principal chief of the Choctaw Nation between 1866 and 1870. Born in 1825, Kiliahote was introduced to Christianity following the death of his mother and father in the early 1830s. Following his conversion to Christianity and a name change to Allen Wright, he was educated in local schools, such as the Choctaw Nation's Spencer Academy. He was then selected for further schooling in New York and Delaware. Wright was ordained into the Presbyterian church in 1856 and then returned to Indian Territory to work among the Choctaw.

Wright served in the Confederacy during the Civil War. Following the war, Wright was elected principal chief of the Choctaw Nation and served two terms, from 1866 to 1870. In 1866, during negotiations for Choctaw and Chickasaw treaties, Wright suggested the name *Okla-homma* for the region, meaning "red people," which became the official name of the state of Oklahoma in 1907. Wright was later elected to public office, serving in the Choctaw House of Representatives, the Senate, and then as trea-

Allen Wright. National Anthropological Archives, Smithsonian Institution.

surer. During the 1870s and 1880s, Wright translated numerous works, including the Chickasaw constitution and codes of law, into English. In 1880, his *Chahta Leksikon*, a Choctaw dictionary, was published. He also completed a translation of the Psalms from Hebrew to Choctaw.

Wright was married to Harriet Newell Mitchell, a missionary from Dayton, Ohio. He fathered eight children, and his son Frank Hall Wright also became a Presbyterian missionary. Allen Wright died on December 2, 1885, in Oklahoma.

Early Life

Kiliahote was born along the Yaknukni River in present-day Mississippi, the son of Choctaw parents. When he was seven years old, he was relocated to the Indian Territory, the present-day state of Oklahoma, with his family. He was orphaned at an early age. His mother died just before the Choctaw removal, which occurred between 1830 and 1833, and his father died soon after arrival in the West, leaving him with one sister. The Reverend Cyrus Kingsbury, a Presbyterian minister, took him in and provided him with an education at local missionary schools. It was the Reverend Kingsbury who gave Kiliahote the name Allen Wright, after Alfred Wright, an early missionary to the Choctaw.

Leadership

Allen Wright was a full-blood, brilliantly educated Choctaw minister who served as principal chief of the Cherokee Nation between 1866 and 1870. After his conversion to Christianity and education in local schools, such as the Choctaw Nation's Spencer Academy, Wright was selected for further schooling in the East. He was an excellent student, he first attended a school in Delaware and then entered Union College in Schenectady, New York, where he received a degree in 1852. In 1855, he graduated from Union Theological Seminary in New York City. In 1856, Wright was ordained into the Presbyterian church, after which he returned home and began work among the Choctaw Nation. Wright became involved in tribal affairs and was elected to the Choctaw House of Representatives and the Senate and later was tribal treasurer.

Following the 1830 Removal Act, the Five Civilized Tribes—the Choctaw, Cherokee, Creek, Chickasaw, and Seminole Nations—were forcibly moved west of the Mississippi River. Part of the land that is now Oklahoma was designated the Indian Nations, or Indian Territory. Forced removal had a devastating effect on the entire Choctaw Nation. They lost 10 million acres of land that comprise the present-day states of Alabama and Mississippi. In exchange, they were promised peace, friendship, and land in the West. They were not compensated for farm buildings, schoolhouses, and livestock that they lost to the Americans who claimed their traditional homelands. The meager compensation they received for their homes and homelands was deducted from relocation expenses and lands in the new territory. They were not compensated for the hundreds of Choctaw who died from exposure to winter blizzards, cholera epidemics, and lack of necessary supplies during the removal and relocation. Once in Indian Territory, the Choctaw were forced to share the new territory with the Cherokee Nation and later the Chickasaw Nation.

In 1862, during the Civil War, Wright served with the Confederacy. After the war, he was elected principal chief of the Choctaw Nation and served for two terms, from 1866 to 1870. In 1866, Wright was sent to Washington, D.C., as a delegate of the Choctaw Nation to negotiate a treaty between the Choctaw and the U.S. government. Wright was influential in wording the terms of the agreement. One of his suggestions was that *Okla-homma*, from *okla* ("red") and *homma* ("people,") be the name for the region. In 1907, the name was adopted, and the state became Oklahoma.

Wright became principal chief of the Choctaw Nation in the fall of 1866, in his inaugural address he called on all law-abiding citizens among his own people and "those who are making their temporary residence among us to unite in establishing industry and good order." He said, "The law would recognize no difference of nationality within the jurisdiction of the Choctaw Nation." Early in 1867, he issued a proclamation warning those who were "abusing the privileges, which for the sake of humanity have been extended to them," and refugees were required to secure temporary permits upon the recommendation of the Choctaw neighbors or they would be subject to removal as intruders. On June 17, 1867 he issued orders to remove a number of intruders, including eleven Cherokee, six Creek, and one freedman family.

His inaugural also reflected the past mistreatment of the Choctaw people. Wright stated,

> This was the second time in our history that the bright future prospect for the Choctaws in the rapid march to civilization—progress of education, and wide spread of religion among them have been impeded and paralyzed by direct and indirect acts of the government of the United States, the direct act being the removal from their ancient and much loved homes in Mississippi and the indirect their own unfortunate internal war, in which the Choctaw became involved.

Wright was a highly respected Presbyterian minister and a scholar whose knowledge of languages included Choctaw, English, Latin, Greek, and Hebrew. During the 1870s and 1880s, Wright translated numerous works. His *Chahta Leksikon*, or Choctaw dictionary, was published in 1880. He also translated the Choctaw and Chickasaw constitutions, legal codes, and several hymnals. Before his death on December 2, 1885, in Oklahoma, Wright completed a translation of the Psalms from Hebrew to Choctaw.

Further Reading

Champagne, Duane. ed. *The Native North American Almanac: A Reference Work on Native North Americans in the United States and Canada*. 1994. Detroit: Gale Research.

Debo, Angie. *The Rise and Fall of the Choctaw Republic*. 1961. Norman: University of Oklahoma Press.

Hirschfelder, Arlene, and Paulette Molin. *The Encyclopedia of Native American Religions*. 1992. New York: Facts on File.

Waldman, Carl. *Who Was Who in Native American History*. 1990. New York: Facts on File.

Thomas Yellowtail

Full Name at Birth: Thomas Yellowtail (Medicine Rock Chief)

Birth: March 7, 1903, near Lodge Grass in present-day Montana

Death: date and place unknown

Education: no formal education

Leadership Position: Crow medicine man and Sun Dance chief

Summary

Yellowtail was born on March 7, 1903, near Lodge Grass in present-day Montana. When he was six years old, Chief Medicine Crow, a renowned war chief and holy man among the Crow, gave him the name Medicine Rock Chief. About 1971, Yellowtail was chosen by the Shoshone holy man John Trehero* (or Truhujo) to succeed him as Sun Dance chief. Trehero instructed Yellowtail in the use of sacred songs. Next, he placed his right fist between Yellowtail's shoulder blades and blew heavily, emitting the shrill call of the elk, thus transferring his Elk power to Yellowtail.

Yellowtail was a highly regarded medicine man and Sun Dance chief but came under criticism and suspicion from some detractors. Among the Crow, the Sun Dance as practiced by Yellowtail was the primary instrument for regeneration of the earth, the continuation of the people, the recovery of those suffering from illness, and other spiritual blessings much as their ancestors had done in previous times. The intent was to show respect for spiritual things.

Yellowtail added innovations to the Sun Dance that caused some concern over doctrinal controversy. This aroused criticism from some Sun Dance leaders. Yellowtail's Sun Dance religion included the use sweat lodges for ritual purification, the vision quest to acquire spiritual power, and daily prayers with the sacred pipe, as well as the actual Sun Dance ceremony. Yellowtail saw the Sun Dance as much more than a three-day ceremony. It was his belief that the Sun Dance religious experience began three or four days before the ceremony and continued throughout the year. In 1984, Yellowtail chose John Pretty on Top to succeed him as Sun Dance chief of the Crow.

Early Life

Yellowtail was born on March 7, 1903, near Lodge Grass in present-day Montana. His family's surname came from a shortened version of his father's name, Hawk with the Yellow Tail Feathers. As a youth, Yellowtail was influenced by elders who had participated in the traditional way of life on the Plains. He observed firsthand the traditional ceremonies of the Crow and listened in awe while the elder Crow war chiefs talked of war exploits and the traditional life of the Crow as they roamed the Great Plains on horseback in search of buffalo or in defense of their homelands.

When Yellowtail was six years old, Chief Medicine Crow, a renowned war chief and holy man among the Crow, gave him the name Medicine Rock Chief. As a child, Yellowtail was also adopted into the Sacred Pipe Society of his people. Years later, in 1924, he was adopted into the Tail Feather Society as well. Crow clans are groups of tribal members of common lineage that are formed to fulfill specific roles within the tribal structure. Clan membership brings with it a close bond and the responsibility to assist fellow clan members in times of crisis and in ceremony. Clan members generally observe special rituals and possess common dress regalia, songs, and ceremonies.

At age eighty-eight, Yellowtail was one of three living members of the Sacred Pipe Society. He stated that "we do not know the exact origin of it [the Sacred Pipe Society] among the Crow. . . . We know that many, many of our great leaders have had sacred visions relating to these rites, and we know too that the blessings we receive from following our sacred ways are very great." The Tail Feather Society was charged with responsibility for maintaining the knowledge and practice of sacred dances.

Leadership

Thomas Yellowtail was a venerated Crow medicine man and Sun Dance chief. He was a member of the Whistling Waters Clan of the Crow Nation and was born during the reservation era, initiated by the federal government through treaties in 1789; it formally ended in 1871 by an act of Congress.

In 1969 Trehero, a Shoshone medicine man and Sun Dance chief, visited Thomas Yellowtail and his wife Suzie. In a ceremonial laying on of hands, Trehero, nearly ninety years old, and ready to retire, transferred his medicine powers to Yellowtail. Trehero instructed Yellowtail until he was able to conduct the sacred work on his own. In one recorded instance, Trehero assisted Yellowtail in a Sun Dance ceremony as late as 1975.

In passing on his sacred knowledge, Trehero said to Yellowtail, "I'm supposed to turn all my medicine powers over to you. I received this order from Seven Arrows." Seven Arrows was the dwarf owner of the Sun Dance. Dwarfs were members of the Without Fires Clan of supernaturals and took their place in the religious cosmology along with the sun, stars, moon, and thunder. The instructions from Seven Arrows validated Yellowtail's right to the Sun Dance ceremony as conveyed by Trehero:

He has picked you,. . . and you are the man to carry on. Seven Arrows has picked you among the Shoshone, Crow, and Bannock. There's a lot of Crows asking me, "John, you're getting old, give your medicines to me." . . . I refused everybody until that time you came into the dance (winter holiday dance). There

came a whisper in my ear. He said, "John, you watch the door and see the couple that comes in. That's the man to receive your medicine. That's the man we pick among the tribes, the Shoshone, Bannock, some Ute. Seven Arrows has been at every Sun Dance and he has picked you."

Trehero instructed Yellowtail in the use of sacred songs and transferred the power of the Elk Person into Yellowtail, thereby making him head and owner of the Elk Lodge and a recipient of his medicines. Yellowtail now asserted a right to primary leadership of the Sun Dance ceremony.

Yellowtail's Sun Dance religion included sweat lodge purification, the vision quest, daily prayer, and the use of the sacred pipe, as well as the actual Sun Dance ceremony. According to Yellowtail, the Sun Dance is much more than a three-day ceremony. Other religious activities must take place throughout the year, including daily prayers, monthly prayer meetings, and ceremonies at the Sun Dance site prior to and following the actual Sun Dance ceremony.

Yellowtail possessed otter medicine powers that endowed him with a mystical affinity for underwater animals. He believed that he could recall the underwater animals that had been trapped to extension from nearby streams. He also possessed a close affinity for the "spike elk," and a young elk became Yellowtail's medicine tailsman after Trehero ritualistically transferred the Elk power to him.

Yellowtail married his wife, Suzie, on April 27, 1929, and they raised many children, including three of their own. Yellowtail referred to Suzie as Grandma; her maiden name is not recorded. In 1952, they traveled to Europe, North Africa, and the Holy Land on a tour sponsored by the U.S. State Department. In 1970, they were jointly named outstanding American Indian of the Year at the All-American Indian Days in Sheridan, Wyoming. Yellowtail's wife, who died on December 25, 1981, rode on horseback during President Nixon's inauguration parade in January 1969. She was the first Indian registered nurse and served on the president's Indian Health Council. She was inducted into the Montana Hall of Fame in 1987.

In 1984 Yellowtail chose the Crow medicine man, John Pretty on Top, to succeed him as Sun Dance chief of the Crow. In 1986, Pretty on Top represented the Native American people at a world prayer meeting held in Italy by Pope John Paul II.

Yellowtail told his life story to his son, Michael Oren Fitzgerald, and it was published in 1991 as *Yellowtail: Crow Medicine Man and Sun Dance Chief*.

Further Reading

Fitzgerald, Michael Oren. *Yellowtail: Crow Medicine Man and Sun Dance Chief*. 1994. Norman: University of Oklahoma Press.

Hirschfelder, Arlene, and Paulette Molin. *The Encyclopedia of Native American Religions*. 1992. New York: Facts on File.

Voget, Fred W. *The Shoshoni-Crow Sun Dance*. 1984. Norman: University of Oklahoma Press.

Appendix A: Native American Spiritual Practitioners and Healers by Birth Date

Unknown

	White Buffalo Calf Woman
active in mid-fourteenth century	Deganawida
active in late eighteenth century	Sweet Medicine
active in early nineteenth century	Akikita
active in early nineteenth century	Two Wolves
active in late 1880s	Big Ike
died 1875	Mamanti
died ca. 1889	Crazy Mule
active from 1869; died 1890	Curley Headed Doctor (or Curly-Headed Doctor)
active at turn of twentieth century	Albert Thomas
active in early twentieth century	Págits
active in early twentieth century	Suwi
active into the 1970s	Peter Catches
died 1976	John (Fire) Lame Deer
ca. 1525–ca. 1575	Aiowantha (Hiawatha)
ca. 1555–ca. 1665	Passaconaway
ca. 1620 to 1630–ca. 1690	Popé (Popay)
1656–1680	Kateri (Catherine) Tekakwitha
ca. 1720–Unknown	Neolin (Delaware Prophet) ("The Enlightened One")
1723–1792	Samson Occum
ca. 1735–1815	Handsome Lake (Skanyadariyoh)
ca. early 1740s-after 1800	Coocoochee
ca. 1744–1816	Molly Ockett
ca. 1760s–1799	Toypurina (Regina Josefa Toypurina)

ca. 1765–1860	Aripeka
ca. 1770s–1818	Josiah Francis
1775–1836	Tenskwatawa ("Open Door")
1788–1858	Eleazar Williams
ca. 1790–ca. 1852	Kenekuk
ca. 1794–ca. 1841	Wabokieshiek
ca. 1795–ca. 1892	Box Elder
ca. 1795–1876	Stone Forehead
1798–ca. 1839	William Apes
ca. 1800–Unknown	Mon'Hin Thin Ge
ca. 1802–ca. 1886	Bull Lodge
1802–1856	Kah-ke-wa-quo-na-by ("Sacred Feathers") (Peter Jones)
1804–1844	Jesse Bushyhead
1807–1881	Stephen Foreman
ca. 1807–ca. 1882	White Bird
ca. 1810–1902	Enmegahbowh
ca. 1810–1877	Toohoolhoolzote
ca. 1812–ca. 1890	Keseruk
ca. 1815 to 1820–1895	Smohalla
1816–1902	Piapot
1817–1894	Ne-sha-pa-na-cumin (Charles Journeycake)
1818–1869	George Copway
ca. 1818–1897/98	Davéko
ca. 1822–1899	Low Horn
ca. 1823–ca. 1883	Black Hairy Dog
1823–1889	James Chrysostom Bouchard
ca. 1825–1881	Nakaidoklini
1825–1885	Allen Wright
1829–1909	Goyathlay (Geronimo)
ca. 1830–Unknown	Wolf Chief
ca. 1835–ca. 1915	Tavibo (Northern Paiute-White Man)
ca. 1837–1921	White Bull ("Ice" or "Hail")
ca. 1839–1922	Skolaskin (or Kolaskin)
ca. 1840s–ca. 1940s	Fanny Flounder
ca. 1840–Unknown	Brave Buffalo (Tatan' ka ohi'tika)
ca. 1840–1896/98	John Slocum
ca. 1844–1873	Calf Shirt
ca. 1844–ca. 1918	Wodziwob ("Gray Hair")
ca. 1845–1924	Short Bull

ca. 1846–1904	Kicking Bear
ca. 1847–1929	Porcupine
ca. 1850–1911	Quanah Parker
ca. 1850–1943	Shoniagizik
1850–1918	Redbird Smith
1853–1931	Philip Joseph Deloria
ca. 1854–1932	Sitting Bull (Haná cha-thí ak)
ca. 1856–1932	Wovoka (Jack Wilson)
ca. 1857–Unknown	Pretty-Shield
1858–1939	Charles Alexander Eastman
ca. 1860s–1910 to 1914	Jake Hunt
1863–1950	Black Elk
1865–1915	Susan La Flesche Picotte
1867–1923	Wassaja (Carlos Montezuma)
ca. 1870–Unknown	Fanny Brown
1874–1987	Juan de Jesus Romero (Deer Bird)
ca. 1875–Unknown	Albert Hensley
ca. 1883–1985	John Trehero ("Rainbow")
1884–1960	Mountain Wolf Woman
ca. 1887–Unknown	Josie Billie
1887–Unknown	James Blue Bird
ca. 1887–Unknown	Nels Charles
1890–1973	Hola Tso
ca. 1891–1989	Frank Fools Crow
1895–1968	Sanapia
ca. 1898–1979	Essie Parrish
1899–1985	Henry Crow Dog II
1901–1990	Vine Victor Deloria, Sr.
ca. 1901–Unknown	John King
1903–	Thomas Yellowtail
1907–1993	Mabel McKay
1909–1999	Thomas Banyacya
1911–1988	Emily Hill
1913–1980	Ruby Modesto
1915–	Rolling Thunder
1933–	Vine Deloria, Jr.
1937–1993	Kee-Kah-Wah-Un-Ga (Reuben A. Snake, Jr.)

Appendix B: Native American Spiritual Practitioners and Healers by Nation or Group

Abenaki
Molly Ockett

Achomawi
Albert Thomas

Apache
Goyathlay (Geronimo)
Nakaidoklini

Arapaho
Sitting Bull (Haná cha-thí ak)

Arikara
Two Wolves

Blackfoot
Calf Shirt
Low Horn

Cahuilla
Ruby Modesto

Cherokee
Jesse Bushyhead
Stephen Foreman
Rolling Thunder
Redbird Smith

Cheyenne
Black Hairy Dog
Box Elder
Crazy Mule
Porcupine
Stone Forehead

Sweet Medicine
White Bull ("Ice" or "Hail")

Choctaw
Allen Wright

Cocopa
Suwi

Comanche
Quanah Parker
Sanapia

Cree
Piapot

Creek
Josiah Francis

Crow
Pretty-Shield
Thomas Yellowtail

Delaware (Leni-Lanape)
James Chrysostom Bouchard
Neolin ("The Enlightened One")
(Delaware Prophet)
Ne-sha-pa-na-cumin (Charles Journeycake)

Fox. *See* **Sac (Sauk) and Fox**

Gabrielino
Toypurina (Regina Josefa Toypurina)

Gros Ventre
Bull Lodge

Hidatsa
Wolf Chief

Hopi
Thomas Banyacya

Huron
Deganawida

Inuit
Keseruk

Kickapoo
Kenekuk

Kiowa
Mamanti

Kiowa-Apache
Davéko

Klickitat
Jake Hunt

Miccosukee
Aripeka

Modoc
Curley Headed Doctor (or Curly-Headed Doctor)

Mohawk
Coocoochee
Kateri (Catherine) Tekakwitha
Eleazar Williams

Mohegan
Samson Occum

Navajo
Hola Tso

Nez Percé
Toohoolhoolzote
White Bird

Nisqually
John Slocum

Ojibwa (Chippewa)
George Copway
Kah-ke-wa-quo-na-by ("Sacred Feathers") (Peter Jones)
John King
Shoniagizik

Omaha
Susan La Flesche Picotte
Mon'Hin Thin Ge

Onondaga
Aiowantha (Hiawatha)

Oto
Akikita

Ottawa
Enmegahbowh

Paiute
Tavibo (Northern Paiute-White Man)
Wodziwob ("Gray Hair")
Wovoka (Jack Wilson)

Pennacook
Passaconaway

Pequot
William Apes

Pomo
Mabel McKay (Cache Creek Pomo)
Essie Parrish (Kashaya Pomo)

Sac (Sauk) and Fox
Wabokieshiek

Sanpoil
Skolaskin (or Kolaskin)

Seminole
Aripeka
Josie Billie

Seneca
Handsome Lake (Skanyadariyoh)

Shawnee
Tenskwatawa ("Open Door")

Shoshone
Emily Hill
Rolling Thunder
John Trehero ("Rainbow")

Sioux
Dakota
Philip Joseph Deloria
Vine Deloria, Jr.
Vine Victor Deloria, Sr.

Lakota

Black Elk
James Blue Bird
Brave Buffalo (Tatan' ka ohi' tika)
Peter Catches
Henry Crow Dog II
Charles Alexander Eastman
Frank Fools Crow
Kicking Bear
John (Fire) Lame Deer
Short Bull
White Buffalo Calf Woman

Taos Pueblo

Juan de Jesus Romero
(Deer Bird)

Tewa Pueblo

Popé (Popay)

Ute

Págits

Wanapam

Smohalla

Winnebago

Albert Hensley
Kee-Kah-Wah-Un-Ga (Reuben A. Snake, Jr.)
Mountain Wolf Woman
Wabokieshiek

Wintu

Fanny Brown
Nels Charles
Albert Thomas

Yavapai

Wassaja (Carlos Montezuma)

Yurok

Big Ike
Fanny Flounder

Bibliography

Books

Axelrod, Alan. *Chronicle of the Indians Wars from Colonial Times to Wounded Knee*. Englewood Cliffs, N.J.: Prentice Hall, 1993.

Bailey, Paul. *Ghost Dance Messiah*. Los Angeles: Westernlore Press, 1970.

Ballantine, Betty, and Ian Ballantine, eds. *The Native Americans: An Illustrated History*. Atlanta: Turner Publishing, 1993.

Bass, Althea. *Cherokee Messenger*. Norman: University of Oklahoma Press, 1936.

Bataille, Gretchen M., ed. *Native American Women: A Biographical Dictionary*. New York: Garland Publishing, 1993.

Bean, Lowell John, ed. *California Indian Shamanism*. Menlo Park, Calif.: Ballena Press, 1987.

Beck, Peggy V., Anna Lee Walters, and Nia Francisco. *The Sacred Ways of Knowledge, Sources of Life*. Flagstaff, Ariz.: Northland Publishing, 1990.

Boyd, Doug. *Rolling Thunder*. New York: Random House, 1979.

Braroe, Niels Winther. *Indian and White: Self-Image and Interaction in a Canadian Plains Community*. Stanford: Stanford University Press, 1975.

Brown, John. *Old Frontiers: The Story of the Cherokee Indians from Earliest Times to the Date of Their Removal to the West, 1838*. Kingsport, Tenn.: Southern Publishers, 1938.

Brown, Mark H. *The Flight of the Nez Percé*. New York: Putnam, 1967.

Calloway, Colin G. *First Peoples: A Documentary Survey of American Indian History*. New York: St. Martin's Press, 1999.

Capps, Benjamin. *The Warren Wagontrain Raid: The First Complete Account of an Historic Indian Attack and Its Aftermath*. New York: Dial Press, 1974.

Carter, Samuel, III. *Cherokee Sunset: A Nation Betrayed, a Narrative of Travail and Triumph, Persecution and Exile*. Garden City, N.Y.: Doubleday, 1976.

Casagrande, Joseph B., ed. *In the Company of Man: Twenty Portraits by Anthropologists*. New York: Harper & Brothers, 1960.

Cassidy, James J., Jr. *Through Indian Eyes: The Untold Story of Native American Peoples*. Pleasantville, N.Y.: Reader's Digest Association, 1995.

Champagne, Duane, ed. *The Native North American Almanac: A Reference Work on Native North Americans in the United States and Canada*. Detroit: Gale Research, 1994.

Cole, Cyrenus. *I Am a Man, the Indian Black Hawk*. Iowa City: Iowa State Historical Society, 1938.

Copeland, Marion W. *Charles Alexander Eastman (Ohiyesa)*. Caldwell, Idaho: Caxton Printers, 1978.

Crow Dog, Leonard, and Richard Erdoes. *Crow Dog: Four Generations of Sioux Medicine Men*. New York: HarperCollins, 1995.

Debo, Angie. *The Rise and Fall of the Choctaw Republic*. Norman: University of Oklahoma Press, 1961.

Deloria, Vine, Jr. *For This Land: Writings on Religion in America*. New York: Routledge, 1999.

———. *Singing for a Spirit: A Portrait of the Dakota Sioux*. Santa Fe: Clear Light Publishers, 1999.

DeMallie, Raymond J., ed. *The Sixth Grandfather: Black Elk's Teachings Given to John G. Neihardt*. Lincoln: University of Nebraska Press, 1984.

Dempsey, Hugh A. *The Amazing Death of Calf Shirt and Other Blackfoot Stories*. Saskatoon: Fifth House, 1994.

———. *Big Bear: The End of Freedom*. Lincoln: University of Nebraska Press, 1984.

Densmore, Frances. *Northern Ute Music*. Bureau of American Ethnology Bulletin 75. Washington, D.C.: Government Printing Office, Smithsonian Institution, 1922.

Dewing, Rolland. *Wounded Knee II*. Chadron, Nebr.: Great Plains Network, 1995.

Dictionary of Indians of North America. St. Clair Shores, Mich.: Scholarly Press, 1978.

Dillon, Richard H. *Burnt-out Fires: California's Modoc Indian War*. Englewood Cliffs, N.J.: Prentice Hall, 1973.

Dorsey, George A. *Traditions of the Arikara*. Washington, D.C.: Carnegie Institution of Washington, 1904.

Du Bois, Cora. *Wintu Ethnography*. Berkeley: University of California Press, 1935.

Edmunds, R. David. *The Otoe-Missouria People*. Phoenix: Indian Tribal Series, 1976.

Erdoes, Richard, and John (Fire) Lame Deer. *Lame Deer, Seeker of Visions*. New York: Simon and Schuster, 1972.

Erdoes, Richard, and Alfonso Ortiz. *American Indian Myths and Legends*. New York: Pantheon Books, 1984.

Fitzgerald, Michael Oren. *Yellowtail: Crow Medicine Man and Sun Dance Chief*. Norman: University of Oklahoma Press, 1994.

Fletcher, Alice C., and Francis La Flesche. *The Omaha Tribe*. Washington, D.C.: Smithsonian Institution, 1911.

Fowler, Loretta. *Shared Symbols, Contested Meanings*. Ithaca, N.Y.: Cornell University Press, 1987.

Gibson, Arrell Morgan. *The American Indian*. Lexington, Mass.: D. C. Heath, 1969.

———. *The American Indian: Prehistory to the Present*. Lexington, Mass.: D. C. Heath, 1980.

Gill, Sam D. *Native American Religions: An Introduction*. Belmont, Calif.: Wadsworth Publishing Company, 1982.

Gill, Sam, and Irene F. Sullivan. *Dictionary of Native American Mythology*. New York: Oxford University Press, 1992.

Gordon-McCutchan, R. C. *The Taos Indians and the Battle for Blue Lake*. Sante Fe: Red Crane Books, 1991.

Graves, Charles S. *Lore and Legends of the Klamath River Indians*. Yreka, Calif.: Press of the Times, 1929.

Grinnell, George Bird. *The Cheyenne Indians: Their History and Ways of Life*. New York: Cooper Square Publishers, 1962.

———. *The Fighting Cheyennes*. Norman: University of Oklahoma Press, 1956.

Haseloff, Cynthia. *The Kiowa Verdict: A Western Story*. Farmington Hills, Mich.: Thorndike Press, 1997. http://www.readwesterns.com/kiowa_verdict_excerpts.htm.

Heizer, Robert F. *Handbook of North American Indians*. Vol. 8. Washington, D.C.: Smithsonian Institution, 1978.

Hirschfelder, Arlene, and Paulette Molin. *The Encyclopedia of Native American Religions*. New York: Facts on File, 1992.

Hittman, Michael. *Wovoka and the Ghost Dance*. Ashland, Ohio: Book Masters, 1990.

Hoebel, E. Adamson. *The Cheyennes: Indians of the Great Plains.* New York: Holt, Rinehart and Winston, 1978.

Horse Capture, George. *The Seven Visions of Bull Lodge.* Lincoln: University of Nebraska Press, 1992.

Iverson, Peter. *Carlos Montezuma and the Changing World of American Indians.* Albuquerque: University of New Mexico Press, 1982.

Jackson, Donald, ed. *Black Hawk: An Autobiography.* Urbana: University of Illinois Press, 1990.

————. *Ma-ka-tai-me-she-kia-kiak, Black Hawk.* Urbana: University of Illinois Press, 1955.

Jackson, Robert H., and Edward Castillo. *Indians, Franciscans, and Spanish Colonization: The Impact of the Mission System on California Indians.* Albuquerque: University of New Mexico Press, 1995.

Johnson, Troy, et al., eds. *American Indian Activism: Alcatraz to the Longest Walk.* Urbana: University of Illinois Press, 1997.

Jones, David E. *Sanapia: Comanche Medicine Woman.* Prospect Heights, Ill.: Waveland Press, 1972.

Josephy, Alvin M., et al., eds. *Red Power: The American Indians Fight for Freedom.* Lincoln: University of Nebraska Press, 1999.

Klein, Barry T. *Reference Encyclopedia of the American Indian.* Nyack, N.Y.: Todd Publications, 2000.

Kroeber, A. L. *Handbook of the Indians of California: The Yurok Land and Civilization.* Washington, D.C.: Bureau of American Ethnology, Smithsonian Institution, 1925.

Landes, Ruth. *Ojibwa Religion and the Mide'wiwin.* Madison: University of Wisconsin Press, 1969.

Linderman, Frank B. *Pretty-Shield: Medicine Woman of the Crows.* Lincoln: University of Nebraska Press, 1972.

Llewellyn, K. N., and E. Adamson Hoebel. *The Cheyenne Way: Conflict and Case Law in Primitive Jurisprudence.* Norman: University of Oklahoma Press, 1941.

Lowe, Robert H. *The Crow Indians.* Lincoln: University of Nebraska Press, 1983.

Lurie, Nancy. *Mountain Wolf Woman: Sister of Crashing Thunder: The Autobiography of a Winnebago Indian.* Ann Arbor: University of Michigan Press, 1961.

Lyon, William S. *Encyclopedia of Native American Healing.* Denver: ABC-CLIO, 1996.

————. *Encyclopedia of Native American Shamanism: Sacred Ceremonies of North America.* Denver: ABC-CLIO, 1998.

Mahon, John K. *History of the Second Seminole War.* Gainesville: University of Florida Press, 1967.

Mails, Thomas E. *Fools Crow.* New York: Doubleday, 1979.

————. *Plains Indians: Dog Soldiers, Bear Men and Buffalo Women.* New York: Bonanza Books, 1985.

Malinowski, Sharon. *Notable Native Americans.* Detroit: Gale Research, 1995.

Markowitz, Harvey. *American Indians. Vol. 1: Abenaki—Hayes, Ira Hamilton.* Pasedena, Calif.: Salem Press, 1995.

Marquis, Thomas B. *The Cheyennes of Montana.* Algonac, Mich.: Reference Publications, 1978.

Matthiessen, Peter. *In the Spirit of Crazy Horse.* New York: Penguin Books, 1992.

McAllister, J. G. *Davéko: Kiowa-Apache Medicine Man.* Bulletin 17. Austin: Texas Memorial Museum, 1970.

McBride, Bunny. *Women of the Dawn.* Lincoln: University of Nebraska Press, 1999.

McGaa, Ed. *Mother Earth Spirituality: Native American Paths to Healing Ourselves and Our World.* San Francisco: Harper and Row, 1989.

McGloin, John Bernard. *Eloquent Indian: The Life of James Bouchard, California Jesuit.* Stanford: Stanford University Press, 1949.

McLoughlin, William G. *Champion of the Cherokees: Evan and John B. Jones.* Princeton, N.J.: Princeton University Press, 1990.

————. *Cherokees and Missionaries 1789–1839.* New Haven, Conn.: Yale University Press, 1984.

McWhorter, L. V. *Hear Me, My Chiefs! Nez Percé Legend and History.* Caldwell, Idaho: Caxton Printers, 1992.

Means, Russell, with Marvin J. Wolf. *Where White Men Fear to Tread: The Autobiography of Russell Means.* Los Angeles: General Publishing Group, 1995.

Meyer, Melissa L. *The White Earth Tragedy: Ethnicity and Dispossession at a Minnesota Anishinaabe Reservation, 1889–1920.* Lincoln: University of Nebraska Press, 1994.

Meyer, Roy W. *The Village Indians of the Upper Missouri: The Mandans, Hidatsas, and Arikaras.* Lincoln: University of Nebraska Press, 1977.

Milloy, John Sheridan. *The Plains Cree.* Winnipeg: University of Manitoba Press, 1988.

Mooney, James. *The Ghost-Dance Religion and the Sioux Outbreak of 1890.* Lincoln: University of Nebraska Press, 1991.

Moore, John H. *The Cheyenne Nation: A Social and Demographic History.* Lincoln: University of Nebraska Press, 1987.

Moulton, Gary E. *The Papers of Chief John Ross, Vol, 1, 1807–1839.* Norman: University of Oklahoma Press, 1984.

Murray, Keith. *The Modocs and Their War.* Norman: University of Oklahoma Press, 1959.

Neeley, Bill. *The Last Comanche Chief: The Life and Times of Quanah Parker.* New York: Wiley, 1995.

Neihardt, John G. *Black Elk Speaks.* Lincoln: University of Nebraska Press, 1979.

Nelson, Edward William. *The Eskimo About Bering Strait.* New York: Johnson Reprint Corporation, 1971.

O'Connell, Barry O., ed. *On Our Own Ground: The Complete Writings of William Apess, a Pequot.* Amherst: University of Massachusetts Press, 1992.

Peters, Virginia Bergman. *Women of the Earth Lodges: Tribal Life on the Plains.* North Haven: Shoe String Press, 1995.

Powell, Peter J. *Sweet Medicine: The Continuing Role of the Sacred Arrows, the Sun Dance, and the Sacred Buffalo Hat in Northern Cheyenne History.* Norman: University of Oklahoma Press, 1969.

Quaife, Milo Milton, ed. *Life of Black Hawk, Ma-Ka-Tai-Me-She-Kia-Kiak.* Chicago: Lakeside Press, 1916.

Rice, Julian. *Lakota Storytelling: Black Elk, Ella Deloria, and Frank Fools Crow.* New York: Peter Lang, 1989.

Ridington, Robin, and Dennis Hastings. *Blessings for a Long Time: The Sacred Pole of the Omaha Tribe.* Lincoln: University of Nebraska Press, 1997.

Roark, Harry M. *Charles Journeycake: Indian Statesman and Christian Leader.* Dallas: Taylor Publishing Company, 1970.

Ruby, Robert H., and John H. Brown. *Dreamer-Prophets of the Columbia Plateau: Smohalla and Skolaskin.* Norman: University of Oklahoma Press, 1989.

Sarris, Gregg. *Mabel McKay: Weaving the Dream.* Berkeley: University of California Press, 1994.

Shoemaker, Nancy. *Negotiators of Change: Historical Perspectives on Native American Women.* New York: Routledge, 1995.

Siclis, Boris. *Passaconaway in the White Mountains.* Boston: Badger Publications, 1916.

Silverberg, Robert. *The Pueblo Revolt.* New York: Weybright and Talley, 1970.

Snow, Dean R. *The Iroquois.* Cambridge, Mass.: Blackwell, 1996.

Stanley, F. *Santanta and the Kiowas.* Borger, Tex.: Jim Hess Printers, 1968.

Steinmetz, Paul B. *Pipe, Bible, and Peyote Among the Oglala Lakota: A Study in Religious Identity.* Knoxville: University of Tennessee Press, 1990.

Stewart, Omer C. *Peyote Religion: A History.* Norman: University of Oklahoma Press, 1987.

Stoutenburgh, John L., Jr. *Dictionary of the American Indian.* New York: Philosophical Library, 1960.

Sturtevant, William C. *Handbook of North American Indians.* Vol. 8. Washington, D.C.: Smithsonian Institution, 1978.

Thornton, Russell. *American Indian Holocaust and Survival: A Population History*

Since 1492. Norman: University of Oklahoma Press, 1987.

———. *We Shall Live Again: The 1870 and 1890 Ghost Dance Movements as Demographic Revitalization.* Cambridge: Cambridge University Press, 1986.

Tong, Benson. *Susan La Flesche Picotte, M.D.: Omaha Indian Leader and Reformer.* Norman: University of Oklahoma Press, 1999.

Trafzer, Clifford E. *American Indian Prophets.* Newcastle, Calif.: Sierra Oaks Publishing Company, 1986.

Trigger, Bruce G., and Wilcomb E. Washburn, eds. *The Cambridge History of the Native Peoples of the Americas. Vol. 1, North America, Parts 1 and 2.* Cambridge: Cambridge University Press, 1996.

Vander, Judith. *Songprints: The Musical Experience of Five Shoshone Women.* Urbana: University of Illinois Press, 1988.

Vecsey, Christopher, ed. *Handbook of American Indian Religious Freedom.* New York: Crossroad Publishing Company, 1993.

Vennum, Thomas. *Wild Rice and the Ojibwa People.* St. Paul: Minnesota Historical Society Press, 1988.

Voget, Fred W. *The Shoshoni-Crow Sun Dance.* Norman: University of Oklahoma Press, 1998.

Waldman, Carl. *Who Was Who in Native American History.* New York: Facts on File, 1990.

Waldman, Carl, and Molly Braun. *Encyclopedia of Native American Tribes.* New York: Facts on File, 1988.

Walker, James R. *Lakota Belief and Ritual.* Edited by Raymond J. DeMallie and Elaine A. Jahner. Lincoln: University of Nebraska Press, 1991.

Walker, Paul R. *Spiritual Leaders: American Indian Lives.* New York: Facts on File, 1994.

Walton, George. *Fearless and Free: The Seminole Indian War, 1835–1842.* Indianapolis: Bobbs-Merrill, 1977.

Washburn, Wilcomb E. *Handbook of North American Indians, Vol. 4.* Washington, D.C.: Smithsonian Institution, 1988.

Weslager, C. A. *The Delaware Indian Westward Migration with the Texts of Two Manuscripts (1821–22) Responding to General Lewis Cass's Inquiries About Lanape Culture and Language.* Wilmington, Del.: Middle Atlantic Press, 1978.

———. *The Delaware Indians: A History.* New Brunswick, N.J.: Rutgers University Press, 1990.

Whitman, William. *The Oto.* New York: Columbia University Press, 1937.

Wilson, Raymond. *Ohiyesa: Charles Eastman, Santee Sioux.* Chicago: University of Illinois Press, 1983.

Yellowtail, Thomas. *Yellowtail: Crow Medicine Man and Sun Dance Chief.* As told to Michael Oren Fitzgerald. Norman: University of Oklahoma Press, 1991.

Articles and Chapters

American Indian Culture and Research Journal 21, no. 2. (1997).

Bruguier, Leonard R. "A Legacy in Sioux Leadership: The Deloria Family." In Herbert T. Hoover and Larry J. Zimmerman, eds. *South Dakota Leaders.* Vermillion: University of South Dakota Press, 1989, pp. 367–78.

Du Bois, Cora. "Wintu Ethnography." In A. L. Kroeber and R. H. Lowe, eds. *American Archaeology and Ethnology 1935–1939.* Berkeley: University of California Press, 1940.

McNamee, Gregory. "Native Voices." *Tucson Weekly* March 9–15, 1995. http://www.tucsonweekly.com/tw/03–09–95/review2.htm

Owsley, Frank L., Jr. "Prophet of War: Josiah Francis and the Creek War." *American Indian Quarterly: Journal of American Indian Studies* 9 (1985): 273–293.

Temple, Thomas Workman II. "Toypurina the Witch and the Indian Uprising at San Gabriel." *Masterkey* 32, no. 5 (September–October 1958).

Web Sites

The Achomawi: http://curtis-collection. com/tribe%20data/achamawi.html.

American Indian Prophecies: A Brief History of the Future of America: ttp://www. texfiles.com/features/prophecies.html.

Apache Nightmare: http://library.ncsu. edu/marion/AJW-8598.

Apache Wars: http://www.historychannel tours.com/tours/thc/apachewrsov.html.

Articles of Agreement between the United States and the Delaware Indians, July 4, 1866: http://digital.library.okstate. edu/kappler/treaties/del0937.htm.

Black Elk, a Great Religious Leader: http://www.cwrl.utexas.edu/~mmaynar d/Voices/blackelk.html.

A Blackfoot Winter Count: http://www. lethfhc.org/winter.htm.

Blood Indians: http://www.newadvent. org/cathen/02603a.htm.

Brave Buffalo and the Sacred Stones: http://members.aol.com/Mnicholas2/ native/buffalo.htm.

Brave Buffalo's Dream: http://www.cyber suds.co.jp/ge/INDIAN/brave.html.

A Brief Summary of Seminole History: Osceola and Aripeka: http://www. seminoletribe.com/history/osceola_ abiaka.shtml.

Chief Frank Fools Crow: http://www.chief. uiuc.edu/foolscrow.html.

Deganawida: http://www.louisville. edu/k-12/camden/conroy/deganawi. html.

Deganawida: http://web.onramp.ca/ rivernen/nation_1.html.

[Enmegahbowh] The Episcopal Diocese of Minnesota: http://www.episcopalmn. org/history.html.

Essie Parrish: http://www.pressdemo-crat.com/extras/top50/parrish.html.

[Fanny Flounder] Shamanism: http://www. cabrillo.cc.ca.us/~crsmith/shaman.html.

George Copway: http://www.george town.edu/bassr/health/syllabuild/guide/ copway.html.

[Geronimo] Meindertsma, P.J., *Geronimo, His Own Story*: http://odur.let.rug.nl/ ~usa/B/geronimo/geronixx.htm.

Handsome Lake: http://nativenet.uthscsa. edu/archive/nl/9209/0001.html.

Henry Crow Dog II: http://www.human rights.de/u/usa/lpart/hcd.html.

[Henry Crow Dog II] Myths and Legends: http://www.santeedakota.org/mythsand. htm.

A Hiawatha and Deganawidah Bookshelf: http://www.aaronshep.com/book-shelves/Hiawatha.html.

Hiawatha and Mondamin: A Native American Legend: http://detnews.com/ menu/stories/17152.htm.

Hidatsa: http://emuseum.mnsu.edu/cul-tural/northamerica/hidatsa.html.

Hola Tso: http://www.lapahie.com/ Hola_Tso.html.

The Hola Tso Story: http://members.tri-pod.com/NATIVELEE/hola.htm.

[Hola Tso] 32nd Native American Church Convention: http://members.tri-pod.com/NATIVELEE/conven-tion.htm.

The Hopi Message to the United Nations General Assembly: http://www.welcome home.org/rainbow/prophecy/hopi.html.

"If you knew the conditions . . ." Health Care to Native Americans: http://www.nim. nih.gov/exhibition/if_you_knew/ if_you_knew_10.html; http://www. nim.nih.gov/exhibition/if_you_knew/if_ you_knew_12.html.

Indian Tribes of Washington County: The Delaware: http://ourworld.compuserve. com/homepages/meadorman/in-dian.htm.

[Jake Hunt] Notes from "The North American Indian," Volume 7: http:// curtis-collection.com/tribe%20data/ klick.

[John (Fire) Lame Deer] Review: *Lame Deer: Seeker of Visions*: http://nativenet. uthscsa.edu/archive/nl/9211/0027. html.

John (Fire) Lame Deer, Richard Erdoes: *Talking to the Owls and Butterflies*:

http://www.colostate.edu/Depts/Writing Center/assignments/co300/99–00/sutton/port1/sum/pop1j.htm.

Kateri Tekakwitha: http://www.ukans.edu/kansas/wn/kateri.html.

Kickapoo History: http://www.diskshovel.com/kick.html.

Kicking Bear: http://www.artsednet.getty.edu/ArtsEdNet/Resources/Maps/battle.html.

Kicking Bear: http://www.pbs.org/weta/thewest/wpages/wpgs680/68_06.html.

Kiowa Drawings: http://nmnhwww.si.edu/naa/kiowa/kiowa.html.

Lakota Dance Ghost Dance Apostles: http://www2.memes.com/artworks/lakota.html.

The Life of the Blessed Kateri Tekakwitha: http://www.bluecloud.org/kateri.html.

Love Made Manifest by Edward M. Cook: 14 Biographies that Constitute "An Aristocracy of Unselfish Service": http://www.vgsales.com/bios.html.

[Mabel McKay] Dancin' on Sacred Land: The Putah-Cache Bioregion Project: http://wdsroot.ucdavis.edu/clients/pcbr/where/doslpres.html.

Marks in Time: Delaware Treaty History: Treaty of 1854: http://members.tripod.com/~lenapelady/deltreaty1854.html.

Modoc Shadows: http://www.multimedia.calpoly.edu/libarts/denglund/1994.html.

The Modoc Wars: http://education.opb.org/learning/ofg/modoc/soldiers.html.

Mohegan Heroes: http://www.mohegan.nsn.us/tribe/s220content.html.

Molly Ockett: The Last of the Androscoggins: http://www.avcnet.org/ne-do-ba/bio_moly.html.

Molly Ockett Middle School Survey April 2000: http://www.msad72.k12.me.us/molly.html.

Mountain Wolf Woman: Sister of Crashing Thunder: http://www.press.umich.edu/titles/06109.html.

Native American Medicine: http://www.alternative therapies.com/select/past/45c.html.

Native Peoples of the Plains: The Return of the Sacred Pole: http://twist.lib.uiowa.edu/plainsind/spole.html.

Nicholson, Shirley, ed. Student Summaries of Chapters in Shamanism: http://www.mwsc.edu/~mullins/250s98/shmnbk.htm.

[Págits] Music from the Smithsonian: http://www2.bitstream.net/~dtrohr/Music%20Minnesota.htm.

Papers of Carlos Montezuma, M.D.: http://sun3.lib.uci.edu/~slca/microform/resources/p-q/p_030.htm.

Passaconaway: http://www.sidis.net/PassContents.htm.

Paul P. Reuben:PAL: Perspectives in American Literature: A Research and Reference Guide. Early Nineteenth Century: William Apes or William Apess (Pequot) (1798–1839). http://lead.csustan.edu/english/reuben/pal/chap3/apess.html.

Peter Jones: http://128.100.124.81/library/special/jones.htm.

Piapot: Powerful Images: http://www.museums west.org/exhibit/piapot.htm.

Piapot: Treaty Biographies: http://www.otc.ca/piapotbio.html.

Popé: http://cbs.infoplease.com/ce5/CE041710.html.

Popé: People in the West: http://www.pbs.org/weta/thewest/wpages/wpgs400/w4pope.html.

Quanah Parker: http://www.stainblue.com/quanahparker.html.

Quanah Parker—A Texas Legend: http://www.lnstar.com/mall/texasinfo/quanah.html.

Redbird Smith: http://www.louisville.edu/k-12/camden/conroy/redbird.html.

Reuben A. Snake, Jr.: American Indian Ritual Object Repatriation Foundation: Founding Trustee: http://www.repatriationfoundation.org/snakev.html.

Reuben A. Snake, Jr.: In Memory of Reuben A. Snake, Jr.: http://www. narf.org/ nill/resources/nlr/nlr20a.htm.

Reuben A. Snake, Jr., Statement of: http://paranoia.lycaeum.org/war.on. drugs/debate/peyote.speech.

Reuben A. Snake, Jr.: Your Humble Serpent: http://www.islandnet.com/~millenia/s nake.html.

[Samson Occum] Preaching to the Indians: http://www.lihistory.com/3/hs326. htm.

Short Bull: http://olc.edu/shortbull/ shortbull.html.

Sovereign People: http://www.clpgh. org/cmnh/exhibits/north-south-east-west/iroquis/handsome_lake. html.

Susan La Flesche Picotte (1865–1915): http://www.worldbook.com/fun/whm/ html/whm071.html.

Susan La Flesche Picotte: woman Spirit: http://www.meyna.com/omaha. html.

Taos Blue Lake Collection Papers: http://libweb.princeton.edu/libraries/ firestone/rbsc/finding_aids/taosblue lake/taosbluelake_1.html.

Taos Indians Thankful for Blue Lake Vote: http://members.aol.com/chloe5/ news-7.html.

Tenskwatawa (Open Door): http://www. newagepage.com/miracle/NOV/ nov24.html.

Tenskwatawa (The Prophet): http://www. npg.si.edu/col/native/tensk.html.

Thomas Banyacya: Hopi Interpreter: http://www.angelfire.com/on/GEAR20 00/tbhopi.html.

Thomas Banyacya: Hopi Traditional Elder: http://www.alphacdc.com/banyacya/ba nyacya.html.

Thomas Banyacya: Remembering Thomas Banyacya: http://www.sonic.net/~ kerry/banyacya/thomas.htm.

[Toohoolhoolzote] Historical Figures: http://www.geocities.com/RpdeoDrive/ 3077/favppl.html.

[Toypurina] Native California: Indian Revolts: http://www.chez. com/batea uxmls/#CHII1e.

Treaty with the Delawares, 1861: http:// digital.library.okstate.edu/ kappler/treaties/del0814.htm.

Vine Deloria, Jr.: http://www. native authors.com/search/bio/biodeloria.html.

Wallace Black Elk: http://www.blackelk. com/

White, Julia. *Woman Spirit*: http://www. meyna.com/mohawk2.html.

White Buffalo Calf Woman: http://indy4. fdl.cc.mn.us/~isk/arvol/lamedeer.html; http://indy4. fdl.cc.mn. us/~isk/arvol/ buffpipe.html.

White Buffalo Calf Woman, The Story of: http://www.cudenver.edu/~ccambird/w hitebuf.html.

Wovoka: People in the West: http:// www.pbs.org/weta/the west/wpages/ wpgs400/w4wovoka.html.

Wovoka's Message: http://www.dream scape.com/morgana/wovomsg.htm.

Index

About the Author

TROY R. JOHNSON is a professor of American Indian Studies and U.S. History at California State University, Long Beach. He is the author, editor, or associate editor of 17 books and numerous scholarly journal articles and has presented a score of papers at scholarly conferences. His area of expertise also includes American Indian activism, federal Indian law, Indian child welfare, and Indian youth suicide.